Across Forest, Steppe, and Mountain

In this book, David A. Bello offers a new and radical interpretation of how China's last dynasty, the Qing (1644–1912), relied on the interrelationship between ecology and ethnicity to incorporate the country's far-flung borderlands into the dynasty's expanding empire. The dynasty tried to manage the sustainable survival and compatibility of discrete borderland ethnic regimes in Manchuria, Inner Mongolia, and Yunnan integrated within a "Han Chinese" imperial political order. This unprecedented imperial unification resulted in the great human and ecological diversity that exists today. Using natural science literature in conjunction with underexploited and new sources in the Manchu language, Bello demonstrates how Qing expansion and consolidation of empire was dependent on a precise and intense manipulation of regional environmental relationships.

David A. Bello is an associate professor of East Asian History at Washington and Lee University.

Studies in Environment and History

Editors

J. R. McNeill, Georgetown University
Edmund P. Russell, University of Kansas

Editors Emeritus

Alfred W. Crosby, University of Texas at Austin
Donald Worster, University of Kansas

Other Books in the Series

Peter Thorsheim *Waste into Weapons: Recycling in Britain during the Second World War*

Kieko Matteson *Forests in Revolutionary France: Conservation, Community, and Conflict, 1669–1848*

George Colpitts *Pemmican Empire: Food, Trade, and the Last Bison Hunts in the North American Plains, 1780–1882*

Micah Muscolino *The Ecology of War in China: Henan Province, the Yellow River, and Beyond, 1938–1950*

John Brooke *Climate Change and the Course of Global History: A Rough Journey*

Emmanuel Kreike *Environmental Infrastructure in African History: Examining the Myth of Natural Resource Management*

Paul Josephson, Nicolai Dronin, Ruben Mnatsakanian, Aleh Cherp, Dmitry Efremenko, and Vladislav Larin *An Environmental History of Russia*

Gregory T. Cushman *Guano and the Opening of the Pacific World: A Global Ecological History*

Sam White *Climate of Rebellion in the Early Modern Ottoman Empire*

Alan Mikhail *Nature and Empire in Ottoman Egypt: An Environmental History*

Edmund Russell *Evolutionary History: Uniting History and Biology to Understand Life on Earth*

Richard W. Judd *The Untilled Garden: Natural History and the Spirit of Conservation in America, 1740–1840*

James L. A. Webb, Jr. *Humanity's Burden: A Global History of Malaria*

Frank Uekoetter *The Green and the Brown: A History of Conservation in Nazi Germany*

Myrna I. Santiago *The Ecology of Oil: Environment, Labor, and the Mexican Revolution, 1900–1938*

Matthew D. Evenden *Fish versus Power: An Environmental History of the Fraser River*

Nancy J. Jacobs *Environment, Power, and Injustice: A South African History*

Adam Rome *The Bulldozer in the Countryside: Suburban Sprawl and the Rise of American Environmentalism*

Judith Shapiro *Mao's War against Nature: Politics and the Environment in Revolutionary China*

Edmund Russell *War and Nature: Fighting Humans and Insects with Chemicals from World War I to Silent Spring*

Andrew Isenberg *The Destruction of the Bison: An Environmental History*

Thomas Dunlap *Nature and the English Diaspora*

Robert B. Marks *Tigers, Rice, Silk, and Silt: Environment and Economy in Late Imperial South China*

Mark Elvin and Tsui'jung Liu *Sediments of Time: Environment and Society in Chinese History*

Richard H. Grove *Green Imperialism: Colonial Expansion, Tropical Island Edens and the Origins of Environmentalism, 1600–1860*

Elinor G. K. Melville *A Plague of Sheep: Environmental Consequences of the Conquest of Mexico*

J. R. McNeill *The Mountains of the Mediterranean World: An Environmental History*

Theodore Steinberg *Nature Incorporated: Industrialization and the Waters of New England*

Timothy Silver *A New Face on the Countryside: Indians, Colonists, and Slaves in the South Atlantic Forests, 1500–1800*

Michael Williams *Americans and Their Forests: A Historical Geography*

Donald Worster *The Ends of the Earth: Perspectives on Modern Environmental History*

Samuel P. Hays *Beauty, Health, and Permanence: Environmental Politics in the United States, 1955–1985*

Warren Dean *Brazil and the Struggle for Rubber: A Study in Environmental History*

Robert Harms *Games against Nature: An Eco-Cultural History of the Nunu of Equatorial Africa*

Arthur F. McEvoy *The Fisherman's Problem: Ecology and Law in the California Fisheries, 1850–1980*

Alfred W. Crosby *Ecological Imperialism: The Biological Expansion of Europe, 900–1900, Second Edition*

Kenneth F. Kiple *The Caribbean Slave: A Biological History*

Donald Worster *Nature's Economy: A History of Ecological Ideas, Second Edition*

Across Forest, Steppe, and Mountain

Environment, Identity, and Empire in Qing China's Borderlands

DAVID A. BELLO
Washington and Lee University

CAMBRIDGE
UNIVERSITY PRESS

University Printing House, Cambridge CB2 8BS, United Kingdom

One Liberty Plaza, 20th Floor, New York, NY 10006, USA

477 Williamstown Road, Port Melbourne, VIC 3207, Australia

4843/24, 2nd Floor, Ansari Road, Daryaganj, Delhi - 110002, India

79 Anson Road, #06-04/06, Singapore 079906

Cambridge University Press is part of the University of Cambridge.

It furthers the University's mission by disseminating knowledge in the pursuit of education, learning and research at the highest international levels of excellence.

www.cambridge.org
Information on this title: www.cambridge.org/9781107068841

© David A. Bello 2015

This publication is in copyright. Subject to statutory exception and to the provisions of relevant collective licensing agreements, no reproduction of any part may take place without the written permission of Cambridge University Press.

First published 2015

A catalogue record for this publication is available from the British Library

Library of Congress Cataloging in Publication data
Bello, David Anthony, 1963–
Across forest, steppe and mountain : environment, identity and empire in Qing China's borderlands / David A. Bello.
pages cm. – (Studies in environment and history)
The multicultural Qing is reconsidered in "multi-ecological" terms of three borderland case studies from northeastern Manchuria, south-central Inner Mongolia, and southwestern Yunnan. Human pursuit of game, tending of livestock, and susceptibility to disease vectors required imperial adaptation beyond the cultural constructs of banners or chieftainships in order to maintain a "sustainable Qing periphery" based on these environmental relations between people and animals. The resulting borderland spaces are, therefore, not simply contrivances of more anthropocentric administrative fiat, but environmental interdependencies constructed through more "organic" and conditional relations of imperial foraging, imperial pastoralism, and imperial indigenism.
Includes bibliographical references and index.
ISBN 978-1-107-06884-1 (Hardback : alk. Paper)
1. Environmental policy–China–History.   2. China–History–Qing dynasty, 1644–1912.
3. Borderlands–Environmental aspects–China–History.   4. Hunting and gathering societies–China–Manchuria–History.   5. Pastoral systems–China–Inner Mongolia–History.
6. Indigenous peoples–China–Yunnan Sheng–History.   7. Ethnicity–Environmental aspects–China–History.   8. Imperialism–Environmental aspects–China–History.
9. Human ecology–Political aspects–China–History.   10. Sustainability–Political aspects–China–History.   I. Title.
GE190.C6B35 2015
304.20951–dc23   2015010604

ISBN 978-1-107-06884-1 Hardback
ISBN 978-1-107-65823-3 Paperback

Cambridge University Press has no responsibility for the persistence or accuracy of URLs for external or third-party internet websites referred to in this publication, and does not guarantee that any content on such websites is, or will remain, accurate or appropriate.

To the memory of my father, Anthony E. Bello
and to my mother, Dorothy J. Bello

Just as it is certain that one leaf is never totally the same as another, so it is certain that the concept "leaf" is formed by arbitrarily discarding these individual differences and by forgetting the distinguishing aspects.

Friedrich Nietzsche, "On Truth and Lies in a Nonmoral Sense"

We select from out of the presented only the aspects of our interest and neglect the rest; to the rest that is neglected we become first indifferent and then blind; in our blindness, we claim completeness for the aspects that we have selected. We seize them as absolute, we cling to them as the complete truth, we become dogmatic.

K. Venkata Ramanan, *Nāgārjuna's Philosophy*

Contents

List of Tables	*page* xi	
List of Maps	xiii	
Notes on Translation and Transliteration	xv	
Acknowledgements	xvii	
	Introduction	1
1	Qing Fields in Theory and Practice	21
2	The Nature of Imperial Foraging in the SAH Basin	63
3	The Nature of Imperial Pastoralism in Southern Inner Mongolia	116
4	The Nature of Imperial Indigenism in Southwestern Yunnan	169
5	Borderland Hanspace in the Nineteenth Century	219
6	Qing Environmentality	266
Works Cited		277
Index		321

Tables

1	Jin and Qing Manpower Raids on Donghai Jurchen, 1631–40	*page* 76
2	New Manchu Banner Companies' Relocation Routes to Ningguta, 1678	89
3	New Manchu Mobilizations to Ningguta, 1676	91
4	Sable Pelt Equivalents for Butha Ula Forage	98
5	Fengtian Forager Annual Quotas	99
6	Major Qing State Pastures in Manchuria and Mongolia	122
7	*Taipusi* Horse Herds, Seventeenth and Eighteenth Centuries	125
8	Vital Statistics, Three-Banner and Dariganga Sheep Flocks, 1739–1760	126
9	Malarial Locales in Qing Southwestern Yunnan	199

Maps

1	Hu Line Ecotone Map	*page* 11
2	China as Great Triple-trunked Dragon	29
3	SAH Basin: Jilin and Heilongjiang	65
4	Qing Inner Mongolia: Select Banners and Leagues	119
5	Yunnan's Southwestern Frontier	171

Notes on Translation and Transliteration

Italicized foreign words in the main text are Chinese pinyin romanizations unless otherwise identified. In general, with some exceptions, Manchu ("Ma") words are romanized according to Jerry Norman's transcription system; Mongol ("Mo") terms have been romanized according to the transcription notes in Atwood, *Young Mongols and Vigilantes*, *xv–xvii*; Russian ("Ru") is romanized in accordance with the transliteration notes in *Russia's Conquest of Siberia, lxxi-ii*.

I have generally followed Janhunen, *Manchuria: An Ethnic History*, for transliteration and correlation of regional indigenous ethnonyms, an inexact science at best (125–28). My own modifications have been made mainly to distinguish between subgroups of the modern Ewenki by adding a hyphenated prefix of the conventional Qing term, e.g., "Solon-Ewenki" and "Kiler-Ewenki." The conventional Qing terms of Hejen and Fiyaka (*He-zhe* and *Fei-ya-ka*, respectively, in Chinese) have been retained because it is difficult to directly link these terms to either of their putative modern ethnic equivalents, the Ghilyak and the Nanai.

Inner Asian, primarily Manchu, words for which I have found only Chinese versions have been rendered in *pinyin* linked by hyphens. This procedure is also used to signify conventional sinicized versions of these words (e.g., the Chinese Mu-lan for the Manchu Muran). Inner Asian toponyms have generally been transliterated in Manchu or Mongol, as appropriate, with some exceptions. Alternate transliterations of various Manchu, Chinese, and Mongol terms can be found in the index.

Aimag and *aiman* refer to Mongol and Manchu (including all indigenous northeastern peoples) "tribes," respectively. Translations from the Chinese in all cases retain "tribe" for *buluo* and "barbarian" or "tribal" xvi *Notes on Translation and Transliteration*

for *yi*. When discussing Uliastai groups before their incorporation into the Qing banner systems, I use *otog*. I use "banner" for all incorporated Mongol groups. Some justification for these usages from archival sources can be found in NFY, KX 2-1676: 276; MWLF, QL 1/9/26 [03-0173-1192-018.1], QL 12/7/19 [03-0173-1078-003], QL 1/9/26 [03-0173-1192-018.1], QL 12/7/19 [03-0173-1078-003], QL 23/12/13 [03-0177-1734-007].

Taxonomic nomenclature for various species mentioned in premodern documents is problematic, particularly in Chinese. *Dongzhu*, for example, can refer to pearls from one or more of several mussel species. *Diao* can refer to the marten genus or to its species category of *Martes zibellina* (i.e., sable). The association of *Panax ginseng* with *rensheng* is also imprecise. With a few exceptions, I have provided this nomenclature in the index only for select entries to provide limited clarification of vague, but important, forage terms.

Acknowledgments

Many people kept this project resilient with minimal disturbance for over a decade. My gratitude is theirs, the errors mine. My advisor and friend John E. Wills, Jr., has ensured that the basic conditions for all of my work have been kept at productive equilibrium from the beginning. Benjamin A. Elman has likewise exerted a long-term stabilizing influence, as has Peter C. Perdue. Robert B. Marks has afforded specialized expertise and generosity at nearly unsustainable levels.

Colleagues who helped nurture various versions of the book at formative stages in presentation or article form include John Shepherd, Tobie Meyer-Fong, Kathryn Bernhardt, Ling Zhang, Lisa Brady, William T. Rowe, Johan Elverskog, Hans Ulrich Vogel, Zhang Jie, Zhou Qiong, and Jack Hayes, who provided welcome disaster relief. Conference conversations with Timothy Brook, Mark Elvin, Micah Muscolino, and Yan Gao were also quite fruitful. Wen-hsin Yeh and Robert P. Weller provided particularly green pastures at the Berkeley Summer Research Institute Workshop, "Bordering China: Modernity and Sustainability." I gratefully learned from all the workshop's participants, particularly my friend Ma Jianxiong. Another fertile field for intellectual development has been the Conference of East Asian Environmental History, where I have become annually indebted to Ts'ui-jung Liu for her support. I also deeply appreciate the poetic presence of my good friend and colleague Wendy Swartz.

I am deeply gratified that the editors of this series, John McNeill and Edmund P. Russell, along with Deborah Gershenowitz and her staff, quickly granted this book a very welcome and distinctive publishing niche. Easy access to material resources was provided by, first and xviii *Acknowledgments*

foremost, annual Glenn and Lenfest research grants from my home institution of Washington and Lee University, which additionally contributed a subvention, for nearly the whole of the past decade. My own History Department also made vital contributions in terms of time, money, and collegiality. Elizabeth A. Teaff and the staff of Leyburn Library tracked down innumerable references across forest, steppe, and mountain with a truly Manchu determination. Elsewhere in Virginia research was funded by a grant from the Foundation for Independent Colleges' Mednick Fellowship and from the University of Virginia's East Asian Collection for a library travel grant. Farther afield, seed money, among many other contributions, was initially provided by a 2002–03 Post-Doctoral Fellowship in Chinese Studies from Stanford University's Center for East Asian Studies under the directorship of Jean Oi, to whom I'm especially grateful for allowing me to revise my proposed project. Support for 2006 research in China came from the American Council of Learned Societies American Research in the Humanities in China/National Endowment for the Humanities for Scholarly Research in the People's Republic of China and from the J. Wm. Fulbright Scholarship Board/Council for International Exchange of Scholars, China Studies Research Grant (Award no. 5110) for Scholarly Research in the People's Republic of China. The Institute for Advanced Study provided the ideal habitat to finish up the book with the support of the Herodotus Fund for membership at the School of Historical Studies in 2014–15 and, especially, of Nicola Di Cosmo.

In China proper, the atmosphere of a dragon's true lair was maintained for me by the faculty, especially Professors Dong Jianzhong and Huang Aiping, librarians, Dr. Wang Xufen in particular, and other staff at Renmin University, the Institute of Qing History, the National Project for the Compilation of Qing History, and the Liaoning Provincial Archives. My ongoing debt to the staff at the First Historical Archives of China remains in arrears and cannot be repaid in silver, grain, livestock, or any other medium of which I am aware. Here I also have only a *baniha* to offer Professors An Shuangcheng and Chuang Chi-fa, whose instruction opened an entirely new expanse of Manchu in the archives for me. As always, Dr. Li Nan provided general onsite relief; Stephanie Ho and David Hathaway, Inner Asian levels of hospitality only they can sustain.

Similar support and fellowship of Rebecca Shea and Hoyt Sze, Troy and Mary Paddock, Michele Thompson, Chia-ju Chang, and Lin Hsiuling in the United States nurtured the project at critical junctures. But most influential of all, across all terrain, is my wife Jeanette Barbieri.

Introduction

I think back afar to Han and Tang, Song and Ming;
Guarding the Great Wall being their sole scheme for tranquility.
Fertile fields in tens and hundreds of thousands of acres thus forsaken in the
  wilderness;
How could there be food enough to cover their myriad populace?
            The Qianlong emperor, *Two Verses on Antiquity*

When he posed this question poetically in the thirtieth year of his reign, the Qianlong emperor was presiding over an empire at its zenith that spanned nearly a quarter of Eurasia. The emperor's question was also rhetorical, given the expansion of his Qing dynasty (1644–1912) that set the teeming "populace" of China proper loose among the "fertile fields" of "the wilderness" of Inner Asia north and west of the Great Wall. In a preface to his 1765 poem, the Qianlong emperor explained that poor Han commoners could now till for a livelihood north of the passes, which had lain outside the mandate of the Qing's four main ethnic Chinese dynastic predecessors. Liberation from the old Chinese restraints concretized by the Great Wall was to be the final Manchu answer to the perennial Han questions of population growth and northern frontier security. The emperor held this achievement to be so distinctive that he claimed his indirectly self-laudatory poem was "not bragging, but simply an expression of awe."[1]

The expanse of Qing dominions was certainly awesome, to Manchu emperors and even to their former Han subjects. Writing 162 years later in 1927 in the wake of ethnic Chinese nationalism that had helped topple the dynasty, the compilers of the *Draft History of the Qing* (*Qingshigao*) paid the Qing what was probably the greatest tribute of Han historiography possible at the time. They praised the geographical manifestation of the dynasty's "imperial radiance," which united Sakhalin Island to the Pamirs and the Greater Hinggan Mountains to Hainan Island, as unprecedented "since the Han and Tang!"[2] Adherence to old Manchu boundaries inscribed in the *Draft History* and other dynastic texts was to be a standard Chinese nation-state response to both post-Qing imperialist and domestic ethnic minority territorial challenges.

Beneath the awesome radiance generated by the manifest hyperbole of both emperor and compilers lies more solid ground. The Qing empire stretched through more than 60 degrees of latitude and about 50 degrees of longitude to encompass a vast diversity. The resulting Qing empire faced distinctive challenges arising from the Manchu unification of this expanse's two main divisions, which can be abbreviated as Inner Asia and China proper. These challenges were not posed solely by human beings, but by this wide-ranging environmental variation of which people were a part. As a result, state control under a fully monocultural or anthropocentric imperial system was impractical. Instead, the state had to recognize that the human "culture" of ethnic identity formation and the "nature" of nonhuman ecology mutually constituted environmental relations of "culture-nature" that inform the historical space of Qing borderlands.[3] This recognition included environmental relationships between humans and animals. Qing borderland space was ostensibly embodied in people, but ultimately dependent on sustaining animal-people interactions that conditioned any human borderland presence. These interactions were primarily existential rather than metaphorical and were not exclusively human social constructs.[4]

I offer three representative case studies of Qing borderland formation to demonstrate the political and historical significance of environmental relations, centered on ties between people and animals: Manchus and game in northern Manchuria, Mongols and livestock in south-central Inner Mongolia, and indigenous peoples and mosquito-borne blood parasites in southwestern Yunnan. Each of these relationships is expressed not simply by human impact on the surrounding ecology, but also by that ecology's impact on the formation of distinct borderland identities. Manchu military skill depends on game. Mongol steppe survival requires livestock. Yunnan indigenous agency is shielded by malaria.

Diverse borderland conditions generally precluded the uniform imposition of China proper's key environmental relationship, namely, ethnic or "Han" Chinese intensive cultivation of cereal plants. Instead, the Qing

Introduction

employed a different strategy, adapted for local conditions, to control each of these borderland zones, which I have metaphorically abbreviated as forest, steppe, and mountain. None of these areas were exclusively human constructs as often implied by their administrative designations as the banner system of Manchuria, the *jasag* system of Mongolia, the system of southwestern native chieftainships (*tusi*), and the network of provinces, prefectures, and districts (the "*junxian*" system) of China proper.[5]

From the perspective of environmental history, a set of wider relationships, which certainly include aspects of all these systems but are not rigidly circumscribed by them, becomes visible. No particular cultural element was definitive, although practices such as ritual, law, and education certainly helped unify and form Qing subjects. These were conducted, however, within a wider dynamic environmental context that required adaptation in order to maintain the hierarchical ranks that defined the empire. Specifically, the Qing state adapted itself to boreal Manchuria's environment through "imperial foraging" to construct a "borderland Manchu" identity. In steppe Inner Mongolia the Qing adapted through "imperial pastoralism" to construct a "banner Mongol" identity. In forested highland (or "Zomian") Yunnan it adapted through "imperial indigenism" to construct a "civilized tribal" identity. Each identity would constitute the human resources necessary to secure borderland spaces and natural resources for the dynasty.

These identity constructs, however, were not entirely determined by dynastic fiat or indigenous resistance or some compromise between the two, because borderland peoples lived off their climates, flora, and fauna. Any ethnic identity formation was, consequently, not just cultural, but also ecological. Some current work in human psychology indicates that the formation of ethnicity is a semiconscious choice by individuals to reductively order the complex diversity of "the social world" into groups to make it more easily intelligible and less uncertain.[6] Such an adaptive reduction is not wholly social, however, because it remains semiconsciously dependent on other nonhuman organic connections. I will abbreviate these connections as "ecological" and consider them mainly as embodied in animals. The internalizations of Qing ethnic identity still remain "products of an imperial culture," which imposes and refines requisite formative criteria, but also remain conditional because they are always born within a larger ecological context.[7]

Ecologies have played a role in the formation of ethnic identities beyond that of mere anthropogenic constructs of "nature."[8] Studies of peoples such as the Gimi of Papua New Guinea, who see themselves as

Across Forest, Steppe, and Mountain

"dialectically connected to" animals, reflect constructions dependent, not imposed, on local ecologies.[9] Although there is a cultural component to this process, it is not culturally determined. If it were, there would be no existential need to protect the biodiversity that shelters indigenous identity.[10] Cultural, rather than environmental, determinism seems the more pervasive analytical obstacle, exaggerated fears of a "downgrade" in "individual agency" notwithstanding.[11] As the Gimi apparently know from experience, culture is not autonomous, but informed by ecological interactions. Similar sorts of culture-nature interconnections also formed Qing borderland space.

ENVIRONMENTAL RELATIONS AND EMPIRE

These environmental interconnections, perceived or not, were critical for the production of difference across borderlands. The Qianlong emperor's grandfather, the Kangxi emperor (r. 1662–1722), provides an example in his 1707 sighs of resignation over the limits of Qing power in Guizhou:

The native chieftains are of myriad types and their customs vary. From antiquity the royal regulations were unable to bind them. It is completely impossible to control them as We do the subjects of the interior and this has been so from the beginning. We must make the best of it and attempt only a general type of control. An excessively stringent application of the law will be the source of endless trouble ... Preventing incidents from occurring must be our main policy, for an excess of incidents will be too costly for Our state to bear.[12]

This was the emperor's response to his provincial Governor Chen Shen's recitation of the native chieftainship system's official formula — the state would "use Han laws to reign in the native chieftains, use native chieftains to reign in [their own] Miao [subjects]," then "use Civilized Miao to reign in the Wild Miao."[13] People remain at the middle of both these ideal and practical views of chieftainships, so state administrative adaptation appears as accordingly "anthropocentric."

As the following chapters will show, however, such appearances, which strongly inform state discourses throughout dynastic borderlands, conceal a wider range of connections that structure "people" problems of various types. The core relationship here is that which "humans share with their environments" as a result of "evolved methods of adaptation."[14] Qing administrators can appear obtuse in this regard when they decry environmental problems, often centered on resource access, as having entirely human causes, such as corruption, negligence, etc. Another expression of the Kangxi emperor's exasperation, a

Introduction 5

1716 vermilion rescript on Ordos droughts and snowstorms, is again exemplary. His anger is entirely undiluted by any consideration that the herds of "greedy" Ordos lamas may have also been too devastated by the steppe's characteristically extreme weather for voluntary donations of any relief livestock to their distressed followers.[15] Such attitudes may have arisen from a kind of expediency that tacitly acknowledged the limitations of state control, which was most effective over people rather than plants, animals, or climate.[16]

Such an anthropocentric mind-set can be defined by the extent to which authorities discount plausible nonhuman causal factors. Such factors were difficult to escape in practice, if often evaded in rhetoric. So Guizhou's mountainous terrain loomed behind even Governor Chen's neat prescription as he acknowledged that his strategy was framed by the fact that these indigenous "myriad types" differed from peak to peak.[17]

The bewildering connection of human diversity to ecological diversity conditioned and restricted, but certainly did not preclude, the Qing borderland construction project in the southwest and elsewhere. In the southwestern ecological context, mountains were certainly one structuring factor. The overlapping reproductive cycles between insects and parasites that spread disease to humans, the theme of Chapter 4, were another, and one that was also influenced by variation in elevation and differential human resistance. These cycles produced a symbiotic "animal," the malarial mosquito.[18] Unaware of these complex cycles, which are not fully understood even today, the dynasty adapted its regional order to rely more exclusively on a human subject that could endure the cycles' malarial results. This so-called civilized tribal identity was, moreover, predicated on a precariously ambitious conversion from indigenous swiddening to Han agrarian practices. There was no comparable attempt to covert "borderland Manchus" and "banner Mongols" into China proper farmers, but both identities were tied to relations with, much more accessible, animals that the state also worked to manipulate.

All three Qing borderland identities can thus be seen either as artificial, even illusory, state impositions on local diversities or as viably malleable adaptations to those same diversities. None, however, were constructed by humans alone. Over the past fifty years work such as that of cultural ecologist Julian Steward and sociologist-anthropologist Bruno Latour have effectively challenged analytical frameworks based on "the fruitless assumption that culture comes from culture" or on "the tautology of social ties made out of social ties."[19] Recently Latour has proposed "Actor-Network Theory" (ANT) in recognition that actions "rarely consist of [solely] human-to-human connections ... or of object-to-object connections, but will probably zigzag from one to the other." Others have gone farther to assert that humans and nonhumans share agency in the formation of nature that encompasses both. Common to such revisions is the recognition that human agency must be qualified by its larger ecological context so as to include "the earth ... as an agent and presence in history."[20]

A number of influential historical studies of imperial relations have subjected human action to such environmental conditioning. William Cronon's *Changes in the Land: Indians, Colonists and the Ecology of New England* shows how distinct sets of environmental relations were formative for the respective ethnic identities and cultures of native Americans and British settlers, with profound effects on North American history. Alfred W. Crosby's *Ecological Imperialism: The Biological Expansion of Europe, 900–1900* portrays nonhuman entities as essential to a formation of empire. More recently, some of these ideas have been developed into critiques of anthropocentric tendencies in modernity. Timothy Mitchell, for example, connects "dams, blood-borne parasites, synthetic chemicals, mechanized war and man-made famine" in often inadvertent and unpredictable interactions that underlie a "techno-politics" based on "the 'social construction' of things that are clearly more than social."[21]

A consideration of China's environmental history using newer approaches also qualifies some established western concepts. It is difficult, for example, to approach structures of Qing domination from Crosby's generally compelling "ecological imperialist" perspective. Much longer periods of closer interspecies contact minimized the biological expansion of neighboring Han Chinese "portmanteau biota" to effect change comparable to the rapid conversion of the Americas and Oceania into "Neo-Europes" central to Crosby's account. On the steppe there was nothing like Crosby's disparity of domesticated animals favoring European colonists over American indigenous peoples. There were not even real bison equivalents, although the voracious grasshopper *Chorthippus* may have leapt at the opportunity to fill the bison's grass-eating ecological niche.[22]

Environmental imperial histories show how environmental relations materially affect the human hierarchy based on ethnic difference that defines imperial relations to produce ungovernable changes over time. An empire's attempt to subject environmental diversity to greater uniformity required an anthropocentric control prone to undermining its own stability through alienation from this same diversity. This formulation is an environmental corrective to postcolonial conceptualizations of imperial relations that often "start with the people as creators of

Introduction

themselves and transformers of their environment."[23] Critical studies of western colonialism have often been predicated on such anthropocentric, if politically understandable, premises. Similar assumptions inform studies of Chinese imperial history where the Han majority appear as mainly self-creators and environmental transformers.

THE ENVIRONMENTAL HISTORICAL TERRAIN OF QING CHINA

Pertinent debates over Sinification, for example, have deliberated the conventionally accepted power of Han culture to assimilate non-Han cultures without being significantly altered by them. The "New Qing History" has played a leading role in this debate through studies emphasizing the persistent influence of Qing Inner Asian, especially Manchu, culture on imperial "Chinese" practice.[24] The New Qing History certainly adopts a more imperially appropriate perspective in terms of ethnic diversity and geographical scale. Yet both sides in this resolutely cultural debate ignore the influence of ecological factors on issues of Han ethnic superiority.[25]

Serious consideration of the environment will not end divisions over contending definitions for key analytical terms such as race, ethnicity, acculturation, and assimilation. An environmental perspective, however, does expose the significance of the anthropocentric assumptions that underlie them. From this alternative vista, multiple dimensions appear beyond the binary of "Manchu-Han" relations, for example. Northeastern peoples who did not accompany the Manchu diaspora to China proper maintained direct connections to northeastern flora and fauna. Differences here did not simply arise from contrasting and constructed cultural interaction. They also arose from physical degrees of alienation or interaction with regional ecologies that distinguished borderland Manchus from all inhabitants, Manchu and Han, of China proper.

Variants of Han identity were likewise formed through regionalized ecological contacts. Consider, for example, the effects of "patchiness" in William T. Rowe's account of dam conflicts in Wuchang below the Han and Yangzi confluence in Hubei. Patches are localized areas within wider landscapes that exhibit a different set of ecological dynamics from their surroundings to promote greater localized diversity.[26]

Wuchang had patches of lakes and marshes that contained annual upsurges in water upstream, complicating standard forms of water control for agriculture. Wuchang residents had adapted in two ways to these conditions over time. One was the usual strategy of wet rice cultivation that was not very successful, and the other was a highly successful fishing economy. The region's preexisting patchiness allowed the emergence of both fishing and farming cultures that "practiced very different lifestyles and lived in very different worlds comparable to those sometimes encountered at ecological frontiers (say between steppe and cultivation, or nomadic gathering and permanent settlement)." Violent conflict, as both groups tried to concentrate water resources for their exclusive benefits, was endemic, with the state, exhibiting a "strong Confucian agrarian bias," tending to favor rice cultivation.[27]

Hills spattered throughout the lower Yangzi provided another patchy zone for the formation of "shack people" (*pengmin*) identity. As Anne Osborne relates, these land-hungry migrants brought "new techniques and crops, which would exploit" agriculturally marginal slopes "through a distinctive adaptation to the highland environment." Unfortunately, this adaptation relied on ephemeral forms of shifting cultivation, causing deforestation and erosion that "threatened the stability of the [existing] agricultural ecosystem" through the promotion of drought and flood. This was Han-style swiddening, far less sophisticated and sustainable than the "slash and burn" practices of hill peoples in the southwest. Han-style swiddening was a product of new relations between cultivators and New World crops that created a new identity, shack people. The state found it difficult to integrate this new identity, because shack people's practice of their constituent environmental relations led to "a downward spiral of reclamation, abandonment and new reclamation which threatened agricultural and social stability" in both the marginal hills and the lowland cores.[28] Restated in terms of environmental relations, the ecological effects of the formation of shack people identity threatened to erode the agrarian basis of the established Han identity.

These examples from China proper's core regions of the middle and lower Yangzi suggestively exhibit a "significant degree of microvariation" in "environmental exploitation" recognizable in Mark Elvin's sketch of a "Chinese style" of "premodern economic growth."[29] All show state and society exerting agency to transform their surroundings, but only within certain ecological limits, set in part by conditions such as patchiness. Once exceeded, these limits exert a counterpressure, in the form of water shortages, erosion, and the like, that may not only vitiate new adaptations, but undermine older ones. Indeed, it is often human attempts to effect excessive concentrations of key resources, while overlooking their wider interdependencies, that inadvertently trigger ecological counterpressures. There is, moreover, evidence to suggest that such counterpressures are inevitable forms of "creative destruction," or "dynamics of

Introduction   9

disharmony," intrinsic to all life processes. These dynamics move to promote wider, more diversifying, and more stable circulations of biomass that might otherwise become precariously overloaded. Vegetation is periodically consumed in naturally occurring forest fires that actually promote ecosystem maintenance in this way.[30] The cultural turn rejected concepts of decontextualized, ahistorical, and "natural" human practices. Environmental science's dynamics of disharmony likewise rejected previous ideas about the ecology's steady-state character, with implications for social science analyses informed by a "new ecology." This approach, which actually has been developing since the 1970s, emphasizes the interdependency and variability of social-ecological action across different scales of time and space in an often "nonequilibrium" fashion significantly beyond human prediction or control.[31]

In other words, the more successful human intervention is at concentrating ecological resources, the more unstable the resulting consolidated environmental relations become over time as this excessive concentration disruptively severs itself from other connections. Zhao Zhen's study of Qing state forest "conservation" policies in the Shaan(xi)-Gan(su) region of northwestern China can be read as exemplary of these inherent contradictions. Attempts to limit deforestation in the region were primarily motivated to ensure ongoing agricultural development, which was itself largely responsible for deforestation in the first place.[32] The direct relationship between the two practices was substantially ignored until the excessive concentration of resources for fields at the expense of forests revealed the limiting factors of their mutual dependency. This does not seem to be an exclusively modern dynamic brought on by advanced technological change, although allowances must be made for differences of scale, speed, and the like. Rather, this dynamic defines a limit on the life expectancies of all human assemblages, empires included, without precluding them entirely. Human cultures are in this way integrated into larger environmental cycles.

Important western work on Chinese environmental history, most notably Robert Marks' interdisciplinary study of South China's socioeconomy, has understandably focused on the Han core as the center of agro-urban transformation extending throughout and well beyond this area.[33] This is largely true of studies in Chinese as well, which also tend to focus on longstanding themes and regions such as disaster relief and the Yangzi basin.[34] Significantly, some recent Chinese scholarship has begun to recognize the historical implications of environmental, not simply cultural, interaction.[35] Yet even exceptional works, such as Qin Heping's study of maize cultivation's effects on demographics of Yunnan indigenous peoples,

Across Forest, Steppe, and Mountain

Luo Kanglong's study of agricultural and ethnic distinctions between various forms of rice cultivation in the southwest, Zhao Zhen's book on ecological change in the northwest, the book by Xiao Ruiling et al. on Inner Mongolian desertification, and Liu Shiyong's study of malarial vectors in Taiwan all proceed from the ecological effects of Han migration.[36]

Overall, this body of work, which influentially informs current Chinese environmental history, is primarily concerned with the effects of a single ethnic group. This can unintentionally reinforce the impression of the Han alone as self-creators and environmental transformers. There is no doubt that this work has firmly established the historical significance of human interactions with various ecologies in many dimensions. It has also shown that these resulting environmental relations at the core of imperial China cannot be severed from expressions of Han ethnic identity. However, in dynastic cases such as that of the Qing, which supervised nature-culture connections well beyond China proper, environmental relations further afield need to be taken into more active account.

ENVIRONMENTAL RELATIONS IN THE QING BORDERLANDS

Qing China's environmental relations were not constituted solely by Han activity, as critical as that was for the empire as a whole. Han migration, for example, would have been severely restricted without the dynastic consolidation and radical expansion of borderland spaces, particularly those just north and west of the ecotone conventionally delineated by the "Hu Line" (*Hu Huanyong xian*).

This geographical concept was first formulated in 1935 by Hu Huanyong, one of the founders of modern demography in China. Hu determined that around 6 percent of China's population lived scattered across 64 percent of the country's land area northwest of a line he determined cut diagonally across China northeast from Heihe County, Heilongjiang Province, southwest to Tengchong County, Yunnan Province. The remaining 94 percent of the population inhabited a mere 36 percent of the land southeast of this line, an area roughly equivalent to the whole of China proper, excluding most of Gansu and the northeastern half of Sichuan. Hu employed both ecological and cultural explanations in his analysis of this condition. Considerable differences in climate due to elevation encouraged more pastoral adaptations in the relatively cool and dry northwest as opposed to agricultural adaptations in the warmer, wetter southeast. In 1987, 96 percent of China's grain was still produced southeast of the line, and 60 percent of its sheep came from the northwest of it.[37]

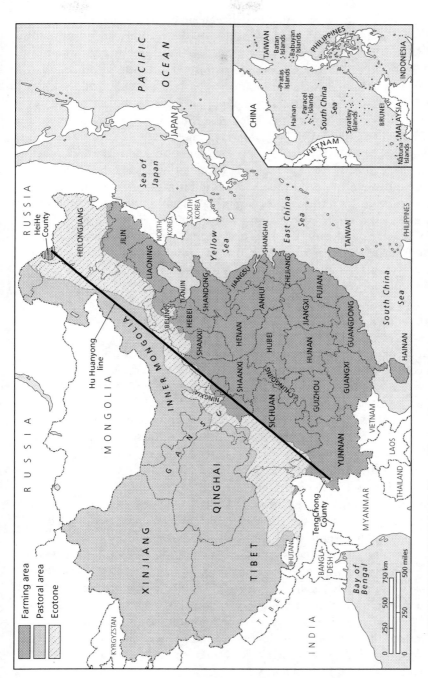

MAP 1: HU LINE ECOTONE MAP (From Zhang, Wei, and Chen, "Mapping the Farming-Pastoral Ecotones in China," *Journal of Mountain Science*, 6.1 [March 2009]: 85.)

The line has also been found to delineate an ecotone zone. This transition area is uniquely defined by scales of space, time, and degree of interaction between adjacent ecosystems that can be broadly described as pastoral to the northwest and agrarian to the southeast.[38] In contrast to more rigid notions of separation between "steppe and sown" arising from steady-state ecological assumptions, it is precisely the ecological malleability of this ecotone that enabled a transformation of borderland environmental relations embodied in Han migrants.[39]

Many Han moved across the line into the most arable parts of Inner Mongolia, primarily, and Manchuria, secondarily, during the eighteenth century. Yunnan's mineral wealth was also attractive during this period, while more of its fertile spaces began to fill up as well. Han settlers, however, were hardly roaming into vast tracts of empty wilderness. The Qing state had already become deeply involved in its own schemes to coordinate the environmental relations of indigenous peoples to construct borderlands in all three areas before Han arrived on the scene to complicate operations further. Forage and, especially in Mongolia, livestock received particular state attention north of the passes. In contrast, coping with an incompletely understood disease environment substantially influenced Qing operations in Yunnan.

Such marginal space under construction has been variously defined in terms of a "middle ground," frontier, or borderland and is often considered a product of "creative misunderstandings" between human actors, when not more conventionally seen as an outcome of one dominant actor's orchestrated design.[40] While rightly emphasizing both the constructed nature and ambiguity of such areas, these concepts tend to underestimate the necessity for human adaptation to prevailing and uncertain ecological conditions as a prerequisite for borderland formation.[41] Although ecological conditions are certainly subject to human manipulation, this manipulation is limited by these same conditions. Relations between humans and the ecology are recursive, and, for all its marginality, borderland space cannot lie beyond them.[42]

Borderland space, however, by definition did lie beyond the influence of the empire's core that was fundamentally configured in agro-urban terms, while including considerable patchy zones. So my three case studies from northern Manchuria, south-central Inner Mongolia, and southwestern Yunnan together are all territories of far less spatial and social centralization. They contain fewer settlement hierarchies patterned by urbanization and intensive agriculture than the corresponding space of the empire's ethnic Han majority.[43]

Introduction 13

This has been a comparative disadvantage, past and present, for these less centralized formations. Structured by more "tribal" types of organization, they "are still widely considered inherently unstable, transitional and incomplete" with "their trajectories unfinished until such time as they become states or ... collapse." Terms and concepts related to tribal and foraging peoples have been relegated to the bottom of this hierarchy of state centralization. Carole L. Crumley has countered that less rigidly ordered organizational forms may be more flexible in responding to periods of marked environmental change.[44] Whatever the truth of this observation, less centralized formations do seem to exhibit more direct, immediate interdependence with their surrounding ecologies.

The imperial agrarian state anchored in China proper was, of course, an inherited legacy of its Han, Tang, Song, and Ming predecessors. Yet, in contrast, the Qing nevertheless did make a concerted, if often conflicted, effort to protect and even nurture networks of environmental relations other than those constituting Han agrarianism. The resulting complexity of merging new and old forms under a single imperial system required continuous dynastic adaptation to maintain the awesome Qing radiance.

Discursive adaptation in the context of the enormous project of reordering connections between peoples and ecologies is a main subject of Chapter 1. The chapter traces these connections as links between culture and nature that produced the empire's primary forms of economic and military power. These links appear as two main forms of environmental relations, "arablism" (or "arable-ism") and "venery," terms that refer to nature-culture interactions informing both agriculture and hunting, respectively. The state constructed a Han identity in China proper on the basis of imperial arablism, while militarized hunting, or venery, formed a similar basis for Inner Asian identity of Manchus and Mongols. Both networks, as more than just "farming" and "hunting," produced the empire's primary forms of economic and military power, respectively. Other networks emerged as state adaptations to more specific regional borderland conditions.

In Chapter 2, one such variant network, imperial foraging, is examined as the main environmental relation producing a borderland order in Manchuria embodied in the "borderland Manchu." The formation of this identity was the Qing response to the seventeenth-century Russian invasion of the Sahaliyan-Amur-Heilong (in Manchu, Russian, and Chinese, respectively, or "SAH") River basin in north-central Manchuria. Initially hunted, gathered, and mobilized under relations of sable pelt tribute, borderland Manchus experienced radical alterations of their environmental ties as alienation from the foraging that had forged them into the empire's premier military human resources. An increasingly "cultured nature" of imperial foraging emerged during the eighteenth century under bureaucratic and political pressures from China proper.

Chapter 3 covers the dynastic construction of "banner Mongol" identity as the embodiment of its order of imperial pastoralism in response to steppe political rivals and extreme weather. The Qing used dependencies of herders on climate, grass, and livestock to construct this order, but state actions to uphold it could undermine themselves. The provision of agrarian aid, in the form of grain and silver, as the main form of state disaster relief and debt recovery for continuously stricken Mongol herds unintentionally alienated people from their livestock. Mongol pastoral identity, critical for dynastic control of the steppe borderland, was commensurately attenuated. The region's fragile, but flexible, econtone also left it vulnerable to another unintended consequence of the Qing incorporation of Inner Mongolia, namely, Han migration powered by an arablism incompatible with imperial pastoralism.

Chapter 4 examines southwestern Yunnan's disease environment as the greatest environmental challenge to Qing borderland formation. "Imperial indigenism" was the main dynastic borderland strategy in a region whose malarial vectors, mosquitoes and blood parasites, remained beyond informed control. These vectors' effectively invisible condition precluded the more direct orchestration of people-animal relations characteristic of imperial foraging and imperial pastoralism. Differential resistance to disease prevented the direct presence in substantial numbers of the empire's main, but susceptible, embodiments of Han, Manchu, and Mongol, while endowing the indigenous population with sufficient staying power. Consequently, the Qing focused on the relatively exclusive construction of a "civilized tribal" identity, whose formation was also inhibited by the region's primary environmental relation, swidden agriculture. Differential resistance to malarial mosquitoes in particular conferred a substantial autonomy on indigenous peoples, who were positioned to exploit yet another imperial rivalry, here with Myanmar, that compelled Qing borderland formation.[45]

Chapter 5 compares my three borderland case studies through brief examinations of nineteenth-century conditions as the consequences of Qing adaptation and maladaptation became more pronounced. The "dynamics of disharmony" that resonated recursively across the state's orchestration of environmental relations during this period originated

Introduction   15

as much from Qing success as from its failure in the process of imperial borderland construction. The realm's primary contradiction between culture and ecology at this time was the spread of Han arablism into the empire's borderlands and its intensification in the imperial core. This spread, however, is examined not in terms of population increase, but as a function of the production and degradation of arable land. Fields may have actually declined in many areas due to unsustainable Han agrarian practices, sometimes dynastically promoted under imperialist, mainly Russian, pressure. I conclude with a consideration of some of the wider implications of all these relations as a Qing "environmentality" that worked to construct each as part of an organic whole.

This study cannot pretend to be comprehensive, even within the limits of its three case studies, whose multiethnic character nevertheless makes some degree of essentialization unavoidable. The more ambiguous terms such as *Hua* and *Xia* have been translated as "Han" in most circumstances. Diverse groups are unavoidably lumped together under rubrics such as "Manchu foragers," "Mongol herders," and "indigenous swiddening peoples," although I have attempted to clarify and qualify these terms where appropriate.[46] The book, however, does expand on the considerable body of existing work on all three regions in a comparative direction that has hardly been mapped. Social and natural science research, including extreme climatology, rangeland sciences, ecological anthropology, and nonequilibrium ecology, has helped to make this approach possible. Above all, Manchu sources have been the prerequisite for a detailed historical analysis, especially of those borderlands where Manchu was the primary language of official communication.[47] Although by no means an argument for an exclusive "Manchu-centric" historiography, the book is an extended demonstration of the language's importance explored in previously published versions of Chapters 3 and 4. I have also used Manchu sources to expand an earlier published version of Chapter 5.[48]

Nevertheless, limitations, individual and structural, have prevented me both from accessing a greater range of the existing record, especially in Russian and Mongolian, as well as from being adequately conversant with all the pertinent natural sciences. Acknowledgment of limitations has been one of the lessons I have learned from the practice of both borderland and environmental history. In many respects exposure to the diversity of its imperial margins seems to have conferred a like awareness on the Qing state, which ceased to expand its frontiers by the closing years of the eighteenth century and which evinced increasing difficulty in keeping

16   *Across Forest, Steppe, and Mountain*

things in tune throughout its existing domains by the onset of the nineteenth. As I hope the following pages will show, however, orchestration was never easy or natural because of the diversity Qing imperial relations sought to harmonize. Yet disharmony became historically audible, especially when the state stopped adapting and started imposing.

Notes

1 *Qing Gaozong yuzhi shi* 8:132b.
2 *Qingshigao*, 8:1891.
3 Dichotomies such as "nature/culture" perpetuate illusory disjunctions, but some such distinctions seem linguistically unavoidable and remain useful with sufficient qualification; Haraway, "The Promises of Monsters," 297–98.
4 In stressing mutually constitutive relations not fully encompassed by humans, this study departs from work in "anthrozoology" that emphasizes how humans "understand animals in the context of human society and culture"; DeMello, *Animals and Society*, 9–11. No one in Qing China socially constructed blood parasites, for example, although some of their malarial effects were so treated.
5 For overviews of these ethnic administrative systems, see Ma Ruheng and Ma Dazheng, eds., *Qingdai de bianjiang zhengce*; Di Cosmo, "Qing Colonial Administration in Inner Asia," 287–309. Regionally specialized studies include Cheng Zhenming *Qingdai tusi yanjiu*; Yang Qiang, *Qingdai Mengguzu mengqi zhidu*; Du Jiaji, *Baqi yu Qingchao zhengzhi lungao*.
6 Hale, *Ethnic Politics*, 50. I am grateful to my colleague, Matthew Gildner for directing me to Hale. Hale's formulation recapitulates with greater precision and interdisciplinary support a more commonsense generalization that "every civilization has an ethnocentric world image in which outsiders are reduced to manageable spatial units"; Dikötter, *The Discourse of Race*, 5. On the utility of the concept of identity in various contexts, see Brubaker and Cooper, "Beyond 'Identity'," 1–47; Elliott, "Ethnicity in the Qing Eight Banners," 32–35; Elliott, *The Manchu Way*, xiv–xv, 8–13; Crossley, "Thinking about Ethnicity," 7–8, 11, 25, 27. I consider "early modern" ethnic identity as semiconscious and not fully formed in a modern sense.
7 Crossley, "Thinking about Ethnicity," 27. See also Brower and Lazzerini, eds., *Russia's Orient*, xv–xvi.
8 For a rejection of nature as a purely cultural construct, see Ingold, "Hunting and Gathering," 117, 129.
9 West, "Translation, Value and Space," 633. For some trends in environmental anthropology, see Headland, "CA Forum on Theory in Anthropology," 605–30; Little, "Environments and Environmentalisms," 253–84.
10 The "environment of Mongolian ethnic culture," has, for example, become an important issue in current development work in Inner Mongolia specifically and in Inner Asia in general; Bilik, "Culture, the Environment and Development in Inner Mongolia," 161–62; Humphrey and Sneath, "Introduction," 2.

Introduction 17

11 Shaw, "Happy in Our Chains?" 1–2. For more informed critiques of, generally popular, accounts based on environmental determinism, see Steinberg, "Down to Earth," 798–820; Blaut, "Environmentalism and Eurocentrism," 391–408.

12 *Kangxichao Hanwen zhupi*, KX 46/2/1, 1:592–601.

13 *Kangxichao Hanwen zhupi*, KX 46/2/1, 1:592–601. Difficulties in precisely defining southwestern indigenous peoples, who are generally abbreviated as "Miao" in dynastic documents, persist to this day; Lombard-Salmon, *Un exemple d'acculturation Chinoise*, 110–17; Diamond, "Defining the Miao," 92–116.

14 Headland, "CA Forum on Theory in Anthropology," 610; Little, "Environments and Environmentalisms," 259. For discussions evaluating adaptation and related concepts in ecological anthropology, see Worster, "History as Natural History," 1–19; Balée, "The Research Program of Historical Ecology," 79; Balée, "Historical Ecology," 13–14; Whitehead, "Ecological History and Historical Ecology," 31.

15 *Kangxichao Manwen zhupi*, #2784, 1103.

16 For a discussion of such limits in a premodern European context, see Paul Warde, "The Environmental History of Pre-Industrial Agriculture in Europe," in Sverker Sörlin and Paul Warde, eds., *Nature's End: History and Environment*, (Houndmills, Basingstoke: Palgrave Macmillan, 2009), 73–78, 88.

17 *Kangxi hanwen zhupi*, KX 46/2/1, 1:592–601.

18 Currently, the scientific notion of "animal" is in flux. Mosquitoes are part of the kingdom "Anamalia," and the blood parasite plasmodium is a microbe of the kingdom "Protista," or "Protozoa." These kingdoms, however, may fall to "supergroups" that better reflect evolutionary relationships between all "eukaryotic" organisms whose cells possess nuclei. Microbes would then be retypecast as "Chomalveolata" and animals as "Opisthokonta"; Parfrey et al., "Evaluating Support for the Current Classification of Eukaryotic Diversity," 2062–73.

19 Steward, *Theory of Culture Change*, 36; Latour, *Reassembling the Social*, 70.

20 Latour, *Reassembling the Social*, 75; Haraway, "The Promises of Monsters," 297; Asdal, "The Problematic Nature of Nature," 60–74; Worster, "Appendix: Doing Environmental History," 289; Mitchell, *Rule of Experts*, 22, 27–31. Works calling for greater analytical integration between "culture and nature" include Little, "Environments and Environmentalisms," 257–59; Chakrabarty, "The Climate of History," 197–222; Hughes, "Three Dimensions of Environmental History," 319–30; Sörlin and Warde, "The Problem of Environmental History," 107–30; Stroud, "Does Nature Always Matter?" 75–81; Soulé and Lease, eds., *Reinventing Nature?*

21 Cronon, *Changes in the Land*; Crosby, *Ecological Imperialism*; Mitchell, *Rule of Experts*, 52. See also Grove, "Environmental History," 261–82.

22 Crosby, *Ecological Imperialism*, 2, 270; Jeffrey A. Lockwood et al., "Comparison of Grasshopper (Orthoptera: Acrididae) Ecology," 8. Peter C. Perdue has made some similar, if more qualified, comparative observations concerning smallpox as a portmanteau biota in the South Pacific and Inner Asia; Perdue, *China Marches West*," 45–47.

18 *Across Forest, Steppe, and Mountain*

23 Cited in Young, *Postcolonialism*, 8.
24 Representative works are reviewed in Waley-Cohen, "The New Qing History," 193–206. Contrasting views of Chinese and U.S. scholars on the somewhat controversial subject can be found in Liu Fengyun and Liu Wenpeng, eds., *Qingchao de guojia rentong*. Liu's introduction concludes that the New Qing History remains a western theory about Chinese history that seems difficult to domesticate (11). Indeed, some Chinese authors have rejected its premises and claims entirely; Zhong Han, "Beimei 'Xin Qingshi'," 156–213.
25 See, for example, Rawski, "Reenvisioning the Qing," 829–50, and Ho, "In Defense of Sinicization," 123–55. I am approaching Sinicization here in a narrower sense than as "a bundle of assumptions regarding the reasons for and manifestations of cultural change throughout a very broad expanse of Asia"; Crossley, "Thinking about Ethnicity," 2.
26 Winterhalder, "Concepts in Historical Ecology," 33.
27 Rowe, "Water Control and the Qing Political Process," 360, 364–66, 368–69.
28 Osborne, "The Local Politics of Land Reclamation," 4, 6, 39.
29 Elvin, *The Retreat of the Elephants*, xxiii–xxiv.
30 Holling and Sanderson, "Dynamics of Disharmony," 61–62; Botkin, *Discordant Harmonies*, 5–13. For insights from fire ecology, see Bond and Keeley, "Fire as Global 'Herbivore,'" 387–94. For a study of Chinese fire management, see Hayes, "Fire and Society in Modern China," 23–35.
31 On nonequilibrium (also called disequilibrium) ecology, see Scoones, "New Ecology and the Social Sciences," 479–507; Rohde, *Nonequilibrium Ecology*. On new ecology, see, Biersack, "Introduction," 5–18; Worster, "Nature and the Disorder of History," 77.
32 Zhao Zhen, "Qingdai ShaanGan diqu de senlin," 262–72.
33 Marks, *Tigers, Rice, Silk, and Silt*. For a more comprehensive analytical bibliography of related works, see Bello, "Environmental Issues in Premodern China."
34 For overviews, see Bao, "Environmental History in China," 475–99; Zhao Zhen, "Zhongguo huanjing shi yanjiu," 122–24; Zhu Shiguang, "Qingdai shengtai huanjing," 51–54. For a more comprehensive analytical bibliography of related works, see Bello, "Environmental Issues in Pre-modern China."
35 See, for example, Zou Yilin, "Lun Qing yidai dui jiangtu bantu guannian," 183–96.
36 Qin Heping, "Yumi," 274–87; Luo Kanglong, "Lun Ming Qing yilai tongyi shuizhi de tuixing," 288–301; Zhao Zhen, *Qingdai xibu shengtai bianqian*; Xiao Ruiling et al., *Ming-Qing Nei Menggu xibu diqu kaifa*; Liu Shiyong, "Cong xuesi chong dao nüyuan chong," 393–423.
37 Subsequent studies based on 1980s data confirm that the basic population ratios and trends that produced them have changed very little since Hu compiled data in 1933; Hu Huanyong, "Zhongguo renkou de fenbu," 139–45.
38 Gosz, "Ecotone Hierarchies," 369; Zhang Jiana et al., "Mapping the Farming-Pastoral Ecotones in China," 78–87. For a critique of the ecotone concept, see Rhoades, "Archaeological Use and Abuse," 608–14.
39 Owen Lattimore's still influential work on China's "Inner Asian frontiers" is the most important expression of a steady-state condition separating China

Introduction 19

proper and the Mongolian steppe. While Lattimore is often more nuanced in his assertions than might be expected in a work that is nearly seventy-five years old, his conclusions tend toward primordial and immutable distinctions between "irreconcilable" conditions that ignore the more malleable state of the Sino-Mongolian ecotone; Lattimore, *Inner Asian Frontiers*, 54–55. On the other hand, his sensitivity to complex interactions between diverse livestock and forage vegetation have drawn the attention and appreciation of rangeland specialists as recently as 2008; Miller and Sheehy, "The Relevance of Owen Lattimore's Writings," 103–15.

40 An influential example of the former is White, *The Middle Ground*. An important example of the latter is Howell, "Ainu Ethnicity," 69–93. For comparative discussions see Chappell, "Ethnogenesis and Frontiers," 267–75; Baud and Van Schendel, "Toward a Comparative History of Borderlands," 211–42.

41 For discussions of borderland formation focused on human agency, see Adelman and Aron, "From Borders to Empires"; 814–41; Parker, "Towards an Understanding of Borderland Processes," 77–100; White, "Creative Misunderstandings and New Understandings," 9–14. For Eurasian perspectives, see Power and Standen, eds., *Frontiers in Question*; Znamenski, "The Ethic of Empire," 108.

42 My sense of "recursive" here is related to that of Giddens, *The Constitution of Society*, *xxiii*, 25–26. See also Bourdieu, *Outline of a Theory of Practice*, 78–87; Postone et al., "Introduction: Bourdieu and Social Theory," 4. Key elements of Giddens's structuration theory, such as "practical consciousness" and of Pierre Bourdieu's work on "field and habitus" seek to explain how individual practice and collective social formations are mutually constitutive. I suggest a similar recursive relationship exists between humans and ecology, although the latter cannot be entirely encompassed by the former.

43 Lower urbanization and related patterns also problematize analyses based on the conventional macroregion model, which is also rooted in questionable steady-state assumptions. For an extended critique, see Cartier, "Origins and Evolution of a Geographical Idea," 79–142. I have attempted to define my spatial units "environmentally," as distinctive interdependencies between people, flora and fauna. These form the locus of interactions between indigenous peoples, the Qing state, and select ecological elements all active within these comparatively patchy, more dynamic spaces.

44 Crumley, "The Ecology of Conquest," 183–85.

45 I use "Myanmar" to designate the region commonly referred to as "Burma" in various English sources in accordance with the Qing term "Miandian" and the Konbaung Dynasty term "Myanma"; Thant, *The Making of Modern Burma*, 83. See also Yule and Burnell, *Hobson-Jobson*, 131.

46 For some useful discussions of complications arising from ethnic terminology, see Abramson, *Ethnic Identity in Tang China*, 2–3; Yang Nianqun, *Hechu shi 'Jiangnan'?* 10–11; Elverskog, *Our Great Qing*, 24–25, 181n; Sneath, *The Headless State*, 65–68, 96–97.

47 For extensive abstracts of works in "Manchu studies" (*Manxue*) globally during the last century, see Yan Chongnian, *20 shiji Manxue zhuzuo tiyao*.

20   *Across Forest, Steppe, and Mountain*

Manchu archives and their organization have been surveyed in Guo Mengxiu, *Manwen wenxian gailun*; Elliott, "The Manchu-Language Archives of the Qing," 1–70. For recent work based on Manchu archival sources, see Oyunbilig, ed., *Manwen dang'an*. A major resource website for Manchu studies is the *Manchu Studies Group*, www.manchustudiesgroup.org.

48 Bello, "Relieving Mongols of their Pastoral Identity," 480–504; Bello, "The Cultured Nature of Imperial Foraging in Manchuria," 1–33; Bello, "To Go Where No Han Could Go for Long," 283–317.

I

Qing Fields in Theory and Practice

In the summer of 1765 a swarm of locusts appeared in the lands of the Pastoral Chakhar Mongol Plain Red Banner just north of the passes and was flitting southward toward the ripening grain fields of northern Shanxi. Plain Red Superintendent Ciriktai's job was to stop the swarm before it crossed into China proper. This required mobilization of a considerable number of his banner troops to conduct eradication operations intended to drive the locusts northward away from Shanxi and out into the steppe. Ciriktai and his colleague in charge of the Bordered Yellow Chakhar Banner, Nawang, were both quite explicit that the swarms were no danger to Mongol pastures, but only to Han fields of the "interior" (Ma: *dorgi ba*). Unbeknown to Ciriktai, however, officials in the Shanxi subprefecture of Ningyuan had rushed out several hundred of their Han charges to conduct an unauthorized operation that succeeded in driving the swarm southward "quite near the cultivated fields of the Han." The ineptitude of China proper's officials had to be corrected by another operation by Ciriktai's Mongols. In conjunction with over six hundred other Pastoral Chakar troops, they successfully redirected the swarm back northward, saving northern Shanxi's fields from devastation.[1]

Inner Asians rescuing north China from steppe invasion would have been a quite unusual occurrence in the vast majority of Chinese dynastic cases. During the Qing, however, it was simply understood as part of the job north of the passes. Ciriktai, for example, did not wait for any directive from Beijing. He personally led his men to take on the swarm on his own initiative, which accounts for the lack of coordination with Han efforts to the south. Such cooperation, whatever its limits, distinguishes the Qing empire in environmental historical practice as Mongol horsemen were deployed to save Han fields south of the Great Wall from northern swarms of various regional species of *Locusta migratoria*. The relation between humans and horses mobilized to preserve that between humans and plants was the central component of this cooperation. As one of Ciriktai's fellow Chakhar officers noted, Inner Asian–inflected mounted hunting practices were required to stop the locusts. Cavalry first "formed up in battue-style" (Ma: *adame jergilefi*) to encircle and drive the swarm into a central space. Then they were finally trampled under the horses' hooves to accomplish what "human strength could not overcome" (Ma: *niyalma i hūsun eterakū*).[2]

Chiriktai's 1765 operation also affords a glimpse of the interdependency between the Qing empire's two main divisions of environmental relations that were constitutive of ethnic Han Chinese and Manchu-Mongol identities. The empire fostered both relations to create a space of distinctively Qing fields where imperial versions of hunting and farming would nurture human embodiments of state authority across Inner Asian steppe and China proper's alluvial plains. This chapter will examine these two main divisions to provide a general context in which to consider the more regionally nuanced case studies that follow.

Mounted bow hunting and its related skills, which enabled Ciriktai's Mongols to crush the locusts, centered on the pursuit of wild animals across uncultivated areas north of the Great Wall. Human military prowess was developed through animal "resistance" as prey fled and hid within a similarly tempering terrain and climate. This "venery" process was necessary for the formation of the empire's paradigmatic Inner Asian identity.

A very different process constructed the corresponding identity embodying the empire's mastery of its other great domain, China proper. Here humans intensively cultivated domesticated cereal grasses. Mainly wheat, millet, and rice were grown on land that had been terraformed for centuries to maximize yields under challenging dynamic conditions of climate, soil quality, and incursions from animals such as *Locusta migratoria*. Simultaneously a particular Han human identity was also cultivated. These *liangmin* ("law-abiding people") were also raised in this process of "arablism" from which the state drew most of its revenue, many of its officials, and nearly all its population, rural and urban.

Although certainly different in many ways, both venery and arablism were integral components the empire required to reconcile considerable

Qing Fields in Theory and Practice

human and ecological diversities to maintain the vast unity of Inner Asia and China proper. In this sense, "from many, one" was the main Qing environmental historical contradiction and challenge. Imperial identities had to be centrally the same for purposes of unity but had to be appropriately different locally to maintain the incorporation of multiple regions. The necessary tension between central uniformity and local diversity drove Qing environmental history.

The ethnic manifestation of this tension between Inner Asian conquest dynasties and their majority Han subjects is first and foremost defined in arablist terms as "Hanspace," then in venery ones, in the discussion that follows. The longer, dominant theory and practice of Hanspace arablism developed under threat of less articulate venery practice, which was, nevertheless, periodically triumphant.

Although pre-Qing imperial arablism grew the same plants, it did not raise the same people in the process. Previous Chinese empires had been much more monocultural both ethnically and ecologically, making Ciriktai's operations unthinkable in the Ming, for example. This monoculture had been formed from the "ruling elite's" reductive ordering of the complex diversity of its mainly Han world, which "throughout history . . . viewed the people of the northern steppes with an almost traumatic apprehension." "Hanspace," became the reductive and apprehensive ethnic-ecological expression of imperial China proper's arablism in comparative isolation from other environmental relations as a type of (super)natural habitat for agrarian Han Chinese.[3] The Qing empire was an unprecedented integration of arablist Hanspace into a more "multi-environmental" association with Inner Asian venery.

GROUNDING HANSPACE

In his manuscript *Huangshu*, Wang Fuzhi described China proper as an ideal Han ecosystem. He envisioned "lofty peaks" flowing together around China like "a surrounding wall" and "mountain torrents" that spill from steep precipices that protect China "like moats." These formed a tight belt of "veins" surrounding a region where "cold and heat regulate one another, language is mutually intelligible, appearances are similar, the 'hundred grains' the source of common nourishment, the 'six domesticated beasts' beget each their kind, [and] commerce mutually proliferates." Mountain ranges all merged to form the "natural unification" of the "central region" (*zhongqu*) of China proper. Wang's description broadly corresponds to what is known in Chinese geomancy as a "dragon's true lair" (*long zhen xue*), where *qi* naturally concentrates.[4]

The nature of *qi* and its related systems of thought are equivocal in their distinctions between material and metaphysical phenomena, a condition I try to convey through use of the term "(meta)physical."[5] Here *qi*'s primary sense is the oscillating natural matter-energy conceived as (meta)physically determining humans and their respective cultural and historical experiences rooted in distinct geographical areas. Wang saw the whole of China proper as a *qi*-saturated "dragon." This process forms "Hanspace," an exclusive historical habitat for the Han.[6] For Wang geographic location defines ethnicity, but the location itself is conditioned by *qi* in an explicit hierarchy:

Barbarians [*Yidi*] were born in a land different from that of the Han [*Huaxia*]; this difference in lands is a difference in *qi*. When *qi* is different, customs are different; when customs differ, everything known or done is also different. Thus, there are intrinsic differences between noble and mean. Lands are distinct, boundaries set, and the atmosphere special such that they cannot be jumbled.[7]

This is a view of mutually conditioning place and "race" not exactly determined by environment, but by *qi*, a (meta)physical substance that establishes an ethnospatial hierarchy that is environmentally compartmentalized. This substance usually comprises two complementary, but also hierarchical, components, *yin* and *yang*. Their interaction is governed by *shen* (the "unfathomable") to produce universal (meta)physical "change" that cannot be fully comprehended or expressed.[8]

Hanspace, as a reductive and apprehensive expression, defined and regulated Han ethnic identity, particularly among elites under authority of Inner Asian conquest dynasties such as the Qing, which men such as Wang resisted so bitterly in hidden word and open deed. It strongly fixed that identity to a particular place, China proper, as the natural ground of their historical action. This ground was geographically, culturally, and metaphysically, in sum "naturally," separate from other places and peoples. Chinese elite responses to incursion by Others into Hanspace reveal both accommodation and oppositional trends, all of which refine, and sometimes redefine, Hanspace under conditions of ethnically disorienting encounters with other human diversity.

Strictly speaking, Hanspace, predating modern science, was not precisely "environmental determinism." It was, rather, a premodern Han environmental construct of heterogeneous elements predicated on a direct correspondence between humans and their (meta)physical environments, which were mutually interpenetrating in an essentializing

Qing Fields in Theory and Practice

fashion. These elements included aspects of Confucian philosophy and historiography as well as less orthodox geomancy (*fengshui* or, more precisely, *kanyu*).[9]

Hanspace was never authoritatively systematized or consistently transmitted. Moreover, the Qing dynasty devoted much effort to banning and eliminating texts that expressed Hanspace oppositionally. A representative outcome demonstrating the equivocal Manchu response to Hanspace is the fact that some authors were honored. The eminent Zhejiang literatus Hu Wei, for example, found a distinguished place in the Qing canon of *Siku quanshu*, and the noted historian and scholar-official Zhao Yi's essays were preserved in the important statecraft work *Huangchao jinshi wenbian*. In contrast, works of dissident Han such as Lü Liuliang were banned – and destroyed where possible – by dynastic authorities under the notorious Qing literary inquisitions. The *fengshui* author Shen Hao openly referred to the inhibiting effects of the inquisitions on traditional Hanspace cartomantic practices of celestial patterns (*tianwen*) and terrestrial principles (*dili*) in his 1712 work.[10] Still other works remained unpublished or underground. Wang Fuzhi's, for example, did not begin to emerge until the mid–nineteenth century.

These facts are certainly testaments to Hanspace's significance but often render the extant record vague and incomplete. It is difficult to determine Hanspace texts' precise content, extent, and influence, although many prominent thinkers were clearly aware of them. At the same time, ambiguity provided an opportunity for a much wider range of reception that accounts for the dichotomous responses to these texts. Han elite constituencies could thus be mobilized to support, or oppose, the imperial conquest state.

A relatively consistent reception along these lines emerges from the "Han-barbarian discourse" (*Xia-yi lun*), deployed by Chinese intellectuals throughout the imperial period.[11] This discourse, formed long before the onset of the post-Tang conquest dynasties, was generally predicated on making rigid, naturalistic, and hierarchical distinctions between the two groups. Consequently, this discourse does not encompass strong accommodationist perspectives such as those more publicly visible and legitimate in the Qing. Indeed, it is precisely the emergence of conquest dynasties that expanded and altered this discourse so radically, which drove its chauvinist manifestations underground or, in many cases, eradicated their texts. The Han-barbarian discourse also does not center on relations between space and ethnicity, although some elements of these relations are certainly present. For these somewhat contradictory reasons of both wider

26 · *Across Forest, Steppe, and Mountain*

applicability and narrower focus, this discourse is not entirely synonymous with Hanspace. The accommodation of accommodationist views was made possible by literally wider perspectives arising from Inner Asian conquest. Hanspace could then rearticulate the Han-barbarian discourse, and its historical variants such as anti-Manchuism, beyond a self-other dichotomy of mere race or ethnicity.

ACCOMMODATIONIST HANSPACE

Hanspace has been visible in Chinese elite cartographic texts since the emergence of antiquity's classical canon, containing the only accounts of the first three dynasties, the Shang, Xia, and Zhou, known in imperial times. One of the most significant portions of these texts, the "Tribute of Yu" (*Yugong*), is generally held to be the earliest classical expression of Chinese geography. In it, Yu, the founder of the Xia dynasty, established the formal boundaries of China proper, known as the Nine Provinces (*Jiuzhou*), after controlling the floodwaters that had inundated the whole region. The "Tribute" account of his postdiluvian renovation of the physical, political, and cultural core of the Han people became a primary Hanspace text.

In later ages, Confucian scholars sought to determine the Nine Provinces' precise location in works sufficiently voluminous to culminate in Hu Wei's self-deprecatingly titled *Yugong chuizhi* (*A Peep-hole View of the "Tribute of Yu"*). Contemporaries considered this work, complied between 1694 and 1697 with maps added in 1705, as the definitive commentary on its subject, mainly the clarification of toponyms. Hu's work has been read as a demonstration of empirical and demystifying "practical learning" largely devoted to evaluating and clarifying the text and its numerous historical glosses.[12] A major rationale for this approach, however, is to affirm empirically and rationalistically a (meta)physical concept of Han imperial space, primarily by linking the Nine Provinces to their contemporary Qing counterparts.[13]

To this end, Hu augmented his extended gloss on each line of the text with forty-seven maps, including a "Map of the Five Domains" (*Wufu tu*), an ethnic schematic of the Nine Provinces, conventionally represented as five concentric squares. Each square comprised an area of five hundred *li* to form the central Domain of the Sovereign (*Dian fu*), then that of the Nobles (*Hou fu*), then the Domain of Pacification (*Sui fu*), then the Domain of Restraint (*Yao fu*), and, finally, the outermost Wild Domain (*Huang fu*).[14] Hu's assemblage is part of a cartographic tradition

Qing Fields in Theory and Practice

unconcerned with precise measurement. Instead it conveys facts that can be read here as a template for the spatialization of Han ethnic identity in a political idiom.[15] The three innermost squares constitute the "core of the state" (zhongbang), regions of exclusively Han residence and administration, with state-subject interaction in the core primarily defined by taxation. This core is the realm of Han authoritative presence by virtue of the proximity of the imperial state's apparatus for the maintenance of administrative and ideological order, zhengjiao. The person of the emperor most visibly embodies this apparatus as he presides directly over the Domain of the Sovereign. Hanspace attenuates as it moves outward from this embodied central domain.[16]

Ethnically significant attenuation, however, begins at the core's outermost square, the Domain of Pacification. Zhengjiao diminishes with distance from the more central Han zones and proximity to the two outer zones, which are almost exclusively inhabited by non-Han "barbarian" peoples under indirect rule of the imperial Chinese state. In other words, both distance and ethnic diversity begin to erode Hanspace. It is in the Domain of Pacification that, in the words of one annotator of the Tribute" whom Hu cites, "the distinction between inner and outer is made" and, consequently, the imperial Chinese frontier and its greater ethnic diversity begins.[17]

Such principles of ethnospatial distinction had governed cartographic practices across dynasties. One of the earliest extant maps, carved on a stone stele in 1136, is a "Map of the Tracks of Yu" (Yuji tu). This map had been produced during the Southern Song, a time when northern China had fallen under Inner Asian domination. This crisis of foreign occupation of Han territory, originating in the late Tang, is an important context for the roughly contemporary production of such Song maps as the Yixing shanhe liangjie tu. The title of the map refers to the Tang Buddhist astronomer-monk Yixing's revision of the system of correspondence between particular celestial bodies and each of the Nine Provinces for divination purposes. Yixing's (meta)geographical work seems to have formed part of the foundation for the textual expression of Hanspace as it existed in the Ming and Qing periods.[18]

Yixing, building on the innovative work of his Tang predecessors such as Li Chunfeng, made a significant and comprehensive revision of the "field allocation" (fenye) system of astral-terrestrial correspondences.[19] Based as it originally was in the late Zhou on relatively unchanging ties between points of earth and sky, field allocation was unable to adapt to expansions and contractions of territory. Li helped initiate the system's revision by linking celestial bodies to contemporary Tang administrative territories while retaining Nine Provinces terminology. Yixing's improvement was to link mountains and rivers, instead of ephemeral administrative divisions, to ruling celestial bodies. The cardinal points of this system were China's "Five Sacred Peaks" or "Marchmounts" (*Wuyue*), as well as its major rivers, chiefly the Yellow and the Yangzi, whose (meta)geographical images (*shanchuan zhi xiang*) directly corresponded to those of the Milky Way and constituted the main barriers between Han and non-Han peoples. The "northern barrier" (*beijie*) was roughly delineated by the Yellow River and the Great Wall "to restrict" the western *Rong* and the northern *Di*. The "southern barrier" (*nanjie*) was roughly delineated by the Yangzi and the Lingnan mountain range to keep out the southern *Man* and the eastern *Yi*. Both barriers ran west to east, reaching to Korea in the north and the coast in the south. Throughout the "stratum" (*ji*) of each barrier circulated a distinctive *qi* force associated with its particular direction. The stratum of the northern barrier "carried" the *yin* force that infused the north's natural conditions within subsurface "terrestrial veins" (*diluo*). The stratum of the southern barrier's terrestrial veins carried the *yang* force that likewise infused the south's natural conditions.[20]

Yixing restored the field allocation system's original basis in physical topography anchored on major geographical expressions as material manifestations of space more resistant to human historical change. Yixing's work also made Hu's project feasible because most subsequent changes were spatially marginal or linguistically nominal. Consequently, despite revisions in the interval, Hu could empirically find that conditions between antiquity and his own time were "quite similar" in correspondences between the Nine Provinces and the contemporary Qing map of China proper.[21] Physical geography, not simply human ethnic difference, played a fundamental role in this process. Indeed, Yixing found a more anthropocentric basis alone was too unstable to preserve the field allocation system, despite the continuity of the celestial component throughout the system's permutations. Hanspace in this way became an enduring expression of the landscape transcending the dynastic cycle, and this influence is seen in later Song maps and subsequent references in the writings of Confucian scholars. Intensified interethnic conflict during and after the Song made it all the more important that the fields allocated according to Yixing's principles were Han fields.

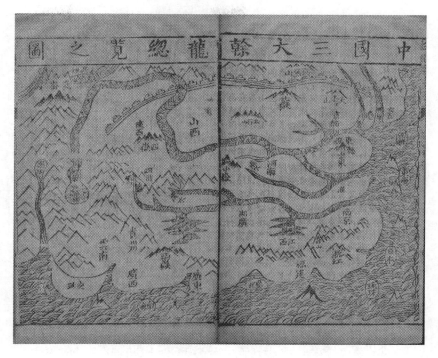

MAP 2: China as Great Triple-trunked Dragon

Some of the geomantic principles Yixing relied on are also visible on Ming maps that envisioned China proper as consisting of the bodies or "trunks" (*gan*) of three dragons of terrestrial *qi* in mountain form. China's dragon trunks are divided along a west-to-east axis by the Yellow River in the north and the Yangzi in the south. The image of "China as great triple-trunked dragon" (*Zhongguo san da gan long*) was also described in detailed provincial terms in Qing geomantic works:

> There are three dragons inside China, called the three trunks; they are the *gen* [northeast], *zhen* [east], and *sun* [southeast] ... The provinces of Shanxi, Zhili, Shandong, and half of Henan are all to the left [i.e., north] of the Yellow River and are the *gen* dragon's [terrestrial] veins. Gansu, Sichuan, Shaanxi, Chang'an, Huguang, Liangjiang, Luoyang, and Kaifeng are all the *zhen* dragon's veins. Yunnan, Guizhou, Fujian, Guangdong, Guangxi, and Jiangxi are all the *sun* dragon's veins.[22]

Here the dragon trunks are nexuses comprising structures both natural, as terrain circulating vital *qi*, and anthropogenic, as administrative divisions and urban spaces. The Hanspace habitat thus existed through an

30 *Across Forest, Steppe, and Mountain*

interdependence of humans and ecology not just by virtue of a Han-barbarian self-other dichotomy.

Even tribute, a primary measure of Hanspace ostensibly defined by ethnically diverse human relations, is bounded by ecological links forged by distance and distinct types of flora, fauna, and minerals. Hanspace manifests itself metaphysically in that it always exists to some degree everywhere and, since the beginning of Chinese recorded history, at every time in essentially the same way. However, it is not absolutely unlimited, and tribute appears as a result of spatial confines and differences. In Hu's view the influence of *shengjiao* extended beyond the empire's physical administrative boundaries (*jiangli*) that encompassed the Nine Provinces. Nevertheless, although "there is no distance [*shengjiao*] does not reach," it was considerably attenuated by distance from the Han core of the state. Indeed, tribute, in its most basic sense as the local produce, flora, and fauna presented by subordinates to superiors, was the primary tangible evidence of the operation of *shengjiao* outside the exclusively Han core of the state.[23] This ethnic core also attenuates through the two transitional outer domains culminating in the "four seas," which are not really bodies of water and entirely inhabited by the non-Han Yi, Di, Rong, and Man peoples. As Hu in effect states, these groups rule their own lands and people.[24]

The force of *shengjiao* nevertheless remains sufficient to tie the Han core and non-Han periphery together and even portend their eventual unification by assimilation:

The lords of the Domain of Restraint and the Wild Domain, which lie beyond [the three domains of the Sovereign, Nobles, and Pacification], ... all present [tribute] in order to express their sincere desire to move toward assimilation by proper emulation ... Tribute relations even extend to the island barbarians of the east beyond the seas and the various western barbarians, who all come to make offerings and be governed ... Tribute should be taken in the sense of wide, of great. For ... taxation is limited to the core of the state, but tribute links the world. To say "taxation" does not include tribute, but to say "tribute" does include taxation. Thus, when historians use tribute for the name of this section [i.e., the "*Yugong*"], they actually mean it in the sense of the greater unity [*da yitong*] from east to west.[25]

Tribute here is the culture that unites the entire world, regardless of distance or ethnic diversity, but depends on both as realized through the distinctive varieties of flora, fauna, and minerals that are its material currency. Taxation, in the form of regular agrarian products from China proper, is a subcategory that is purely Han.

Tribute is also the conduit through which *shengjiao* travels to incorporate new territory and peoples into the Nine Provinces. Hu asserts,

Qing Fields in Theory and Practice

against commentators who would permanently restrict Han hegemony to the Five Domains (*Wufu*), numerous historical examples of the Sinification of previously barbarian regions. Min (i.e., Zhejiang), which was not part of the original Han core, is one such example of how this hegemony has persisted to "turn hearts toward the true Way, so that they are daily farther away from beasts."[26] Such incorporation is central to an accommodationist interpretation of Hanspace as it emerges under Inner Asian conquest, a significance not lost on Hu's contemporaries. A preface to the *Chuizhi* by Xu Bingyi notes that "our state continues Yu's [achievement of] subjection so that *shengjiao* extends everywhere to far exceed that of the Xia dynasty." In Hu's reading this view is validated by, for example, the *shengjiao* transformation of the Tang "Western Regions" (*Xiyu*), which lay in the two outer domains, into Qing Xinjiang eighty-odd years later.[27] Hanspace could thus serve the interests of a non-Han dynasty in a way the Han-barbarian discourse could not. Hanspace terrain, however, was sufficiently unstable to allow the formation of dissenting views, and ultimately, of a dissident Han identity.

DISSIDENT HANSPACE

Hanspace was existentially informed by *qi*, a dynamic substance circulating in shifting concentrations throughout Hanspace with both ecological and political effects. *Qi* was thus the key link between nature and culture in Hanspace and was primarily responsible for the dynastic cycle as it declines in one region to concentrate in another. This flux of *qi* can be, for Ming loyalists such as Wang Fuzhi, a catastrophe as *qi* drains away from China proper. For Qing loyalists, however, this flux progressively flows to the northeast to empower the rise of the Manchus beyond the Great Wall.

Geomantically *qi*'s effects were visible as relatively stable mountains and rivers. Below ground, however, this "terrestrial *qi*" (*diqi*) was not in a steady state. It could flow in unpredictable directions through subterranean veins, such as those that defined Yixing's strata, with manifest political disruption on the surface. Accommodationists could view such disruptions as progressive. Zhao Yi, for example, read monumental shifts in Chinese dynastic history based on the principle that "the waxing and waning of terrestrial *qi* inevitably changes over time." *Qi* became dispersed in the northwest, the center of previous Han Chinese dynasties and their capitals, and ultimately reconcentrated itself in the northeast, homeland of his overlords, the Manchus. Zhao located this tipping point in the late Tang when "the ground [of the dynastic capital of Chang'an] became unsteady and unstable, an indication of the exhaustion and unceasing dispersal of its *qi*." The Qing dynasty was thus a historical result of a natural process of one to two hundred years of *qi* flow from the northwest to the northeast. Over this period, a steady succession of Inner Asian conquest dynasties first gained "part" of China proper under the Liao, then "half the empire" under the Jin, and then the whole territory under the Mongols. The Qing alone, however, enjoyed the full political benefits of consolidated sovereignty over China proper as *qi* reached maximum accumulation in the northeast. The Qing was now able to displace the Ming, occupy China proper, and then expand control beyond it. Manchu Qing legitimacy was thus "naturally" derived by an extrapolation of traditional Hanspace dynamics into Inner Asian territory. China proper nevertheless remained at the center of this process, the culmination of *qi* as imperial political authority.[28]

Zhao's *qi*, however, was distinctively Qing and not Ming. In contrast, Ming Taizu could exult over his expulsion of the Mongols from China proper as a natural occurrence of the same basic historical mechanics of *qi*:

Since the overthrow of the Song throne, the Yuan used the barbarians of the north to invade and rule China, and there was no one within or beyond the Four Seas who was not subjugated. How could this be human strength; for it was actually conferred by heaven … Now at this time celestial fate has revolved around, and the *qi* of the central plains flourishes. From amid the myriads, there is now a sage incarnate [i.e., Ming Taizu, himself] to drive out the northern barbarians and restore Han China [*Zhonghua*].[29]

In a similar spirit Lü Liuliang, whose anti-Manchu thought resonated beyond the grave in the Zeng Jing case, believed that the rise of a sage occurred once every five hundred years in response to the waxing of *qi*.[30] Such views formed the basis of a dissident Hanspace articulated during the Qing in latent contest with public accommodationist expressions such as Zhao Yi's.

It is obvious from these contrasting views that Hanspace was partly a state of mind and, so, subject to interpretation. Both sides, however, concurred on many of the basic historical mechanics of *qi* as well as some of its effects.[31] Hanspace remained the common intellectual property of the empire's Han constituency but also reflected the diverse responses of that constituency to Inner Asian conquest. As a result, dissident and accommodationist variants, all still based on the same *qi* mechanics, could arise simultaneously in response to Khitan, Jurchen, Mongol, or Manchu domination.

Qing Fields in Theory and Practice

During the Han imperial intervals between Inner Asian rule, particularly during the Ming, a broader consensus on the inviolability of Hanspace could arise, but the necessity of explaining previous periods of extended non-Han rule qualified even the most chauvinistic assertions. So Ming Taizu could reject human agency in the face of the natural conditions created by revolutions in "celestial fate." Such problems were confronted amid the loftiest peaks of historiographic inquiry during the Ming and served to compel adaptation of the traditional discourse to account for unprecedented "violations" of Hanspace and even for ethnogenesis itself.

Hu Han, one of the Ming compilers of the official Yuan dynastic history, augmented views similar to Yixing's that seem definitive of the contemporary state of Hanspace concepts. In his explanation of macrohistorical change, Hu stressed the importance of the topographic ethnic divide embodied in "terrestrial strata" (*diji*), which "distinguish between China and the barbarians, between inner and outer." When Han ruled non-Han, each remained in their proper place, especially because "barbarians live beyond the [Yellow and Yangzi] rivers where there is a different atmosphere and customs are also different." Even the efforts of enlightened rulers such as Shun and King Wen could not overcome these barriers, with ethnogenic consequences: "the sages were unable to unite with these peoples in benevolence. Thus, their races became possible."[32]

Wang Fuzhi, who had lived through the trauma of the Qing conquest, refined a number of concepts visible in Hu's formulation to produce what is probably the most comprehensive extant synthesis of dissident Hanspace. In broad historical analytical surveys such as *Song lun* and *Du tongjian lun*, as well as in shorter works such as *Huangshu*, Wang's synthesis included many of the ideas visible or latent in Hu Wei, Zhao Yi, Hu Han, and Yixing. Without asserting a conscious intellectual linear continuity between all these thinkers, it is possible to see how Hanspace provided room for the formation of Han identity in dissident, as well as accommodationist, mode. Wang's writings can certainly be read as classic expressions of crypto-anti-Manchu and protonationalist thought, but this tends to obscure Hanspace's larger effects that contributed to the construction of both dissident and accommodationist Han identities.[33] Wang, unable to exert public influence during his lifetime, could not redefine the whole of Hanspace ideology as anti-Manchu, despite his influence on late Qing antidynastic movements. He does, however, reveal in unusual detail dissident Hanspace ideology that the Qing state considered seditious, capable, that is, of forming dissident Han identities.

Wang's views are informed not only by human actions, the Manchu conquest chief among them, but also by the ecology of China proper, particularly its terrain. A complex, and not always consistent, interplay of culture and nature forms a version of the Hanspace construct so innately powerful that it renders long-term non-Han residence in China unnatural. "Numinous natural defenses" (*tiangu*), especially potent south of the Yangzi, made it physically impossible for non-Han to exist in China over the long term. Non-Han "naturally know that this is not their land" and that their incursion violates "a natural law [*tianji*] ... by abandoning the land where they can properly dwell and thereby endure."[34] In some respects here and elsewhere, Wang invokes a type of ethnic cleansing for China proper naturally effected by the region's own ecosystem.

Humans, however, play an active role in their own formation as a distinct group when "early in the life of a people ... they unite ... and keep harm at a distance by expelling their mongrels." It is also critical for a ruler to establish unity within this newly emergent "ethnos" (*lei*) by controlling their "own territory" through their "own principles" to "bring forth the creative *qi*-force of celestial *yang* and terrestrial *yin*." An ethnos takes active advantage of its natural surroundings to reinforce itself. Rulers thus "employ the substance of *qi* to consolidate their natural territories," especially in terms of siting the dynastic capital.[35] Subsequent dynastic history is conceived as a struggle to maintain this formative and pristine environmental relationship against incursion.

Space, especially as distance, is a critical category for ethnic identity because it can preserve or erode an ethnos. The *Rong* and *Di* were actually ethnic casualties of just such an erosion in Wang's view. Both had been "people of China" until "they declined over generations, and the Way [i.e., Han culture] failed until they sank to a different race." This decline occurred as a direct result of isolation from a disjointed imperial center, comparable to Hu Wei's "core of the state" and the attenuated effects of its *shengjiao* over expanding distances. When the center fragmented at the end of the Zhou dynasty, "lords of mountain crannies and shorelines were established on heights and, confident in such defenses, did not attend at court audiences." The subjects of these ineffectual polities, including the *Rong* and *Di*, became "scattered across the streams, mountains, forests, and valleys of China, constantly ranging about so that they became wandering peoples."[36] Physical isolation within China proper, augmented by defensible natural terrain of remote mountains and shores, blocked the court center's ideological hegemony of *shengjiao* through the ritual media of distinctively Han culture such as "court audiences."

Qing Fields in Theory and Practice

Destabilizing ethnic diversity is the direct result of a corrosive confluence of ecological and anthropogenic conditions.

Wang's remedy is a proper Han habitat consisting of an established agrarian order mediated by the *junxian* system of provinces, prefectures, and districts for security and taxation to restrict itinerancy into spaces too isolated for the state's control apparatus. His program for the reclamation of all Hanspace in China proper under ethnically appropriate principles would be to settle the surplus population of "migrants" on a commensurate amount of arable land, "delineate its fields and boundaries," and then "indoctrinate the youth to settle their natures and enable them to attain their aspirations." The result would be a habitat that would "enable the stabilizing of agricultural production, the constancy of the gentry, and the regularization of state revenues." In effect, Wang's Hanspace is intended to re-Sinicize locals by restoring relations between humans and cereal plants. Wang even cites some locales in contemporary Guizhou supposed to have undergone such conversion.[37]

It is notable that Wang's ideal Hanspace is ethnically homogenous, unlike Hu Wei's "Tribute" Hanspace encompassing peripheral non-Han. This ethnic distinction is the consistent difference between dissident and accommodationist Hanspace. Yet two vital common links persist. One is the emphasis on historical continuity of imperial identity in classical Chinese terms. Wang expresses this in his conclusion that "everywhere in the Nine Provinces from mountain peak to winding shore, all are become the great Xia."[38]

The other common link is *qi* mechanics, although the dissident view considers the natural depletion of "pure" (*chun*) *qi* that sustains Hanspace as an ethnoecological catastrophe. Pure *qi* is undifferentiated, and its natural circulation in China nurtures political unity among its "unmiscegenated" (*tonglei*) people. Once *qi* is exhausted, however, a corresponding political vacuum results, attracting incursions of "motley" (*za*) and "chaotically differentiated" *qi* embodied in non-Han "mongrels" (*yilei*), spawned from the endemic disorder beyond China. Incursion is ultimately fatal to the outsiders, for whom "the land is unsuitable and heaven unhelpful," but also pollutes China proper.[39]

The ethnic ecology of differential *qi* provided a framework for historical explanation of Inner Asian conquest. In the eyes of the authors of one Ming geomantic manual the motley *qi* of the Jin and Yuan precluded Jurchen and Mongol long-term residence in China's "northern dragon" trunk. The imperial polity was only properly reestablished with the construction of Ming Beijing in the region, held the most environmentally

36 *Across Forest, Steppe, and Mountain*

suitable for (Han) Chinese capitals as far back in antiquity as Yao and Shun.[40] Here *qi*'s permutations provide the narrative of a dissident Hanspace history.

Wang explores this narrative in traumatic detail as he conventionally locates a watershed in the late Tang when "after several centuries, the land's virtue decayed and gradually became saline." Exhaustion was considered inevitable and was integral to geomantic understandings of *qi* mechanics that limit the geographical tenure of a dynastic capital as it draws on "royal *qi*" (*wang qi*). In this instance, however, *qi* depletion resulted in something "beyond calculation" as "the Jurchen [Jin] and Tartars [Mongols] received the mandate" to take up imperial residence in north China.[41] This is Wang's unnatural disaster for a narrow, monocultural Hanspace, which Zhao Yi divined as a naturally progressive development for a wider, multicultural Hanspace.

Such conflicting identities, formed in a common Hanspace tradition, were Han embodiments of the new environmental relations engendered by the establishment of the Qing dynasty in 1644. Whether viewed as natural law or crime against nature, the fact of the Qing conquest imposed itself on Hanspace, which was itself so imposing that the Manchu conquerors were forced into their own accommodations and oppositions to control Han ethnic identity formation.

The Qing Throne's Struggle for Hanspace of Its Own

The Qing literary inquisitions conducted from the Shunzhi into the Qianlong reigns are extended testimonies to the Qing state's concern over Han elite identity formation.[42] The role of Hanspace in this concern is exemplified by the 1729 Zeng Jing case, which was personally and publicly supervised by the Yongzheng emperor.[43] The case was a unique instance of "debate" between Han and Manchu over conflicting versions of Hanspace. The emperor was moved to publish his official version as the *Dayi juemi lu* (*Record of the Great Counsel to Enlighten the Deluded*).

The accused Zeng Jing was an unsuccessful degree candidate from Hunan working as a teacher, who decided to overthrow the Qing in 1728 after reading some of Lü Liuliang's writings that were subtly critical of Manchu rule. Zeng felt a particular urgency due in part to a series of natural disasters, which he interpreted as the traditional celestial opposition to an illegitimate dynasty, that struck Hunan and nearby provinces in that same year. Zeng had actually gone so far as to send a letter to the

Shaanxi-Sichuan governor-general Yue Zhongqi urging he lead a rebellion as the descendant of the famous Song general, Han ethnic hero, and martyr Yue Fei, who had fought the Jurchen Jin. Yue Zhongqi turned Zeng in, and he was interrogated and ultimately spared after his public retraction, which was also published as part of the *Dayi juemi lu*.

In the process of denouncing the intellectual heirs of thinkers such as Lü, the Yongzheng emperor made a direct refutation of dissident Hanspace concepts. The emperor rejected the notion that there should be any discriminatory distinction "between Han and barbarian [*Hua yi*]" because the Qing has received the mandate of heaven to rule both "within and beyond China [*zhongwai*]." So it was "particularly inappropriate" to treat anyone who acquiesced and became a loyal subject differently on the basis of ethnic identity. The emperor also objected to ideas that sought to "erect barriers" between Manchus and Han, because they were rooted in ignorance of the fact that "Manchuria is like one of China's native territories."[44]

The emperor's father, the Kangxi emperor, had helped to set a precedent for this assertion, although the Yongzheng emperor made no direct reference to it. A 1677 expedition had been dispatched to Manchuria to determine the precise location of the Changbai Mountain range (Changbaishan; Ma: Golmin Šanggiyan Alin), in part to confirm its location as the numinous center of the Manchu's original homeland. Upon its discovery, the Kangxi emperor decreed that "the mountain's mystic power" should be formally recognized through the institution of ritual sacrifices to its officially designated spirit, so that Changbai's "ritual codes will be like those of the Five Marchmounts."[45] The cardinal points of Hanspace were in this way extended northeast in the form of a Manchurian Marchmount.

The Kangxi emperor, however, expressed a significantly different orientation in a conversation with his senior court officials in 1709. The emperor queried one of his Grand Secretaries, Li Guangdi, as to the geographic origin of Shandong's terrestrial veins that formed its mountains. The emperor authoritatively corrected Li's reply that these ran from locales in Shaanxi and Henan. He asserted that all of Shandong's mountains, including the chief of the Five Marchmounts, Taishan, were ultimately rooted in the Changbai range. Terrestrial veins ran under the Gulf of Bohai to form a "dragon of surpassing extent." Li accordingly deferred to the emperor's "wide and comprehensive" canonical knowledge.[46] Qing rule was literally redrawing the map of Hanspace and impressing it on Han elites, whose reception, sincere or not, was certainly public. Quantitative, and even locational, revision was not new to

38 *Across Forest, Steppe, and Mountain*

Marchmount geography, which had plotted only four, for example, during the Warring States period. Marchmounts by tradition expanded "in direct relation with the expansion of the imperium" and so allowed enough space to accommodate a Qing imperial relandscaping.[47]

The result was a contradiction in Han-barbarian discursive terms, a Qing Hanspace. Behind the Yongzheng emperor's assertion that Manchuria was like a Chinese province towered the fifth sacred peak of Changbai. Beyond it lay his successor the Qianlong emperor's future assertion in his rereading of Ming versions of Jin and Yuan history that "the eastern *Yi*, the western *Rong*, the southern *Man*, and the northern *Di* all are names derived from places, no different from ... Jiangnan or Hebei." The emperor even made a historic break with the past to distinguish between "the China [*Zhongxia*] of the Han, Tang, Song and Ming dynasties" and "the China [*Zhongxia*] of our imperial dynasty" when dealing with Inner Asian peoples such as the Zunghars.[48]

Reinforced through exploration, interrogation, and correction, Qing Hanspace was intended to encompass a less reductive, less apprehensive group of ethnic identities to embody the diversified hierarchy of a larger empire. The Han-barbarian discourse was much narrower in all these respects. The Qing read this discourse as a symptom of dynastic weakness, not a cure for it, as the Yongzheng emperor informed the Han public. He said that the Han-barbarian discourse had persisted in subsequent times of partial unification (*pian'an*), such as the Jin, Song, and Six Dynasties periods, when "there were many states, all equal in size and virtue, none being able to dominate the others." Consequently "northern people slandered the southerners as 'island tribals,' and southerners referred to the northerners as 'captives with queues.'" People of these times were unconcerned "with cultivation of virtue or acts of benevolence." They "merely adhered to quarrels and mutual slander." So the Han-barbarian discourse had long been discredited as "an extremely low and narrow doctrine."[49]

Even *qi*, the common currency of both Han dissident and accommodationist identities was subjected to revision. Like Wang Fuzhi, Zeng contended China proper's *yin* and *yang* aspects of *qi* were balanced enough to form virtuous people, whereas *qi*'s imbalance outside rendered non-Han animals. The emperor rejected the notion that regionally different *qi* determined the creation of humans or animals, because Confucianism clearly considered awareness of social ethics as the primary difference.[50]

Qi, however, was not irrelevant for interpreting historical change, but the dynastic watershed for the Manchu throne was the Ming, not the

Qing Fields in Theory and Practice

Tang of Han convention. The emperor asserted that from the Jiajing reign (1522–66) on, there was a blockage of *qi* circulating in the cosmos that manifested as a deterioration in Ming human relations resulting in political and social chaos. He attributed subsequent stabilization to the cosmically appropriate assumption of Qing rule.[51] In the process the Qing had effectively reoriented Hanspace, rendering the Han-barbarian discourse obsolete:

> Since antiquity, during ages when China was unified, the unassimilated dwelling in the midst of lands of inconsiderable expanse, like the *Miao* or the state of Chu, were denounced as barbarians; lands now known as Hunan, Hubei, and Shanxi. Who in these places can now be considered barbarians? At the height of the Han, Tang, and Song, the northern *Di* and the western *Rong* were traditionally considered the scourges of the frontier whose territory had never been subjected, and this distinction constituted the basis of the frontier between here [China] and there [barbarian territory]. Since our dynasty entered into the lordship of the central lands to rule over the empire, Mongol tribes of the farthest frontiers have all become subjects on our map. The frontiers of China having been extended so far to the great good fortune of all China's subjects, how can there still persist the principle of division between Han and barbarian, or center and periphery![52]

This was a radical rejection of many basic categories informing Hanspace used throughout Chinese history to reinforce an ethnic hierarchy of Han over non-Han. So influential were these categories that the Manchu state itself had to adapt.

In its imperial practice, however, the Qing continued to operate along more traditional, if certainly less metaphysical, lines. The Manchu banner system from boreal forests, the beg system from Xinjiang oases, the native chieftainship system from the empire's southwestern mountainous jungles, the Mongol *jasag* system from the steppe, as well as the *junxian* system from the fields of China proper – all attest to elaborate administrative mechanisms to spatially order ethnic diversity as determined by a combination of history, culture, and human interaction with the surrounding ecology. One basic justification for distinct state-supported ethnic spaces, for example, was the concern to maintain an ethnically pure Manchuria by restricting Han immigration. The most environmentally critical justification, however, concerned the mutual incompatibilities between Han agriculture and alternative practices, such as Mongol pastoralism, more suited to borderland ecologies.[53]

Consequently, Hanspace of some sort required delineation for the preservation of Han and other ethnic identities. This Han identity was not simply rooted, however, in what many scholars past and present have often nebulously called "Chinese culture." For Han elites, the essence of their identity was empirically and historically rooted in the very ground upon which they stood. Hanspace embodied the natural law of Han nature physically realized primarily by agriculture of a very distinctive type by a very specific sort of person. As the material basis for the construction and maintenance of Hanspace, agriculture was almost a type of wilderness "terraforming" intended to render a space Han habitable in both ecological and cultural, that is, environmental, terms. Arablism environmentally constituted China proper as the empire's distinctive Han core.

ARABLISM

The agrarian relations of the Han core have been the primary focus of Chinese environmental history for obvious and compelling reasons. Agriculture was the basis both of urbanization in premodern China and of the imperial system itself. So Chinese agriculture and empire are inextricably linked.[54] This relationship fosters a particular character of both land and people to produce an easily manageable revenue, ideally in the form of grain or silver, for the state. The immense ecological and cultural diversity existing within dynastic boundaries, however, complicated the concentration of this diversity within a single polity, which had to adapt accordingly.

Imperial arablism was the Qing adaptation to the environmental conditions connecting people and plants that formed China proper. This cultivation of crops and culture related people to land so as to effect their mutual constitution as Han commoners, or *liangmin*, whose cultivation of grain fields produced sustenance, revenue, and identity. *Liangmin* cultivated and were themselves cultivated in the process to realize a Hanspace that sustainably connected China proper to Inner Asia.

The imperial Chinese state, from its inception, was fully conscious of the existential significance of arablism. One of the most straightforward expressions of the conscious need for state management of environmental ties binding imperial relations can be found in Legalist writings, such as those of the *Shangjunshu* (*Book of Lord Shang*).[55] The second chapter, "Orders to Clear Wilderness for Cultivation" ("Ken ling"), presents a classical program for such management to effect an intense and sustainable concentration of resources, centered on grain. Upon deciding on legal reform as the basis for mobilizing state power, the ruler Duke Xiao's first act is to "issue an order to clear wilderness for cultivation." This is the material initiation of the general Legalist principle, that "the means by

Qing Fields in Theory and Practice

which a state is made prosperous are agriculture and war." The orders are a series of tactics to be employed to compel universal cultivation. One significant tactic is for the state

"to take exclusionary control of mountains and moors, so that the people who hate agriculture, the tardy, the lazy, and the greedy, will have no [other] means of subsistence. So they must become farmers, thus, ensuring waste lands will be brought under cultivation."[56]

Legalism totalizingly envisions the uniform transformation of people and land into two monoculturally interdependent components as its basis. With due qualification for change over time, especially urbanization, and rhetorical excess, this foundational interdependency continued to form the monolithic core of the multiethnic, ecologically diverse imperial Chinese project as embodied in Han farmers' and China proper's fields. A rather narrow and persistent arablist "fundamentalism" was expressed in this excerpt from a Ming agricultural manual: "registered wasteland is wasteland. Having reeds and grasses still makes it wasteland. Yet some lazy people ... go after the minor profit of reeds and reject the great treasure of crop cultivation."[57]

As Chen Jian has recognized, legalist agrarian theory's main product was not simply produce, but people, who had been made "guileless" (*pu*), and so were easy to rule, through farming. Chen's conceptualization of this as a "spiritual physiocracy" (*jingshen zhongnongzhuyi*) should not, however, obscure the fact that this condition arises from a state-orchestrated environmental relationship between people and plants that seeks to construct both in service of imperial continuity.[58] Accounts of the ongoing, latent influence of Legalism, as various forms of regulation, on subsequent Confucianized imperial institutions have generally ignored Legalism's similarly influential articulation of the environmental relations of empire.[59]

Of course, every aspect of this articulation did not remain relevant, as Legalist thinkers themselves would have recognized. The Chinese imperial system nevertheless sought to maintain a basic and remarkable continuity of arablism in the face of continuous change. Certain core values such as "guilelessness" could thus be expressed differently, as "diligence" (*qin*), for example, for largely the same ends of imperial stability. Such a variation is visible in the management of farmer and field, which necessitated ongoing administrative determinations of whether problems were ecogenic or anthropogenic, an issue not always amenable to an unqualified determination. In 1750, for example, the Qianlong emperor noticed on an imperial progress through Henan that some places had not yet sown their fall wheat crop, but he could not decide if this was due to "lazy farmers' lack of diligence" or the unsuitability of the soil. Henan Governor Oyonggo's response confirmed the existence of both problems.[60] Scarcity of arable land in China proper made it vital to arrest anthropogenic problems, which, if allowed to persist, would ruin good soil.

Cultural concepts centered on values such as "diligence" were basic components of *liangmin* identity that not only related people to the soil, but enabled them to relate appropriately to a wider variety of soils and climate conditions not well suited to cultivation. Administrators could easily, if not reasonably, come to feel that culture of a sufficient intensity could overcome a nature of inadequate fertility. Thus, Oyonggo's predecessor Šose insisted in 1744 that although sandy, alkaline soil would not support "cultivation of the five grains," the "stupid" residents, who "indolently feared difficulty," and their local officials, who had "made no effort to exhort them," had not tried to plant trees. Their flaws were the main reason for "an increase in wasteland."[61] Such imperial arablism did not always prevail but did inform cultivation culturally and ecologically.

Diligence was, of course, considerably augmented by enormous and pervasive state administrative structures. Water control was probably the most general form, but there were also regional variant structures. Conflicts between north China cultivators and locusts, for example, received considerable attention, which included formal systems for reporting and managing outbreaks, semiofficial "locust cult" shrines, and even local financial incentives. Shandong residents, for example, were offered two hundred coppers by provincial authorities for every *sheng* (roughly one liter or 0.03 bushels) of locust larvae peasants could dig out from snowy fields. Zhili officials offered rice and copper, which, according to one 1742 report, caused "the people to pursue profit like ducks [taking to water] and all energetically searched" for the larvae.[62] The metaphor was quite appropriate because ducks were employed to consume locust larvae and nymphs in watery areas too difficult for humans to reach. For example, more than four thousand ducks, augmented by freelance frogs and swallows, were "hired" and marched in two ranks over some infested northern Anhui districts in 1824.[63]

Even the highest dynastic authorities nevertheless came to recognize that diligence had its natural limits, although they did so while remaining firmly within an imperial arablist discourse. One of the Kangxi emperor's

Qing Fields in Theory and Practice

sacred edicts, issued in 1673, can stand as a representative expression of the basic assumption of cultivation relations as an ever-expanding process for the maintenance of the imperial state: "From antiquity, there has been no task more primary for the long-term tranquility and order of the state than the people's material prosperity. It is thus necessary that fields be cleared in such a way that the treasury has a surplus without levies that entirely exhaust such efforts."[64]

It is significant here that the prosperity of those the emperor subsequently identifies as the "little people" (xiao min), or the average Han commoner of "the provinces," is assumed to come from fields, specifically those that have been newly cleared. The corollary to this imperial pronouncement is that if there is no virgin land to open for cultivation, there will be no more law-abiding Han and, therefore, no more Qing state. By 1716, however, the emperor felt that the arable limits of China proper had been reached: "since an era of great peace has long endured, the population [of China proper] has multiplied considerably, but the land has not increased ... Those who speak of clearing land do not know that China proper actually has no such space." Perhaps this change in perspective arose from the Kangxi emperor's own encounter with what he reckoned were "several hundred thousand" Shandong cultivators and peddlers during a 1681 imperial tour beyond the passes. The territorial imperative for sustaining cultivation, however, remained intact because the emperor's solution was to permit further Han migration beyond the passes.[65]

The year 1716 was also around the time that double-cropping paddy rice was successfully introduced on a large scale in the Yangzi Delta. However, such intensification of cultivation, along with similar and more established practices elsewhere in places such as the middle Yangzi Valley, does not seem to have been an adequate adaptation to contain the Han population within China proper. For the eighteenth century overall, a period of great economic stability, there was hardly a grain crisis as such. However, there was a burgeoning population of overwhelmingly Han peasants, produced by factors such as the extension of double cropping, that was of increasing state concern. Indeed, as Robert B. Marks has pointed out, the Qing "substantial achievement" of minimizing the effects of climate change on food supply to reduce mortality may have contributed to subsequent problems linked to high population. The outlines of such a dynamic are visible in the rejection by officials of the Yongzheng emperor of tighter restrictions on Han northern migration in 1724. They held that if commoners from Zhili, Gansu, and Shandong went north to cultivate Mongolian lands, this would "spread out the population of China proper, and provide a greater surplus of grain."[66]

"Grain," of course, could include wheat, barley, and millet, the primary grains grown north of the Yangzi, as well as a variety of others. Paddy, or wet, rice was mainly restricted to areas south of the Yangzi. During the late imperial period, its intensive cultivation was made possible mainly by the introduction in the eleventh century of early ripening and drought-resistant Champa rice from Vietnam. All major crops coming into China from Southeast Asia or the New World, including maize, peanuts, and potatoes, effectively increased arable land area because they could be grown on hillsides, in relatively saline soils, and on other types of "waste-lands."[67] Humans and crops interacted to transform all marginal areas into fields wherever opportunities presented themselves.

In the overall process of Han arablist development, limiting and ethnically distinctive interdependencies were also formed between Han cultivators and their crops, expressed both biologically and culturally. One example is lactose intolerance, which persists to this day among 75 to 80 percent of Han Chinese and appears to be genetically differentiated by ethnic group. Lactose intolerance is, in other words, a condition that distinguishes Han Chinese from other groups such as Mongols and Uighurs, who are predominately lactose tolerant.[68] The Kangxi emperor, in his 1716 musings, ponders the cultural expression of this condition for Han residence in pastures beyond the passes. Noting there were many potential areas of residence that were "not arable" but had "water and grass," the emperor speculated that "commoners could pursue a livelihood by emulating Mongol herd-raising." He decided, however, that the "average Han" (*laobaixing*), "being accustomed solely to cultivation, could not do this." Shandong relief officials were less delicate, stating that "there are people who could stand beside a cow and not know how to milk it . . . waiting to fall over dead."[69]

The emperor's conclusion that this incapacity "is due to nothing more than habit" reflects a comparatively ethnocentric view that is certainly reasonable for his time and place. However, this view obscures particular types of Han environmental relations that literally embody greater intimacy with plants rather than mammals and, so, limit places to which Han can adapt themselves while preserving their identity. Han, however, to the alternating gratification and dismay of dynastic officials, responded not by adapting themselves to grasslands, but by terraforming grasslands into fields abetted by certain adaptable and familiar plant species.

Qing Fields in Theory and Practice

The state recognized the distinctive efficacy of this combination in imperial arablist terms expressed as an ethnic hierarchy topped by Han grain cultivators. This hierarchy was particularly pronounced in borderlands in general and in southern Mongolia in particular, where, unlike southern Manchuria, sustained Han cultivation was a comparatively recent introduction in the wake of the 1644 conquest. A distinction between Mongol and Han styles of agriculture soon arose, substantially in response to the first wave of Han migration, authorized and otherwise, beyond the Great Wall.

Two poems penned by the Qianlong emperor on themes of "Wild Fields" ("Huang tian;" 1754) and "Mongolian Fields" ("Menggu tian;" 1782) are based on a very general Qing arablist conviction that Mongols were casual cultivators by (pastoral) nature, a characteristic expounded upon in particular detail in "Wild Fields":

> Originally a land of hunting and herding,
> Now farming fields is steadily given weight.
> With no knowledge of weeding and hoeing, each works diligently.
> Merely saying dearth and plenty always depend on Heaven,
> They move out in pursuit of grass and water all summer long,
> Returning just before the autumn harvest;
> They plow indifferently for an indifferent result.

The preface to this poem defines what it terms the Mongol agrarian cultivation of "fields that rely on heaven" (kao tian tian), where "no attention is paid" to weeding and hoeing. Mongols instead "sow fields, then go herding and hunting in every direction and only during the autumn harvest do they return." The fact that they bother to cultivate at all is inaccurately attributed to "the long period of peace" after the Qing conquest that has resulting in using "mountains for fields." The act of farming itself is thus portrayed as "not the original source of Mongol livelihood," but arising from the Qing pacification of Inner Asia and China proper.[70] This theme also appears in the imperial poetic commentary on one of a number of poems entitled "Beyond the Passes" ("Kouwai," 1775). Here the Qianlong emperor writes that ever since "center and periphery" became "one family ... pastoral peoples have obtained no benefit" from the vast territory opened to initially unrestricted Han access.[71] This familial pacification has profound consequences for Mongolian interaction with the land, as further elaborated in "Mongolian Fields":

> When Mongols planted fields in the past,
> They casually sowed, then departed.
> "Depending on heaven," it was called.

When ready in autumn, they return to reap it.
Their departure was not without reason;
Some for hunting, others to mind herds.
Yet now it is like this no longer and
All are accustomed to the tasks of the plow.
They consider rain and assess fair weather,
Having worries no different from common farmers,
And so actually abandon herding and hunting,
Thus forgetting their origins.[72]

One reason for this departure was because hunting and pasture areas were being converted into agricultural fields. A number of the Qianlong emperor's poems make this point and, in contrast to the sentiment expressed in "Wild Fields," seem to lament it. In "What I Saw" ("Suo jian;" 1759), for example, the emperor begins by observing "Virgin land everywhere reclaimed/ Fields in the mountains/ No forests left." He then comments aside that thirty years before "all mountains beyond the passes were forested and could be hunted in," but now land was "everywhere cleared so that there are no forests to be seen." So battue hunting "cannot be practiced outside of restricted areas like Mu-lan." In "Tigershoot River" (*Shehu Chuan*), he observes that "the three-sided drive with bow and arrow has ceased in the wilds." The emperor then appends the comment that during the long Qing peace there has been "no piece of land that has not been cleared for farming." This is a decline from the early years of the Kangxi period when this territory [around Wutaishan] still had wild animals that could be hunted battue style." The poem then resumes with the line that "everywhere huge fields are plowed and lined with mulberry by ten thousand households." Poetic license aside, pastures and hunting grounds persisted through the Qianlong emperor's reign but were contracting under stress, including official pressure for cultivation such as a 1749 request to convert some Ordos pastures.[73]

It is probably unnecessary to enumerate each of the Qianlong emperor's considerable number of essentializations of Mongol identity appearing in an imperial arablist idiom. Interpretation, however, must be qualified by the historical context that renders this body of poetry a progressive expression of interethnic affinity unimaginable during the preceding Ming.[74] It is also important to note that practices similar to Mongol cultivation were not always reprehensible, as in Gao Shiqi's favorable account of like neglect of fertilizing and weeding among Manchus in Butha Ula (Da-sheng Wu-la) in Jilin. Gao concluded this was practicable due to the great fertility of the soil, although he also noted the "diligence" of the locals in the execution of their agricultural and foraging tasks.[75] The environmental relations arising from the intersection of the Mongol "character" with sedentary agriculture appears somehow less acceptable.

The Kangxi emperor was even more prosaically indiscriminate in his evaluation of Mongol arablist capacities when he asserted in a 1698 edict to "educate Mongols" that "the Mongol character is indolent. Once seed is broadcast on the fields they go to various places to herd and, although the grain ripens, do not attend to reaping its harvest. Nor when frost falls do they gather in the harvest, but instead declare a bad year."[76]

In diametrical contrast the Kangxi emperor was moved to somewhat self-congratulatory poetic effusions over the exertions of paradigmatic Han cultivation outside its natural habitat. His "Beyond the Passes Outposts of Cultivation Steadily Become Settlements" (*Kouwai she tun gengzhi juluo jian cheng*) can stand as the state's endorsement of proper cultivation relations under steppe conditions:

> Along the border, a vast wilderness
> That no policy can well forsake.
> Founding settlements through the years
> To concentrate civilized instruction
> By laying out fields along paths running east, west, north, and south.
> Diligently plowing and hoeing in spring and summer;
> Stocking up livestock in fall and winter;
> Harvesting glutinous millet just as the frost starts to thicken;
> Reaping wheat in the final moments of warmth.
> In soil both solidly fertile and stony
> Human effort transforms a barren waste.
> Having springs flow down from the mountains,
> Setting up pig sheds behind cottages,
> All done on time and tirelessly.
> Thus, population registers fill up.
> Rulers since antiquity, I fear, had no
> Such means for transformation by cultivation.[77]

All such characterizations, good and bad, are important manifestations of imperial arablism in the steppe context and, as such, serve to reinforce an imperial borderland hierarchy based on ethnically determined cereal farming. In practice, of course, ethnic and spatial distinctions were not so uniform. A 1743 report from Heilongjiang described some Manchu Solon-Ewenki and Mongolian Dagur rotating in and out of Hulun Buir as "crude" in their cultivation and "entirely ignorant of hoeing."[78] Han farmers in China proper itself were also criticized for their own version of "fields that rely on heaven," although their form of arablist malpractice was expressed in the Anhui common saw "looking to heaven for a harvest" (*wang tian shou*). Like Mongols, Anhui peasants did nothing between sowing and harvest, although, significantly, this was attributed to "fooling around" (*xiyou*) rather than herding or hunting.[79] The pervasive arablist hierarchy is nevertheless operative even in this instance. Mongols "naturally" have trouble with environmental practices not traditionally theirs, and Han have inexcusable problems with their own native usages.

The essential Mongol character is thus constructed as unsuited to intensive agriculture by nurture and nature, inherent climate, and inborn laziness, and is also predisposed to herding and hunting. Interaction with Han can effect a progressive agrarian assimilation rendering the two groups indistinguishable. Yet the Qianlong emperor's conflicted reaction to this outcome mirrors broader state contradictions in the formation and implementation of agrarian and pastoral policies north of the Great Wall, where relations different from those of imperial arablism had originated.

VENERY

Fields beyond the Great Wall were constructed differently from those in China proper. Ecological conditions of this vast area, dominated by comparatively dry and cold forest and steppe, precluded agriculture as the primary means of environmental interaction. This had a commensurate effect on cultural expressions. In contrast, more direct links with animals, rather than with plants, formed core elements of the Mongols and Manchus, the two major categories of northern ethnic identity in the Qing.

Of course, plants were certainly a part of these northern networks as animals were a component of those to the south. The focus of human intervention in the northern ecology, however, was not converting "wasteland" into cropland, but managing animal populations, specifically in the form of herding and hunting. This focus was a response to ecological conditions that tended to favor diversification centered on some form of foraging or herding rather than agricultural specialization. As one 1736 report from Heilongjiang explained, groups relying on herding and hunting could endure harsh winter conditions, a regular phenomenon north of the passes, far more effectively than those exclusively dependent on grain fields.[80]

Subsequent chapters will divide practices along ethnic lines to examine how herding constructed banner Mongol identity and foraging borderland Manchu identity. However, this is a somewhat artificial distinction

Qing Fields in Theory and Practice

in practice, because both groups, to say nothing of their complex and variegated subdivisions, hunted and herded. The following section will qualify this distinction through a brief examination of venery, a term intended to describe hunting relations that construct human identity in dynamic interdependency with prey as mounted hunter-soldiers. Venery was the environmental tie common to both groups as inhabitants of ecosystems north of the passes.

Venery was, moreover, central to the imperial construction of non-Han borderland identity, whereas herding tended to be more regionally and ethnically specific in application. Qing rulers such as Nurhaci, addressing Khalkha *otog* in 1619, could certainly assert that "Mongols raise animals and eat meat ... but [Manchus] plow fields and eat grain," but such attitudes were selectively held.[81] In fact, meat eating itself seems to have been a Manchu characteristic in the view of their imperial predecessors, the Ming. One Ming official, Song Yihan, contemptuously observed a few years later around 1621 that "these Jianzhou tribals [i.e., Jin Jurchen] live rough, eat meat, and are unable to farm the land they acquire."[82] Yet Nurhaci's and Song's diametrical views both assume the superiority of agriculture, and, in this respect, both are expressions of imperial arablism across an ethnic boundary.

Hunting, however, in the Manchu view was never entirely yoked to agriculture, but was held a vital, indeed strategic, component of both Manchu and Mongol identity. This is clear even before the conquest in the numerous adjudications of hunting cases that appear in the records of the early Qing.[83] Some of these cases involved restricting Manchu elites from hunting excesses, involving trespass into battue fields or simply breaches of discipline stemming from clamorous rivalry to bag the quarry first, which scared off game. Mongol enthusiasm had to be likewise disciplined, as in the *Lifanyuan* (Court of Territorial Affairs) decision in 1638 to limit the number and type of game tribute presented to the throne to avoid excesses that would burden Mongol nobles' subjects and exhaust their horses.[84]

Venery was not comparable to arablism in the imperial environmental scheme of things in scale and general influence. It did, however, receive heavy patronage during the Qing as part of the dynasty's efforts to accustom arablism to the empire's newly expanded boundaries. These included efforts to preserve a "Manchu" identity that was often amalgamated with banner members of various ethnicities, including Mongols. Indeed, there were actually several distinct banner systems simultaneously in operation mainly distinguishable by their degree of autonomy, always limited, from central state control. I will prefix the Manchu term for banner, "*gūsa*," to distinguish those formations, such as the Pastoral Chakhar, that were under direct central state military authority. The Mongolian term for banner, *hoshuu*, will be attached to less militarized and state centralized groups such as the *jasag* Forty-nine Banners, who could, for example, tax their own subjects and pass on hereditary offices.[85] So, although both banner groups are ethnically Mongolian, they are ethnic administratively distinct as "Manchu" state *gūsa* banners and Mongolian local *hoshuu* banners, respectively.

Perhaps the most dramatic and enduring of example of Qing venery patronage was the imperial hunting park of Muran (Mu-lan). Located at Chengde, the imperial summer capital beyond the Great Wall, Muran was used for 140 years (1681 to 1821) as the center for ritualized political and military activities as well for subsistence and elite foraging.[86] Chengde has been viewed as "a composite landscape that reproduced the map of the Manchu empire." "The geographical provenance" of the complex's "microclimates" was contrived to be sufficiently diversified to permit visitors to experience a select part of the complex as a "reduced version of their own landscape." Although this may be one of Chengde's general effects, the Qing rulers most responsible for its construction, the Kangxi and Qianlong emperors, viewed the "secondary landscape" of Muran from a nativist, rather than universalist, perspective that could also apply to the whole Chengde complex.[87] Muran was founded on the conviction that hunting was the primary expression of ethnic identity north of the passes in service of imperial borderland maintenance across generations. The Qianlong emperor bequeathed a representative statement of this concern to his successors in 1782, carved in the stone stele of the Yongyou temple at Chengde.

Fearing his posterity would forget the reserve's main purpose, as originally articulated by its founder the Kangxi emperor, the Qianlong emperor disclosed that Muran had been constructed mainly to preserve military skills, as exercised by mounted bow hunting. This role furthermore distinguished Muran from its imperial Chinese hunting park predecessors, which had been lavishly maintained "since the Tang" purely for personal pleasure to the ruin of state finances. In contrast, the Muran-Chengde complex's "Mountain Retreat" (*Shanzhuang*) had been deliberately located beyond the passes to "give appropriate weight to military practice, not to excessively esteem" literati culture. The emperor's immediate concern arose from the 1778 elevation of Chengde to a prefecture and its attendant Confucian cultural institutions.[88] The whole Mountain Retreat complex was explicitly and deliberately not Hanspace. Nor was it, strictly speaking, conceived even as a space where "center and periphery were as one family" (*zhongwai yi jia*), in the idiomatic expression of Qing multiculturalism.

Muran itself was primarily intended as a space for Inner Asian venery, its undeniably important, and somewhat paradoxical, Buddhist dimension notwithstanding. Of course, Buddhism was an integral part of stable imperial relations with Mongols that produced "transethnic Buddhist" manifestations of a nineteenth-century "Pan-Qing identity."[89] The Qianlong emperor, nevertheless, made his preference for more mundane identities clear on another Yongyou stele when he stated the continuity of military practice was the essential significance of his grandfather the Kangxi emperor's "imperial tours" (*xunshou*, literally "patrolling and hunting"). This, rather than the propagation of Buddhism, was the state's most pressing duty to be passed on to future generations.[90] The practices constituting Muran here appear as Inner Asian manifestations of a militant "patrimonial-bureaucratic empire" much more explicit than their high Qing China proper counterpart, the southern tours.[91]

Integral to these practices, from a particularly Han point of view, was Mongol "pacification" effected mainly through the reserve's hunting, rather than its religious, rituals. This was the view of the prominent historian Wei Yuan, who considered the Muran hunt the "grandest of all the ceremonies used to pacify the Mongols." Zhao Yi went so far as to assert that the emperor's annual hunting activities were not to train banner troops, but "actually to keep a yoke on the Mongols," in an elaborate display of culturally appropriate prowess and pomp.[92] Such views should be qualified, especially prior to the nineteenth century, in light of more nuanced assertions from the throne.[93]

Manchus and Mongols shared a form of environmental relations expressed in venery spaces beyond the passes through mounted bow hunting in banner formations. As a 1726 *Lifanyuan* entry acknowledged, both the Chakhar banners and the "banner people of China proper went battue hunting in one body ... dutifully exerting themselves throughout."[94] In many respects, there was little straightforward "pacification" involved as opposed to a common identity formation of Inner Asian hunter-soldiers critically dependent on interaction with wild steppe fauna. "Mu-lan's Battue System," as described in the essays of Zhao-lian, certainly portrays the elaborately ritualized multiethnic military coordination between Manchu and Mongol that characterized formal Qing battue hunting. However, the many hierarchical distinctions noted are usually based on hunting experience or social status rather than simple ethnic difference. Such differences are difficult to discern in an account that, for example, states both "Mongol vassal tribes" and the "Khorchin" must supply 1,250 huntsmen for the Muran ceremonies. The prerequisite for expressing these distinctions at all is Muran's "1,000 *li* of dense forests and abundant grassland and water" that attract "herds of wild beasts to breed there." Only under these conditions does Muran become "a truly heaven-sent area for military training and pacifying the distant."[95]

Pacification by venery could also domesticate Han elites, such as Gao Shiqi, who in 1682 accompanied the emperor on an eastern tour and was suitably impressed by Manchu hunting prowess. Encounters with tigers seem to have been especially opportune for this purpose. He describes how the Kangxi emperor and his immediate retinue pepper a tiger with arrows from elevated positions, "so that there is not one that is not slaughtered," or how fearless dogs are set on tigers concealed in high grass, or how guardsmen advance on tigers with spears. Gao marvels that "in the past, people said that the power of tigers and panthers of the mountains could not be matched, but now fighting them is extremely easy. Several tens have been killed over the past month or so, something unknown to previous generations."[96] This was, of course, an exaggeration, as Han agricultural clearance had been devastating tigers in places such as Shaanxi since at least the Ming dynasty. One study suggests a correspondingly precipitous drop in the tiger population south of the passes that easily exceeded the Kangxi emperor's lifetime score of 135 tigers bagged that he reckoned up in the fifty-eighth year of his reign. Southern Manchuria was similarly affected from the early eighteenth century.[97]

The emperor had the educational role of game in mind when he made this statement of his hunting record in 1719, which included twenty bears, twenty-five panthers, ninety-six wolves, 132 wild pigs, several hundred deer, and, in one day, 318 rabbits. This had been his practice since his childhood, and he admonished his guardsmen to apply themselves with like diligence. A generation later in 1749 Suiyuan General Buhi expressed a similar concern in his request to arrange joint annual hunting exercises beyond the passes for Manchu banner troops stationed south of the Great Wall and regional Mongol banner troops. Buhi was concerned that the troops, who normally cultivated fields, had "no wild animals" to hunt and so were losing vital military skills. He proposed that these men be deployed for hunting in the vicinity of Pastoral Chakhar and *hoshuu* areas where "there are still wild animals like

Qing Fields in Theory and Practice

rabbits, foxes, and gazelles in the mountain valleys and empty steppe." Their pursuit would "suffice for battue training" that would enable the troopers to "move through the wilderness." Fusengga, the military governor of Heilongjiang, made similar observations about inexperienced Solon-Ewenki and Dagur troops in 1764.[98]

Such "predator-prey" networks delineate what the Qianlong emperor meant in a 1754 poem by "close relations" (*qin*) that "construct a suitable similitude" (*jian kan tongli*) with Mongol vassals to create an "intimacy" (*jinqing*) that cannot come from "loose reigns on the borderlands."[99] While expressed in hierarchical, and even Manchu nativist, terms, these relations are rooted in multiethnic Inner Asian hunting practices. Consequently "close relations" reflect and reinforce a common venery subculture of "Mongols and Manchus who mainly hunt with bows from horseback." This Manchu-Mongol practice is thus distinguished from the "Oirads and East Turkestanis" who mainly "practice falconry."[100] In this sense, Manchu-Mongol venery was an exclusive bond even within the wider Inner Asian hunting context.

This bond also included concern for sustainability. The Kangxi emperor, for example, decreed in 1682 that "spring being the time that wild animals are pregnant," shooting female deer within encirclements would be prohibited then. This was a more practical manifestation of the poetic sentiment expressed in the Qianlong emperor's 1757 poem "Letting Deer Go." The poem's first lines indicate that Muran had a role in managing wild animal populations: "If female deer number beyond the norm, / Lift the battue, / Let them cut out for the underbrush, / Having learned thus from King Xuan's example of herding." This point is elaborated on in the commentary that follows, which states that "the beasts of Mu-lan are basically like those herded in a game park. They are intentionally reserved to breed and also, when taken, are intentionally not entirely hunted out."[101] By maintaining conditions neither completely domesticated nor entirely feral, preserve managers were constructing a particular type of animal "identity" that would in turn produce a corresponding human identity, both in service of the venery vital to the Qing's exercise of empire. Some complications in the formation of this human identity are revealed in a 1717 decree by the Kangxi emperor that Mongols, rather than "New Manchus" (*Xin Manzhou*; Ma: *Ice Manju*), were to be used on Muran patrols. The emperor was concerned that these newly recruited northeastern indigenous peoples would not only neglect enforcement of hunting prohibitions on trespassers, but would pursue game on behalf of their own officers.[102]

Appropriate venery relations were formed from a complex network of human and nonhuman elements. The dynastic emphasis, however, was not on animal conservation for its own sake, but to forge a particular bond between Inner Asian peoples. This bond was based on a banner identity centered on mounted bow hunting that was often broadly characterized as militantly "Manchu," but that also included Mongols.[103] Moreover, Manchu-Mongol venery was entirely dependent for its viability on game. Prey had to be elusive, and that required sufficient space with sufficient forest cover and even prohibited the use of firearms. The Qianlong emperor held that elite Solon-Ewenki troops were defined by their archery skills during the hunt because firearms made it too "easy to take beasts." His 1750 ban on firearms during battue encirclements was backed with silver, used to buy back his hunter-soldiers' guns at a tael each. Another seventy-nine Heilongjiang, Solon-Ewenki, and Dagur were similarly bought off in 1764.[104]

Wild animals had to have both space and chance to live to preserve borderland Manchus. Preservation, moreover, had to cover a particular ecology and culture, which no longer existed south of the Great Wall and were coming under increasing pressure north of it from the first decades of the eighteenth century. These environmental interdependencies conditioned the maintenance of the empire's northern borderlands but could not be neatly kept in total isolation from other conditions that linked the empire across its administrative boundaries. So northern venery periodically had to be redeemed with southern silver.

CONCLUSION

In July 2008 more than thirty-three thousand people were mobilized to deal with locust outbreaks across 240,000 hectares of land in southern Inner Mongolia. Eradication teams included herdsmen who deployed chickens, a traditional insect control method, en masse to eat the locusts. Such operations, which evoke something of Ciriktai's efforts nearly three and a half centuries before, helped to keep locusts from the Beijing area for several years.[105] Qing fields and their relations within and across both ecosystems and administrative boundaries continue to resonate in a way that recalls more of the Yongzheng emperor's integrated and multicultural Hanspace than Wang Fuzhi's monocultural preserve.

Nevertheless, the environmental relations structured by imperial arablism effectively constituted a fundamental, if not absolute, ethnic divide between Han and the venery peoples north of the passes. Imperial

Qing Fields in Theory and Practice

arablism networked cultural and ecological elements to construct ethnic and spatial hierarchies whose most enduring material legacy are the vast grain fields radiating from China proper into borderland space.

Spatially in this respect, Qing grain fields and their cultivators did differ from their dynastic predecessors to effect an unprecedented expansion of imperial arablism in terms of extent and duration. Mongol and Manchu military superiority proved ephemeral in this context, although it crucially, and unwittingly, made this Han expansion possible. This difference is not simply one of disparate human numbers, but also of critical human ties to more portable domesticated plants. Wild animals, in contrast, needed to stay in northern forested terrain to stay wild or just stay alive, and Inner Asian hunter-soldiers needed them to stay this way as well. These needs excluded wild animals and, ultimately even Inner Asian hunter-soldiers, from Hanspace almost as effectively as any of Wang's "numinous natural defenses."

Han of China proper, however, could not ignore venery and were actually indebted to it for opening arable expanses beyond Yixing's northern barrier. Venery and arablism thus conditioned each other to form part of the larger network of the Qing empire. The greater expanse and transformative effects of China proper's definitive environmental practices, however, has tended to overshadow, and even eclipse, the borderland networks without which the Qing empire would not have existed. The following chapters will attempt to track the environmental relations within the forests, steppe, and mountains looming beyond these Qing fields.

Notes

1 MWLF, QL 26/6/17 [03-0178-1880-012], 26/7/3 [03-0178-1883-009], 26/7/8 [03-0178-1883-021]; 26/7/9 [03-0178-1883-022]. For a historical overview of locust plagues in China, see Zhang Yihe, *Zhongguo huangzai shi*.

2 MWLF, QL 26/7/9 [03-0178-1883-022].

3 Dikötter, *Discourse of Race*, 4. Hanspace can be seen as an ideological response to social stresses that formed identities in a way compatible with Hale's ideas cited in the Introduction; cf. Geertz, *Interpretation of Cultures*, 193–220. Viewing Hanspace as ideology, however, anachronistically places it within a range of modernist psychological concepts from "false consciousness" to "cynicism" to "fantasy"; Žižek, *Sublime Object*, 28–30. Here ecology "is never 'ecology' as such, it is always enchained in a specific series of equivalences" that are ultimately political – socialist, feminist, capitalist, etc.; Žižek, ed., *Mapping Ideology*, 12. With such dismissal of nonhuman factors in identity formation, ideology becomes a "fantastically" anthropocentric concept. Hanspace was not "enchained" in these modern "psycho-political" terms.

56   *Across Forest, Steppe, and Mountain*

4 Wang Fuzhi, *Huangshu*, 12:532; Zhao Tingdong, *Dili wujue*, 56, 65. For an overview of work on Wang in Chinese, see Sky Liu, "Studies of Wang Fuzhi," 307–30. For Wang's views on ethnicity as anti-Manchu thought, see Fa-ti Fan, "Nature and Nation," 417–19, and Dikötter, *Discourse of Race*, 25–29.

5 For a significant qualification of the materialism of Wang's thought, see Black, *Man and Nature*, 63–74. Benjamin A. Elman and Richard J. Smith have noted the interpenetration of empirical and metaphysical concepts in Qing systems of thought that seriously challenge assertions of an unambiguous "decline in Chinese cosmology" during the late imperial period; Elman, *Cultural History of Civil Examinations*, 295–96, 311–26; Smith, *Fathoming the Cosmos*, 192–94.

6 For Wang's own (meta)physical concept of *qi*-based change, see Black, *Man and Nature*, 70–74.

7 Wang Fuzhi, *Du tongjian lun*, 10:502. For similar views from the Southern Song, see Hoyt Cleveland Tillman, "Proto-Nationalism in Twelfth-Century China?" 403–28.

8 Black, *Man and Nature*, 71–73.

9 The orthodox or heterodox status of *fengshui* in late imperial China is particularly difficult to determine. The prominent literatus Wei Yuan, for example, criticized the Jiangxi school's emphasis on topographical "formations and contours" (*xingshi*) in what appears to be an attempt to articulate a more orthodox Confucian practice of geomancy; Wei Yuan, "Dili gangmu xu" and "Zhi long cheng qi lun xu," 12:239–40 and 12:241–42, respectively. Even the Kangxi emperor expressed ambivalence, acknowledging that while many doctrines were mere fabrications, "such techniques cannot be completely dispensed with." Cited, along with many other examples, in Bruun, *Fengshui in China*, 65–66. Recent studies include Bruun, *An Introduction to Feng Shui*; Field, "In Search of Dragons"; Yu Xijian and Yu Tong, *Zhongguo gudai fengshui*.

10 Shen Hao, *Dixue*, 1a.

11 The term also appears as *Hua-yi* or *Xia-yi guan*. For an extended pre-Qing example of this discourse, see the Jin dynasty essay "Xi Rong lun"; *Jinshu*, 5:1529–34. Recent scholarship in Chinese has attempted to historicize this discourse in linear fashion, which qualifies notions of Sinification; see Li Dalong, "Quantong yi-Xia guan," 1–15; Yu Fengchun, "Hua-yi yanbian," 21–34; Zhang Shuangzhi, "Qingchao huangdi de Hua-yi guan," 32–42. Works in English have taken chronologically limited approaches, e.g., Wiens, "Anti-Manchu Thought," 1–24. Some recent work, however, surveys the transdynastic context; see Dikötter, *Discourse of Race*, 1–30.

12 For an account of the contexts for practical learning in evidentiary scholarship (*kaozheng*) and statecraft practices, see Elman, *From Philosophy to Philology*.

13 Hu's attitude in this respect is strikingly similar to that of Zhu Xi's approach to *Yijing*; see Kidder Smith et al., eds., *Sung Dynasty Uses of the I-Ching*, 169–205. Wang Fuzhi's relationship to *Yijing*, and to Zhu's views on it was similarly complicated, as was Hu's own; Smith, *Fathoming the Cosmos*, 175–77.

14 Legge, *The Shoo King*, III:142–51.

Qing Fields in Theory and Practice   57

15 Yee, "Chinese Geographic Maps," 2:35–70; Yee, "Chinese Maps in Political Culture," 2:74–76, 87; Henderson, "Chinese Cosmographical Thought," 2:203–27.

16 Hu Wei. *Yugong chuizhi*, 14 (preface), 682.

17 Hu Wei, *Yugong chuizhi*, 677.

18 Lü Liuliang, *Lü Wancun wenji*, 2:6.18a–b; Wang Fuzhi, *Huangshu*, 12:534; Chavannes, "Les Deux Plus Anciens Spécimens," 214–47; Yee, "Chinese Geographical Maps," 46–47.

19 The following discussion of the field allocation system follows Edward H. Schafer, *Pacing the Void*, 75–76. For a helpful traditional explication see, Gu Zuyu, *Du shi fangyu jiyao*, 11: 5508–21.

20 *Xin Tangshu*, 3:817–18. For a Song-era map with reproduced text from the *Tangshu*, see *Songben lidai dili zhizhang tu*, 84–85.

21 Hu Wei, *Yugong chuizhi*, 642.

22 Zhao Tingdong, *Dili wujue*, 131–32.

23 Hu Wei, *Yugong chuizhi*, 678, 698–99. "Tribute" (*chaogong*) here means regional produce submitted by vassal states that are not under direct administration of the Nine Provinces as originated in the "*Hua-yi*" foreign relations of the Han dynasty; Fu Baichen, *Zhonggguo lidai chaogong*, 1–3.

24 Hu Wei, *Yugong chuizhi*, 14, 685, 699.

25 Hu Wei, *Yugong chuizhi*, 3.

26 Hu Wei, *Yugong chuizhi*, 678.

27 Hu Wei, *Yugong chuizhi*, 682–83.

28 Zhao Yi, "*Chang'an diqi*," 3.1921b. For Zhao, flights from Tang capitals resulting from major rebellions are particularly significant evidence for the depletion of regional *qi*. *Qi* fluctuation was also held to influence dynastic succession; Yang, *Studies in Chinese Institutional History*, 14–15; Zhao Yi, *Nianer shi zha ji*, 95.

29 *Mingshilu*, 1:127a–b. For an extended, variant version, see Chen Jian, *Huang Ming tongji*, 1:104–7. Ming Taizu's reign has been considered a peak of ethnocentric Han thought; Wiens, "Anti-Manchu Thought," 3–4; Li Dalong, "Quantong yi-Xia guan," 7.

30 Lü Liuliang, *Tiangai lou si shu yu lu*, 1:474a. Ming Taizu believed that by the 1350s *qi* was concentrated on the south bank of the lower Yangzi, where he would establish the dynastic capital, and that his state's subsequent prosperity and territorial expansion "derived solely from shifts in the *qi* of the mountains and rivers"; *Mingshilu*, 1:104b.

31 Gu Yanwu relied on similar *qi* mechanics to reach the conclusion that *qi* had been moving toward the southeast from the northwest, which thereupon became a wasteland; Gu Yanwu, *Ri zhi lu*, 627. For Gu's general views, see Santangelo, "*Collected Papers*, 183–99. For a contrasting Ming period concept of *qi*'s historical role, see Xu Jishan and Xu Jishu, *Dili renzi xu zhi*, 36.

32 Hu Han, *Hu Zhongzi ji*, 1:4a–b. Versions published in official Qing compilations omit these passages of "Han-barbarian discourse."

33 See, for example, Wiens, "Anti-Manchu Thought," 10–14; Fa-ti Fan, "Nature and Nation," 417–19; Du Weiyun, *Qingdai shixue yu shijia*, 69–72.

34 Wang Fuzhi, *Du tongjian lun*, 10:455.

58   *Across Forest, Steppe, and Mountain*

35 Wang Fuzhi, *Huangshu*, 12:538.

36 Wang Fuzhi, *Song lun*, 132.

37 Wang Fuzhi, *Du tongjian lun*, 10:436–37.

38 Wang Fuzhi, *Du tongjian lun*, 10:437.

39 Wang Fuzhi, *Du tongjian lun*, 10:454–55; Wang Fuzhi, *Huangshu*, 12:537. Wang refers to a number of Inner Asian conquest dynasties, including the Yuan, whose descendants were able to remain in their natural habitats in "the northern deserts" and "beyond the passes" long after these regimes had vanished from China proper.

40 Xu and Xu, *Dili renzi xu zhi*, 42.

41 Wang Fuzhi, *Huangshu*, 12:538–39; Xu and Xu, *Dili renzi xu zhi*, 43.

42 For a general and comparative account of the literary inquisitions of these respective reigns, see Guo Chengkang and Lin Tiejun, *Qingchao wenzi yu*.

43 For recent accounts of the case in English, see Zelin, "The Yung-Cheng Reign," 189–92; Spence, *Treason by the Book*. For a detailed historical analysis, including the original text of the *Dayi juemi lu* and related official documents, see Shanghai shudian chubanshe, ed., *'Dayi juemi lu' tan*.

44 Shanghai shudian chubanshe, ed., *'Dayi juemi lu' tan*, 133–34.

45 *QSL*, KX 16/9/2, 4.880a, KX 17/1/18, 909b.

46 *Da Qing shi chao shengyu*, 1:202. See also the Kangxi emperor's essay on the topic; "Taishan shanmai yi Changbaishan lai," in *Qing Shengzu yuzhi shi wen*, 6:339b–40b. For a description of geomantic alpine geneaology see Yuan Shouding, *Dili dan zhe lu*, 17, 21, 244. The emperor's formulation implies a (meta)geological elevation of Changbaishan above Taishan's as the latter's ultimate source or "patrilineal ancestral mountain" (*zushan*). His argument could resonate a century later with senior Han officials such as Min-Zhe and Yun-Gui governor-general Zhao Shenzhen, who cited a Song *fengshui* authority to affirm the emperor's view; Zhao Shenzhen, *Yuechao zazhi*, 84.

47 James Robson, *Power of Place*, 42.

48 *Guochao gong shi xubian*, 2:868; Zhang Shuangzhi, "Qingchao huangdi de Hua-yi guan," 35–36; Gaozong, *Yuzhi shi wen shi quanji*, 37.

49 Shanghai shudian chubanshe, ed., *Dayi juemi lu*, 134.

50 Shanghai shudian chubanshe, ed., *Dayi juemi lu*, 155. *Yin* and *yang* distortions were considered characteristic of frontier areas at least as far back as the Han. Compare the "completely unsuitable frigid, saline, and sandy frontier prefectures" with "materially abundant" China proper's location at "the cosmic center where *yin* and *yang* converge" in the famous salt and iron debates; *Yan tie lun*, 695:527a.

51 Shanghai shudian chubanshe, ed., *Dayi juemi lu*, 134. See Chapter 5 for a translation of this passage.

52 Shanghai shudian chubanshe, ed., *Dayi juemi lu*, 135.

53 See, for example, MWLF, YZ 10/10/2 [03-0173-1027-010]; QL 12/2/6 [03-0173-1082-002].

54 The variations on this theme are considerable and run throughout imperial China's extant corpus. For highlights, see Xu Guangqi *Nongzheng quanshu*, 1–54. For its manifestations in Qing practical statecraft, see He Changling,

ed., *Qing jingshi wenbian*, 2:884b–885b, 888b, 895a–898a, 918a, 950b, 951a, 961b.

55 "Legalism" is a problematic term but has been retained here because of its persistent common usage. For a critical analysis, see Kidder Smith, "Sima Tan and the Invention of Daoism, 'Legalism,' *et cetera*," 129–56. For discussions of topics related to legalism and early agrarian thought, see Graham, "The Nung-chia 'School of the Tillers'," 66–100; Wang Zhennian, "Fajia zhengzhi sixiang," 209–13; Zhang Linxiang, "20 shiji *Shangjunshu* yanjiu shuping," 10–14.

56 *Shangjunshu zhuyi*, 18, 23, 31. A slightly different translation can be found in Elvin, "Unsustainable Growth," 19. For an English translation of the text, see Duyvendak, *The Book of Lord Shang*.

57 Xu Guangqi, *Nongzheng quanshu*, 124–25, translated, with slight variation, in Vermeer, "Exploitation of New Farmland," 233.

58 Chen Jian, "'Jingshen zhongnongzhuyi' 99–104; Zhang Jingshu, "Nongye jiaoyu sixiang tanxi," 124–27; Niu Yinshuan et al., "Fajia 'zhongnong' sixiang tanxi," 59–61.

59 See, for example, Yan Li, "Fajia sixiang zai Zhongguo," 112–13; Chen Song, "Lun Songdai shidafu jiecent falüe sixiang," 116–25.

60 Ge Quansheng, ed., *Qingdai zouzhe huibian*, QL 15/11/12, 118.

61 Ge Quansheng, ed., *Qingdai zouzhe huibian*, QL 9/4/6, 81.

62 Wang Jiange, "Qingdai Huabei de huangzai," 100–107; Shin-Yi Hsu, "The Cultural Ecology of the Locust Cult," 731–52; Sun Jiagan, *Sun Wending Gong zoushu*, 1:497–502; Ge Quansheng, ed., *Qingdai zouzhe huibian*, QL 6/3/19, 49.

63 Tao Zhu, *Tao Wen Yi Gong (Zhu) ji*, 2:891–95.

64 *QSL* 12/11/5, 4:580a–b.

65 *QSL*, KX 46/6/28, 6:303a–b, KX 51/4/18, 478a, KX 55/ic3/22, 629a–30a. Such absolute statements are qualified by ongoing clearance of marginal land (literally "land between the cracks," *xidi*) within China proper long after the emperor's reign, even in such primordial agricultural areas such as Shaanxi; Ge Quansheng, ed., *Qingdai zouzhe huibian*, QL 6/4/26, 51. However, as Chapter 5 argues, the sustainable productivity of such land, which usually required years of subsidy, is questionable.

66 *Yongzhengchao Manwen zhupi*, no. 1474, 1:816–17; Li Xu, *Li Xu zouzhe*, 182, 233, cited in Zhang Yan, *Qingdai Jingji Jianshi*, 344; Myers and Wang, "Economic Developments, 1644–1800," 568–69, 611–12, 641–45; Marks, "It Never Used to Snow," 445. Requests from Mongol elites to put bannermen to work cultivating arable fields around pastures were by no means discouraged. One such request in 1732 from Khorchin, Aukhan, Ongni'ud, Tümed, and Kharachin nobility was granted without any deliberation; *Yongzhengchao Manwen zhupi*, no. 4137, 2:2145.

67 Bray, *Agriculture*, 493–95; Ping-Ti Ho, "Early-Ripening Rice," 200, 201, 210, 216–17. For an overview of Chinese scholarship on New World crops, see Cao Ling, "Ming Qing Meizhou liangshi zuowu," 95–103.

68 Shukla, "Lactose Intolerance in Health and Disease," 66–70; Zheng Jiaju et al., "Lactose Malabsorption," 284–86; Zheng and Rosenberg, "Lactose Malabsorption," 1–6.

60   *Across Forest, Steppe, and Mountain*

69 *QSL*, KX 55/ic3/22, 629a–30a.

70 *Qing Gaozong yuzhi shi* 4:265b.

71 *Qing Gaozong yuzhi shi* 4:265b–66a, 12:52b.

72 *Qing Gaozong yuzhi shi* 14:167b–68b. A gloss later in the poem on an expression of "secret worry" explains that because contemporary Mongols have become as agrarian as Han, they are no longer the ferocious warriors feared from the Han to the Ming and would now be useless as soldiers.

73 *Qing Gaozong yuzhi shi* 5:344a, 6:379b–80a; Ge Quansheng, ed., *Qingdai zhouzhe huibian*, QL 14/11/10, 112. "Three-sided drive" (*sanqu*) refers to the tradition of surrounding game on only three sides, thus benevolently allowing prey an escape route. Here it is likely a general reference to battue hunting.

74 For a similar reading of Qianlong's Mongolian poetry influenced by the PRC's contemporary multiethnic discourse, see Xi-yong-jiao, "'Qin fanzhong jian kan tongli, waiyu jimi qi jinqing'," 76–78.

75 Gao Shiqi, *Hucong dongxun riji*, 111–12.

76 *QSL*, KX 37/12/17, 5:1027b–28a.

77 *Qing Shengzu yuzhi shi wen*, 1:179a.

78 MWLF, QL 8/2/3 [03-174-1514-001]. Different reports on this group, comprising one thousand Solon-Ewenki, Dagur, and Bargut each, give different accounts of the agricultural abilities and dependencies, especially of the Dagur; MWLF QL 6/10/5 [03-175-1558-033]. All three thousand seem to have been conscripted from "huntsmen" (*buthai hahasi*), which raises the question as to why Dagur sometimes appear as unreliant on any meat; QL1/12/11 [03-174-1481-001]. Nevertheless, overall deliberations in 1736–43 accepted that the Dagur were generally cultivators whereas the Solon-Ewenki and Bargut were generally pastoralists and foragers. The record is consistent in its assertion that climate conditions in Hulun Buir precluded sufficient Dagur cultivation and that 168 Solon-Ewenki and Dagur were dismissed from cultivation to return to "sable tribute." "Tribute" probably included hunting for food in this context.

79 Ge Quansheng, ed., *Qingdai zhouzhe huibian*, QL 3/11/29, p. 17.

80 MWLF, QL 1/12/11 [03-0174-1481-001].

81 *Manbun rōtō*, 1:201–2.

82 Chen Zilong, ed., *Huang Ming jingshi wenbian*, 6:5124a. Whatever their own capabilities, contemporary Manchu troops certainly relied on Han peasants, "who understand agriculture," to assist them in establishing military agricultural colonies; *Qingchu neiguo shiyuan Manwen dang'an*, 1:149.

83 For examples, see *Qingchu neiguo shiyuan Manwen dang'an*, 1:200, 269, 280, 287–88, 308, 316, 328, 394, 400–401, 403, 431–32. Issues in such cases could include whose arrow actually hit a tiger, letting game escape, breaking battue formation to pursue game and even, incredibly, a dispute between an imperial guardsman and the khan Hong Taiji himself over whose deer was bagged and whose deer got away. The guardsman was imprisoned, but pardoned from execution after an appeal by his family; ibid., 1:431–32.

84 *Qingchu neiguo shiyuan Manwen dang'an*, 1:46, 54, 448; Zhang Ruizhi and Xu Lizhi, eds., *Shengjing Manwen dang'an zhong de lüling*, 2:282.

Qing Fields in Theory and Practice   61

85 Jiang Yongjiang, "Lun Qingdai monan Menggu," 33–35. The terms "*hos-huu*"and "*jasag*" are also transliterated, more technically, as "*qošiyun*" and "*jasay*," respectively.

86 Important anthologies in Chinese on the Chengde complex include Bishu Shanzhuang yanjiu huibian, ed., *Bishu Shanzhuang luncong*; Dai Yi, ed., *Qingshi yanjiu yu Bishu Shanzhuang*.

87 Forêt, *Mapping Chengde*, 18, 23. Chengde was not fully "multicultural," being a place where "the Manchu ruling elite often associated with their Inner Asian subjects . . . more closely than they did with Han Chinese"; Dunnell and Millward, "Introduction," 3–4.

88 "Bishu Shanzhuang hou xu," in *Rehe zhi*, 2:831–33. For an alternative English translation of this preface, see Hedin, *Jehol*, 158–59. The Kangxi emperor was much more explicit in an edict from the last year of his life in 1722 when he asserted that annual battue hunting exercises were essential for military preparedness. He went on to attribute his victories over the Zunghars to his devotion to peacetime hunting beyond the passes; *Rehe zhi*, 3:1842–43. The "Hou xu" also notes that the Yongzheng emperor shared this view of hunting, although he never went to Chengde himself.

89 Elverskog, *Our Great Qing*, 135–39, 145–46; Elverskog, "Wutai Shan," 252.

90 *Rehe zhi*, 4:2635–39. The Qianlong emperor's personal and public commitments to Buddhism are controversial. For a recent study, see Luo Wenhua, *Longpao yu Jiasha*. Luo sees a critical distinction between political policy and personal piety that can resolve the emperor's otherwise contradictory expressions.

91 Chang, *A Court on Horseback*, 7–18, 87–91, 138. Significantly for my point here, Chang cites two versions of the "decisive" sources of patrimonial domination, military and judicial or military and fiscal; ibid., 12. This emphasis on arms does not exclude other considerations but certainly suggests an order of priority.

92 Wei Yuan, *Shengwu ji*, 1:100; Zhao Yi, "Menggu zha ma xi," *Yanpu zaji*, 13–14.

93 In rejecting a 1741 a proposal to abolish imperial battue hunting rituals, for example, the Qianlong emperor reiterated their import for both military training and Mongol relations. He also specified that hunts were a critical component the traditional strategies of imperial foreign relations of "cherishing those from afar" (*huaiyuan*) and "pacifying" (*huairou*) vassal states; *QSL*, QL 6/2/8, 10:961a–b.

94 *Qianlongchao neifu chaoben 'Lifanyuan zeli,'* 27.

95 Zhao-lian, "Mu-lan xingwei zhidu," *Xiaoting zalu*, 219–21. The Khorchin's distinct status most likely is based on their special marriage relations with the imperial house.

96 Gao Shiqi, *Dongxun riji*, 106.

97 Cao Zhihong and Wang Xiaoxia, "Ming Qing Shaan nan yimin kaifa," 11–17; *Rehe zhi*, 1:502; Zhang Shizun, "Kangxi shiyi nian 'dongbei hu'," 99.

98 *Rehe zhi*, 1:502; MWLF, QL 14/4/9 [03-171-0311-001]; QL 29/10/16 [03-181-2113-006].

99 *Qing Gaozong yuzhi shi* 4:257b. For further evidence, see Wang Chuihan, "Guoyu qishe yu Manzu de fazhan," 61–62.

100 *Rehe zhi*, 1:195.

101 Gao Shiqi, *Dongxun riji*, 107; *Qing Gaozong yuzhi shi* 5:143b.

102 *Kangxichao Manwen zhupi*, no. 3098, 1239.

103 For some of the Qianlong emperor's representative Manchu nativist expressions, see *QSL*, QL 6/2/8, 10:961a–b, QL 6/9/28, 1167b–68b. Hunting's significance is generally subdivided for ethnically distinct purposes, such as Manchu identity and Mongol pacification; Ning, "The Lifanyuan and the Inner Asian Rituals," 60–92, although note 69–70; Wang Sizhi, "Bishu Shanzhuang de xingjian," 100–117. For contrasting comprehensive and transhistorical characterizations, see Allsen, *The Royal Hunt*; He Pingli; *Xunshou yu fengchan*.

104 *QSL*, QL 15/10/8, 13:1129b–30a; MWLF QL 29/7/25 [03-0181-2099-018].

105 "Inner Mongolia Fights Rampant Locusts."

2

The Nature of Imperial Foraging in the SAH Basin

The Changbai Mountain Nature Reserve was established in 1960, but the region's special status long predated the PRC. The reserve is centered on the original homeland of Jurchen, later Manchu, peoples who established the Qing dynasty. Some of its historical continuities appear in an ecological form that recalls the dynasty's restricted resource enclaves like "ginseng mountains" and "pearl rivers." Legitimate and illegal resource extraction by humans from the area's considerable biodiversity also persists.[1] In contrast, however, the dynasty intervened to culture this enclaved nature to ensure a vital supply of resources, both human and otherwise. State-managed foraging became a primary and often conflicted strategy for the sustainable exploitation of these unique, interdependent northeastern resources.

Northeastern ecological biodiversity was not the passive background for the play of human agencies, but instead interacted with humans in vital, and sometimes unanticipated, ways. Manchu identity and space were products of northeastern nature and culture, not simply of Qing fiat or compromises with indigenous peoples and outside invaders. Broadly speaking, variation in environmental interaction is how and why "Manchus" in China proper became different from northeastern peoples left behind in the wake of the 1644 conquest. Moving south of the Great Wall altered cultural and natural, or "environmental," contexts. A borderland Manchu identity was accordingly formed north of both the Great Wall and the Willow Palisade (*Liutiaobian*) separating southern Manchuria from Jilin and Heilongjiang.

63

64   *Across Forest, Steppe, and Mountain*

Borderland Manchus were a particularly valuable human resource formed under these conditions. They embodied the empire's Manchurian borderland, ideally as its quintessential northeastern hunter-soldier unspoiled by residence in the agro-urbanized south. "New Manchus" were the most militarized manifestation of borderland Manchu identity, which also included indigenous pelt tributary peoples not normally subject to military service. New Manchus ideally combined vernery skills in service of the dynasty's regional order.[2] This distinction in identity differentiates those indigenous groups who left trapping behind when they took up arms and residence in Qing *gūsa* banner companies from other groups who remained on the hunt, but not the attack, in their native villages. Administrative space reflected these differences during the seventeenth and eighteenth centuries. The mid-SAH settlements were stripped by direct recruitment and transfer of New Manchus while those of the lower SAH persisted in place under traditional clan organizations subject to periodic supervision.[3] Modern scholars have characterized exchange relations with this latter group as "rewarding pelt tribute with goods." Such "tribute relations" became an increasingly commercialized trade of pelts for the textile products overseen by authorities at Ilan Hala in the Qianlong period.[4]

Nevertheless, borderland Manchu identity remained fluid in practice because it was based on a regional venery experience that permitted the dynasty to draft and demobilize indigenous hunters. Units like Heilongjiang's "Hunting Eight Banners" (*Bu-te-ha baqi*), composed mainly of Solon-Ewenki, Dagur, Orochen, and Bargut, were training reserves. As soldiers they could be relieved of their regular pelt tribute to grow grain, but authorities recognized hunting as the prerequisite skill for all elite banner troops. A 1732 edict offers a concise rationale for the state's venery construction of its soldiers: "it has been heard that the able-bodied men of Butha Ula have multiplied to two or three thousand. Since all hunt for a living, they are inured to toil and hardship ... select 1,000 of those in their prime as soldiers." Foraging ability enabled hunters in Heilongjiang and Jilin to be deployed in strategic, unarable, territory such as Hulun Buir.[5]

Embedded in regional ecological conditions through foraging, indigenous peoples were among the resources most fiercely contested during the Romanov-Qing conflict over the SAH river basin in the latter half of the seventeenth century. This imperial fight for space, pelts, and people accelerated the dynasty's formation of a borderland Manchu

The Nature of Imperial Foraging in the SAH Basin

identity as it regimented various indigenous peoples as New Manchus into *gūsa* banner units. This mobilization, however, also initiated the substantial alienation of these peoples from their previous environmental relations. Moreover, this alienation continued even after the successful Qing integration of its Manchurian borderland. Integration, in turn, promoted both greater Han migration into southern Manchuria and imperial foraging's bureaucratized hunting and gathering practices. Alienation and integration transformed the Qing's carefully cultured nature of Manchurian space and identity in ways that the dynasty had not intended.

This chapter examines the process of how this network of cultured nature was formed on the basis of a forager identity and its subsequent modifications under the exigencies of, first, Russian incursion and then imperial foraging. Despite its obvious import, Han migration will be downplayed here to focus on comparatively unexamined dynamics shaping regional Manchu identity and borderland space.

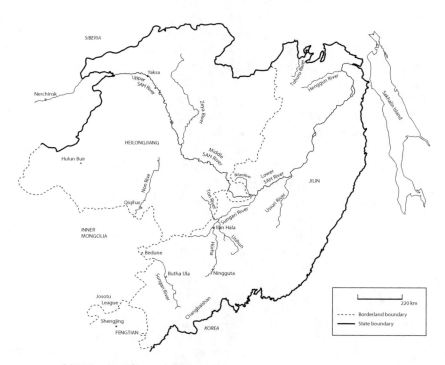

MAP 3: SAH Basin: Jilin and Heilongjiang

FORAGING AND MANCHU IDENTITY

Qing authorities sought to preserve ecological ties to their northeastern homeland among the Manchu diaspora despite the physical separation entailed by the conquest of China proper. Foraging was integral to the ongoing formation of a distinct, unified, and imperial Manchu identity across the Great Wall that dynastic authorities considered the apex of their state's ethnic hierarchy.

In the view of Qing rulers such as the Yongzheng emperor, Manchus were of the "greatest concern" because they were the "root of the state" and, as such, "comparable to no others."[6] The formation of Manchu identity was, moreover, not a passive process for the participants. The dynasty's ethnic exemplars, bannermen, were thus commanded "to do their utmost to become studied in Manchu frugality, the Qing [i.e. Manchu] language, mounted archery, labor service [and] the arts of drill and ritual usage."[7] Many of these practices, including foraging skills like archery, could be pursued only under certain social and ecological conditions that required maintenance of amenable spaces sufficiently isolated from the empire's Han Chinese majority.

Manchuria's eastern and northern expanses inevitably became the empire's main reserve for Manchus to be insulated from "contamination," by "Han customs," including the drinking, gambling, cockfighting, and profligate expenditures, so decried by Qing rulers.[8] Hybridization into a new composite identity through proximity to Han culture distinguished diasporic from borderland Manchus.[9] Unlike Fengtian (modern Liaoning province) and its capital Shengjing to the south, Jilin and Heilongjiang had not been subjected to large-scale Han migration and were considered relatively pristine, if endangered from the mid–eighteenth century.[10]

Even before the Qing conquest of China proper dynastic authorities sought control over the forage resources of the Jurchen/Manchu home territory, roughly centered in southeastern Jilin around the Korean border. Nurhaci formulated one of the earliest dynastic rationales for such control on March 3, 1623:

Formerly, all sorts of pelts, eastern pearls, and sable were foraged by one hundred men sent out by the eight *Beile* Princes' households, each of which retained its own respective catches. So for fear of internal disorder, all sorts of forage from the year 1622 like eastern pearls, sable, lynx pelts, tiger pelts, wolf pelts, otter pelts, and squirrel pelts were all equally divided into eight portions.[11]

The Nature of Imperial Foraging in the SAH Basin

Here the progenitor of the Qing imperial house acknowledges the importance of foraging for the formation of Manchu political relations within the first decade of the Later Jin state's foundation. As authorities such as Liu Xiaomeng have recognized, such interventions were important indications of Jin centralized state-building efforts.[12] Foraging was too sensitive to be left to the comparatively random intersection of people and nature existing before 1623. Instead, a more equitable distribution of forage would be enforced for the state's ultimate benefit. This is one early manifestation of an imperial foraging policy in the northeast and of the critical role played by these resources in structuring Jin politics.

Within a decade or so, the throne was exerting even greater control of foraging space, often making even elite subjects' access dependent on imperial approval. Nurhaci's son Hong Taiji (r. 1627–43) prohibited unauthorized entry into hunting grounds through regulations issued on the eve of a hunt in Kaiyuan in 1633.[13] From "the early years of the state," access was restricted to imperial clansmen. Ranks from prince (*wang*) to duke (*gong*) had the privilege of sending out foragers into Jilin's Butha Ula region for unique Manchurian produce, especially the so-called "three Northeastern treasures" (*Dongbei sanbao*), "eastern," or river, pearls (*dongzhu*; Ma: *tana*), sable (*diao*; Ma: *seke*), and ginseng (*renshen*; Ma: *orhoda*). Access by such elites' foragers was gradually restricted or eliminated, and their numbers were limited by rank from 15 to 140.[14]

Unauthorized foreign access was, of course, prohibited entirely. Nevertheless, in 1635 alone, in addition to several cases of illicit hunting and fishing, Manchu troops confronted at least thirty-two Korean ginseng poachers in four separate incidents. After several exchanges of diplomatic notes, a Korean state investigation in midyear discovered over seventy more of its subjects involved in the traffic.[15]

These incidents were particularly disturbing to the Jurchen in the context of their contemporary, intensifying struggle with Ming China, which Korea was being pressured to support. Ginseng made a critical economic contribution to the Jurchen ability to carry on this conflict. In fact, many of the northeast's principal forest products were so important that by 1617 conquests of nearby Jurchen rivals enabled the Jin state to control the trade in "ginseng, pine nuts, river pearls, and marten pelts, which daily increased its wealth and power" until it was beyond Ming control. Fragmentary statistics from 1583–84 indicate a balance of trade in overwhelming favor of Jurchen traders. The more than thirty-two thousand taels of silver brought in by ginseng alone paid for the Han agricultural products purchased nearly forty times over.[16] It is hardly surprising, then, that a 1635 Qing official diplomatic protest about poaching to King Injo (*Renzu*; r. 1623–49) of Korea's Chosŏn dynasty expressed the fear that "subjects of the Great Ming are also moving into our territory to dig ginseng."[17] Regional poaching of ginseng by Han subjects of the Ming had actually been going on for nearly a century earlier at the expense of the Qing's Jurchen forebears. Han, circa 1538, were already poaching marten pelts and fish in "their search for profit" north of the Ming's Liaodong border. Ming Chinese were still engaged in illicit foraging activities in 1616, the year the Jin was founded.[18]

Conflicts generated by unique northeastern natural resources between Han, Koreans, and Jurchen were thus endemic, almost traditional, by the mid–seventeenth century, and poaching was mutual.[19] The Jin attempt to restrict access to strategic resources, both economically profitable and politically critical, was compatible with regional historical trends extant for at least a century or so by the mid-1630s.

Banner lands, and their subdivisions of specialized foraging preserves such as ginseng mountains, pearl rivers, and imperial hunting grounds, developed within this milieu. Korean officials had already commented on the Jurchen forager construction of northeastern space in 1536: "the barbarian [i.e., Jurchen] custom is to defend separate mountains and derive benefit from their produce. Should any fail to hold their traditional mountain, they have no dwelling place."[20] Under such conditions Jurchen identity and mountain microecosystems were existentially related.

Of course, mountains teeming with forage would not remain an existential prerequisite for Jurchen, particularly once they began to expand beyond their immediate home territory. The Jurchen-Manchu relation to their foraging spaces certainly changed over time, particularly as Jin power expanded into Qing. Nevertheless, foraging space continued to contain an inevitably idealized Manchu identity even as large numbers of indigenous peoples moved physically and culturally farther from the northeast.[21]

The pristine nature of the region and its peoples is easily exaggerated, perhaps most famously in the Qianlong emperor's 1754 poem "The Willow Palisade." The dynasty's northeastern "quarantine policy" (*fengjin zhengce*) was rooted in the palisade's dense thickets, planted to delineate the boundary between Han-inflected southern Manchuria and the "Manchu" north. This policy has been interpreted in terms ranging from absolute to superficial depending on the sources and periodization employed.[22]

The Nature of Imperial Foraging in the SAH Basin   69

Analysis of pristine foraging has also been problematic for contemporary western anthropology. Scholarship from the late 1980s challenged prior assertions of the existence of "primary" hunter-gatherers, who only foraged and never needed to farm or trade. In contrast, "secondary" hunter-gatherers are understood as diversifying their subsistence activities, although some scholars dismiss the category of forager altogether as a purely subjective construction of modern observers. More recently, a basic consensus has emerged on retaining hunter-gatherers in a less essentialized and anachronistic conceptual form to accommodate the diversity of their lifeways, especially today.[23]

Different levels of the Qing state made conflicting distinctions between foragers as well, discussed in greater detail below. While reflecting past and present categorical ambiguities, the evidence suggests the existence of particular northeastern foraging practices that required space to maintain interconnected human and natural resources. Such enclaves could be existential prerequisites for the preservation of a forager identity depending on when, where, and how this identity is defined. From the perspective expressed in the Korean account of 1536, individual forage mountains in Jilin were necessary to the physical survival of any Jurchen *aiman*, who all appear as pristine foragers. From the Ming perspective in 1617 amalgamated forage was critical to the political survival of the Jin state, which by that time was clearly engaged in secondary foraging augmented by agriculture and herding. Once the Qing state had overcome both the Koreans and the Ming to consolidate itself in China proper, the significance of foraging areas diminished in these brute existential terms. However, it increased, from the dynasty's eighteenth-century perspective, for the preservation of the embodiments of "the old, pure and honest Manchu traditions." This deliberate state policy to preserve, even determine, foraging culture for purposes other than immediate survival was the basis for a third borderland identity constructed through "imperial foraging."[24]

IMPERIAL FORAGING: THE ADMINISTRATIVE SPACE OF CULTURED NATURE

After 1644, the environment for best cultivating imperial foraging lay in parts of Jilin and Heilongjiang that could be kept largely isolated from corrosive non-Manchu elements, especially Han agro-urban practices. In fact, incompatibility between Han farming and Manchu hunting had already left a preconquest record and legacy.

70 *Across Forest, Steppe, and Mountain*

Conquest dynasties long before the Qing had been confronted with such conflicting environmental interests, as in the Khitan Liao throne's decree in 996 that military personnel could not hunt when it would affect agriculture.[25] In 1642, when elite hunters' horses damaged fields, Hong Taiji could already reminisce that in his father's time this offense merited a whipping, and even execution if sufficiently serious. Nine years previously during a fishing trip in Fushun the emperor had the ears of two offenders pierced when he saw their horses freely grazing in peasant fields. In 1635, again harkening back to a ban from his father's reign, Hong Taiji scolded clansmen for hawking near fields and livestock. He declared that when he "deployed troops for the hunt, all bivouac in the outskirts, even in seasons of bitter cold, and do not enter villages lest they harm people and property."[26]

Hong Taiji's son, the Shunzhi emperor, faced a similar problem under different conditions once the Manchus rode south to occupy China proper. A March 1651 decree reflected growing pressures on traditional Manchu foraging practices amid Han fields:

[Han] commoners ... all rely on the land for sustenance. We have heard that commoners' fields are being everywhere enclosed to provide bivouacs for hunters passing through. Now while hunting is a military exercise to which the people of old held, We fear it will inevitably cause agricultural grievances to the detriment of commoners' affairs. How can commoners carry on with their places now wrested from the plough and hoe, and their route to food and clothing cut off. This is a great burden Our heart cannot bear. The Board of Revenue will immediately order local officials to return the whole of the lands previously enclosed to their original masters and charge them to cultivate it as opportunity permits.[27]

In this instance, enclosure, a major controversy between Manchu and Han in the wake of the conquest, possibly amounting to over 1.6 million hectares (more than four million acres) mainly in the greater Beijing area, appears as a deliberate extension of northeastern foraging spatial practice into China proper.[28] This practice was already interfering with important agricultural activities in Fengtian locales such as Fushun before the conquest but had become unsustainable in north China during the Shunzhi reign.

Nevertheless, live Manchurian fauna continued to embody attempts to maintain some semblance of northeastern foraging conditions south of the Great Wall. Amur tigers, Manchurian brown bears, and Amur leopards (*Panthera pardus orientalis*) were caught and sent to Beijing until 1822, when captures were limited to tigers used to stock the Nanyuan hunting preserve near the capital for banner training exercises. Other animals went for breeding stock, such as the five different types of Manchurian fish fry

The Nature of Imperial Foraging in the SAH Basin 71

procured in the early 1750s or the ten Manchurian moose calves captured in the Kangxi reign.[29]

It was during the same reign that a bureaucratic transformation took place as the Qing administrative apparatus shifted its center from Shengjing, which became an auxiliary capital, to Beijing. A Shengjing branch of Beijing's *Neiwufu* (Imperial Household Department) emerged to manage northeastern foraging space, in addition to managing other crown lands. The bulk of this immense territory was intended for the plow, ideally guided by demobilized bannermen on fields set aside for them. Banner serfs would labor on the imperial clan's own manor farms in southern Manchuria.[30]

The Beijing *Neiwufu* was separated from the regular bureaucracy to manage the extraction of wealth for the extended imperial household and staffed by the emperor's own "three superior banners," namely, the Plain Yellow, the Bordered Yellow, and the Plain White. These, along with five "inferior banners" in service of noble households, pursued elite foraging activities in the northeast. Such units were composites of preconquest household bondservant and banner companies, some of which were formally consolidated into the Shengjing branch of the *Neiwufu*, established in 1752.[31]

To supervise the imperial house's northeastern dominions, the Shengjing branch worked with a number of subsections of the Beijing *Neiwufu* as well as with parts of the regular Six Board bureaucracy, including offices under the *Gongbu* (Board of Works).[32] The most important subsection was the *Duyusi* ("Office of the Imperial Hunt"; Ma: *Buthai Jurgan*; known as the *Caibuyamen* from 1661–76), coordinating foraging matters between Shengjing and Beijing. Finally, administrative elements of the local banner system also participated.

A brief bureaucratic anatomy of fish foraging in the Butha Ula enclave may convey some of the system's complexity. The sixteen specialized fishing "detachments" (*zhu-xuan*; Ma: *juhiyan*) would turn catches over to their immediate superior, the Butha Ula Superindendant. He would then have sturgeon conveyed to Beijing, "fine-scaled" fish to the Shengjing Board of Rites, and sea perch to the *Yuchashanfang* (Palace Larder), a subbranch of the Beijing *Neiwufu* that served up imperial meals. The foragers' supply needs, mainly grain and salt, were requisitioned through the Shengjing *Neiwufu*, which could even provide wives for single foragers.[33] Fishing in Butha Ula involved elements of the local banner system, the Shengjing regional and Beijing central bureaucracies, while contributing little to the direct subsistence of the foragers involved.

Across Forest, Steppe, and Mountain

Escalating elite imperial demand approached mass consumption of forage over time. The earliest function of Butha Ula units from roughly the 1620s to the 1640s had been to acquire forage for sacrifice at dynastic temples and tombs. In 1700 fish foragers had to procure only sixty fine-scaled fish for this purpose, in addition to their sturgeon-catching duties, imposed four years earlier. By the early 1880s, foragers were scouring ten rivers to obtain their quota of 5,382 fine-scaled fish.[34]

The scale and complexity of operations such as Butha Ula fishing is another distinguishing characteristic of imperial foraging, but the uses to which such immense amounts of forage were put were also distinctive. Fine-scaled fish were not intended simply for consumption, but for veneration of dynastic tombs, as were the sable and otter pelt tribute from indigenous peoples such as the Hejen and Fiyaka.[35] Indeed, the very act of hunting and gathering these products was intended to nurture the corresponding "Manchu" virtues among the various inhabitants of northeastern foraging spaces. Imperial foraging in these terms was one postconquest strategy to maintain ecological and cultural conditions for the preservation of the dynasty's preconquest ethnic identity. Consequently, a fundamental prerequisite for imperial foraging was sufficient, and sufficiently isolated, space, which preconquest resource competition had already established as the cores of imperial foraging enclaves. These enclaves, often defined by geographic features such as mountains and rivers, fell into three basic classifications.

Each of the eight Manchu banners had access to ginseng mountains (*renshen shan*), foraging mountains (*caibu shan*), and battue hunting mountains (*weilie shan*) of between two to nineteen in each category. Sometimes several banners shared access to a particular enclave. The two red banners, for example, shared ten battue hunting grounds between them. Of twenty-six foraging enclaves and forty-five battue hunting enclaves appearing in banner records, most of those that can be located lie scattered across the border between eastern Fengtian and southwestern Jilin over much of the core of the original Manchu homelands. Mountains defined such enclaves in this generally subboreal region, possibly because their elevated boreal microclimates nurtured distinctive flora and fauna. Korean ginseng (*Panax ginseng* C. A. Meyer), for example, is a product of the mixed broadleaf-conifer forests of southeastern Manchuria.[36]

These resource enclaves were special administrative subdivisions of northeastern space for military and foraging purposes integral to the pursuit of a banner lifestyle. The most important, the Butha Ula enclave, was established "in the early years of the state" as a specialized foraging

The Nature of Imperial Foraging in the SAH Basin 73

banner region that was probably comparable in expanse to a small modern prefectural municipality.[37] Units processed forage while executing military duties, such as patrols used to maintain enclave integrity. Enclave authority was complicated. It overlapped for certain purposes and at different times, mainly between the *Neiwufu* and Jilin's military governor, who could not, for example, levy taxes on Butha Ula. The enclave's garrison was ranked under the *Neiwufu* military hierarchy of the three superior and five inferior banners. These could be subject to different foraging regulations, a statutory complexity that partly reflected environmental diversity.[38]

Specialized distinctions also arose between soldiers and foragers that had not previously existed and that often altered relations between people and animals. In 1682 upon returning from an imperial tour through Jilin, the Kangxi emperor decided to reduce the burdensome foraging duties of regular banner troops, probably about twenty-five hundred men around this time, also stationed in Butha Ula.[39] Henceforth, the capture of nestlings of eagles and hawks, usually pursued in early spring to "the detriment of agriculture," would be abolished. Foraging of "sturgeon and other fish," however, would continue with specialized forager *juhiyan* duly assigned in 1666. Finally, hunting, as the primary form of military exercise for banner troops, would continue, but not "incessantly." The paramount concerns here were the preservation of the horses' condition and protecting personnel from "undue harm" when "encountering wild beasts."[40]

The emperor's decision to scale back trooper's foraging duties was made in the context of more than a decade of Cossack incursion into the SAH basin, which the Qing ended through military operations in the mid-1680s and the Treaty of Nerchinsk in 1689. This victory required an unprecedented military and administrative mobilization into regions far north of Butha Ula, where previous dynastic presence had been sparse. The mobilization resulted in the establishment of the territorial administrations of Jilin and Heilongjiang, in 1653 and 1683, respectively. An increased emphasis on standing armies, a local agrarian logistical infrastructure, and a commensurate reduction in any activities such as foraging that hindered these measures duly ensued.[41]

The conditions that arose in Jilin and Heilongjiang intensified the influence of the imperial state on local foraging practices, traditional indigenous expressions that had not made such absolute distinctions between hunting, gathering, and fighting. Moreover, this cultural contraction in what activities legitimately distinguished a soldier from a

74 *Across Forest, Steppe, and Mountain*

forager did not arise from Han migration, usually denounced as the main agent for the erosion of traditional Manchu identity. Instead, stress reverberated from the political summit of the Manchu diaspora in response to military exigency under particular ecological conditions.

IMPERIAL COMPETITION FOR THE SAH BASIN: FIRST STAGE

The imperial borderland of Qing dynasty Manchuria was still forming in the second half of the seventeenth century, along with its attendant Manchu identity, as a result of interactions between indigenous peoples and subjects of the Russian and Chinese empires in the SAH basin. Manchu identity and Qing dynasty themselves remained somewhat recent notions, having only been formally declared in 1635–36.[42]

At this same time Russia's Romanov dynasty (1613–1917) sought Eurasian empire through eastward Siberian expansion into the SAH basin, initially spearheaded by the Cossack raiders of Vasilii Poiarkov in 1643. This expansion then stalled from a combination of indigenous resistance, Cossack rebellion, and Manchu arms, all abetted by sheer distance from authorities in Moscow.[43] After a major defeat by Qing forces in 1658, however, Russians had steadily, and largely without authorization, infiltrated back into the basin in the 1660s. By the early 1670s an official Cossack stronghold at Yaksa (Ru: Albazin) on the SAH River had been built. Such local departures from the tsar's authority are symptomatic of the contemporary limitations of Russian centralization in the wake of the political turmoil of the "Time of Troubles" and the consequent improvisational nature of Siberian expansion. By this time a number of ill-conceived and futile missions, begun in 1654, had been sent to the Qing court to formally assert Romanov imperial authority over the basin and its resources.[44] The renewed Russian challenge compelled the Qing to incorporate the SAH basin in less ambiguous terms.

The complexities of this incorporation were embodied in the dynasty's attempts to reorder the identities of inhabitants of a river basin that already had three distinct names in Manchu, Russian, and Chinese. In 1676 thousands of these inhabitants, generically termed "Warka" in Manchu documents, accordingly found themselves undergoing a not entirely voluntary removal southward under Qing auspices.[45] Like the ginseng, river pearls, and sable pelts enriching their forest habitat along the SAH tributary of the Sungari River, thousands of indigenous peoples were being hunted and gathered by both the multiethnic Romanov and Qing empires.[46]

The Nature of Imperial Foraging in the SAH Basin 75

Warka and the other Donghai, or "Savage" (*Yeren*), Jurchen lived intermixed between the Sungari-Hūrha (-Mudan, in Chinese) and Ussuri-SAH confluences. They all had been exposed to manpower raids, which were not always resisted, by the nascent Manchu state decades before the arrival of Russian competitors. Raids on these *aiman* were launched as early as 1607, when the Weji were attacked. A main objective of such raids into the SAH basin, virtually annual during the 1630s, was the enlistment of captured males, supplemented by other human and natural resources taken at the same time.[47]

These state-building raids were the first of two regional mobilizations by the Manchu state. Raids in the first half of the seventeenth century ultimately abetted the conquest of China proper, and raids in the century's second half provided for the defense of the SAH basin against Russian incursion. Both mobilizations expanded and consolidated Manchu territory through the transformation of diverse indigenous identities into "New Manchus," whose composition and incorporation differed in terms of the pre- and post-1644 conquest contexts.[48]

Although all operations against SAH peoples prior to 1644 can be seen as central to the Jin-Qing "unification" of Manchuria, indigenous peoples who avoided removal from their native places were not fully subjugated. They could even become restive, as the Solon-Ewenki centered on the upper SAH reaches did in a final uprising in 1639–40. The Qing suppression operations in 1640–41 captured at least 3,385 adult males, along with 4,296 dependents. Probably many of the Donghai Jurchen captured that same year were also picked up in the process.[49]

Manpower raids perhaps most perfectly exemplified the Manchu concept of hunting as warfare and also exhibit the imperial state's treatment of their captives as human resources. Hong Taiji, for example, decided that 557 newly captured "Warka" men in 1634 (identified as "Hūrha" in Table 1) "need not be equally distributed in eight equal parts," one for each banner as usual, but apportioned to understrength banners as needed.[50] The seventeen raids listed in Table 1, conducted against the "Warka" and other Donghai Jurchen peoples, were regulated by a series of statutes governing the foraging of human beings.[51] A 1638 report most explicitly prescribes capital punishment for officers who "failed to capture a single person." One soldier was punished for a lack of vigilance that had allowed a mass escape from "the pen constructed to restrict all the able-bodied males captured from the designated villages." Another officer was rewarded "because the males captured were more than the number originally fixed." This rather blithe revelation implies the existence of a quota for

76 *Across Forest, Steppe, and Mountain*

TABLE 1 *Jin and Qing Manpower Raids on Donghai Jurchen, 1631–40*

Raid Date	*Aiman* Raided	Captive Males	Additional Captives	Other Plunder	Source (*QSL*)
1631	Warka	1,219	1,887	G, P	2:113b
1632	Ujala[a]	N/A	700[b]	L, P	2:177a–b
1633	Ujala	N/A	565[c]	L, P	2:181a–b
1634	Hūrha	1,116	2,424	G, L, P	2:242b, 268a–b
1635	Warka	5,534	4,819	L, P	2:301a, 329b–330b
1636	Warka	1,896	1,479	L, P, G	2:356b, 369b, 375a
1638	Warka, Gūaleca	1,520	2,952	L, P	2:519b–20a, 538b–39b, 546a
1640	Hūrha, Kurka, Ujala	2,954	6,129	P	2:675b–76b, 688a–b, 691b–92a, 695a–b
Total		14,239	20,955		

Notes: G = ginseng, L = livestock, P = pelts.
[a] Clan name.
[b] Includes men women and children.
[c] Age and gender unspecified.

adult male captives that may have appeared in the first year of the Kangxi emperor's reign. This is one indication that manpower raids continued after 1644.[52] Officers involved in operations launched from Ningguta were rewarded based on the number of households subjugated, ranked at five ascending levels of twenty-unit increments from twenty to one hundred.[53]

Although subject to quotas that included punishment for shortfalls and rewards for overfulfillment like any other forage, indigenous captives, as Hong Taiji emphasized to 2,541 of his raiders in 1634, shared with their captors a common language and descent. Consequently, they would be "pacified ... with fine words" expressing these ties. Prisoners would be "taken in hand," so they would "submit en masse" for "employment on our behalf." They were valuable resources to be treated well, not subjected to abuse.[54]

The Jurchen and other *aiman* groups had been conducting such raids for nearly two centuries at least to obtain another, southern type of valuable human resource, Han farmers. More than one hundred thousand were estimated in 1543 to have been killed or taken in ninety-seven raids during the Ming Chenghua emperor's reign (1464–87) alone.[55] They were a considerable addition to what a Ming official envoy to the Jurchen in 1443 reported as the "many Chinese in the Jurchen savages' households compelled to till the land."[56]

The Jurchen acquired much of their fifteenth-century agricultural capacity, critical for their subsequent rise, directly from Han, and also Korean, captives, who were the main workforce of Manchuria's sixteenth- and seventeeth-century "manors" (Ma: *tokso*). As late as the 1680s, Han taken from operations against the Three Feudatories in Guangdong and Fujian were being sent north to work Shengjing's burgeoning manors, although Manchu records state that many "were not acclimated to the region" and did not even know how to farm.[57] Long-term agrarian relations qualify the formation of a "Jurchen" or "Manchu" identity as purely arablist or venery. However, Gao Shiqi's diary and the Qianlong emperor's poetry, along with other postconquest records, indicate that Inner Asians generally did not devote themselves so wholeheartedly to farming in the ethnically distinctive way that Han did because of more intimate connections to foraging, herding, and regional ecology.

Manchurian conditions required devoted farmers. As one study in the 1930s understated it, "structurally the Manchurian soils are not ideal" for agriculture. In addition to alkaline soils that render about 10 percent of the Manchurian plain unarable, seasonal extremes in temperature, relatively short growing seasons, poor drainage, substantial zones of permafrost, and meager precipitation in short intensive bursts considerably restrict the scale and type of cultivation possible in many places. The western Songnen grasslands, for example, spend about 140 days a year frozen to a depth of ten centimeters. Changbai in the southeast also spends five to six months of the year at subzero temperatures, during which, as one 2009 account again understated it, "agriculture rests." Consequently, the arablist possibilities for the cultivation of Han staples such as cotton are limited to the milder climes of southernmost Manchuria.[58]

Manchurian conditions hardly precluded agriculture everywhere but did inhibit its state-building potential in the rather cool seventeenth century. The critical source of Jin economic power was the hunting, gathering, and trafficking of unique northeastern forage, an exclusively Inner Asian enterprise grounded in a militant equestrianship and pastoralism, not in cereal cultivation. By this time, however, Manchu foraging was neither pristine nor subsistence, but it had introduced new arablist relations into its society through the hunting and gathering of agrarian Han and Koreans.[59] In this respect, hunting and gathering enabled Manchu identity to diversify beyond exclusively hunter-gatherer relations. Like its military, Manchu agriculture was a product of foraging.

Conflicts over regional human and natural resources were, consequently, not new by the mid-1600s, but their scale and complexity had

78 *Across Forest, Steppe, and Mountain*

grown with the development of imperial rivalry between major Eurasian states. Russians, too, raided for their own human resources, as in 1652 when they captured 361 Dagur women and children.[60] The Qing, in response, expanded their influence over the relatively unsubjected peoples in the lower SAH reaches as well as strengthened their control of semisubjects on the mid-SAH.

Indigenous peoples were in this way compelled to take sides, and their political relationships deliberately altered for purposes of imperial incorporation. This process of transformation from *aiman* to *gūsa*, however, also required manipulation of these peoples' ecological ties, which would likewise undergo not always predictable change. Contacts linking basin peoples and their surroundings produced a diversity that not only complicated the construction of a more centralized Manchuria, but also conditioned the extent to which the region could be incorporated into either a Romanov or a Qing empire. The state's limited control over regional diversity defined Manchuria's status as a borderland under construction where relatively uncoordinated foraging practices prevailed. The imperial core, in contrast, had been long dominated by intensive agricultural activities under intricate state supervision.

Consequently, methods used to turn Han peasants into imperial subjects could not be applied to SAH basin foragers without considerable modification, a process further complicated by Russian competition for these same human resources. Traditional foraging practices, sable tribute most prominently, were critical for the development of the basin's human resources, but hampered their further refinement for empire.

SABLE-CENTERED ENVIRONMENTAL RELATIONS

For any aspirant rulers of the region, the political was necessarily the environmental in the sense that relations between sovereign and subject were traditionally maintained through sable (*Martes zibellina*) pelt tribute. Tribute as guest ritual has generally been examined within the context of interstate diplomacy rather than as a form of environmental interaction creating complex ties between people and their surrounding ecologies. However, *gong*, the Chinese word for tribute, was not synonymous with *alban*, a Manchu term that could also mean "tax" or even "official duties." So the Manchurian practice retained to varying degrees in different circumstances the sense of all three definitions. Its foraging bureaucracy collected a wider range of remittances (see Table 4) than the mainly grain and silver taken in by its China proper counterpart, the

Hubu (Board of Revenue).[61] Northeastern "tribute" as used here thus describes general hunter-gatherer obligations, often reciprocated by rewards, under special conditions of imperial foraging. As John E. Wills, Jr., has advocated for maritime Sino-European relations, "tribute" is understood here to focus on indigenous practices in the process of studying an "interactive emergence" between cultures.[62]

Sable, a primary material incentive for imperial incursion into the basin's northern reaches, was a critical resource for uniting fragmented regional groups into a borderland order defined by foraging rather than cultivation. Subjugation in this context was ritually and materially tied to a unique regional resource, which indigenous peoples were especially well situated, by nature and nurture, to acquire through hunting, not planting. Tribute in the SAH basin required a different assemblage of elements that included both hunters and forests.

The social significance of pelts was grounded in the necessities of basic subsistence in a boreal environment. Although residents consumed them for a variety of purposes, pelts for clothing were a prerequisite for human habitation of the northern basin, especially for farming and soldiering. Officials requested "fur coats" (Ma: *jibca*) as vital both for forty-seven Cossacks taken prisoner at Yaksa in 1684 and for five hundred Qing troops working the land in Heilongjiang in 1688.[63] Within a few generations, however, shortages had appeared in the territory. A 1750 report explained that Solon-Ewenki and Dagur were so numerous that fur-bearers became too scarce to supply clothing. Their previous existence as "hunters and foragers who ate the flesh of wild animals and wore hides" with "little use" for cloth" had consequently become unsustainable. Since the climate was "too cold for cotton cultivation," it urged that indigenous people be taught Mongolian methods of felt production from livestock to avoid expensive purchases from merchants.[64]

Of course, furs, sable being the most prized, were also needed for trapping fur-bearing animals during cold weather when pelts were at their maximum thickness. There were several methods for obtaining pelts, all of which necessitated extended periods of outdoor exposure for hunters, whether they smoked sable out of their lairs or ran them down with dogs.[65] The local production of basic necessities such as clothing for life in the basin meant foraging amid a semiboreal ecology.

The biodiversity of this ecology is immense for an area so far north (roughly between 41° and 55°). These natural endowments, many of them regionally unique, are scattered across an area of more than 2 million, largely mountainous, square kilometers drained by the more than forty-four hundred kilometers of the world's ninth longest river. Manchurian mixed forests and the boreal or taiga forests, two of fifteen distinct ecological regions formed from the combined climatic effects of monsoons, oceanic currents, and mountains, are among the most important cradles of this biodiversity. Forests in the Changbai Mountains, for example, consist mainly of mixed stands of Korean pine and a range of indigenous deciduous trees to produce an ecoregion that gives rise to other rare species such as ginseng, unique to this type of forest. These forests also distinctively contain larger stands of larch and pine conifers that in turn provide a food-rich habitat for rare mammals such as the Amur tiger, the leopard and, most significantly for seventeenth-century Eurasian empire, the sable.[66]

Sable are adapted for SAH forests. A recent study of sable in northern Heilongjiang province found that the animals showed a marked preference for stands containing both larches and birches, which facilitate resting and feeding. Overall, sable almost exclusively favored old-growth stands that provide substantial cover, especially in winter. They tended to avoid unforested areas or even where saplings predominate.[67]

Sable are intimately and intricately dependent on distinctive tree species whose intermixture substantially defines boreal and Manchurian mixed forests, which in turn helps to constitute the ecoregion. Over time, humans have interacted with this biodiversity in ways that can augment or reduce it, but always as to gradually integrate themselves within it, even if just to keep warm. So foraging skills, rather than cultivation skills, are far more important for the accumulation of the three Manchurian treasures, which formed part of the material basis for regional control. Control, however, was also based on hunting skills for the militarization of human resources. The Qing had amply exploited the synergistic potential of both natural and human foraging resources in their mobilization for the 1644 conquest of agrarian China.

Human interactions with sable and other forage were, consequently, conditioned by a range of cultural and ecological factors that could be put in service of imperial state ends but required appropriate orchestration of more than just human acts. Human and natural resources could be mutually enhancing so that a state needed to control their linkages to obtain the means to construct a stable regional order.

Human-sable interaction was a fundamental component of this order, with sable tribute acting as its traditional and primary expression. The Qing inherited this system, which can be traced as far back as the Han dynasty. Manchus both modified and expanded the system to form

The Nature of Imperial Foraging in the SAH Basin

subject "tribute sable tribes," an administrative abbreviation for a diverse group of indigenous peoples, including the Solon-Ewenki, Hejen, Fiyaka, Kiler-Ewenki, Orochen, and Dagur, under nominal dynastic authority.[68] One common and distinctive characteristic among them was, of course, the possession of a particular range of hunter-gatherer skills. Hong Taiji exulted over this range near the conclusion of his dynasty's initial subjugation of basin peoples in 1642: "along the seacoast from northeast to northwest, to the Reindeer Herder (*Shilu*) and Dog Keeper (*Shiquan*) tribes, ... the lands that produce black fox and black sable, which do not plow and sow but customarily hunt and fish for their livelihoods ... everywhere has been subjected."[69] This preliminary subjection was maintained through sable tribute.

QING PELT TRIBUTE

As noted in Chapter 1, taxation was tangible evidence of the efficacy of *shengjiao* in the hierarchical construction of Hanspace. This arablist view was substantially altered within the northeastern venery context, for which tribute, not taxation, was the primary political tie. It was more a matter of *alban* than *gong*. *Alban*, especially *seke alban* ("sable tribute"), unlike *gong*, did not construct peripheral vassals but core soldiers.

The early Manchu state's incorporation of the basin was thus padded with sable. Pelts were presented in at least forty-nine of sixty (82 percent) tribute missions between 1626 and 1643, sometimes in quantities as large as that of a 1634 Solon-Ewenki presentation of 1,818 sable pelts.[70] This practice continued as the Qing extended its authority northward. Official entries for thirty-eight indigenous tribute missions from the SAH basin from 1644 to 1673 indicate that all presented sable pelts, which were the sole tribute items in twenty-eight (74 percent) of these cases.[71]

Qing pelt tribute usually required that an *aiman* mission travel to an administrative center, Ningguta, and later Ilan Hala, in Jilin or Qiqihar in Heilongjiang. Tribute could be assessed from one to fifteen pelts per adult male annually, depending on an adult male's status as nominal hunter, banner soldier, elite forager, reservist, etc. In Kangxi-era Jilin a mix of banner company and hunter households turned over 2,649 sable pelts, as recorded in a 1678 tribute list that also acted as a crude census. A similar list from Heilongjiang records 3,187 Solon-Ewenki and Dagur adult males presented one pelt per man in 1791. Tribute sable was generally sorted into three grades with differing quotas. Officers receiving these pelts on behalf of the emperor reciprocated mainly with textiles from

82 *Across Forest, Steppe, and Mountain*

China proper, including robes, hats, boots, saddle cloths, belts, sashes, and fans. Quota shortfalls were sometimes punished by withholding gifts, other times simply carried over to be repaid the following year. A feast was also a regular part of the proceedings. Once the ritual was concluded, the tributary delegation was permitted to trade the remainder of their various pelts, which could amount to thousands, and other goods with resident private merchants.[72]

Qing pelt tribute ritual, as the preceding Ming exchanges before it, was primarily intended to subjugate SAH basin peoples. Profit was, technically, secondary. Regular commerce in pelts nevertheless reached immense proportions during the Ming. 47,243 sable pelts were traded in just six months between 1583 and 1584 despite the dynasty's limited degree of control restricted to the basin's southern fringes. This scale ensured the Ming tribute system suffered from local profiteering that cheated indigenous peoples. This undermined what one contemporary critic called the pelt tribute system's fundamental principle of "sending [tributaries] back with more than they came with."[73]

A more direct Qing presence permitted a more ambitious agenda for the transformation of tributary identities into New Manchu bannermen. The role of pelt tribute in the construction plan for embodiments of an imperial borderland was especially visible when ritual norms were violated, as they were by the Hejen and Fiyaka tributary missions in 1675. These groups were inhabitants mainly of the lower reaches of the SAH and nearby Sakhalin Island, which were the extreme and tentative northeastern edges of dynastic authority in the basin. The Kangxi emperor had himself bluntly recognized the vacuum of Qing norms among these two groups three years earlier in 1672. As part of a contemporary mobilization against resurgent Russian incursion, he charged Jilin's first military governor, Bahai, "to spread a civilizing influence and employ all means to enlighten them" because "although they are submissive, they are actually savage and it would be best to guard against them." This order was similar to one the emperor also sent to Bahai around the same time to civilize the equally "savage" and "crafty" Warka and Hūrha.[74] The "savage" identities of all three peoples were to become "cultured" through more supervised interaction with their surroundings. Bahai duly employed pelt tribute to effect this change, but a misunderstanding, possibly deliberate, exposed the limits of tribute as an instrument of ethnic transformation. A mid-1676 report complained that Fiyaka and Hejen representatives had unilaterally violated tribute etiquette by presenting their sable pelts not at Ningguta, but at an outpost much farther north. Because of their ritual impropriety, these "ignorant people"

The Nature of Imperial Foraging in the SAH Basin   83

(Ma: *mentuhun urse*) would not witness Ningguta's impressive concentration of military power that customarily formed the backdrop of pelt tribute proceedings there. Such a display was thought particularly timely to discourage the Hejen and Fiyaka from plundering the "new people" (Ma: *ice urse*), a reference to the Warka, who were then in the process of being relocated southward to Ningguta for protection and mobilization.[75]

Assault, however, could reinforce indigenous identity as Qing subjects. As early as 1653, a group of five Cossacks were sent out to explore routes to China in order to obtain its emperor's submission to the Tsar. En route the Cossacks demanded horses and guides from what they called a "Ducher" village. They also declared the tsar's proposal that Heilongjiang be divided roughly in half, with Russia taking the territory east of the Non River (Nenjiang). As their tributary mission later reported in an imperial audience in Beijing, the villagers, probably known to the Qing as ethnically akin Hūrha, decided that they could not maintain livelihoods as Cossack tributaries. So, in gratitude for state gifts of clothing and horses bestowed for their pelts, the villagers killed the Cossacks and added their victims' fox and sable to augment their own annual tribute. After admonishing them to spare further Russian emissaries, the throne sent the delegation off with their statutory gifts of clothing.[76]

Although the villagers' ethnicity is not clear from the record, it is apparent that they were indeed Qing subjects who were willing, under the express motive of the pelt tribute system, to resort to violence to maintain a Qing Manchuria against imperial rivals. Lower SAH basin groups such as the Fiyaka and the Hejen, who had not been as exposed to this system, were, in contrast, unlikely to uphold the Qing regional order so militantly. Here is one indication that pelts were more than simply articles of commerce or consumption. Pelts were sovereign wares, commodities whose semiritualized exchange could help establish and maintain hierarchical power relations, and their requisite suzerain-subject identities, without further supervision or coercion.

ROMANOV PELT TRIBUTE

The Russians were more heavy-handed in manipulating relations between indigenous peoples and sable pelts. Villager reaction to Cossack visitors was accordingly violent in 1653, and this also facilitated Qing mobilization of the SAH basin against Russia more than twenty years later. Pelts in general and sable in particular conditioned Romanov expansion in eastern Eurasia to such an extent that some scholars have characterized this historical process as "the exhaustion of hunting grounds, the discovery of new ones and their subjugation to Russian authority." State policy in general has, moreover, been characterized as "essentially subordinated to the goal of exacting tribute" from indigenous peoples, who are all seen as "direct or potential providers of fur tribute." Russian state officials themselves could even be partly paid in pelts. Fur certainly was the explicit medium of subjugation for Erofei Khabarov's 1649–53 expedition, the second major SAH incursion following Poiarkov's. He was specifically ordered to compel the peoples of the basin to pay tribute, called *yasak*. *Yasak* was a core policy for Russian steppe penetration whose origins can be traced back several hundred years to the Mongol Golden Horde. Russia imposed it as a generic levy, whose medium differed by locality, on non-Christians. Consequently, the basin would pay in furs, in contrast to Khabarov's previous operations where there had been "no sable, foxes, beavers or otters in the steppe." Of course, Russian eastward expansion was not entirely determined by fur, which nevertheless has been characterized as its chief economic motive. So steppe dwellers were not to be exempted from *yasak*, but pay "in whatever precious goods the land may offer," for "they must not think that because there is a scarcity of animals for *yasak* that they will not come under the [Russian] Sovereign's mighty hand."[77]

Russian Eurasian expansion was, in this way, conditioned, rather than determined, by the biodiversity of distinct ecoregions, as reflected in the qualification in Khabarov's orders regarding the issue of fur-bearing animals. Differences in the biodiversity of steppe and forest diversified Russian Eurasian expansion in this respect. This suggests additional consideration of forest foraging practices for restructuring accounts of regional conflict between the Russian, Manchu, and Zunghar Mongol empires during what Peter C. Perdue calls "the decisive turning point in steppe-settled interactions."[78] An important part of this interaction, contributing to the Romanov defeat, was the mobilization of basin peoples mainly on behalf of the Qing in a conflict that occurred in and over the fur-rich forests of the SAH basin, not out on the steppe.

Consequently, the way in which Russian empire would be constructed within the basin's boreal and Manchurian mixed ecoregions was substantially conditioned by the presence or absence of fur-bearers. Human consumption of fur-bearing animals was decreed as the distinct, boreal idiom of incorporation within Romanov imperial space, which remained in the grip of a veritable "fur fever" from 1585 to 1680. During this period, which nearly encompasses the span of Sino-Russian conflict in the

The Nature of Imperial Foraging in the SAH Basin 85

basin, pelts, mainly sable, represented about 7 to 10 percent of Romanov total revenues.[79]

The Russian pelt tribute system, however, was weakened, like the Ming's, by extortion predicated on an exchange of pelts for indigenous hostages. *Amanat* was another Golden Horde inheritance, although indigenous steppe peoples saw this Cossack hostage taking as integral to nonaggression agreements between equals rather than as assurance of political submission as the Russians would have it. Poiarkov duly kidnapped Dagur and Hejen he came across while collecting "the Sovereign's *yasak*," and searching "for new non-*yasak*-paying people." His expedition was hampered by the contradiction between his method of collection and his men's dependence on locals to supply food. Crippled by food shortages that antagonized locals did nothing to remedy, Poiarkov foray into the basin ended by 1646.[80]

Khabarov continued to try constructing a Romanov Amur based on a relatively crude exchange of hostages for pelts, running as high as fifty per head. This tribute system was presumed adequate for a sustainable regime based on maximum sable extraction. To this end, Khabarov's expedition was charged to compel indigenous peoples to hand over as much *yasak* tribute "as circumstances allow." Taking "their leaders as hostage" would compel the *aiman* to "pay the Sovereign's *yasak* ... for all time to come." Although the order defined a range of acceptable *yasak* pelts, including sable, fox, ermine, beaver, and otter, the vast majority of the Russians' *yasak* was collected in sable, and this preference was reinforced in subsequent orders.[81]

The brutal inefficiency of Romanov pelt tribute is casually revealed in Khabarov's August 1652 report of attempts to impose *yasak* on a Dagur group living on the Jingqili (Ru: Zeya) River. After pursuing and killing some of the people they encountered, the Cossacks seized around 170 villagers. Khabarov then informed *aiman* leaders that if the Dagur "would give the *yasak* to our Sovereign and be obedient and submissive in all ways," they would not be killed but protected. Dagur leaders, including one "Prince Tolga," reluctantly agreed, and swore an oath accepting "eternal *yasak* servitude," but almost all the new subjects soon ran off. After futile attempts to torture the remaining Dagur leaders into recalling their people, the Russians, having antagonized their main provisioners, were forced to withdraw from the vicinity.[82]

Khabarov had overestimated the capacity of hostages and oaths to transform Qing subjects into Romanov subjects and underestimated the difficulties of basin foraging in general. The Dagur quickly adapted to the

86 *Across Forest, Steppe, and Mountain*

challenge by manipulating Russian vulnerability to both nature and custom. The Dagur made Khabarov, who stated that both sides had been "living together as one family" and associating "frequently," believe they accepted Russian domination by giving their word, pelts, and food. These submissions gave most the chance to flee. The Dagur had deprived the Russians of vital human resources, a strategy culminating in the suicide of Tolga and his fellows.[83]

Russian dependency also reveals why pelts alone were insufficient for a sustainable Romanov Amur. Instead, pelts and indigenous peoples, along with other local resources such as food, formed an integrated whole that would have to be more carefully managed without crude extortion before Russia could realize its ambitions. Regional domination would emerge only for the imperial power that could reorder all the critical components of boreal diversity for its own benefit. So, after the initially confused stage of Qing-Romanov conflict from the 1640s to the 1660s, each power sought to reorder its control of pelts and peoples to adapt to the new challenges posed by the other.

IMPERIAL COMPETITION FOR THE SAH BASIN: SECOND STAGE

Both Qing and Romanov forces received unambiguous indications through their respective pelt tribute systems that the indigenous peoples of the basin were under pressure to subject themselves to one side or the other in the 1650s. This decade saw the formal establishment of the Qing military administrative region of Jilin and the outbreak of five military clashes between Romanov and Qing forces between 1652 and 1660. The indigenous peoples most directly involved lived along the Sungari River, part of Jilin's southwestern border with Heilongjiang, and the SAH River's middle reaches. None of these peoples were entirely unified or entirely subjugated by either empire, but by the 1650s they had become some of the SAH basin's most compelling resources.

In 1657 Ningguta's commander Šarhūda, prompted by Cossack raids' erosion of sable tribute, submitted a memorial to the throne to urge an expedition along the Sungari. Šarhūda wanted preemptive conquest of various *aiman* of unsubjugated Hejen and Fiyaka and defense of existing Qing vassal *aiman* from subversion. His warning that "it would be no easy matter" to resubjugate subverted *aiman* indicates the limits of the contemporary tribute system's ability to construct reliable Qing subject identities. Indeed, Russia had already "recruited" new Dagur "Cossack servitors" in 1652, and scattered records indicate a subsequent expansion

The Nature of Imperial Foraging in the SAH Basin   87

in servitor ranks. Šarhūda's fears were confirmed two years after his own major 1658 victory, the fourth military clash between the two powers since 1652. A fifth clash in 1660, won by Bahai, also required the "pacification" of 15 Fiyaka villages of more than 120 households near the Sungari-SAH confluence in western Jilin.[84]

For a generation starting in the 1650s Qing sable tribute underwent a decline in terms of both quality and quantity that reflected dynastic losses in territory. Sable shortfalls began to appear among the tribute of the Dog-Keepers and other *aiman*, persisting into the 1680s. Starting around 1653, incidents, including Cossack operations that scattered locals and disrupted their hunting, contributed to tributary shortfalls. Cossack predation became less systematic after Šarhūda's defeat of the main, authorized Romanov forces under Onufrii Stepanov, but independent, often rebellious, Cossack bands continued to move aggressively into the basin. There was little practical distinction, however, between these two types, and Qing authorities only really began to note differences around 1669. By this time, pressure for full mobilization of dynastic forces against the resurgent threat had formed and was expressed by one official proponent directly in terms of pelts and peoples. Censor Mo-luo-hong justified his request for an increase in Ningguta's Manchu garrison by asserting that "the Cossacks have frequently violated the lands beyond Ningguta and within Heilongjiang where the people who present sable pelt tribute live."[85]

Large-scale military action remained difficult for both sides during the 1670s mainly because of problems elsewhere, including unrest in China proper and a major conflict with the Zunghar Mongol leader Galdan (r. 1671–1697). Both taxed Qing capacities far more than Russians ones. So the deterioration in dynastic pelt quality and quota shortfalls continued largely unabated throughout the 1670s, an unambiguous sign that Russian incursion had made critical territorial inroads along the mid-SAH. When dynastic officials questioned Solon-Ewenki about such declines in the 5,089 tribute pelts due for 1680, for example, it was confirmed that Cossacks had cut off access to the best hunting grounds.[86]

Russian and Manchu progress in creating imperial space in the basin was in this way explicitly measured in pelt gains and losses. Tribute structured the process of this competition and the new historical space it was creating. One of Khabarov's Qing prisoners affirmed during his interrogation that indigenous peoples had come to Ningguta to petition for protection, saying that if the Qing would not defend them, "we will be forced to pay the *yasak*" to the Russians.[87] Such appeals were a primary reason for the dynastic mobilization of indigenous peoples as ethnically remodeled New Manchus.

88 *Across Forest, Steppe, and Mountain*

The removal of Donghai Jurchen from the mid-SAH during the 1670s was the operational centerpiece of this mobilization. By this time both the Qing and Romanovs had received warnings and appeals for intervention via their indigenous tributary systems.[88] Such records, dating from the 1670s until the Russian expulsion from the SAH in 1687, suggest a polarization of direct imperial struggles for basin resources.[89]

The Qing state issued an appeal to indigenous peoples and implemented drastic measures as early as 1653–54 when many "Solon" were relocated southward to the Non River where they would form the Hunting Eight Banners. Several hundred households were also moved in 1665. Details on relocation, however, are scant before the 1670s, coinciding with the apparent peak in Cossack Yaksa's ability to collect *yasak*.[90] The Russians sometimes likely misinterpreted the wholesale abandonment of villages before their impending and often dreaded descent as Manchu-initiated. Actually, as for example in 1653, authorities were sometimes informed of indigenous flight to Qing territory after the fact through routine communications of pelt tribute exchanges.[91]

Relocation, which could involve shifts of thousands of people and animals over hundreds of kilometres, was logistically complicated and potentially traumatic. Table 2 provides demographic statistics on the 1676 relocation operation. Under the leadership of the Meljere clan leader Januka, forty-five New Manchu banner companies of 2,768 men were raised from a population of more than thirteen thousand. This whole group was shifted from an area roughly stretching more than two hundred kilometers from the Ton River above Ilan Hala north to the the Bičan River, just above the SAH-Sungari confluence.[92] So began a systematic process of relocation that continued to form, shift, and reshift New Manchu banner companies of mid-SAH residents to points as far south as Beijing up to 1791.[93]

At such a scale and under the exigency of Russian incursion, problems, including active resistance to relocation, were inevitable. By 1678 officials were still reviewing demographic registration information (outlined in Table 2) that was required to complete mobilization for eighteen of the banner companies. Some of these had already been split into new formations.[94] Many ostensibly logistical problems were actually rooted in the abrupt severance of indigenous peoples' existing environmental ties, especially with game, in the process of reconstituting their identity as mobilized Qing subjects.

Upon their arrival at Ningguta some Warka officers, for example, petitioned resident dynastic officials for funds to purchase a large number

The Nature of Imperial Foraging in the SAH Basin 89

TABLE 2 *New Manchu Banner Companies' Relocation Routes to Ningguta, 1678*

(Clan)/Banner Company[a]	SAH Home Village	No. of Households	No. of Adult Males	Initial Destination[b]
(Meljere)				
Kelde	Ektin	28	90	Sungari
Hangko	Ice	30	102	Sungari
Dundei	Ektin	31	72	Sungari
(Heye)				
Calbišan	Oogiyan	27	77	Sungari
Noona	Oogiyan	"	81	Sungari
Anai	Oogiyan	23	101	Sungari
Beikune	Oogiyan	21	98	Sungari
Loban	Gitan	35	88	Utun
Ulingge	Lefuke	31	115	Sungari
(Tokoro)				
Imnece	Tumetu	29	84	Sungari
Hureni	Kitkin	29	97	Sungari
Cimao	Kitkin	32	77	Sungari
Teoce	Kakū	37	116	Sungari
Lahida	Hilhū	13	56	Sungari
Arašan	Elge	30	100	Sungari
Neone	Gūbkatin	47	151	Sungari
(Ujala)				
Tehulde	Getehun	41	111	Hūrha
Nendiokin	Ebuda	22	65	Hūrha
Total: 18	14	533	1,681	

(*Source:* NFY, KX 5–1678: 4–17)
Notes: [a] Each company is indented under its parenthesized clan.
[b] First river stop in a series of multistage village transition points to Ningguta.

of cattle to be used for meat broth, an important staple that the Warka "were accustomed to eating." The new recruits asked that food cattle be purchased for them because their agricultural duties producing food for Qing military operations left no time for hunting. Indeed, Warka officers had been explicitly ordered to ensure that "when these ignorant people go hunting, they have not been careless in cultivation."[95] These exchanges indicate Warka foraging culture's disruption by an imperial arablist agenda that required adaptation as New Manchus to a new ecological and cultural habitat.

The Warka could also resist adaptation by "desertion," as the Manchu regulars dispatched to apprehend them called it. Some newly arrived

90 *Across Forest, Steppe, and Mountain*

Warka, instead of submitting formal complaints, decided to slip back to their homes while ostensibly out hunting, fishing, or herding around Ningguta. At least forty-six males from twenty-six separate households from eight banner companies made tactical use of their old way of life to escape the new set of obligations that effectively required the Warka to leave off foraging and become full-time soldier-farmers (see Table 3). Some of the fugitives were eventually caught heading back to their homes on the Bičan. When questioned, the fugitives revealed a cultural gap that had opened between the two groups of Manchurian forest peoples. When Qing troopers asked their Warka captives if they had deserted because of conflict with long-established residents in Ningguta, the fugitives instead explained that "we were unable to get meat broth and stew to eat" in Ningguta. In their "native place ... abundant grass and trees" had enabled them to hunt for the requisite meat ingredients. They had deserted because they "missed" their own food, which was unobtainable in their new, comparatively treeless home.[96]

It is not entirely accurate to view this incident as evidence that the Warka were literally, purely, and immutably products of their pristine boreal environment – namely, that they were "primary hunter-gatherers" in more technical and controversial anthropological terms. It is actually impossible to speak of "the Warka" as a highly and consciously unified people in a Qing or Romanov sense, making it difficult for both modern scholars and imperial contemporaries to categorize them.

Nevertheless, one Warka *aiman* officer's report made it quite clear that relatively arablized areas such as Ningguta were ecologically unsuitable in his people's terms. He complained that in their normal

existence our people are partial to [hunting/eating] wild animals and fish working only a little in the fields. Some people do not work the fields at all, but are pastoral. Now since we moved to Ningguta, however, we have come to depend only on fields, [but] oxen and plows are insufficient so we cannot engage in cultivation.[97]

These Warka in their natural habitat were not uniformly hunter-gathers, pastoralists, or agriculturalists. Instead, they manifested a number of ecologically conditioned practices that probably maximized their chances of survival. The state itself actually used some such distinctions. Officials initially decided that if the Cossacks moved toward the various lower SAH Hejen *aiman*, none would need evacuation "since these people do not farm and so are able to move anywhere out of the way."[98] Yet the dynasty finally used an essentialized agrarian identity as the determinant for indigenous removal. Problems emerged when Warka who were only

The Nature of Imperial Foraging in the SAH Basin 91

TABLE 3 *New Manchu Mobilizations to Ningguta, 1676 (NFY KX 3-1676:101-11)*

(Clan)/Banner Company[a]	No. of Households	No. of Members	No. of Adult Males
(Meljere)			
Januka	28	361	62
Kelde	28	306	63
Kišeo	13	175	45
Olboco	29	294	62
Abtai	27	329	64
Dedušen	16	197	45
Kilede	18	219	50
Wario	19	253	44
Tumju[d]	32	344	57
Hangko	33	406	66
Dundei*[c]	20	215	52
Ulgina*	33	381	66
Ninggune*	28	285	61
(Heye)			
Bukteo	28	290	53
Calbišan	24	253	55
Sajuna	25	241	53
Gelio	17	297	67
Soldon	29	359	72
Lobaka	35	276	69
Anai	21	295	58
Naicungga	38	298	69
Ulingge	24	388	76
Beikune	24	406	74
Cokita	17	185	43
Noona[b]	26	303	68
Noona[b]	30	279	59
Faju	32	272	68
(Tokoro)			
Imnece	25	247	57
Giyaciha	35	468	85
Kisuku	28	383	82
Baniokan*	33	287	66
Lahida	12	182	40
Hureni	26	307	44
Werhemu*	21	193	45
Cimao	32	231	61
(Ujala)			
Tehulde	37	434	87
Celdei	14	191	45

92 · Across Forest, Steppe, and Mountain

Table 3 (cont.)

(Clan)/Banner Company[a]	No. of Households	No. of Members	No. of Adult Males
Nendioken	22	236	43
Šulduha	25	247	49
Nikšan	27	283	54
(Gaijing's Ujala)			
Buku	31	377	74
Kabai	40	446	94
(Bayara)			
Tahana	29	356	73
Tolonggo	17	172	42
Nadana	36	483	83
Total:[c] 45	1,196	13,518	2,768

Notes: [a] Each company is indented under its parenthesized clan.
[b] One of these companies is probably a mistranscription of "Nona" (NFY 1-1676:117).
[c] Totals include figures from parts of the Daidaha and Nohai companies, which appear auxiliary and have been otherwise excluded from the table (cf. NFY KX 1-1676: 115–20). They amount to twenty-three men from twelve households containing eighty-eight members.
[d] Tumju: company implicated in desertion attempts (NFY 2-1676: 39–54).
[e] Dundei*: company containing fugitive households (NFY 2-1676: 225–29).

semiagricultural at best tried to adapt to regions where the prevalence of agriculture was relatively monocultural. Something of the same problem seems to have emerged with Russian management of the mainly pastoral Yakuts, whom officials nevertheless compelled to hunt sable.[99]

In sum, there were, and are, practical pressures to make groups such as the Warka "legible," to use James Scott's term for oversimplifications that abbreviate human and ecological complexity to facilitate state control.[100] The Qing state oversimplified Warka agrarian practices to make diverse basin peoples more legible for relocation. The resulting desertions, whose precise extent remains unclear, were reportedly occurring "one after the other" and affecting Ningguta's security.[101] Although hardly "mass" in the scale shown in Table 2, these desertions, like those reported among new Sibe and Dagur recruits in the 1690s, reveal ongoing difficulties with incorporating multiethnic New Manchus into a more uniform set of arablist practices rooted in deforestation.[102]

Some desertions were likely related to the precipitous implementation of mobilization policies to rapidly deploy indigenous peoples at the expense of time and resources they needed to adapt to Ningguta's new conditions. During their unit formation, some New Manchus complained that new

The Nature of Imperial Foraging in the SAH Basin   93

cultivation duties and constant shifts between outposts had left them "no time to obtain shelters." There were other requests that New Manchu troops be moved from "temporary" residences in Ningguta's outskirts to houses within the town to permit them to "understand its ways."[103]

Relocation also disrupted the Qing pelt tribute system. By 1678 Qing officials sought to stop Ningguta's "new people" from trading pelts with Fiyaka and Hejen groups, which they held responsible for the poor quality of tribute pelts that year. They also feared the state would permanently lose exclusive access to high-quality pelts.[104] In this instance, Qing response to Russian incursion necessitated increased dynastic regulation of inter-*aiman* trade to preserve the integrity of tribute and to monopolize foraging of premium sable.

Dynastic officials, however, found they could not opportunistically reorder relations between peoples and pelts by decree. In fact, sable pelts were so much a part of basin quotidian existence that some banner officers felt pelt exchanges could not be prohibited because sable was used as dowry and to pay debts, in effect as currency for major transactions.[105] Some people, such as the Warka deserters, even felt compelled to move back to game-filled forests, in spite of other people's objections. Connections between game and peoples were not wholly subject to state, or even human, manipulation, which overlooked the ecological fact that the Warka's new residence of Ningguta, likely critically deforested, was not prime sable habitat.[106] Limitations on imperial power arose from such interdependency between indigenous culture and biodiversity rather than simply from human action.

Cossack incursion pressured the dynasty to resort to relocation, a denial of the human resources that also embodied, however tenuously, Qing territory. A more decisive reassertion of a Qing borderland would require different embodiements, based on restructured tributary identities and new constructions from indigenous peoples such as those Fiyaka, Hejen, and Kiler-Ewenki who had never been imperial subjects. This restructuring had to go beyond an alteration of pelt tribute relations. It required a more drastic transformation of indigenous peoples' forager identities into highly regimented military-administrative garrisons almost exclusively dependent on cultivation. Some of this transformation's consequent problems were already visible in issues of game, agriculture, and town residence that appeared within the first several years of the Warka arrival in Ningguta. Additional problems, however, would emerge once a more direct Qing presence was established along the northern reaches of the basin during the final expulsion of Romanov forces. This expulsion had begun with the

94 *Across Forest, Steppe, and Mountain*

mobilization in the mid-1670s that relocated the Warka and restructured their identity, a process that continued beyond Russian departure in 1689.

Russia benefited from indigenous discontent with Qing relocation policies. One such manifestation was the 1682 appearance of leaders of more than four hundred Qing tributaries at Nerchinsk, the Russian administrative equivalent of Ningguta, petitioning to transfer their pelts to the tsar. The leaders explicitly referred to Qing relocation policies as their motive, stating that the dynasty was "driving them out and planning to take them from their encampments to their Bogdoi empire, together with their wives and children."[107] Russian reconstruction of such indigenous tributary identities was, of course, precisely what the Qing relocation policies were intended to avoid.

A dynastic counterattack was thus commensurately urgent. Its primary thrust was aimed at Yaksa, Russia's main, if modest, outpost on the SAH since the early 1780s. Once reconnaissance and logistical preparations were completed, Qing forces moved forward in 1683 to clear Russian forces from the basin and began the assault on Yaksa in 1684. This assault was successfully concluded in 1685, but the Cossacks reoccupied Yaksa's stockade until Qing forces decisively expelled them in 1686–87. By this time, direct negotiations between the two imperial powers had been initiated, culminating in the historic Treaty of Nerchinsk that ceded most of the basin to the Qing.[108]

During these operations Qing forces had several encounters with the Russians' indigenous allies, the Kiler-Ewenki, and took several of them prisoner. One encounter revealed a population of forty-seven Cossacks and eighteen Kiler-Ewenki, one adult male, two adult females, twelve boys, and three girls, all living and fishing together on the Tuhuru River, more than 250 kilometers west of the mouth of the SAH River in northern Jilin. The officer in charge of the main operation, which also returned these nineteen "Russian prisoners" to their homes, acknowledged that "this is the first time we have pacified these ninety-nine males of thirty-one Kiler-Ewenki households." He declared that although they "lived in the mountains and forests like wild beasts and birds," "all would submit in droves" once they were subjected to "Milord's civilization." Another pacified group contained both Kiler-Ewenki and Orochen. There was also an indigenous group of eleven unweaned infants, forty-five adult males, sixteen adult females, nineteen girls, and twenty boys among the Yaksa garrison when it first fell in 1685. Three boys and thirteen girls among them had been "sired by Cossacks" from "women taken captive."[109]

These *aiman* women, possibly hunted down like sable or any other valuable boreal animal, were being used to produce new human resources for the Romanov incorporation of the SAH basin to deploy indigenous fighters against the Qing. Reports make it quite clear that the regional order envisioned by the dynasty had a limited tolerance for a foraging lifestyle, defined as people living "like wild beasts and birds." Such an existence sustained the ethnic fragmentation that Qing officials felt made the region vulnerable to foreign incursion and obstructed their own efforts to construct reliable New Manchus. The dynasty even exploited the ambiguities of Cossack identity by taking Russian prisoners into Qing ranks to redeploy them against Romanov forces.[110]

Foraging, a way of life adapted to residence in the basin's forest ecology under preimperial conditions, required the devotion of considerable dynastic resources to alter this practice and its embodiments before, during, and after the final conflict with the Russians in the 1680s. The Kangxi emperor implicitly acknowledged the incompatibility of forager and imperial identity when he remitted the penalties for the 1685 defaults in Solon-Ewenki and Dagur pelt tribute. He acknowledged that "the Solon and Dagur act as the great army of Heilongjiang and staff its military postal relay stations. In consideration of their efforts, they will be spared censure and receive their statutory rewards." Recognition of this incompatibility was even more explicit in a 1690 decision that because one thousand new Dagur recruits for expanded regional garrisons "would not be able to hunt or fish for themselves, their presentation of sable tribute should be stopped. They will be issued money for rations as per regulations on provincial capital garrisons."[111]

There were also instances of mobilizing foragers as farmers or soldiers, then demobilizing them back to hunters. In 1743 "hunting" (Ma: *buthai*) Solon-Ewenki and Dagur who had been cultivating state fields resumed pursuit of sable and other game, as did hunter-soldiers withdrawn from "outposts" (Ma: *karun*) in 1698. The general trend, however, was to transform foragers into sedentary stipended consumers of grain just like garrisons in China proper. Forager tribute had become far less important than mobilization of forager bodies.[112]

Such bodies were, nevertheless, raw materials for "great army" service. Many, like the impoverished Solon-Ewenki shifted to Ningguta in 1690, required special "instruction" because they had "never understood working fields nor lived in houses," but instead lived "like wild beasts and birds without resting places." Even in 1735, Solon-Ewenki and

96   *Across Forest, Steppe, and Mountain*

Bargut hunter recruits deployed to Hulun Buir, used to "living in the wild," "had trouble understanding" orders if they were "too detailed." Other poor Solon-Ewenki and Dagur, even when seemingly fit for duties such as manning five new postal relay stations in Heilongjiang, still had problems adjusting to a more regimented way of life. These "ignorant new people" nearly starved in 1688 because they "did not know how to reckon the time" needed to apportion their rations. Just locating forager recruits proved time-consuming. That same year mobilization of 332 Solon-Ewenki and 86 Dagur, all "willing" and "poor," required three months' delay until these hunters returned.[113]

Foraging, poverty, and military enlistment seem to have combined to provide the Qing with voluntary, but unusually raw, recruits. They would undergo a traumatic seasoning when stationed in relatively sedentarized places where "poor people, because they fish and hunt for a living, would not be able to sustain a livelihood."[114]

Incompatibilities between forager recruits and the Qing imperial infrastructure are a sign that the SAH basin was in a state of environmental transformation in the latter half of the seventeenth century. At this time, Qing-Romanov competition was drastically altering, and at times even severing, relations between humans and basin biodiversity.

A BORDERLAND CONSOLIDATED; FORAGING BUREAUCRATIZED

These alterations are most visible throughout Manchuria in the wake of the final Qing victory over the Romanovs. The onset of the eighteenth century witnessed the systematization of imperial foraging as the dynasty consolidated its borderland order. Administrative structures built up throughout Manchuria within the first fifty or so years after the conquest and mainly in response to Russian incursion afforded the Qing state greater access to human and natural resources via a foraging bureaucracy that spanned the northeast. Han settlers also inadvertently gained easier entry into what had been a violently contested zone. The peacetime activities of both the Qing state and its Han subjects put further, and sometimes contradictory, pressures on indigenous peoples and natural resources that continued to transform foraging relations.

Dynastic policy continued to regiment traditional interaction with the ecology through the formation of specialized hunter-gatherer detachments. In addition to twenty-five ten-man detachments gathering mainly pearls,

The Nature of Imperial Foraging in the SAH Basin 97

fish, pelts, and ginseng in Butha Ula in the late seventeenth century, Shengjing had forty-five otter pelt hunters operating in nine *juhiyan*, thirty Siberian salmon fishermen, ten stork hunters, fifteen bee-keepers, thirty game hunters, and fifty-five wild honey foragers. Sixty-five fishermen were based in Niuzhuang in southern Fengtian. There were also fox hunters and falconers hunting pheasants.[115] Northeastern ginseng and honey hunters were frequently supplemented by foragers sent from Beijing.[116] Some *aiman* were also operating outside Fengtian in Heilongjiang and Jilin, mainly trapping sable, and some small groups were operating on the north China frontier primarily as falconers. Finally, military *gūsa* banners continued to engage in foraging, especially hunting.

Although devoted to specialized activities, these forager groups could be reassigned. In 1710, for example, Butha Ula *juhiyan* were deemed to be gathering enough wild honey to suspend the activities of the manor honey producers, and virtually all of Shengjing's fishermen, banner personnel and commoners alike, were disbanded in 1726. In 1686, these *juhiyan* were ordered to end the "hardship" of trapping sable, which had been garnering mainly low-quality pelts, and to start gathering pearls. By 1693, they had been shifted to alternate years of honey gathering and ginseng digging.[117]

The Butha Ula foragers' tribute had originally been fixed by statute solely in terms of pelts, fifteen per man annually, raised to twenty in 1653. Thus, the 192 pelt foragers active in 1685 would have owed 3,840 pelts. Although some foragers, like those ordered to grow crops or specialize in sturgeon, were excused from this tribute altogether, most continued to pursue their quarry under an elaborate system of substitute forage that the trappers could turn over to meet their basic sable pelt obligations.[118]

Table 4 shows that this system of equivalents in effect rendered sable pelts a unit of account that persisted even after the actual use of pelts as a medium stopped. Subsequent surpluses or shortfalls in Butha Ula pearl quotas, for example, were still expressed in sable pelts because "if there are no sable equivalents made for pearls, apportioning reward and punishment will be difficult." This situation was probably compounded by the elimination of the other equivalents in 1682, when foraging was suspended for ten types of "animals useless for sacrifice" (*wuyong shengwu*) whose pelts or pinions would no longer be convertible into sable. Silver as well could enter into wider regional circulation through the quota system's normal operation, which generally allotted cash rewards for surpluses, although cloth awards were also common.

98　　Across Forest, Steppe, and Mountain

TABLE 4 *Sable Pelt Equivalents for Butha Ula Forage (Huidian (KX), 727: 6596-99)*

Forage	Sable Pelt Equivalent	Forage	Sable Pelt Equivalent
River pearls		Otter pelts	
<8 fen–1 qian	10/fen	Top grade	3/pelt
8 fen	80	Second grade	2.5/pelt
7.5 fen	67.5	Third grade	2/pelt
7 fen	63	Fourth grade	1.5/pelt
6.5 fen	52	Fifth grade	1/pelt
6 fen	48	Fifth grade	1/pelt
5.5–0.5 fen	5/fen; 2/half fen	Bottom grade	0.5/pelt
>0.5 fen	as pearls		
Pearls	1/fen	Leopard pelts	
		Top grade	5/pelt
		Second grade	4/pelt
		Third grade	3/pelt
Lynx pelts		Tiger pelts	
Top grade	6/pelt	Top grade	4/pelt
Second grade	5/pelt	Second grade	3/pelt
Third grade	4/pelt	Third grade	2/pelt
Fourth grade	3/pelt	Fourth grade	1/pelt
Fox pelts	2/pelt	Squirrel pelts	
		Top grade	20/pelt
		Bottom grade	25/pelt
Wolf pelts		Eagle pinions	2/pair
Top grade	3/pelt		
Second grade	2/pelt		
Bottom grade	1/pelt		
Raccoon dog pelts	0.5/pelt	Stork pinions	1/pair
Jackal pelts	1/pelt		

Shortfalls earned lashes. Such provisions distinguish forage *alban* from regular taxes.[119]

A different quota system existed to the south in Fengtian that was not based on sable pelts, primarily available only much farther north. There were fewer equivalents and a much wider range of forage with specified quotas. Equivalents were specific to some forage categories: two otter cubs the equivalent of one adult or a sea eagle equivalent to two storks. Rewards were expressed in terms of silver taels for salmon, for example, with an award of 0.2 of a tael for every five fish over quota. Shengjing's "honey raisers," probably beekeepers, were also rewarded with money.[120]

The Nature of Imperial Foraging in the SAH Basin 99

TABLE 5 *Fengtian Forager Annual Quotas (Hei-tu dang, 5:18.20, 6:3.2–4, 8:16.56–58, 17:30.41–42)*

Forage Type	Annual Quota	Shortfall Penalty (Lashes)	Foragers Assigned (Men)
Fish	32,500 jin (19,396 kg)	3/20 jin	65
Otter pelts	75	5/otter	45
Pheasants	3,000	n/a	30
Siberian salmon	1,500	n/a	30
Storks	150	3/2 birds	10
Wild honey	15,600 jin (9,310 kg)	5/2 bottles	312

The Qing state sought to subject ginseng, the single most valuable forage item in the northeast, to a more complicated system of control, albeit one limited by unauthorized human action and environmental change. Systemic adaptation was particularly necessary during the Kangxi period, exemplified by the exhaustion of ginseng in Butha Ula and Ningguta between 1684 and 1685, although only 156 Shengjing diggers were active. The reasons are not difficult to comprehend if a 1694 report of more than five thousand authorized foragers gathering root on behalf of their noble patrons or contemporary assertions by Heilongjiang military governor Sabsu of more than thirty thousand diggers are accurate. The state had already reduced banner authority over alpine ginseng fields. It ended the allocation of specific ginseng mountains to each of the eight banners for exclusive foraging around the same time exhaustion surfaced in 1684. The apparent motive was to tighten field access, certified through a permit system largely instituted during the Kangxi reign, to stop infiltration by illicit diggers. The natural limits of these measures, however, is suggested by the shift of gathering to new and rich, but less convenient, locales farther northeast on the Ussuri River, which was facilitated by the expulsion of the Russians.[121]

Another major change occurred in 1709 when foraging was formally militarized with the certification of thirteen hundred Butha Ula "Manchu troops" in thirteen units with an annual quota of one thousand *jin* (about 597 kilos). Any surplus would be at the disposal of these self-supporting units. Shengjing would dispatch another four thousand Manchu troops. They, in conjunction with four thousand others from Ningguta and two thousand from Butha Ula, would engage in state-supported forage of

100   *Across Forest, Steppe, and Mountain*

another one thousand *jin*, mainly for the *Neiwufu*. Butha Ula foraging, the last major form of banner ginseng gathering, would formally end in 1750. The three hundred remaining foragers, whose annual ginseng duties had been resumed in 1746, included one hundred troops, who could not find their way to the fields without forager guides. In 1749, exclusive reliance on these troops resulted in a 72 percent shortfall of the three thousand *jin* quota. A year later that the emperor decided that Butha Ula ginseng digging was going on "in name" only and sent the three hundred foragers to gather pearls exclusively.[122]

Despite administrative differences between foraging regimes, there was a common bureaucratic principle at work reconstituting relations between foragers and their forage. Under this system it was possible to deliberate whether gathering pine nuts and pine cones were distinct activities or to be merged with others. Hunting dogs were assigned state rations.[123] Pearls and stork pinions could be equated in terms of sable pelts, or storks themselves in terms of sea eagles. Some animals could be dropped from these equations entirely as "useless" or be rarefied into accounting abstractions when their real numbers declined. Such "unnatural" relations indicate that the state tried to make northeastern forage more exploitable, or legible, even as it sought to preserve a Manchu cultured nature within a wider, largely uncontrolled ecological context.

IMPERIAL FORAGING: THE SUSTAINABILITY OF CULTURED NATURE

Nevertheless, various administrative regimes imposed on foragers do not seem unambiguously intended to preserve a borderland "Manchu" identity. At least some forager groups, like some banner units, were multiethnic. Ratios between the two basic ethnic categories of Han and Manchu are often unclear.[124] Some units give the impression of ethnic uniformity, as among a group of Han fox, goose, and eagle hunters newly settled in Mukden in 1663, or as among a number of Manchu banner units looking for pearls in Jilin in 1686.[125] Qing authorities themselves were sufficiently uncertain about the Butha Ula ranks to order a detailed inquiry in 1662. One group of 114 was almost equally divided between Han and Manchu troopers, intermixed with a few Koreans.[126]

Whatever their actual ethnic composition, forager groups generally operated within the sphere of the Manchu banner system in lands exclusively set aside for the livelihoods of banner members and technically barred to Han commoners. The Kangxi emperor bluntly expressed this principle

The Nature of Imperial Foraging in the SAH Basin 101

in 1712 when he asserted that "Manchu troops can go dig ginseng, Han cannot." Consequently, all banner personnel, regardless of their ostensible ethnicity, were pursuing a "Manchu" lifestyle, defined by venery practices that distinguished them from the Han of arablist China proper.[127]

This lifestyle was profoundly affected by the demands of state foraging within the larger regional ecology, as exemplified in a fox-hunter group's 1668 application for transfer from a Shengjing banner company. The hunters had ended up in Shengjing after a series of state-mandated transfers had split them off from their original group. The hunters' petition described the "intolerable" conditions requiring them to spend the entire fall and part of the winter, about four months, hunting foxes. An additional two months was needed to convey the tribute pelts to Shengjing and return to their homes. Monthly musters in Shengjing for mandatory inspection consumed the rest of the year for the hunters. These time-consuming obligations compelled them to traverse an area too large to leave them enough time to fulfill their other tribute duty, grain cultivation. Their main complaint was that Shengjing-imposed obligations both to hunt foxes and to grow grain constituted an "unbearable" double tax.[128]

Tribute demands imposed on fox hunters may have upset a balance that depended on limited cultivation as a supplement to foraging. A similar dynamic is visible among Solon-Ewenki and Dagur hunters in Heilongjiang, who successfully petitioned in 1743 to resume hunting for subsistence and pelt tribute precluded by their previous reassignment to cultivation of state fields. It had already been decided in 1732 that cavalry units stationed in Qiqihar and other major towns in Heilongjiang could not be expected to engage in battue hunting operations and grow their own grain, so recruits less proficient with the bow were demobilized to free them for cultivation. Hunter-gatherers did not normally have to spend months each year relaying their tribute and assembling at distant administrative centers for inspection to supervise additions or reductions in personnel. Furthermore, if the experiences of a group of Tümed tributary fox hunters in 1718 is indicative, a petition to the throne was even required for permission to shift hunting grounds to trap south of the Willow Palisade.[129]

The sheer scale of imperial foraging, in terms of expanse, quantity, and administrative complexity, rendered northeastern hunting and gathering difficult to sustain. There is no better admission of this in dynastic records than the 1744 assertion that "the *fengshui* of Changbaishan is not conducive to the implementation of foraging, so it will be strictly prohibited" in response to the exhaustion of local ginseng fields.[130] Although it is impossible to be certain, there are indications that intensification of hunting and gathering combined with poaching and environmental degradation to deplete resources. Both Han migration, broadly responsible for filched resources and deforested terrain, and Manchu state foraging's pressure to fulfill excessive annual quotas were unsustainable in this respect.

Official concern over resource exhaustion was centered on poaching, which could undermine resource management efforts. In 1684 "large masses" of ginseng poachers threatened catastrophic depletion of Butha Ula sable and pearls and may have actually caused a steep decline in regional fish and pearl forage a decade later.[131] A series of regulations was issued between 1730, the year when banner gathering was formally ended, and 1802. They attempted to implement a system of ginseng mountain rotation, with an area subject to two years of gathering, and then allowed one year of recovery. By 1783, however, it was admitted that poaching had undermined this system in Shengjing's jurisdiction. By 1802 ginseng mountains in Jilin had ceased rotation.[132]

Poaching, however, was not the only likely source of exhaustion. In 1686 Shengjing foragers were relieved of their pine nut tribute, which was to be taken up by Butha Ula, a decision probably influenced by quota shortfalls that began to emerge around 1669.[133] The *Duyusi* proposed that the shortfall in the annual two-hundred-kilogram tribute be made up by purchase on the private market in autumn when pine nuts were cheap.[134] This suggests that although pine nuts were still common in Fengtian as a whole, they may have been difficult to find in banner areas reserved for comparatively intense and highly organized hunter-gatherer tribute operations.

The *Duyusi* tended to interpret shortfalls in anthropogenic terms that were centered on human idleness, incompetence, or malice. Thus, it suspected a 1670 shortfall in the wild honey quota might be due to "lazy people." These culprits might not make consecutive searches of designated hills as a statutory forager group, but unofficially split up to cover multiple locales simultaneously, and much less comprehensively. It also suspected its honey gatherers were being diverted by their own personal foraging activities. Such doubts reveal the *Duyusi*'s hostility to informal foraging, which it held interfered with imperial quotas. The solution was an increase in administration through the appointment of an official to oversee honey-gathering activities by this group.[135] In 1690, officials came to a similar conclusion about pine nuts, deciding that some of the throne's own foragers were diverting tribute nuts to Fengtian commerce.

The Nature of Imperial Foraging in the SAH Basin 103

In 1747 the Qianlong emperor himself concluded from pelts whose "color was not like it had been" that his pelt foragers were "concealing the good ones" because past poaching by "Russian Orochen" peoples had been stopped.[136]

The emperor's suspicions regarding his foragers are certainly plausible and doubtless often accurate. They are not, however, always the only possible, or even the most plausible, environmental explanations, which must include considerations of anthropogenic resource depletion caused by the normative operations of imperial foraging. Such considerations seem to have exceeded the capacity of the bureaucratic imagination, which was limited even in anthropocentric terms.

A general intensification of human labor was the standard bureaucratic response to hunter-gatherer shortfalls despite strong evidence of ecological dearth. The failure of Shengjing's thirty pheasant hunters to fulfill their annual quota of three thousand by nineteen hundred fowl in 1668 brought a reprimand and an order to go out and try again. The fact that captured birds were considered too skinny did not affect the *Duyusi's* deliberations, and it simply issued a standard order that surpluses would be rewarded and shortfalls punished.[137]

A more pronounced decline occurred in the stork (*guan*; Ma: *weijun*) quota, which was supposed to be fulfilled by ten men bringing in 150 birds each year. In 1673, the men brought in 116, in 1674 44, and in 1675 a mere 23.[138] The *Duyusi's* solution was to press the hunters to overfulfill the normal quota to make up for previous shortfalls, despite a report explaining that the previous shortfalls arose from there being too few male storks and too many females. Males were probably most sought after because of the size of their pinions. The *Duyusi's* response was an exhortation to overcome these conditions of what was probably overhunting.[139]

Storks were among the ten "useless" animals whose capture would be suspended in 1682, four years after this exhortation was issued. Given the precipitously steady decline in the stork quota from 1673, in addition to considerable shortfalls for 1669 and 1670, it may be that storks became useless only after they became scarce.[140] The Kangxi emperor made a relatively unambiguous demonstration of this type of rationale in 1695 in response to a shortfall in the Butha Ula sable tribute. The emperor noted that "for the past several years sable have decreased because of frequent hunting ... yet [pelts] are not a necessity, and We have no pressing need for them."[141]

An even more explicit acknowledgment of the excesses of imperial foraging came a century later in 1796 when the newly enthroned Jiaqing emperor was told that the only way to obtain pine nuts and pine cones was to cut down trees, then being done throughout the northeast. The emperor decreed an end to this practice, which also pertained to honey gatherers, and ordered that "a method must be established to climb the trees" instead.[142] Bannermen had actually been climbing pines as far back as 1647 and, significantly, had been rewarded for their skill. Given their preference for old growth forests, sable may also have been driven elsewhere or reduced by pine-felling over time.[143] Some such combination of these cultural and ecological factors fomented incidents such as that in 1754 when nineteen Hunting Solon-Ewenki, failing to find any quarry in their Heilongjiang forests, poached 253 sable pelts from a Jilin preserve to meet their tribute obligations.[144]

Although it is difficult to trace the ultimate causes of many accounts of resource depletion in the historical record, shortfalls in pheasants, storks, pine nuts, and sable indicate that imperial foraging, rather than Han poaching, could play a primary role in ways not exclusively attributable to human violation of regulations. This is certainly not to minimize evidence for Han encroachment into banner resource enclaves, particularly in search of valuable ginseng and most evident from the mid-eighteenth century on. Banner personnel nevertheless poached as well. Foragers had been duly and regularly warned by the *Gongbu* since at least 1666 that they were not permitted to cut down trees containing honey, fish, or even carry bows and arrows when on ginseng-gathering expeditions. Yet ginseng cases involving banner foragers emerged, such as that of the twelve Plain White Banner honey gatherers apprehended in the wave of violations investigated in the first decade of the eighteenth century.[145]

However, a relatively exclusive focus on ginseng tends to divert attention from dearth of other resources and, so, from other causes such as imperial foraging.[146] Imperial foraging and Han encroachment could synergistically operate to erode Manchu tradition as well as foraging space. The connections between tree-climbing and the gathering of pine nuts and honey are representative. Abandonment of the foraging skill of tree-climbing and a commensurate rise in tree-felling may be a response to the steady or increasing demands of bureaucratized hunting and gathering. Commercial markets substantially sustained by Han consumption may, meanwhile, develop in tandem. Human resources, tree-climbers in this instance, are simultaneously degraded as skills incompatible with demands are abandoned. Deforestation soon affects other members of the ecosystem, such as sable, creating further declines. A distinct and more

The Nature of Imperial Foraging in the SAH Basin   105

sustainable form of relations between people and their ecology is gradually eroded, mainly to produce substantial quantities in a relatively short time to supply both tribute and commerce.

This sort of intricate environmental interdependency was also operative in connections between marten species and honey foraging. Deforestation triggering a decline in these species could undermine the search for honey because foragers found many wild honey hives by following the tracks of hungry yellow throated martens (*mishu*, lit., "honey rat"; Ma: *harsa*). This tracking skill, in turn, depended on an adequate snowfall to see the prints. A more than 50 percent shortfall in the 1668 honey quota was actually attributed to inadequate snowfall for *harsa* tracking. Lack of snowfall, as well as too much, was also periodically invoked to explain sable tribute shortfalls.[147]

Interconnections in such instances were vulnerable to vagaries of natural conditions and to the larger program to culture Manchurian nature for the dynasty's exclusive use. The Kangxi reign was a critical period for the onset of pressures and contradictions arising from these factors, driven in substantial measure by Qing attempts to maintain privileged access to the northeast's human and natural resources. Although by no means permanently exhausting even the most valuable resources, such as ginseng and sable, which persist in an endangered condition today, the scale of the dynasty's northeastern extractions proved insupportable by the early nineteenth century.[148]

This unsustainable consumption, in addition to Han migration propelled less by culture than by agriculture, reconfigured northeastern space to hybridize a putatively pristine borderland Manchu identity. Effects are especially visible in Fengtian's farmland to population figures, which indicate that the ratio between registered land cultivated by banner people and Han commoners decreased rapidly between 1644 and 1734 from almost 44:1 to a little under 8:1. Such a drop likely helped to push nearly 30 percent (just over 734,000) of the whole of Manchuria's population of just under an estimated 2.5 million people into Jilin and Heilongjiang by 1820.[149]

The significance of scarcity goes beyond a shortage of forage such as pine nuts or even ginseng for imperial kitchens or coffers. The cultured nature that the regime maintained in Manchuria formed a network of imperial foragers who relied on snow to track marten to acquire wild honey to be taken from intact trees back for ritual presentation and royal consumption in Beijing. The range of interconnections between species, climate, and culture represented in this single streamlined

106   *Across Forest, Steppe, and Mountain*

example ensured that a forage crisis would inevitably include an identity crisis. The ultimate unit of account for northeastern forage was not sable pelts, much less an equivalent in storks or raccoon dogs, but Manchus, who were in critically short supply by the nineteenth century. By this characteristically Qing measure, imperial foraging had become unsustainable.

This destabilization presented a serious adaptational challenge for the Qing Manchurian borderland and its attendant hunter-soldier identity. Nevertheless, such change emerged as part of the very process of construction, a dynamic also visible in another Qing borderland defined by distinctive environmental ties, Inner Mongolia.

Notes

1 Yang and Xu, "Biodiversity Conservation in Changbai," 885, 896; Tang et al., "Landscape-Level Forest Ecosystem Conservation," 171–73.
2 Important works on New Manchus include Yang Xulian "Jianlun Qingdai Kangxi shiqi de xin Manzhou," 192–96; Liu Jingxian et al., "Qing Taizu shiqi dexin Manzhou wenti," 102–07, 116; Zhang Jie, "Qing chu zhaofu xin Manzhou shulue," 23–30; Zhang Jie and Zhang Danhui, *Qingdai dongbei bianjiang de Manzu*, 59–93.
3 "Frontier people" (*bianmin*) is a term often applied to unregimented groups mainly inhabiting the lower SAH River and Sakhalin Island, especially to those 2,398 households officially registered as pelt tributaries by 1750. These multiethnic groups included Fiyaka, Hejen and Ainu. For administrative studies see, Yang Xulian et al., *Qingdai dongbei shi*, 140–47; Matsuura, *Shinchō no Amūru*, 222–79.
4 In 1791, for example, Han merchants were seeking to transport 16,567 pelts they had purchased for sale in China proper; Wang Peihuan and Zhao Degui, "Qingdai Sanxing," 199. For related studies, see Guan Jialu and Tong Yonggong, "Qingchao gong diao shang wu-lin zhidu," 93–98; Wang Dehou, "Qingdai Sanxing difang maoyi shulun," 177–83.
5 Zhou Xifeng, *Qingchao qianqi Heilongjiang*, 113–16; Lee, *The Manchurian Frontier*, 52–53; QSL, YZ 10/4/21, 8:556b–57a,YZ 10/3/10, 8:543a MWLF QL 7/3/19 [03-0172-0610-005]. For a study of the Hunting Eight Banners, see Han Di, *Qingdai Baqi Suo-lon*.
6 (*Qingding*) *Baqi tongzhi* YZ 5/4/13, 1:194.
7 (*Qingding*) *Baqi tongzhi*, YZ 2/3/28, 1:174.
8 (*Qingding*) *Baqi tongzhi*, YZ 5/4/13, 1:194–95. For further examples of Han contamination, see ibid., YZ 4/12/27, 1:190; QL 58/4/19, 1:278, QSL QL 48/4/3, 23:790b.
9 Bhaba, *The Location of Culture*, 4, 193, 219; Moore-Gilbert, *Postcolonial Theory*, 129–30, 181-82, 192–95; Gladney, *Dislocating China*.
10 For official comments on the spatial dimensions of Han Manchurian migration, see, for example, QSL, QL 42/6/21, 21:868a–b, JQ 9/2/11, 29:700b–

The Nature of Imperial Foraging in the SAH Basin   107

701b. An important early study of ethnic conditions beyond Fengtian is Wada Sei, "Natives of the Lower Reaches of the Amur," 41–102.

11   *Manbun rōtō*, 2:644. This new regulation was put into practice a day later; *ibid*, 2:645–46.

12   Liu Xiaomeng, *Manzu cong buluo dao guojia*, 264–68, 344–47.

13   *Qingchu neiguo shiyuan Manwen dang'an*, 1:46.

14   Da Qing huidian (KX), 727:6593–94.

15   *Qingchu neiguo shiyuan Manwen dang'an*, 1:157, 159, 173, 178, 179, 215–16; Guan Jialu et al., eds., Tiancong *jiunian dang*, 117. For a studies of Qing-Korean conflict, see Kim, "Ginseng and Border Trespassing," 33–61; Li Huazi, *Qingchao yu Chaoxian guanxi*, 14–26.

16   Peng Sunyi *Shang zhong wenjian lu*, 3:9; Yang Hu, *Mingdai Liaodong dusi*, 133; Symons, *Ch'ing Ginseng Management*, 9–10. "Marten" here and throughout is used for the Chinese term *diao* when it occurs in a context that may not exclusively refer to sable (*martes zibellina*), which shared northeastern habitats with other species of the genus *martes*, such as the less-prized yellow-throated marten.

17   Guan Jialu, *Tiancong jiunian dang*, 91.

18   *Liaodong zhi* (Jiajing), 559a; QSL, TM 1/6/1, 1:65b.

19   Korean records from the 1540s into the 1590s reveal violent clashes with Jurchen violating Korean space in efforts to poach valuable ginseng and hunt; *Chŏson wangjo sillok*, Chungjong (Zhongzong) era, 36.12.28 (Western date January 13, 1542) 18.537b–538a; Myŏngjong (Mingzong) era, 3.9.14 (Western date October 15, 1548) 19.613a; Sŏnjo (Xuanzu) era, 28.8.23 (Western date September 26, 1595) 22.545b–546a and 28.10.7 (Western date November 8, 1595) 22:575a and 28.11.7 (Western date 12.7.1595) 22.593b and 29.1.30 (Western date February 27, 1596) 22.640a–44b and 29.2.29 (Western date March 27, 1596) 22.653b–654a.

20   *Chŏson wangjo sillok*, Chungjong (Zhongzong) era, 31.1.6 (Western date January 28, 1536) 17.628b–629a.

21   For the complex relations between Manchu identity and the historical space of Manchuria, see Elliott, "The Limits of Tartary," 603–46.

22   Edmonds, "The Willow Palisade," 599. For a survey of quarantine, see Zhang Jie and Zhang Danhui, *Qingdai dongbei*, 295–305.

23   Barnard, "Hunter-Gatherers in History, 4–5. For general discussions, see Stiles "The Hunter-Gatherer Revisionist Debate," 13–17; Bird-David, "Beyond the 'Hunting and Gathering Mode of Subsistence'," 19–22.

24   QSL, QL 42/6/21, 21:868a–b. For the significance of hunting preserves in particular for Manchu identity and the Qing imperial order, see Menzies, *Forest and Land Management in Imperial China*, 55–64; Ning, "The Lifanyuan and the Inner Asian Rituals," 60–92.

25   *Liaoshi*, 1:148.

26   QSL, TC 5/6/9, 9/6/25, CD 7/6/5, 2:123a, 311a, 830a.

27   QSL, SZ 8/2/28, 3:424b.

28   Ding Guangling, *Qingchao qianqi liumin*, 39–44; Wakeman, *The Great Enterprise*, 1:469–75; Ma Fengchen, "Manchu-Chinese Social and Economic Conflicts."

108 *Across Forest, Steppe, and Mountain*

29 *QSL*, DG 2/i.c. 3/5, 33:569a; *Kangxi chao Manwen zhupi*, #3706, p. 1537; MWLF, QL 16/5/13 [03-0172-0684-001]. The fish fry included sturgeon (Ma: *kirfu*), Siberian salmon (Ma: *niomošon*), and chum salmon (Ma: *dafaha*).

30 *Da Qing huidian shili* (GX), 12:680a–b; Qi Meiqin, "Guanyu Shengjing Neiwufu," 98–100; Isett, *State, Peasant and Merchant*, 56.

31 Tong Yonggong, "Qingdai Shengjing shang san qi bao-yi," 224–26; Tong Yonggong, "Shengjing *Neiwufu* de sheli," 221. For *Neiwufu* overviews, see Torbert, *The Ch'ing Imperial Household Department*; Qi Meiqin, *Qingdai Neiwufu*.

32 Shengjing also maintained five boards corresponding to the traditional Six Boards, minus the Board of Personnel. The five sometimes overlapped with the Shengjing branch's management; Xie Huijun, "Qingdai Shengjing cheng liubu," 54–58.

33 *Da Qing Huidian shili* (JQ), 700:7940–41; Hei-tu dang, KX 5:40.56–59; 8:23.72–73.

34 *Da-sheng Wu-la zhidian quanshu*, 14, 96–97; *Da Qing huidian* (KX), 727:6594–95.

35 *Huidian shili* (GX), 6:1041a. For ethnographic contexts, see Juha Janhunen, *Manchuria: An Ethnic History*, 115, 126; Zhou Xifeng, *Qingchao qianqi Heilongjiang*, 187–202. Matsuura, *Shinchō no Amūru*, 330–32.

36 (*Qingding*) *Baqi tongzhi*, 2:1265-68; Cong Peiyuan, *Dongbei sanbao*, 76–80. For suggestive analyses of climate and corresponding species variation in Manchuria's boreal subzone, see Grishin "The Boreal Forests of North-Eastern Eurasia," 17–19; Yang and Xu, "Biodiversity Conservation in Changbai," 887–89.

37 Using a ratio of 0.5 kilometer/*li*, Butha Ula, with a perimeter of over four hundred *li*, would cover an area of roughly sixty-four hundred square kilometers.

38 *Da-sheng Wu-la zhidian quanshu*, 23–25; *Da Qing huidian* (YZ), 787:13,434–35.

39 *Baqi tongzhi*, 1:527. During the Kangxi reign Butha Ula garrison troops numbered between an initial seven hundred in 1670 and a peak of over thirty-nine hundred around 1692 (ibid.).

40 *QSL*, KX 11/5/21, 5:32a–b.

41 Niu Pinghan, *Qingdai zhengqu yan'ge zongbiao*, 95, 110.

42 *QSL*, TM 9/10/13, 2:330b–31a, CD 1/4/11, 360b–361a.

43 For Russia's Siberian expansion, see Lantzeff and Pierce, *Eastward to Empire*; Forsyth, *A History of the Peoples of Siberia*; Ledonne, *The Grand Strategy of the Russian Empire*, 29–37, 74–81, 122–23, 130–31, 220–21.

44 For studies of Sino-Russian relations in this period, see Sun Xi and Zhang Weihua, *Qing qianqi Zhong-E guanxi guanxi*; Mancall, *Russia and China*.

45 NFY, KX 2–1676: 74–79. The move involved peoples and livestock resident in the Sungari, Hūrha, Wengkin, Bahūrin, and Sumuru regions.

46 Although technically known as the "Tsardom of Muscovy" or "of Russia" during this period, Russia was an expansionist Eurasian empire in the making. Empire was not formally declared until 1721; *Russia's Conquest of Siberia*, xxxv.

The Nature of Imperial Foraging in the SAH Basin 109

47 *QSL*, WL 35/5/1, 1:49a. For raids on the Donghai Jurchen, see Yuan Lükun et al., *Qingdai qian shi*, 2:707–24; Matsuura, *Shinchō no Amūru*, 224–26; Zhou Xifeng, *Qingchao qianqi Heilongjiang*, 26–29, 38–42. The Warka, Hūrha, and Weji, comprise the main Donghai Jurchen groups of the Ming, but their precise ethnographies are contested; Janhunen, *Manchuria: An Ethnic History*, 101-02; Zhou Xifeng, *Qingchao Qianqi Heilongjiang*, 187–88; Matsuura, *Shinchō no Amūru*, 135, 289–90. I employ the term "Donghai Jurchen" broadly, and somewhat anachronistically, to encompass these peoples.

48 One exemplary difference is a typical confusing overlap in basic terms of reference— some Donghai Jurchen groups, called "New Manchus" before the conquest, became "Old Manchus" after the conquest when the new "New Manchu" units, which also included some Donghai Jurchen, were being formed to fight the Russians; Zhou Xifeng, *Qingchao qianqi Heilongjiang*, 38.

49 *QSL*, CD 5/3/24, 2:678b–79a, CD 5/12/13, 714b–15a.

50 *Qingchu neiguo shiyuan Manwen dang'an*, 1:111. This source also states that there were 557 men captured, as opposed to the 550 recorded in *QSL* TC 8/5/17, 2:242b. Unfortunately, I have not been able to consult the original Manchu text to resolve the discrepancy.

51 For a discussion of early Qing regulations on the incorporation of subjected peoples, see Zhang Pufan and Guo Chengkang, *Qing ruguan qian guojia falü*, 131–46.

52 *Qingchu neiguo shiyuan Manwen dang'an*, 1:325; *Chongde san nian Manwen dang'an*, 154.

53 *Jilin tongzhi*, 5:3407–08 cites the text of this quota from an unidentified edition of the collected statutes, but this citation may be an error by the gazetteer's compiler. For an example from a 1643 raid into Heilongjiang that includes detailed statistics on captures of 2,552 people, their possessions and the rewards meted out to Qing troopers, see *Qingdai dang'an shiliao congbian*, CD 8.9.3, #6, 14:106–110.

54 *QSL* TC8/12/10, 2:280a–b.

55 Chŏson wangjo sillok, Chungjong (Zhongzong) era, 38.1.2 (Western date February 5, 1543) 18:645a–b. For an analysis of Jurchen agricultural development, see Liu Xiaomeng "Mingmou Nüzhen shehui," 66–76.

56 Fang Kongzhao, *Quan bian lüe ji*, 197.

57 Tong Yonggong, "Qingdai Shengjing Neiwufu liangzhuang gaishu," 236–38, 255–56.

58 Murakoshi and Trewartha, "Land Utilization Maps of Manchuria," 480–81; Ripley, Wang, and Zhu, "The Climate of the Songnen Plain," 13, 19; Ren Meie, *Zhongguo ziran dili gangyao*, 135; Isett, *State, Peasant and Merchant*, 216–17.

59 For an analysis of the interplay of many of these factors, see Yuan Lükun et al., *Qingdai qian shi*, 1:115–22.

60 *Lishi wenxian bubian*, #14, 60–61.

61 Chinese-language statutes often elide differences by describing state collection of forage under *Neiwufu* purview in terms related to taxation (*zhengqu, nafu*); *Huidian* (YZ), 787:13432; *Huidian shili* (JQ), 700:7934.

62 Wills, "Maritime Asia, 1500–1800: The Interactive Emergence of European Domination," 102, 104. For tribute in the context of interstate relations, see Wills, *Embassies and Illusions*; Hevia, *Cherishing Men from Afar*.

63 HJY, KX 1-1684:190–91, KX 1-1688:482–86.

64 MWLF, QL 15/11/5 [03-0172-0699-001].

65 Yang Bin, *Liubian jilüe*, 3:8a; Gao Shiqi, *Hucong dongxun rilu*, 106. Some Manchurian peoples still smoke sable out of trees, often cutting them down first; Ka-li-na, *Xunlu Ewenke ren*, 88.

66 Simonov and Dahmer, eds., *Amur-Heilong River Basin Reader*, 3, 8, 10, 50–53; Xiu Yang and Ming Xu, "Biodiversity Conservation in Changbai," 888–90.

67 Buskirk et al., "Winter Habitat Ecology of Sables," 323–24.

68 Cao Tingjian, *Cao Tingjian ji*, 1:33–34, 178–79. For ethnographies, see Janhunen, *Manchuria: An Ethnic History*, 50–52 (Dagur), 61, 125 (Kiler-Ewenki), 68–70 (Orochen), 101–02 (Solon-Ewenki).

69 *QSL* CD 2:804b–06a, 2:828a–30a. The terms "Reindeer Herder" and "Dog Keeper" tribes conflate a number of ethnic groups. See Janhunen, *Manchuria: An Ethnic History*, 59–74, 126 for an attempt to distinguish them.

70 *QSL*, TM 2:30a, TC 2:54a, 55b, 56a-b, 60a-b, 64b, 72b, 99a, 104b, 123b, 124a, 125b, 174b, 198b–99a, 215b, 215b, 221a, 239b–40a, 270b, 278b, 280a, 287a, 301a, 307b, 308b, 358b, 360b, CD 438a, 438b, 448b, 506a, 511a, 518a, 519a, 530a, 542b, 549b, 580b, 585a, 587a, 591a–b, 592b, 593b, 643b–44a, 658b–59a, 706a, 714a, 719a–b, 728b, 793a, 793a–b, 793b, 797a, 798a, 807b, 835b, 878a–b, 857a–b, 882b–83a, 3:38b.

71 *QSL*, SZ 3:46a, 67, 225a, 229b, 313b, 362a, 394a, 519b, 571b, 579a, 608ab, 625b, 669b, 730a, 752b, 813a, 815a, 838b, 862b–63a, 865b, 894a, 944b, 959a, 972a, 983b, 1026a, 1036a, 1088b; SZ 4:70a, KX 4:142a, 171a, 195b, 237b, 249b, 263a, 380b, 572b, 581a–82b.

72 NFY, KX 5-1678:163–207; *Da-wo-er ziliao ji*, 9a:204–13; Wu Zhenchen, *Ningguta jilüe*, 731:608a. For the pelt tribute system in the early Qing, see Zhang Pufan and Guo Chengkang, *Qing ruguan qian guojia falü*, 387–97.

73 Yang Hu, *Mingdai Liaodong dusi*, 131–32; Ch'iu Chung-lin, "Xipi yu dongpi," 109.

74 *QSL* KX 10/10/3, 4:494b, KX 10/10/14, 495a.

75 NFY, KX 1-1676:143–48, 205–10.

76 *Shiqi shiji Shae qinlue*, 111–12; *Qingdai Zhong-E guanxi dang'an, Diyi bian*, 1:9.11, 1:13.14–15. Compare a Russian version in *Russia's Conquest of Siberia*, #84, 304, which includes the names of the five Cossacks. For discussions of the identity of Ducher and Hūrha, see Janhunen, *Manchuria: An Ethnic History*, 101–05; Zhang Jie and Zhang Danhui *Qingdai dongbei*, 11–12.

77 Fisher, *The Russian Fur Trade*, 34; *Russia's Conquest of Siberia*, #75, 239–40; Khodarkovsky, *Russia's Steppe Frontier*, 60–63; Lantzeff and Pierce, *Eastward to Empire*, 17; Etkind, *Internal Colonization*, 81; Znamenski, "The Ethic of Empire," 114. Znamenski shows tribute policies could also, under special circumstances, apply to ethnic Russian peasants in Siberia.

78 Perdue, *China Marches West*, 8. Perdue and Barfield have both explored the multiethnic significance of interactions between regional empires and

The Nature of Imperial Foraging in the SAH Basin   111

ecologies; Perdue, *China Marches West*, 44–50; Barfield, *The Perilous Frontier*, 16–20. For a political-military study from the perspective of Russian sources, see Bergholz, *The Partition of the Steppe*.

79 Fisher, *The Russian Fur Trade*, 29, 120. For larger estimates ranging from 20 to 25 percent, see Etkind, *Internal Colonization*, 80.

80 *Russia's Conquest of Siberia*, #67, 209, 213–15; Lantzeff and Pierce, *Eastward to Empire*, 156–58; Khodarkovsky, *Russia's Steppe Frontier*, 56–60. Khordarkovsky characterizes indigenous views of *amanat* as an occasionally necessary evil, assuaged with Russian gifts, which may arise from differences in time and location. Basin peoples were not so tolerant, nor Cossacks so restrained there. For a portrayal of much less harmonious seventeenth-century Siberian relations, see Glebov, "Siberian Middle Ground," 129–33.

81 *Lishi wenxian bubian*, #14, 76; *Russia's Conquest of Siberia*, #75, 238–39; #81, 277–78, 315; Forsyth, *A History of the Peoples of Siberia*, 41.

82 *Russia's Conquest of Siberia*, #81, 264–67.

83 *Russia's Conquest of Siberia*, #81, 264–67.

84 An Shuangcheng, "Qingchu zai Lafa dukou zhizao zhanchuan gaishu," 82–83; *Russia's Conquest of Siberia*, #81, 273, #92, 344–45; Melikhov, "How the Feudal Rulers of the Ch'ing Empire Prepared Their Aggression," 62; *QSL*, 3:1068a–b.

85 *Qingdai Zhong-E guanxi dang'an*, 1:1.2, 2.3, 7.10, 21.21.

86 Huke shishu, 212:KX 20.8.24.

87 *Russia's Conquest of Siberia*, #81, 271.

88 *Russia's Conquest of Siberia*, #106, 386. The Russians' regularized system of tribute collection from some Dagur *aiman*, in operation for several years by 1654, had been stopped by local resistance and Qing forces no later than 1655; *Russia's Conquest of Siberia*, doc. #84, 306, 311.

89 See, for example, Matsuura, *Shinchō no Amūru*, 288–89; Yang Xulian, *Qingdai dongbei shi*, 94–103.

90 *Chŏson wangjo sillok*, Hyŏnjong (Xianzong) era, 6.5.8 (Western date June 20, 1665) 37.447b–48a; *Zhong-E guanxi*, 1:10.12, 14.16–17.

91 Russian and Chinese reports often do not clarify whether or not Qing relocations were voluntary; *Lishi wenxian bubian*, #24, p. 111; *Russia's Conquest of Siberia*, #85, 311; He Qiutao, *Shuofang beisheng*, 16.28a. There are also some ambiguous references to relocations in the 1650s; Yang Xulian, *Qingdai dongbei shi*, 86–87; *Russia's Conquest of Siberia*, #84, 305; *Lishi wenxian bubian*, #17, 92; Lantzeff and Pierce, *Eastward to Empire*, 168. A 1658 Korean source, for example, refers to the "flight" of indigenous peoples from the "Yaksa" area; Sin Yu, *Pukchŏngnok*, 5a.

92 NFY KX 2-1676: 39-54, KX 3-1676: 101–11, KX 5-1678: 4–17.

93 NFY, KX 3-1676: 101–11, KX 4-1678: 238–43; Matsuura, *Shinchō no Amūru*, 288–301; Zhou Xifeng, *Qingchao qianqi Heilongjiang*, 96–99.

94 NFY, KX 3-1676: 101–11; KX 5-1678: 4–17.

95 NFY, KX 1-1676: 120–25; KX 2-1676: 122–23.

96 NFY, KX 2-1676: 39–54, 91–93, 98–102, 102–05, 225–29. Around this same time other "Warka" were being shifted from outposts where they lived on the

112   *Across Forest, Steppe, and Mountain*

Usihun River to occupy new outposts to the northeast at the Sungari-Hūrha confluence; NFY KX 2–1676: 70.

97 NFY, KX 2-1676:276–77.

98 NFY, KX 1-1676:143–48.

99 Glebov, "Siberian Middle Ground," 136–37.

100 Scott, *Seeing Like a State*, 2–3.

101 NFY, KX 2–1676:188–89.

102 For examples, see *Xi-bozu dang'an*, KX 33/2/12, KX 37/5/9, 1:43–44, 68; Zhou Xifeng, *Qingchao qianqi Heilongjiang*, 100–102.

103 NFY, KX 2-1676:197–99; KX 4-1678:174–76.

104 NFY, KX 4-1678: 251–53.

105 NFY, KX 4-1678: 251–53.

106 An account of Ningguta in the 1680s noted that "ginseng and marten pelts were originally produced from the deepest and furthest regions" of a nearby mountain, but had become completely exhausted; Wu Zhenchen, *Ningguta jilüe*, 731: 607b.

107 *Russia's Conquest of Siberia*, #117, 450.

108 Lantzeff and Pierce, *Eastward to Empire*; 173–80; Sun Xi and Zhang Wei-hua, *Qing qianqi Zhong-E guanxi*, 60–115. For a study of the Nerchinsk negotiations see Sebes, *The Jesuits and the Sino-Russian Treaty of Nerchinsk*.

109 HJY, KX 1-1684:41–53, 140, KX 2-1686:69–71.

110 Huke shishu, 241:KX 24.10.23; HYJ, KX 1-1684: 41–53, KX 1-1685:133–37; *Baqi tongzhi*, 1:38. For Cossack identity, see Witzenrath, *Cossacks and the Russian Empire*, 34–36.

111 QSL, KX 24/10/2, 5:294a; *Xi-bozu dang'an*, KX 30/7/3, 1:28. There is also evidence that, by the mid-Qianlong period, some demobilized Dagur and Solon-Ewenki were being pensioned off at half rations to hunt sable in places like Hulun Buir; QSL, QL 25/4/2 16:855a.

112 MWLF, QL 8/6/22 [03-0174-1514-003], QL 8/8/18 [03-0174-1514-004]; *Qingdai E-lun-chun zu Man Han wen dang'an*, #28, 539.

113 HJY, KX 1-1690:19–20, KX 2-1688:306, 397–98, KX 1-1688:180–83; MWLF, YZ 13/1/28 [03-0174-1511-003].

114 *Xi-bozu dang'an*, 1:36. One Manchu document suggests that poverty deter-mined whether or not personnel in bondservant banner companies could move to Beijing or would stay behind in Shengjing when the capital was shifted; Tong Yonggong, "Shengjing *Neiwufu* de sheli," 205.

115 *Qingdai Neige daku sanyi dang'an*, 1:19.327-28; Hei-tu dang, KX 7:14.22–23, 17:30.41–44; *Shengjing shenwu dang'an*, KX 30.9.18, 62. There were 361 fox and 8.5 pheasant hunters in 1661; *Huidian shili* (JQ), 700:7,935–37. Manpower numbers varied, mainly due to population increase and mortality. Fractional headcount figures may reflect discounted tribute obligation.

116 For example, fifty-seven Beijing personnel joined fifty-five others from a manor to collect honey in 1648; in 1650, 282 ginseng gatherers also arrived from Beijing; *Manzu lishi dang'an*, #28, 106, #50, 117.

117 *Huidian* (YZ), 788:14,919, 14,871; *Da Qing huidian shili* (QL) (Shanghai, 2003), 625:311a; *Qingdai Neige daku sanyi dang'an*, 1:19.327. One or more

The Nature of Imperial Foraging in the SAH Basin   113

of several mussel species native to the SAH basin, *Unio mongolicus* as well as *Unio* (or possibly *Margaritifera*) *dahuricus*, were the most likely pearl sources.

118 *Da-sheng Wu-la zhidian quanshu*, 85; *Huidian* (KX), 727:6594–95. Butha Ula's population probably had a total of 399 foragers in 1685, including fifty-seven sturgeon fishermen, one hundred honey gatherers, and fifty "new men" whose duties are not enumerated. This coincides almost exactly with the figure of four hundred said to be operating prior to 1664, but contrasts starkly with the figure of 1,871 cited in a 1670 document on a regional grain supply shortfall, which also mentions 954 foragers in 1651; *Da-sheng Wu-la zhidian quanshu*, 43, 85; Hei-tu dang, KX 8:19.63–65. There is a further estimate of 3,993 foragers active in 1791, with 3,347 gathering pearls and the remaining 646 catching fish; *Da-sheng Wu-la zhidian quanshu*, 43.

119 *Qingdai Neige daku sanyi dang'an*, 1:19.327, 331; *Huidian* (KX), 727:6595.

120 Hei-tu dang, KX 8:16.56–58, 17:30.41–42, 21:21.20–24, 22:16.12–14.

121 Yang Bin, *Liubian jilüe*, 3:6b; *Shengjing shenwu dang'an*, KX 23.11.20, 30, KX 24.3.10, 31, KX 33.7.17, 62; Tong Yonggong, "Qingdai Shengjing shenwu," 260. On permits, see *Shengjing shenwu dang'an*, KX 11.6.28 p. 6, KX 18.6.8, 13; *Huidian shili* (GX), 3:727a–b; Symons, *Ch'ing Ginseng Management*, 42; Cong Peiyuan, *Dongbei sanbao*, 75, 85.

122 Symons, *Ch'ing Ginseng Management*, 11–12; Cong Peiyuan, *Dongbei sanbao*, 65, 72; *Huidian shili* (JQ), 700:7943; *Huidian shili* (QL), 624:100b; *Huidian shili* (GX), 726b–727a.

123 Hei-tu dang, KX 7:35.91, 11:14.22–24. Dogs were used for otter, sable, and tiger hunting; Hei-tu dang, KX 11:14.22–24, Yang Bin, *Liubian jilüe*, 3:3.8a; Gao Shiqi, *Hucong dongxun riji*, 106. Fang Shiji, *Longsha jilüe*, 8:4173. Shengjing's game hunters, who mostly pursued deer and wild boar, were literally known as "people who set dogs on game" (Ma: *niyahašara urse*); Hei-tu dang, KX 13:18.18.

124 See, for example, a 1649 Butha Ula casualty list; *Manzu lishi dang'an*, #39, 112. Banner detachments sent on elite foraging operations may have been more uniformly Manchu, if the apparently Manchu names of nineteen pine nut gathering troopers from the two yellow banners who were rewarded for their tree-climbing abilities are representative; ibid., #10, 98.

125 *Qingdai Neige daku sanyi dang'an*, 1:286, 311–18.

126 *Qingdai Neige daku sanyi dang'an*, 1:283–84. The composition of the Butha Ula military garrison in the late eighteenth century was 85 percent Manchu troops, 11 percent Bargut, and 4 percent Hanjun; (Qingding) *Baqi tongzhi*, 2:612–13. "Old" and "New" Bargut, Mongol subgroups, were driven into Manchuria in successive waves by Russian expansion from around the 1680s into the 1730s. The Qing incorporated them into the banner system and relocated some of them; Janhunen, *Manchuria: An Ethnic History*, 120–21; Zhou Xifeng, *Qingchao qianqi Heilongjiang*, 93–94.

127 *Shengjing shenwu dang'an*, KX 51.3.27, 105. Manchu also makes some nuanced, if not entirely consistent distinctions between northeastern peoples with banner or *aiman* affiliations, who are usually called "*niyalma*" and Han

114 *Across Forest, Steppe, and Mountain*

commoners, called "*irgen*," although both are generic terms for "people." See, for example, HJY, KX 1-1684:228.

128 Hei-tu dang, KX 6:29.39–43. Hunting was not the only lengthy and complicated foraging activity. Ginseng diggers were sent out for six months, which created considerable supply difficulties; Tong Yonggong, "Qingdai Shengjing shenwu," 260–61.

129 MWLF, QL 8/8/18 [03-0174-1514-004], YZ 11/7/27 [03-0171-0167-010]; Hei-tu dang, KX 7:19.32–33; *Kangxichao Manwen zhupi*, #3249, 1323–24.

130 *Huidian shili* (QL), 624:109a.

131 *Qingdai Neige daku sanyi dang'an*, 1:19.327; *Shengjing shenwu*, KX 23.1.24, 26.

132 *Huidian shili* (GX), 3:722b–23b.

133 *Huidian* (JQ), 700:7939.

134 Hei-tu dang, KX 7:36.91–92. Of course, the 1694 and 1686 depletions indicate only a decline near or below the level of practicable imperial foraging but do not necessarily mean absolute resource exhaustion.

135 Hei-tu dang, KX 8:18.60–62. Wild honey was known as "Manchu honey," probably to distinguish it from the "Chinese (Ma: *Nikan*) honey" raised by beekeepers.

136 *Wu-la quanshu*, 86; *QSL*, QL 11/11/18, 12:641a.

137 Hei-tu dang, KX 6:3.2–4, 36.55–56.

138 Hei-tu dang, KX 10:41.40.

139 Hei-tu dang, KX 11:11.20.

140 In 1669, seventy-nine storks were caught; Hei-tu dang, KX 7:14.22–23. In 1670 only thirty-nine storks and four sea eagles, which were the administrative equivalent of eight storks, were caught; Hei-tu dang, KX 8:16.56–58.

141 *QSL*, KX 34.12.19, 5:838a–b.

142 *Da-sheng Wu-la zhidian quanshu*, 86.

143 *Manzu lishi dang'an*, #10, 98, #25, 105, #45, 114; *Da-sheng Wu-la zhidian quanshu*, 86.

144 *Qingchao qian Lifanyuan Man-Meng wen tiben*, 5:345–50.

145 *Shengjing shenwu dang'an*, KX 5.6.11, 1, 43.10.12, 99–100. Violations began to emerge just after a 1699 imperial decree suspending all ginseng gathering; ibid., KX 38.2.28, 67.

146 For an exceptional study, see Jiang Zhushan, "Shengtai huanjing, rencang caiji yu guojia quanli."

147 Hei-tu dang, KX 6:26.35–37; *Qingdai E-lun-chun zu ManHan wen dang'an*, #200, 645–46, #202, 646, #203, 647.

148 As late as the early twentieth century, *Panax ginseng* C. A. Meyer is believed to have existed in the wild across a vast area of Manchuria from latitudes 40° to 48° north and longitudes 125° to 137° east; Koren et al., "Inheritance and Variation of Allozomes in Panax Ginseng," 189. This is approximately the area encompassing the entirety of Qing dynasty Jilin and roughly two-thirds of Qing Heilongjiang north-south along the SAH river. However, the quantity, quality, and accessibility of this ginseng, which might include species of different chemical properties like Siberian ginseng (*Eleutherococcus senticosus*), in imperial foraging terms are unclear. Currently wild ginseng has

almost disappeared from the whole area. In 2014, I talked to local vendors of forest products in the Changbaishan reserve region who believed ginseng could be found only on farms.

149 For figures, Liang Fangzhong, ed., *Zhongguo lidai hukou, tiandi, tianfu tongji*, 273; Diao Shuren, "Shilun Kang Qian shiqi liumin chuguan yiken," 3 (1990): 227–28; Reardon-Anderson, *Reluctant Pioneers*, 49–50. For some discussions, see Isett, *State, Peasant and Merchant*, 26–27; Diao Shuren, "Lun Qingdai dongbei liumin," 165–85.

3

The Nature of Imperial Pastoralism in Southern Inner Mongolia

In 2001, the *Taipusi* Banner of the Shili-yin Gool League was contemplating restoring its fields, configured for agricultural mass production, to pastures. The main rationale was that prevalent environmental conditions were more suitable for herding than for the intense, and ecologically debilitating, agriculture that had generally characterized the area for much of the preceding century.[1] I have found no more eloquent statement of the transhistorical environmental limitations on human agency that helps to explain the necessity for adaptation, both by the Qing dynasty and by the PRC to grassland conditions.

As the modern condition of the Taipusi Banner implies, the socio-economic dimension of Mongol identity has not been limited to a single expression.[2] In a general sense identity was certainly fluid, but overall steppe conditions favored pastoralism as the primary, if not only, mode of human adaptation. It is certainly true that although in sixteenth- and seventeenth-century Mongolia there was no unified Mongol *ulus* or nation, contemporary sources make it impossible "to suggest that 'Mongols' did not exist at this time or that the Qing 'created' the Mongols."[3] Nevertheless, a distinct variant of Mongol identity emerged under dynastic auspices, fashioned in dynamic tension with existing nature and culture.

This Qing Mongol identity was formed within the larger environmental framework of imperial pastoralism as the basis of a northern imperial borderland. This framework's period of formation roughly coincides with the dynasty's conquest of the Mongol steppe from the late seventeenth to the mid–eighteenth centuries. Inner Mongolia became the core of the Qing pastures north of the Great Wall during this time, which also

The Nature of Imperial Pastoralism in Southern Inner Mongolia 117

encompassed the full development of the herding system intimately linked with these and other regional military operations. Local ecological and cultural change, as manifested in Han arablism that disrupted this herding order, gradually emerged from this period as well. Arablism's main effects, however, become fully visible only in the nineteenth century. Ironically, this change was effected partly by imperial pastoralism's successful incorporation of the steppe through exposure to state agrarian administrative influences, especially disaster relief.

This chapter will focus on the formative period of imperial pastoralism as it developed in "Inner Mongolia." This is a somewhat anachronistic term for the vast region that Qing documents often called "south of the desert" (*monan*) divided among "the Forty-Nine Banners" (*Sishijiu qi*) of the inner *jasag* (*nei zha-sa-ke*) as grouped into six leagues (*meng*), two Tümed banners, and the Eight Banner Pastoral Chakhar.[4] At this time imperial pastoralism was forming in the face of three major adaptive challenges of military conflict, the encompassing steppe environment of extreme weather, and Han migration. The chapter begins with the initial Qing consolidation of people and herds in response to the first two of these challenges and concludes with an examination of the various pastoral-agrarian resource conflicts that defined the third challenge. The main Qing object throughout was to manage disruptive strife over pastures and control herder-livestock relations in the face of both human and climatic pressures.

Steppe conditions ensured that ecological considerations were inextricable from ethnic administration. Hanjun *Neiwufu* bannerman Fu Ge incidentally outlines this interdependency in his explanation of the "Nine Whites" (*jiubai*), the annual Khalkha tribute of iconic steppe herbivores to the Qing throne: "The court pacifies its subjects by lavish emolument and light obligation. As the Mongol lands are in the desert where there is little produce, each noble presents eight head of white horses and one white camel."[5]

In this formulation relations are tempered by "desert" conditions, partly self-existent and partly constructed, that necessitate particular attention to the nature of ritual exactions. Consequently, rituals requiring tribute of regional flora or fauna that are unobtainable in terms of quality or quantity actually corrode the human relations they are meant to maintain. The Nine Whites tribute was certainly structured and maintained by humans, but not by humans alone. Inseparable as they were from the steppe, even artificial constructs such as tribute or leagues were conditioned by steppe ecology. The primary set of steppe links holding imperial pastoralism together did

118   *Across Forest, Steppe, and Mountain*

not simply connect people of *hoshuu* and *gūsa* banners but was a network also connecting banners and their herds.

IMPERIAL PASTORALISM: CONSOLIDATING BANNERS AND HERDS

Dynastic military power was needed to unify the Inner Mongolian *aimag* as the social basis for the Manchu state's northern borderland. Such unification under Qing authority was not completed until 1636.[6] The Qing defeat of the last would-be Mongol unifier, the Chakhar khaghan and Chinggisid heir Lingdan Khan, in 1632 effectively legitimized dynastic domination of Inner Mongolia. Uprisings among the Khorchin in 1634, the Tümed of Guihua (Hohhot) in 1635, and the Chakhar revolt under Prince Burni in 1675 were ineffectual.[7] By 1636 the Qing was consolidating its steppe borderland to deal with the remaining two major Mongol conglomerations, the Oirad of the west and the Khalkha of the north.

The *Lifanyuan* was the main government organ for the mediation of differences with, and between, Mongols, who were administered under the *jasag* system of leagues and *hoshuu* banners.[8] Regulation encompassed court audience and tribute protocol, lama affairs, judicial and commercial regulation, and military mobilization. Codified as a series of Mongol legal statutes from the 1630s, these regulations were intended "to put an end to the legal differences among the Mongols" and were "binding on all Mongols under the authority of the Manchus."[9]

Such statutory uniformity, however, expressed only the amalgamating letter of Qing Mongol law, not its divisive spirit. The 1691 Dolon Nuur assembly, under the exigency of Galdan's 1687 Zunghar invasion, extended controls north of Inner Mongolia to the Khalkha *otog*, whose relations with the Qing began in 1638.[10] Final conquest of the Zunghars would not be completed until 1757 when this last and most powerful Oirad polity was defeated in Xinjiang. *Hoshuu* banner proliferation and diversification, however, defined ensuing *Lifanyuan* consolidation. Khalkha banners, for example, were increased from an initial fifty-five in 1691 to seventy-eight no later than 1756, then to eighty-two by 1764.[11]

Qing authorities were most gratified by this "unprecedented" submission of "all the Mongol tribes," even if it the Oirad would remain recalcitrant for nearly the next seventy years. The dynasty was nevertheless saddled with a "vast territory and numerous populace" and "ordered

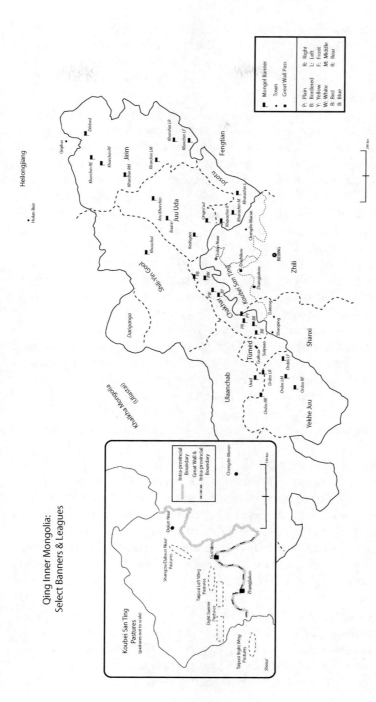

MAP 4: Qing Inner Mongolia: Select Banners and Leagues

every" new banner "to guard their own territory and attend annual court audiences to offer tribute." The prerequisite for carrying out these activities, however, was the fixing of banner pasture boundaries. In this material sense, the league system itself was really an outcome of pasture consolidation and not its agent.[12]

The *Lifanyuan* oversaw pasture allocation, which substantially reduced the frequency and scale of inter-banner strife. Regulations expressed the basic principle of delineation in apparently simple and natural terms: "Pastures near mountains and rivers can use them as boundaries. Pastures without mountains and rivers can use cairns (*e-bo*; Mo: *obō*) as boundaries." Trespassers paid fines in livestock with rates determined by social rank.[13] Modification was inevitable, especially to take account of human response to ecological change. From 1680, for example, *jasag* territories "without grass" would have to apply to the *Lifanyuan* for permission to move to greener pastures in a nearby banner, and only after both areas had been inspected to confirm their conditions. Pasture space could also be reallocated and expanded as a form of disaster relief.[14]

Pasture control was an established principle of herder control. Ming frontier officers had long exploited their Mongol and Jurchen opponents' military dependency on grasslands by regularly "firing the wilderness" (*shaohuang*) in autumn to deprive horses of the grass that fueled them for raids on Ming territory. One Ming commander in 1442 held that "nothing was better as a defense against" such raids than severing this connection because Inner Asians "depend on horses, and horses depend on grass."[15]

In definitive contrast, the Qing, as an Inner Asian dynasty, sought to exploit these dependency networks through pastoral management. Nurhaci made such arrangements, which included access to fodder and grazing land, for a group of "newly subjected Mongols" in 1622. Boundary disputes, such as the trespass by the newly subjected Aru Khorchin, were being handled no later than 1634, around the time that the first *jasag* were being appointed among the Forty-nine Banners.[16] All banner and league formation required grazing space and, therefore, large-scale delineation of Qing banner Mongol grazing areas. This occurred that same year when dynastic officials were sent to consult with subject Mongols on banner boundaries. In addition to the eight Mongol *gūsa* banners, the leaders of ten more banners met at Šongqor in the Khorchin Left Rear Banner to work out boundaries for those bordering Jin territory, estimated at more than 25,200 households.[17] The formative period of

The Nature of Imperial Pastoralism in Southern Inner Mongolia 121

imperial pastoralism was devoted to confining itinerant Mongols through delineating the space of their environmental relations, based on the connections between people and their livestock.

Of course, the *Lifanyuan*'s pasture delineation did not end disputes, and *jasag* had to be periodically admonished, as in 1783, to not to violate boundaries.[18] If anything, management became more complex in the interim period of nearly a century following the Šongqor conclave with the introduction of more groups into Inner Mongolia, many of them northern Khalkha driven south by the Qing-Zunghar conflict. Western Inner Mongolia was filled in this manner by the Alashan Ööled banner in the mid-1680s and the Ejene Gool Torghut banner in the early 1730s.[19] Some of these refugees, such as those moving through established Urad banner pastures in 1732, simply began herding in areas already occupied and even "selected the plump ones" from Urad livestock they encountered "to steal and eat." The *Lifanyuan* responded by quickly erecting boundary outposts (Ma: *karun*) between new Khalkha and old Urad fields.[20]

Inner Mongolia was critical for logistics and for the resettlement of refugee Khalkha, whose lands had been a primary target of Zunghar operations since their commencement in 1687–88. Inner Mongolian pastures thus came under greater human and livestock population pressure as the Zunghars put imperial pastoralism to the test under a succession of expansionist rulers, Galdan, his nephew, Tsewang Rabdan (r. 1697–1727), and Rabdan's son, Galdan Tseren (r. 1727–45). Initial Qing problems with the Zunghars in the late 1670s arose directly from resource conflicts. The southward flight of several thousand to ten thousand "tents" of defeated Mongols triggered these conflicts.[21] Even Zunghar diplomatic and trade missions, ranging from several hundred to several thousand individuals, caused great ecological disruption. They traveled the long route from Xinjiang to Zhangjiakou and Guihua, "pasturing livestock where they pleased, trampling and grazing in the grain fields."[22]

Herder-livestock management being the basis of the empire's steppe borderland, there was increasing concern with controlling interaction between the two, whatever their administrative context. State *gūsa* herding, mainly under *Neiwufu* supervision, was distinct from *hoshuu* herding presided over by the *Lifanyuan*, which managed *jasag* banner and league boundaries if not their animals. Over time, however, the two forms could blend together, particularly as more refugee Mongol groups were settled within state herding zones. These zones became in many respects sanctuaries for the welfare of displaced pastoral Mongols.

Across Forest, Steppe, and Mountain

TABLE 6 *Major Qing State Pastures in Manchuria and Mongolia*

Name	Locale	Established	Administration	Main herd types
Yangxi	Fengtian	1669	*Neiwufu*	Horse, Cattle, Sheep
Daling He	Fengtian	1669	*Neiwufu*	Horse
Taipusi L&R Wings	Koubei San Ting	1644	*Taipusi*	Horse, camel
Dariganga	Inner Mongolia	1700	*Neiwufu* (*Shangsiyuan* and *Qingfengsi*)	Horse, camel, sheep
Shangdu/ Dabsun Nuur	Koubei San Ting	Shunzhi period	*Neiwufu* (*Shangsiyuan*)	Horse, camel, cattle, sheep[b]
Chakhar Eight Banners	Inner Mongolia	c. 1636[a]	*Lifanyuan*	Horse, camel
Three Upper Banners	Koubei San Ting	Shunzhi period	*Neiwufu* (*Qingfengsi*)	Cattle, sheep

Sources: Da Qing huidian (GX), 624b, 667b-68a, 856a–b, 870b; *Da Qing huidian shili* (GX), 10:1010b, 11:886a, 12:1008b, 1009b, 1010a–b, 1011a.
Notes: [a] Source: Dalizhabu, "Qingdai Baqi Chakhar kao," 2002.
[b] MWLF YZ 10/5/22 [03-172-0665-007], (sheep flocks); QL 13/8/14 [03-172-0681-002] (cattle herds).

These immense state complexes often overlapped to accommodate expedient transfers of excess livestock between the densely packed herd zones, clustered just north of the Great Wall, with some outlying pastures in Fengtian and Jilin (Table 6). Most of the main complexes, the state's *Taipusi* (Court of the Imperial Stud), the banners' military herds, and the emperor's own *Neiwufu* Shangdu/Dabsun Nuur pastures, were administratively under the Zhili prefecture of Koubei San Ting. Culturally and ecologically speaking, however, these complexes were Mongolian grassland reserves staffed by Mongolian herders, and large parts of these pastures lie within today's Inner Mongolian Autonomous Region (IMAR) boundaries. The other major, and the largest, complex of Dariganga sprawled over approximately twenty-three thousand square kilometers well to the north on the Inner Mongolia side of its border with Uliastai.

Congenial cultural and ecological conditions also promoted convergence between *gūsa* and *hoshuu* herds, as is visible in the management of the Eight-Banner Pastoral Chakhar. Their old *aimag* lands, "suitable for pastures," had become the core of state herd complexes during Chakhar subjection in the 1630s. In the wake of their 1675 uprising, the defeated Chakhar rebels were relocated from their home territories to areas in Xuanhua and Datong subprefectures and reformed into two wings under direct *Lifanyuan* authority. The Chakhar *hoshuu*, consequently, became *gūsa* banners without a hereditary *jasag* ruling elite. All Chakhar grazing lands became part of the state military system, albeit nominally distinct for certain purposes.[23] Steadily increasing state orchestrations of environmental relations was the trend for the formation of all Qing banner Mongol identity, *gūsa* and *hoshuu*.

The operation of state herd complexes, which were subject to the most sustained supervision, is representative. The *Taipusi* pastures were the core of a larger complex collectively called the Imperial Horse Pastures (*Yumachang*) that included the regular Manchu Eight Banner *gūsa* herds and those of the Board of Rites. The complex was mainly for *gūsa* banner horse herds, although camels also grazed in their own pastures. The complex's primary distinction was between mare (*kema*; Ma: *geo*) and gelding (*shanma*; Ma: *akta*) herds (*qun*; Ma: *adun*). Geldings were used for most regular tasks, while mare herds were breeding grounds that included stallions (*erma*; Ma: *ajirgan*), colts, and foals. Most male colts were gelded at three years and sent to gelding herds.[24]

Breeding, not consumption, was the primary relational nexus between humans and livestock in the state pastures and, so, was regimented accordingly. Management was complicated by different livestock species' varying nutritional requirements and optimal breeding seasons. Even their illnesses were treated by "Mongol physicians" (*Menggu yishi*), who were veterinarians in practice, if not in name.[25] All herds were subject to annual inspections to determine birth and mortality rates, culminating in a major herd reorganization (*junqi*), or round-up, every three years for horses and sheep, every six years for camels and cattle. Round-ups were intended to ensure that female livestock could meet their own statutory reproductive obligations beyond natural rate of replacement.

Three mares or ewes were to produce one offspring between them every three years while the quota for cows or mare camels was set at one every six years. Such rates governed fluctuations in numbers of herds. In 1740, for example, eight new mare herds and sixteen new gelding herds were added to accommodate an 18 percent increase of 7,224 horses over the forty-thousand head norm. Number of head within a herd was subject to similar changes as in a 1766 decision to increase the average *Taipusi*

124   *Across Forest, Steppe, and Mountain*

herd size to four hundred head from much smaller groups ranging from 230 to 312 head prevalent since 1725.[26]

Although breeding was promoted by altering herd size, it was reinforced for human herders through the structure of herd personnel management, which ultimately reached to Beijing and the *Neiwufu*. Results of annual censuses and periodic round-ups brought rewards in sable, satin, or cloth for exceeding breeding quotas. Punishments of lashes, fines, or demotions were meted out for failing to meet quotas. Complicated methods to standardize surpluses and shortfalls, calculated from 1725 in "units" (*fen*) of five hundred and two hundred animals, respectively, were imposed to facilitate evaluation of herder husbandry.[27] This system was the primary state instrument to compel humans and animals to conform to imperial pastoralism.

The effects of this system appear in relatively precise measurements of livestock vital statistics, as in the data of Table 7. Sheep flocks grazing in the Dariganga and Shangdu/Dabsun Nuur pasture complexes can be tracked over a twenty-one-year period of relatively complete figures. These flocks were the largest concentrations of state pasture livestock and statutorily set at 210,000 head organized in 410 flocks in Shangdu/Dabsun Nuur and 100,000 head, probably in 80 flocks, in Dariganga.[28]

The figures in Table 8 reveal that these statutory norms were rarely achieved. During this period overall Shangdu/Dabsun Nuur flocks averaged 169,764 head, or 19 percent below their official strength, and Dariganga flocks averaged 65,260 head, or almost 35 percent below their official strength. The flocks managed an average annual growth rate for this twenty-one-year period of only 1.2 percent, although this figure does not represent reproduction alone. Large flock declines during 1753–54, for example, occurred mainly because of transfers of 105,000 head to army encampments. Direct comparison of birth and mortality figures suggests a much larger increase of 5 percent on average.[29]

Livestock populations could also fluctuate wildly in response to the steppe ecology. When the population of sixteen mare camel herds dropped almost 43 percent from 1730 to 1736 in Shangdu/Dabsun Nuur, Mongol herders soon complained that "the local water and grasslands were not suited to" camel breeding. The camels were duly sent back to better pastures in Dariganga, where they had been productively grazing up to 1732. In this instance, pastoralism could not adapt sufficiently to the Shangdu/Dabsun Nuur grasslands, which may have been overgrazed, although drought and disease were also factors.[30] The only solution under such conditions was new space, rather than intensifying use of existing

The Nature of Imperial Pastoralism in Southern Inner Mongolia 125

TABLE 7 Taipusi *Horse Herds, Seventeenth and Eighteenth Centuries*

Date	Mare Herds	Gelding Herds
Early Qing	40	8
1688	64	8
1694	80	8
1695	84	8
1701	87	8
1706	93	8
1710	120	8
1711	128	8
1723	152	8
1725	152	16
1740 (35,000/5,000)[a]	152	16
1749[b] (30,766/13,117)	160	32
1750[b] (22,535/11,486)	160	32
1761	160	32
1764	94	16
1766[c] (37,600/6,400)	94	16
1770	94	22
1773	104	30
1776	108	30
1779	116	30
1785	116	24
1794	120	26

Notes: [a] Figures in parentheses record mare herd/gelding herd limits, in head of livestock, when available
[b] Figures for these years come from MWLF, QL 15/7/4 [03-171-0374-008], QL 15/7/4 [03-171-0374-009].
[c] Maximum number of head per herd fixed at 400.
Source: Da Qing huidian shili, 11:889a–890b

space. Herding in this way was less subject to human manipulation than agriculture, which could employ a wider range of intensive techniques.

The coordination of Mongols in banners and leagues and livestock in flocks and herds was not exclusively determined by human constructs, but formed in a dynamic, networked relation to steppe ecology. This ecology, in combination with local Mongol action, complicated the state's implementation of imperial pastoralism and forced it to adapt, often by proliferating banners and herds. State inability to maintain its own sheep quotas is one measureable ecological limitation. Study of these grassland adaptations and limitations under the region's extreme weather conditions more precisely delineates the effective boundaries of the dynasty's steppe borderland.

TABLE 8 *Vital Statistics, Three-Banner and Dariganga Sheep Flocks, 1739–1760*

Date[a] (Qianlong)	Mortality (%)	Remainder (Head)	Births (%)	Round-up (Head)	Change from Previous Year (%)
4/10/6[b]	18,358 (17)	87,832	23,557 (21)	134,513	22
[03-171-0362-012]	2,591 (13)	17,409	12,470 (62)	40,044	100
QL 5				171,284	
				50,120	
6/9/26	24,889 (14)	142,718	35,798 (21)	179,232	5
[03-175-1558-028]	6,555 (13)	43,565	16,357 (33)	60,169	20
7/10/2	20,986 (12)	147,484	33,467 (19)	182,731	2
[03-172-0647-003]	7,822 (13)	52,305	16,028 (27)	68,654	14
8/10/29	20,905 (11)	158,451	29,732 (16)	191,721	5
[03-175-1560-003]	9,950 (14)	58,704	18,228 (27)	77,235	12
9/10/18	19,838 (10)	168,129	28,838 (15)	199,540	4
[03-172-0676-002]	9,887 (13)	66,948	17,978 (23)	85,229	10
10/10/26	21,831 (11)	165,106	30,855 (15)	210,000	5
[03-172-0677-003]	23,184 (27)	51,585	9,014 (11)	61,199	−28
11/7/18	39,938 (19)	168,239	24,445 (12)	192,924	−8
[03-172-0678-001]	9,059 (15)	52,040	11,769 (19)	67,520	10
12/7/9	20,573 (11)	166,774	30,750 (16)	199,276	3
[03-172-0680-003]	15,172 (22)	52,348	15,199 (23)	71,150	5
13/8/14	17,218 (7)	178,136	29,212 (15)	207,348	4
[03-172-0681-002]	11,012 (15)	60,108	12,147 (17)	76,056	7
14/7/7	53,471 (26)	150,401	27,795 (13)	178,196	−14
[03-175-1565-009]	10,670 (14)	65,385	11,778 (15)	77,466	2
QL 15				140,656	
				78,889	
16/10/24	13,375 (10)	120,628	21,760 (15)	142,388	1
[03-172-0684-005]	12,082 (15)	66,807	12,849 (16)	79,959	1
17/9/13	17,052 (8)	187,101	25,952 (12)	213,095	1
[03-172-0685-006]	10,975 (14)	68,905	11,795 (15)	81,017	1

Table 8 (cont.)

Date[a] (Qianlong)	Mortality (%)	Remainder (Head)	Births (%)	Round-up (Head)	Change from Previous Year (%)
18/9/7	15,997 (7)	192,122	23,685 (11)	215,807	1
[03-172-0686-001]	10,704 (13)	70,228	12,691 (16)	83,254	3
19/9/6	17,390 (8)	124,518	21,196 (10)	145,714	-32
[03-172-0687-002]	10,596 (13)	28,668	12,349 (15)	41355	-50
20/9/11	13,673 (9)	130,021	16,340 (11)	146,361	0
[03-172-0688-003]	10,078 (24)	29,777	12,230 (30)	42,297	2
21/i.c. 9/20	21,648 (15)	104,598	17,768 (12)	122,778	-16
[03-176-1618-004]	12,148 (29)	28355	14,477 (34)	57,263	35
22/8/24	14,137 (12)	88,111	19,101 (16)	109,149	-11
[03-172-1653-002]	13,201 (23)	34,992	15,560 (27)	50,830	-11
23/6/17	18,085 (17)	56,337	14,286 (13)	70,623	-35
[03-173-1097-002]	10,281 (20)	38621	12,813 (25)	51,649	2
24/8/1[c]	5,136 (3)	136,675	32,551 (22)	172,286	15
[03-178-1779-029]	3,082 (6)	46,655	13,781 (27)	60,644	17
25/10/19	5,828 (3)	156,988	49,191 (29)	209,181	21
[03-178-1845-022]	2,272 (4)	54,843	17,940 (30)	73,717	22

Notes:
Within an entry the top set of figures refers to Dabsun Nuur herds and the bottom set to Dariganga herds. Round-up figures for entries lacking month/day dates, which indicates that no report was found for that year, were compiled from recap sections of reports from the following year.

[a] All year/month/day dates and serial numbers correspond to MWLF documents.

[b] The round-up figures from the previous year (QL 3/9/5) were 110,165 head for Shangdu/Dabsun Nuur and twenty thousand head for Dariganga, respectively. Birth and mortality percentages for QL 4/10/6 are based on these figures. All other birth and death percentages are calculated from the previous year's round-up figures.

[c] Figure for Shangdu/Dabsun Nuur flocks at the beginning of this year was reported as 150,000 head, rather than the figure that would normally be carried over from the previous year's round-up, 70,623 head reported as the QL 23/6/17 round-up in this case. This discrepancy probably indicates a major transfer of 79,377 head to Shangdu/Dabsun Nuur from elsewhere in the interim.

INNER MONGOLIA'S EXTREME WEATHER

In environmental terms, imperial pastoralism was the particular adaptation required by grassland diversity that the dynasty had to undergo in order to establish and maintain its regime from Manchuria to Xinjiang. Temperature and precipitation are the most ecologically significant factors. Grasslands cover about 70 percent of today's IMAR, which as China's third largest province sprawls over 1.18 million kilometers^2 or 12 percent of its territory. 870,000 km^2 of this expanse comprises between 25 percent and 33 percent of China's grasslands. These temperate steppes, which mainly lie across a plateau confluence of dry alpine rain shadows to the west and wetter ocean winds to the east, are "extremely sensitive to interannual variation in climate and land-usage change." This position creates a marked precipitation gradient that declines from east to west over this Mongolian plateau itself. Overall, IMAR temperate steppe zones are generally colder (average annual temperature –2° to 4°C) and drier (250 to 400 millimeters per year) in winter than their North American prairie equivalents.[31]

These average differences, however, mask extraordinary figures that render steppe winters measurably harsher than prairie winters. In modern terms this works out to fluctuation across a range of as much as 30°C in a single day. Qing sources affirm a continuity in these conditions, exhibiting only a nominal difference in degree: "There is extreme cold in the early morning and late evening, while at noon there is a sudden heat so that there can be a difference of forty "degrees" (*du*) between these periods."[32]

In summer the area receives almost all its precipitation, and it is possible for about 30 percent of the annual rainfall to hit an area during one hour in some parts of Mongolia with commensurate flooding and erosion. In general, wetter areas in the east taper off to drier areas in the west. This "strong seasonal" tendency has a commensurate effect on plant cover as well as the animal populations that subsist on it, particularly in winter and spring when the food supply can drop to starvation levels to cause mass herd mortality.[33]

These conditions also contribute to extreme weather events across relatively short time spans. The dynamic relations that produce these conditions remain incompletely understood. For example, until 2009 it had been generally, and incorrectly, assumed that one of the most pastorally devastating of these events, drought, somehow precipitates another catastrophic event, the Mongolian *dzud*. The *dzud* is the notorious steppe winter event produced by extreme cold temperatures that causes mass mortalities of livestock, mainly by impenetrably freezing out forage. The last time such a

The Nature of Imperial Pastoralism in Southern Inner Mongolia 129

"perfect storm" of drought and *dzud* occurred, in 1999–2001, it killed off 30 percent (about 8–10 million head) of Mongolia's total herd population, the worst natural disaster in its recorded history.[34]

A recent 2009 study, based in part on the 1999–2001 event, concluded there was no empirical connection between drought and *dzud*. The region's extreme weather is likely connected somehow to dynamics between its aridity, highly seasonal summer precipitation, enormous annual temperature range, sparse vegetation, and unusual geographical position. The Mongolian plateau lies at an elevated northern latitude far from any ocean, indirectly affected by the Qinghai-Tibetan plateau's rain shadow, and exposed to Siberian high-pressure fronts. Some of these conditions date back to the last major glacial period, the Pleistocene era (13,000 years BP). The resulting dynamics, however, do not necessarily produce cyclic disturbances such as drought and *dzud* in what is otherwise a steady state of ecological balance that inevitably reasserts itself. In terms of regional precipitation, the 2009 study concluded that the precipitation index in Mongolia's South Gobi province defined the area as a nonequilibrium zone that failed to meet the minimum requirement for stable plant and animal ecosystem interactions.[35]

Preindustrial pastoral practices, especially high mobility, that create interdependencies between people and animals have been the primary human response to the steppe's definitive extreme, and often nonequilibrium, weather events. Disaster relief has, consequently, been critical, but reactive. So expedience has tended to prevail over pastorally appropriate measures. In attempting to adapt to substantially ungovernable steppe conditions the Qing state naturally inclined toward those most amenable to human intervention. With its economic and political heartland located well to the south in the agrarian and marketized alluvial plains of China proper, eighteenth-century imperial Chinese human intervention arrived as grain and silver, not livestock. It was not so much Mongol subjection to banners, but Mongol dependency on livestock, that was the prerequisite relation for the stability of imperial pastoralism. This connection subsisted most immediately on grass and water, which, in turn, were most imperilled by nonequilibrium drought and *dzud*.

RAIN, GRASS, AND RELIEF

The steppe's already harsh environment probably became even less hospitable during the Ming-Qing period (mid–fourteenth through nineteenth centuries). Inner Mongolia's general spell of dry cold air at this time could

130   *Across Forest, Steppe, and Mountain*

be related to the so-called Little Ice Age or to more localized climate variation. China is held to have experienced significant climate change, with many chronological and regional variations fluctuating between warming and cooling trends, over a period of the last half millennium.[36] Yet, whatever the precise causes behind Inner Mongolia's climate over the past 350 years, water has been the primary limiting factor, as it generally seems to be across grasslands.

An emphasis on the effects of climate aridity, particularly as opposed to those of excessive grazing, reflects the influence of nonequilibrium rangeland ecology.[37] The grasslands are certainly sensitive to both anthropogenic and "ecogenic" (i.e., nonhuman) factors that can operate synergistically. Consequently, there is a general consensus that China's grasslands in their entirety, which make up about 41 percent of the country's total area, have suffered varying degrees of degradation, especially in the twentieth century. Yet there is considerable disagreement over just how, and in what proportions, these two factors interact. Some even express skepticism concerning the fragility of grassland ecosystems.[38]

Without asserting the irrelevance of all other ecosystem conditions, it can be said that water is the prerequisite resource for growth of all grassland biota that is in most limited or uncertain supply, regardless of how many animals browse the land. So water's highly variable abundance or scarcity substantially determines how much grass, and by extension how much animal forage and ultimately how many animals, there will be in a season. The erratic, possibly nonequilibrium, nature of rainfall prohibits the emergence of an equilibrium or sustainable steady-state consistent grass to grazer ratio.

As a result, grassland pastoralism has historically been critically dependent on seasonal rains, a fact reflected in the regular weather reports submitted to the Qing throne by its state herd officials. One such report submitted in September 1748 by Vice Commander in Charge of the Imperial Pastures Dasungga succinctly summarized vital connections between grass, water, and livestock:

Although there has been little rain and it has yet to seep into the ground, snows for 2 months the previous spring have maintained the grasslands and water in the grassy hillocks and along the riverbanks ... From July 9th to 15th there was a slight steady rain throughout all the herd areas. And although not comparable with grass produced in abundant years, [the blades] were able to reach 3–4 *urgun*, which was just enough to get by. Consequently, there is no possibility of a drought.[39]

Such connections, whose margins as in this case could be measured by the length of a blade of grass, were often quite precarious. Moreover, before the late nineteenth century, these connections were less subject to massive

The Nature of Imperial Pastoralism in Southern Inner Mongolia 131

human intervention such as industrial-scale Han migration or agriculture. Under the relatively unmitigated steppe conditions before this time, attempts to assemble networks of human, animal, plant, and water resources into Qing state herds were constrained by extreme conditions that could produce drought, snowstorms, and sandstorms within a few months of each other.[40]

This was the weather pattern flowing through the Chakhar Plain White Banner horse herds from winter into spring of 1748–49, a few months after Dasungga's general report of fine pasture conditions. Plain White herds were hit by a month-long snowstorm, probably a *dzud*, in mid-December of 1748 just after suffering a drought of indeterminate length. A sandstorm then struck the already damaged herds in mid-April, transitioning to another snowfall on the 3rd of May. By this time only 30–40 percent of the horses were left alive, and some sheep had actually been buried in the sand. As of mid-May livestock were still dropping in the pastures, probably because they could not easily get to the sand-choked grass after their long winter and spring of little or no fodder. Six months of steppe weather that gyrated between drought and snowstorms left the Plain White Banner herds unable to sustain themselves without a state grant of a year's worth of provisions as well as funds for the replacement of livestock losses.[41]

Such grants were the main form of human adaptation to extreme steppe conditions under the dynastic system of pastoral management. Although similar in many respects to the system of disaster relief operating in the farm fields of China proper, disaster relief in the Mongolian grasslands was further complicated by cultural differences. Interaction with the same conditions of climate and topography, often exacerbated by military conflict that made relief necessary in the first place, spawned many such differences.[42]

Even relief for Mongols largely dependent on agriculture posed a distinctive challenge because their fields were located in the wide expanse of the steppe, far from sources of supply. The July 1733 plight of agrarian Dörbed Banner Mongols is a comprehensive, detailed saga of these challenges. Snowstorms and then crop failure had deprived the Dörbed of plow oxen and seed grain. Frozen rivers had delayed transport of 1,840 *hule* (*shi*) of relief seed grain needed by 3,057 distressed households until spring thawed supply routes from neighboring Heilongjiang fields. Distance prevented the timely purchase and safe delivery from zones beyond the disaster area of almost 45 percent of the 1,409 oxen needed by 2,817 households for spring sowing. Even selling off penalty livestock, held by neighboring Khorchin banner *jasag*, to add to the five thousand taels granted for replacement oxen was deemed more practical than driving

132   *Across Forest, Steppe, and Mountain*

the animals to the Dörbed. Finally, within a few months some of these same Khorchin would likewise need aid in the wake of a drought that ruined their own fields.[43]

If anthropogenic disaster, from excessive land clearance or failures in water control, was common in China proper, natural calamities from extreme weather were the norm on the steppe. This difference not only made steppe disaster more difficult to avoid but also made relief efforts more complicated. Rugged terrain, comparatively undeveloped communications infrastructure, and sheer distance from administrative centers often precluded exact compliance with China proper statues that, for example, mandated food aid during "the most difficult [i.e., winter] months of the year."[44]

Ecological conditions on both sides of the wall compelled the state to abandon some of its management principles in practice. Even in the lower Yangzi core, harsh winter weather could hamper or preclude marketized relief solutions, such as grants of silver for food purchases, by blocking vital transport arteries. Differences nevertheless persisted. Although it tried to monitor and limit local Han gentry's vital, but potentially exploitative, participation in relief, the state actually obliged the steppe's local elites, the *hoshuu* banner *jasag*, to afford relief directly.[45]

Although I have found no literal statement to this effect, regulations and reports concerning Mongolian disaster relief strongly imply that local elite participation was essential because there was no other ready source of relief livestock. The relevant regulation required the elites of a stricken banner "to establish means for aid." If insufficient, their aid would be augmented by similar donations "of cattle and sheep" from sources throughout the banner's league. Only after several years of dearth would the *Lifanyuan* intervene, funded, however, through deductions from the salaries of the *jasag* officials concerned.[46] Overall, it is clear that the nature of the disaster is assumed to affect livestock, and elites are directly responsible for its replacement. The state merely contributes loans for timely animal purchase. In fact, in the few cases on record that have come to light where the state did contemplate providing livestock directly, as it did in the 1733 case, local elites held all head on the behalf of the dynasty. These animals had been assessed from various Mongol offenders as fines of penalty livestock.[47]

The state was also reluctant in certain instances even to provide grain, if the Kangxi emperor's petulant response to a 1716 request for grain aid to distressed Ordos Mongols is any guide. The emperor remonstrated in vermillion ink that in the season for military operations, which required grain, such requests were inappropriate. Moreover, "in Ordos the rabbits are quite numerous" and the region enjoyed an abundance of root

The Nature of Imperial Pastoralism in Southern Inner Mongolia 133

vegetables. The emperor's inclination to, in effect, "let them eat rabbits" was reinforced by his conviction that "rich" Ordos lamas, who "generally arrogate the Mongols' livestock," had donated nothing for relief.[48] The spirit of Qing relief regulations for Mongolia in the early eighteenth century was reliance on local elites and resources as much as possible to free up strategic resources such as grain. State grain could be used if necessary, as in the 1733 Dörbed and other cases, but was not the only, or even the first, recourse if there were rabbits to take down, roots to dig up, or lamas to shake down.

The reluctance of the Qing state to involve itself with direct transfers of livestock is made somewhat more comprehensible in view of the scale of disasters such as that which struck the Urad Banner Mongols, pasturing west of Hohhot in the Ulaanchab League, a year later in 1734. A vast snowstorm, likely a *dzud*, killed around 70 percent of the livestock, and its aftereffects threatened to finish off the remainder. During this event 5,054 households numbering 24,501 people lost all their herd animals. Of these, 2,015 households of 9,116 people had been taken in by other households relatively unaffected by the disaster, leaving the state to deal with the remaining 3,039 households of 15,385 people. At rates employed in the 1733 calculations of 1 team of 2 oxen for every 4 households, the remaining Urad in need required 1,519.5 animals, about 8 percent more than the number the Dörbed needed.[49]

The Urad were clearly not, however, primarily agricultural, but were herders dependent on a fairly common combination of horses, cattle, and sheep. They may even have needed cattle in a greater proportion of one ox per household than the agrarian Dörbed. But even this increase of over 200 percent in oxen required for the 3,039 Urad households would be dwarfed by their need for sheep. Although not entirely clear, data from other aid operations suggest that 5 sheep per herding household was a minimum.[50] The Urad would thus also have needed 15,195 sheep, a number representing almost 12 percent of the 130,165 sheep in the whole of the main imperial flocks grazing in the Shangdu/Dabsun Nuur and Dariganga pasture complexes between 1738 and 1739.[51] Such numbers seem to have been exclusively reserved for military operations, although the emperor occasionally granted up to several thousand head to individuals.[52] Instead the Urad were granted a six-month supply of more than 7,244 *hule* of state grain.[53]

In the case of disaster relief for state herds, where maintenance and expansion of head was the priority, neither grain nor silver was an entirely adequate response. This could compel pasture administrators to attempt a direct replacement of lost livestock. Unfortunately, livestock could not be

134   *Across Forest, Steppe, and Mountain*

stockpiled in a pastoral version of an ever-normal granary to provide such emergency aid. Instead, the main source of relief livestock was purchased from private inner *jasag* herds, which could either be equally distressed if conveniently close by, or too distant to be quickly or safely transferred. Inadequate grasslands between the source of relief and the site of disaster often obstructed such transfers as well. Many such problems hindered the 1749 relief efforts when replacement horses brought in from Daling He, in southwestern Fengtian, were likewise devastated in succession by snowstorms en route. In 1752, administrators were still trying to work out the finances and logistics of replacement livestock purchases from inner *jasag*.[54] There is also evidence from relief operations in Mongolia proper that even the dispatch of silver for local livestock repurchase simply raised prices of what few head were available. This problem was apparently serious enough to terminate this form of relief in some locales.[55]

It becomes easy to see why Qing regulations limited aid in practice to grain and silver transfers. Details of state pasture relief operations reveal that, despite obvious and critical differences, both Qing agrarian and pastoral management had great difficulty adapting to natural disasters in a consecutive two-to-three-year period.[56] In this respect, imperial food security north and south of the passes remained materially subject to weather. This fact may explain instances of dynastic preference for silver in general, which did not require the specialized handling of organic substances such as livestock or grain.

The problems created by silver and grain relief, however, were ultimately more complex. State grain aid to herders bereft of herds and flocks raises the question of the extent to which such assistance, albeit inadvertently, eroded Mongol pastoral identity.[57] It would have been difficult for the Qing throne to make good such losses in a timely fashion even if it had been willing to do so at any cost to its existing strategic reserve of livestock, in part because the state herds and flocks were not immune to similar catastrophes. In 1762–63, for example, an epidemic killed nearly 50 percent of the 184,490 sheep in Shangdu/Dabsun Nuur pastures. Banner herders, as per regulations, were expected to make good these tremendous losses of nearly 91,203 sheep.[58]

These regulations reflect the Qing administrative habit of holding humans ultimately responsible for all mortalities among state herds. Aside from limited provisions to account for natural wastage, livestock mortality was never really written off to natural causes.[59] The most onerous of these regulations was the requirement that state herders restore the lost animals. This was another statutory dynamic that encouraged convergence between *hoshuu* and state herds. Banner livestock was also often purchased out of advances of annual herder provision funds in the form of "loans" (Ma: *juwen*) to make good these state herd deficits, as well as enable herders to purchase their own animals, or "personal property livestock" (Ma: *hethe ulha*). Herders of the *Neiwufu*'s Plain Yellow Banner who were held responsible for losses from a 1750 epidemic among state cattle droves resorted to both types of loans to effect stable repayment over more than five years. Herders were held similarly responsible for restitution of losses from the snowstorms of 1749–50, which presiding officials considered the result of carelessness.[60]

Qing officials clearly recognized the excesses of their uncompromisingly anthropogenic stance. When *Taipusi* Right Wing herders were "held responsible for restitution of horses ravaged by wolves" in 1744, central officials acknowledged that "wolf ravages are unavoidable." They believed, however, requiring repayment would prevent laxity and so minimize inevitable losses, even if full restitution extracted from their state provisions might incite "all sorts of malpractices" by disgruntled state herders. Some quarters, moreover, believed that herders falsely invoked wolf attacks to cover their own negligence.[61] The state's insistence on the ultimately anthropogenic origins of resource losses, a mentality also visible in imperial foraging, reveals an institutional tendency to reduce complicated environmental connections, rarely fully transparent, to an overly simplified problem of personnel management. This tendency regularly surfaced as policies of monetization that narrowed diverse environmental relations to more anthropocentric ones. In the Inner Mongolian case, provision and repayment practices comprising a bureaucratically manageable state pastoralism attenuated herders' relations with their traditional embodiments of wealth, personal property livestock. As in its management of relations with Manchurian indigenous peoples, Qing state attempts to maintain a Mongol herding identity compatible with the administrative requirements of an imperial borderland simultaneously strained that same identity.

Herder agency, however latent, also played a role in these dynamics, which the state tried to control through enhanced surveillance. It ended the three-year tours of Manchu wing superintendents rotated in from the capital who were "totally ignorant of herding methods and [the] Mongolian" language. Local matters would be supervised by a Pastoral Chakhar Mongol who could not be deceived through his "ignorance of both herding horses and methods for sustaining Mongols."[62] Whatever the truth of an incident, both herders and the state used steppe ecology,

136 *Across Forest, Steppe, and Mountain*

here the inevitability of wolf attacks, to assert their own conflicting agencies. Outcomes were nonetheless conditioned by this same structure that neither side could alter because plausible wolf ravages continued.

Despite their 1675 uprising, the Pastoral Chakhar continued to predominate in state pasture complexes as the best human resources available to handle both culture and nature. Dynastic statutes themselves indicate that the Chakhar made up the majority of state pastoral Mongols, although the Chakhar's own lands and the overlapping state pasture complexes certainly included other Mongols as well.[63] A 1731 document on state relief for "Chakhar lands" breaks down their 14,934 eligible residents as 5,215 people of the Pastoral Chakhar, 6,845 people of state herding households in the Shangdu/Dabsun Nuur pasture, and 2,874 people, mainly identified only as "Mongols who exist hand-to-mouth" (Ma: *angga sulfame banjire Monggoso*). Here 1,204 of these had appeared from the Khalkha inner *jasag* banners.[64] As Chakhar lands and state pasture complexes became havens for various displaced Mongol pastoralists, Pastoral Chakhar banner identity, sometimes conferred not inherited, became a main human embodiment of the imperial borderland's environmental interconnections.

The broader Qing Mongol identity, in both state and *hoshuu* pastures, was constantly confronted by harsh conditions that human intervention, such as disaster relief or herder regulation, could only partially offset. The Qing state's inability to fully control steppe herd mortality and reproduction on what might be called an imperial scale led to compromises such as grain aid. In turn, grain aid could alter banner Mongol identity away from more pastoral and toward more agrarian forms or toward a greater dependency on ethnic administrative structures that eroded the state's preferred version of pastoralism.

The Qianlong emperor expressed such a concerned preference in a 1741 edict:

The *Lifanyuan* has investigated and memorialized to the effect that from 1681 to 1722 Mongolia has received disaster relief over forty times. From 1723 to 1735 the banner personnel of the inner *jasag* have received disaster relief fifteen times; the Khalkha, three times. From 1736 to 1741, the inner *jasag* and Khalkha, have received aid fourteen times. Mongol livelihood depends on abundant livestock. They do not rely on silver and rice ... There is now report of distress among the banners, and although We grant aid without concern for the wealth of the state, the outer *jasag* have long been accustomed to have no pity at all for these tribes. Ordering them to spend time breeding more livestock will increase their tax levies. Yet, relying only on Our grants for a livelihood cannot be a permanent strategy, and must result in the loss of their original way of life.[65]

The throne's evaluation of its two basic strategies for providing virtually annual disaster relief for Inner Mongolia reveals a potential identity crisis among the region's pastoralists that arises not just from human interrelations, but from networked relations connecting humans and their ecology. The emperor is clear that livestock relief is preferable to silver and rice to preserve a pastoral identity. The only practical source of that livestock, however, are the droves of Mongols farther to the north and west whose southern ties are already under great tension, especially in the midst of contemporary Qing-Zunghar diplomatic maneuverings. These fragile relations with the outer *jasag* would be put under potentially catastrophic stress by dynastic exactions of extra livestock to relieve the inner *jasag*. Furthermore, increasing Inner Mongolian dependency on Qing state relief in a form that erodes their pastoral identity by acclimating them to an arablist consumption of silver and rice would denature the *hoshuu* banner Mongol as embodiment of the steppe borderland. In sum, disaster and its relief constrained imperial pastoralism.

Indeed, in many respects imperial pastoralism was disaster relief, which one study has identified as the major check on *hoshuu* banner economic self-sufficiency.[66] Grain dependency, however, was not effected through coercive commercial manipulation that, for example, used Japanese cultivated cereals to undermine Ainu foraging.[67] Mongol grain dependency was a result of Manchu concern for banner integrity and traditions. Although this type of dependency did not arise by dynastic design, the Qing did deploy relief quite deliberately to maintain the imperial steppe in a relatively steady state.

To this end, relief could be distributed to preserve or even restore Mongol pastoral identity. This generally happened when Mongols unaffiliated with the dynasty turned up in Qing lands or when large numbers of impoverished herders were discovered among state subjects. In 1732 Qing officials were concerned to discover that 86 households of 170 men and their dependents led by a lama had negligently lost their livestock and were trying to get through the winter by itinerant trade just north of Zhangjiakou. Officials eventually rounded up 275 households and 54 single men wandering unauthorized between Zhangjiakou and Xinping on the Shanxi-Zhili border. Some had been driven onto banner pastures because of famine; others had been apprehended with 1,463 horses, 215 cattle, and 3,200 sheep that they had probably rustled. Altogether around 650 of these men were put in service with various local nobles, 550 of them in 3 banner companies. Officials noted that "since these sort of people depend on livestock to live on the Mongol steppe,"

138 *Across Forest, Steppe, and Mountain*

they would be so supplied from the confiscated animals. Each household received three large animals and ten sheep; single men got one large animal and five sheep. Officials handed out 879 horses and cattle along with 3,020 sheep to accompany their new owners to the grasslands of their new lords.[68]

In a sense, these 275 households were human resources that were recycled into imperial Mongol pastoralists by a state redistribution of livestock to ensure they would not overburden their new lords. Some were trying to maintain an inappropriate pastoral identity by rustling from Qing herds or residing illicitly in Qing pastures. Those led by the lama had entirely lost this identity once their livestock had died. None of these lifestyles was considered suitable for the maintenance of the imperial borderland beyond the Great Wall. So officials duly converted all these people into proper Qing pastoralists by restoring appropriate relations between steppe humans and livestock. This 1732 relief operation seems the type that the Qianlong emperor had in mind when he issued his edict nine years later in 1741.

The fall of 1732 was particularly significant in the history of comparatively anthropogenic threats to Qing Mongol identity from the steppe. Relief aid was a fundamental part of the dynastic strategy in response. In the summer of 1731 Qing forces had suffered a major defeat at the hands of the Zunghars at Hoton Nuur, west of Khobdo, where they lost eight thousand of ten thousand men. The Yongzheng emperor was so dismayed by this reverse that he considered abandoning the dynasty's decades-long war. As the Zunghars began to exploit their victory by moving south and east, many Khalkha were driven from their lands and fled to the relative safety of Qing Inner Mongolia. Although the marauding Zunghars were in turn defeated by the dynasty's Khalkha allies at Erdene Juu in October 1732, the effects of their incursion were felt for years afterward in the pastures south of the desert as the Qing state sought to restore proper conditions.[69]

One or all of the groups found wandering just north of the Great Wall in November 1732 were probably fleeing the war. At least 390 Khalkha households requiring resettlement in January 1733 certainly had been in headlong flight since the previous year from their old pastures that had come under Zunghar harassment. These Khalkha, whose livestock had also been ravaged by a snowstorm as they fled to southern Uliastai in 1732, could not shift again to their new Ordos pastures being prepared for them in Qing territory without further aid. Dynastic authorities provided them with more than twenty-one thousand taels

The Nature of Imperial Pastoralism in Southern Inner Mongolia 139

for purchase of livestock and grain and even obtained wives for those who had lost them.[70] Other refugee groups, such as the Torghut subjects of Beile Lubsang Darja, were even allowed to stable their livestock within the passes in winter, when agriculture was suspended. In summer they could go out beyond them again to graze. This "temporary" expedient dragged on for eight years until 1740 was made possible only by the relatively small number of two hundred households involved.[71]

Balancing the interests of various groups of humans, livestock, and plants within the larger context of the region's various ecosystems required extensive coordination on a challenging scale. Military conflict, of course, further complicated state management. Inner Mongolian pastures were duly opened as a critical, if precarious, haven for refugee northern and western banners, who, like the Torghuts, needed a great deal of assistance to integrate into the existing set of local relations with minimal disruption. Assembling resources that even a relatively small group of two hundred households required under these conditions to maintain a proper identity is just what made the construction of an imperial steppe borderland so complex and difficult to sustain.

Extreme weather and livestock dependency fundamentally structured these stressful conditions. When initially left to themselves in the wake of their 1739 livestock losses, desperate Urad families sold off 371 men, women, and children to neighboring Khalkha and Kharachin Mongol troopers in exchange for livestock, grain, tea, cloth, or money. Asking prices were as low as 0.2 taels per person around the same time that livestock repurchases cost between 0.5 to five taels per head. Qing relief officers obtained permission to use some of the five thousand taels in livestock replacement silver to redeem the new slaves from their new masters. The Urad *jasag* were also dressed down for permitting their banner people "to roam scattered about and even be sold off."[72]

The Qing state's capacity for the sustainable complexity necessary to dominate such vast and diverse areas was quite high in the 1730s, much higher than their Zunghar opponents, and was a critical factor in the dynasty's final victory.[73] Forging a working relation between Mongols, Manchus, and Han was certainly one important dimension of this capacity. However, based as it was on other relations between these human groups and their interpenetrating environments, the resulting system was subject to internal conflicts over resources critical for maintaining a stable banner Mongol identity. These conflicts arose from the intricate and intimate relations between humans and livestock that enabled both to survive in large numbers on the steppe.

HERDER-LIVESTOCK RESOURCE COMPETITION: MILK

Milk was one such contentious resource. Qing policies in Mongolia were generally conditioned by the existing environmental relations between people and animals that long predated Qing domination. Milk and dairy products derived from it were important material expressions of these relations because this animal protein was the primary staple for both Mongols and young livestock.

One such conflict between livestock, state, and local human priorities emerged in 1736. Central authorities found that colts of two to five years among state herds in Shengjing and Inner Mongolia were so small and physically debilitated that many would be useless for any of their official transportation or breeding tasks. Mares' milk was the critical resource in question because it was a source of both equine and human nutrition. Mongols' "illicit milk consumption" (Ma: *hūlhame sun be jetere*) had increased "to the extent that the colts cannot get enough to eat." State investigators' proposal was direct, if impractical for steppe conditions: Simply order local state pastures to ban their Mongol herders' consumption of mares' milk.[74]

The superintendant in charge of the Shangdu/Dabsun Nuur pastures, Ušish, explained the human-animal relationship that precluded the proposed ban. He stated that in the first ten or so days after foaling, young horses were permitted to run about to nurse freely. After this period, however, they were tied up to prevent them from nursing. This quickly taught them to rely on grass and water to pass the winter safely when mares' milk was exhausted. They were freed again at night to resume nursing, but in the interval when they were under restraint, Mongol herders would milk the mares for human consumption. This would help people securely pass the winter themselves by preserving some of the milk in the form of sour fermented cakes (Ma: *kūru*).[75]

Milk's seasonal availability in summer and fall regulated living patterns in the pastures and so became a factor in official deliberations over these patterns. During a 1752 exchange on how to deal with more than three hundred poor Mongols in the companies of the Chakhar Plain Yellow Banner, the banner's superintendant, Ušiba, argued that it would be too difficult to integrate these poor people. More economically established banner families would have trouble taking in refugees because they would be unable to handle the increased consumption demands in winter and spring when livestock gave no milk. The unavoidable result would be internal strife.[76] Indeed, the winter-spring dearth was one of the main

The Nature of Imperial Pastoralism in Southern Inner Mongolia 141

motivations for adaptations like foal forage training Mongols such as Ušish's charges habitually engaged in. In this way humans, animals, and their surrounding environment were mutually conditioning, and their relations conditioned policies intended to bring them under more systematic state control.

Beijing authorities had clearly been aware of milk's significance before 1736. Indeed, "milking mares" (Ma: *sun sara geo*) constituted an intrinsic part of a Mongol military banner unit's own regulation complement of livestock.[77] Ušish, however, was compelled to remind Beijing of its own pertinent rules covering herders, which had been issued more than twenty years before. In 1714, the *Shangsiyuan* (Palace Stud; Ma: *Dergi Adun i Jurgan*) allocated fifty milking mares to each gelding and gelding camel herd to provide for human consumption. Ušish proposed that "moderate milking" of mares in these herds, as well as existing prohibitions against "unauthorized milking," be allowed to continue with mares rotated when and where appropriate. Ušish stressed that the lack of milking mares was "a situation harmful to both horse herds and Mongols" and asserted herders could be effective only when they "obtain enough milk with which to pass the winter."[78]

Ensuring a balance between the interests of humans and animals was a fundamental principle of Qing state control on the steppe in general. It was also, as in this case, often critical for the preservation of military resources that were the region's ultimate contribution to the Qing order. Some sort of sustainable method to apportion this limited resource thus needed to be worked out.

The general method seems to have been to maintain a very large proportion of mares for both breeding and milk production. This emphasis is visible at its most basic level in the ratio of mare herds to the other major subcategory of state horseflesh, geldings. Herds in the *Taipusi* pastures in 1723, for example, were fixed by statute at no more than 152 mare herds of thirty-five thousand and no more than sixteen gelding herds of five thousand to maintain a ratio between them of 7:1. A few years later in 1731, the Shangdu/Dabsun Nuur herds numbered 130 and 18, respectively, at ratio of about 6:1.[79] Even when the mare population is reduced to take account of the statutory internal herd proportion of mares to studs at 5:1, the ratio remains a significant 5.6:1 in favor of mares. Yet another 1738 statistical report indicates that only 47 percent of a "mare" herd was actually mares.[80] Early Qing ratios of 40 mare to 8 gelding herds nevertheless suggest the relative importance of

142   *Across Forest, Steppe, and Mountain*

mares, and this proportion was maintained or even increased, as in the 170 mare and 32 gelding herds maintained in 1747.[81]

Officials such as Chakhar Plain White Banner superintendant Daši explicitly recognized the importance of mares, as well as cows, in their milk-producing capacity. A month-long snowstorm, suggesting a *dzud*, soon followed by a sandstorm lasting more than a week wiped out 60 to 70 percent of horses alone in his jurisdiction in 1749. Daši then submitted a warning that revealed concerns focused on two critical livestock functions. He alerted central authorities that "the Mongol livestock devastated by the disaster has reached the condition such that no riding horses for state service, milch cows (Ma: *uniyen*), or milking mares are obtainable."[82]

Of course, neither Mongols nor their livestock lived by milk alone, but if the Mongol trooper interviewed by Zhao Yi was any authority, the vast majority of his people led substantially meatless existences. Probably while accompanying the Qianlong emperor on his 1757 imperial progress to Muran, Zhao asked a Mongol, who "could speak Chinese," whether or not Mongols could always eat mutton. Zhao termed both mutton and milk "Mongol traditions." His acquaintance replied that only the nobility ate meat. "Poor tribals" (*qiongyi*) such as himself generally ate it no more than once a year and even then had to split a single sheep between several families. He added that people "ordinarily subsisted on the milk of horses and cattle," two bowls of which were steeped in tea, boiled, and consumed twice a day, at morning and at night. From this account Zhao concluded that such repasts served as the Mongols' "rice porridge" (*zhanzhou*).[83] Judging from the Qianlong emperor's angry response to the 175 skinny milch cows that gave "very little milk" sent him from Dariganga for consumption at Muran in 1761, milk was certainly an important comestible for the annual imperial hunt.[84]

Zhao's anecdote gains considerable if qualified confirmation from a 1736 Hulun Buir report that local Solon-Ewenki and Bargut troops "had always hunted and herded, relying on the milk of sheep and cattle for their existence." It is impossible to generalize about the diversity of environmental relations all across Manchuria and Mongolia. The report, for example, also stated Dagur troops in the same area were "all dependent on grain for their existence."[85] It seems possible, nevertheless, to affirm that dairy products were a primary, and often the primary, staple of a pastoral lifestyle.

Milk in this respect constituted a common bond, as a shared source of critical nutrition, between humans and young livestock. Comparable

The Nature of Imperial Pastoralism in Southern Inner Mongolia 143

sources, mainly meat or grass, could sustain only one side or the other and were, consequently, not staples interconnecting this relation in the way that milk was. Moreover, milk ensured endurance through the cold seasons endemic to the pastures and to producing the armed power that maintained domination over them. From this perspective, any order aspiring to control Inner Mongolia, whether engaged in breeding livestock, mediating social inequality, or alleviating interspecies competition, had to be sustained by milk.

Given milk's significance it is not surprising that dairy products also took on considerable symbolic significance within the Qing regional order. The Qianlong emperor provides a rich expression of milk as synecdoche for Mongols as a distinct people who were also Qing subjects in his poem "Passing through the Mongol Tribes" ("Guo Menggu zhubu"), composed in 1741:

> ... the road above the passes is long and in full wintery frost
> Through the cold forests of mountain persimmons.
> Smoke blows through the downy hide tents
> The livestock scent of milk and cheese ...
> The feast ends with a joyful shout ...
> Then, food and clothing, regional tribute offered as in the old canons.
> The milk of livestock and *rubing* (*kūru*) all express sincere submission.[86]

After moving through an unpopulated late autumn landscape north of the Great Wall, the emperor encounters Mongol culture immediately and primarily in its intimate proximity to herd animals as producers of dairy products. These products, however, are not simply for human or animal consumption, since they are representative of a region and, by extension in a classical imperial Chinese idiom, regional sovereignty. Qianlong's allusion to these products as tribute calls attention to continuities between past and present imperial practices in the immediate context of Inner Mongolia, which presented certain dairy products from certain banners as tribute by statute.[87]

The fluidity of Mongol identity is clearly observable in many of the previous examples of agrarian Mongols and commercial Mongols as well as pastoral Mongols. Yet the Qing state is likewise clear in its express preference to keep the majority of its Mongol subjects pastoral, if not nomadic, in *hoshuu* or *gūsa* banners. One primary motive for this preference was to maintain appropriate levels of manpower and livestock able to cope with steppe conditions and exigencies. A "natural" pastoral lifestyle, under dynastic sponsorship, was the best way to construct a sustainable Qing borderland, but such a lifestyle could not be imposed by the state or even modified beyond certain limits. Some of those limits were drawn in milk.

Other limits were both ineffectively drawn, and effectively violated, by people. Perhaps the most dramatic and ironic of these was the restriction the dynasty attempted to place on Han agrarian migrants, whose 1644 "defeat" afforded them unprecedented access to the untilled pastures of the Sino-Mongolian steppe ecotone. Significantly, Han migrants did not consciously seek to directly alter Mongol identity, but simply to use steppe resources in a comparatively unrestricted fashion. Moreover, Han migration alone did not undermine Mongol herding, already under pressure from the internal contradictions of imperial pastoralism. Given the environmental interdependencies, it was nevertheless inevitable that shifts in relations between peoples and resources would effect commensurate changes in the identity of those same peoples.

MONGOL-HAN RESOURCE COMPETITION: GRASSLAND AND ITS PRODUCE

Most standard Chinese accounts of Han steppe migration stress the ensuing agricultural development as socioeconomically progressive. An emerging critical view, skeptical of agrarian sustainability, is probably informed by many current evaluations of the causes of Inner Mongolian desertification and grassland degradation.[88]

The Qing state faced many of these same issues, and much of the record exhibits a similarly equivocal character. Divergence is particularly evident in the dynasty's almost continuous stream of edicts and regulations. These sought to limit or entirely restrict northward Han agrarian migration in principle while acquiescing to Han resident farmers beyond the Great Wall in practice and attempting to adapt pastoralism accordingly. Numerous studies take different positions on the chronology and character of this migration.[89] Nevertheless, it is possible to state generally that the Kangxi to Yongzheng regnal transition in 1722–23 was probably the watershed for eighteenth-century Han migration, and mid-Qianlong constitutes a similar divide for the corresponding development of agriculture in southern Inner Mongolia. *Junxian* subprefectures to manage Han populations were regionally established between these two periods. The subprefectures were intended to handle legal and financial matters associated with Han urban-agrarian society as well as assist in handling interethnic disputes.[90] They were the primary units of ethnic

The Nature of Imperial Pastoralism in Southern Inner Mongolia 145

administration dynastically imposed in response to migration's arablist consequences. Subprefectures were also prerequisites for handling larger waves of Han migration of the nineteenth century. Furthermore, the period from late Kangxi to mid-Qianlong as a whole encompasses a series of natural disasters and the span of the Zunghar conflict that were critical for the dynamics of migration. Dynastic prohibition on Han migration was largely ineffective in the face of this dual impetus.

Of course, Han agrarian and commercial migration to Inner Mongolia did not begin in the Qing. There may have been, for example, between fifty to one hundred thousand Han resident there in Altan khan's reign (1521–82). Facilitated as it was by Manchu control of both sides of the Great Wall, however, Qing migration was unprecedented in scale and stability. So, unlike the migrations of the Ming and of other conquest dynasties, Han settlers in the Qing "literally submerged the Mongols of Suiyüan and Chahar."[91]

Ecological factors in the process of migration proved particularly persistent. The major long-term challenge for the dynasty, well before the Zunghars' defeat, was to balance potentially disruptive agrarian and pastoral interests. This challenge was taken up as early as the 1720s, although the state had dealt in ad hoc fashion with major waves of Han migration as early as 1712. At this time a belated mandate to "henceforth" register Shandong migrants beyond the passes was issued in the wake of a report that "over 100,000" were clearing farmland in the region.[92] During the 51 years of the Kangxi reign up to 1712, Shandong experienced 220 droughts and 186 floods, an annual average of 4.3 droughts and 3.6 floods, aside from periodic frosts, pestilences, earthquakes, and the like, annually.[93] Although not all these disasters necessarily generated refugees and not all of the refugees they generated fled to Inner Mongolia, officials reasonably believed that disasters were the primary impetus for migration beyond the passes. Moreover, actual events such as the 1746 flight of Shanxi Han refugees from the twelve floods and eighteen droughts that struck the province the previous year continued to reveal the connections between natural disaster and disruptive Han migration beyond the passes. These refugees soon took up disruptive residence as aggressive beggars in Hohhot and its environs.[94]

The Qing state began to take more systematic measures during the 1720s in the succeeding Yongzheng reign. In consequence, many important herding areas beyond the Great Wall fell administratively within prefectures and subprefectures of "China proper," the areas of northern Shanxi and northern Zhili. Guihua, now the IMAR capital Hohhot, was the

146 *Across Forest, Steppe, and Mountain*

administrative center for two of Shanxi's six conglomerated subprefectures known collectively as Gui(hua)-Sui(yuan) Liu Ting in the northwestern corner of the province. The town and subprefecture of Suiyuan was founded in 1739, and Guihua, founded in the Ming, became a subprefecture in 1741. These two, along with both Shuoping prefecture, established in 1725, and part of Datong prefecture, administered Shanxi north of the Great Wall. The corresponding space in Zhili was, in its western half, under the administration of the three subprefectures of Zhangjiakou, Dolon Nuur, and Dushikou, together making up Koubei San Ting and established in 1724, 1732, and 1734, respectively. To the east sprawled Chengde prefecture, initially set up in 1723 as Rehe subprefecture and including some of the present-day IMAR and Liaoning province. It was also the site of the imperial hunting complex of Chengde-Muran.[95]

Junxian formation served as poetic inspiration to the Qianlong emperor, who lauded the consequent environmental relations in a poem entitled "Country Inns" ("Ye dian"). "Country inns and mountain villages" were sited amid what had been "Mongol pastures" that had now become "fields where the Han multitudes [*qimin*] "plowed land and dug wells." An interlinear gloss notes that this alludes to a former hunting area in the Khorchin banner lands converted first into fields and then, in 1729, into the subprefecture of Bagou ting. The subprefecture managed Han-banner interaction and "now nourished the people" (*xiuyang shengxi*) with "millet-filled fields no different from that of China proper." It goes on to praise the "*jun* and *xian*, newly established," a reference to the elevation of Rehe subprefecture to Chengde prefecture in 1778, that "are nearly rich enough for commerce."[96]

Thus, from about 1723 to 1741 the state's establishment of these subprefectures was an administrative concession to a major demographic transformation of steppe areas immediately north of the Great Wall. The Han migrant populace clearing land in Chakhar territory just north of main passes such as Zhangjiakou has been estimated at around fifty thousand people. This was a dramatic manifestation of what Zhang Yongjiang has called the "interiorization" (*neidihua*) of the Mongolian "vassal tribes" (*fanbu*). In this process distinct borderland ethnic administrative structures steadily come under a ubiquitous, uniform *junxian* administration that is agriculturally rather than pastorally predisposed.[97] Steppe subprefectural conversion over this roughly twenty-year span probably, as Zhang has argued, created a "dual" system of Han-Mongol administration that ethnically influenced relations at all levels.[98] This dual system, however, emerged because both Han and Mongols could utilize

The Nature of Imperial Pastoralism in Southern Inner Mongolia 147

grassland resources, albeit in fundamentally different ways. Interethnic competition ensued and lasted over the next 130 years.

This competition was one historically visible sign that Inner Mongolia's administrative and ecological boundaries were incongruent. It was relations between humans and resources, rather than those between humans and state administrations, that mainly resulted in Han migration north of the Great Wall, even in the late nineteenth century under the exigency of Russian colonialism.[99] The material, rather than political, concerns of the Han masses ensured that the region of Inner Mongolia that would experience the greatest influx of Han migrants in the eighteenth century was the ecotone along the Hu Line.

This ecotone had long drawn migrants. The Chinese red pine, for example, is indigenous to northern China centered on the Yellow River basin. Red pine nevertheless did actually "migrate" into southeastern Mongolia, an area technically beyond the limits of the northern monsoon climate that conditions the distribution of this tree species. The pines appeared with the onset of the monsoon's northward shift, and commensurate increases in temperature and precipitation, nearly eight thousand years ago, and then declined about forty-two hundred years ago. This is also the approximate time frame for the general replacement of woodlands by grasslands. In microclimates created by valleys, however, higher water tables and related conditions permitted isolated pine stands to persist "along the current ecotone and into the steppe." These stands now inhibit soil erosion associated with widespread desertification.[100]

Southeastern Inner Mongolia is an ecotone in part because it is periodically capable of changing just enough to make limited accommodation to species such as the red pine, with an enhancement in diversity that further distinguishes the region. Such patchy diversity is what sustained Mongol herders and what drew Han farmers in the process of their own much more expeditious northern migration in the early eighteenth century.

Of course, agriculture and pastoralism were not monolithic practices, ethnically or spatially. There were pastures south of the Great Wall and cultivation among Mongols, especially the Tümed, although thirteen of their semiurbanized sixty-two "agrarian" banner companies were actually pastoral.[101] Differences north and south among all these practices, however, abounded and were conditioned by both cultural and ecological factors. Han cultivation, as noted in Chapter 1, for example, was distinct from Mongol cultivation, particularly in terms of scale.

148   *Across Forest, Steppe, and Mountain*

Additionally, authorities like the Yongzheng emperor recognized that it was more difficult, even in normal times, to raise horses in the south than in the north. The import of this critical environmental difference on ethnic identity has been explored in Yan Gao's exemplary work on horse pastures in Hubei's Jingzhou garrison. Anthropogenic and ecogenic problems, including population pressure for conversion to grain fields and calcium-deficient water and soil that debilitated herds, compelled radical reductions in pastures and horses from the mid–eighteenth century. Garrison pastures, which could sprawl eighty-four thousand *mu* across the six pastures of the Hangzhou garrison or twenty thousand *mu* of the Jingzhou garrison's spread, had been established with comparatively modest goals of simply feeding rather than breeding horses.[102]

For many large garrisons south of the Great Wall, and especially in the humid climate south of the Yangzi, however, even this goal was unattainable by the mid–eighteenth century for mainly ecological reasons. The Fuzhou garrison's herd of 5,018 head was cut by 66 percent to 1,698 head in 1731 and again by 50 percent five years later. These losses were all attributed to the region's "sweltering weather" that could inflict annual mortality rates of 30 to 36 percent, as had happened in the interim in 1734. Unfavorable climate also induced an identical pattern of reduction in the Jingzhou garrison, which cut its twelve thousand head by 66 percent in 1742, and cut the remainder again by 50 percent in 1833. In 1766, the Hangzhou garrison culled its 10,227 head by 45 percent, which rose to 55 percent three years later. The Guangzhou garrison held out until 1771, when it reduced its three thousand head by 78 percent. Guangzhou was losing horses to the climate, which "was no different from Fuzhou's," so fast that 17 percent of the original three thousand had died by the time the proposal was approved.[103]

The brevity of equine life expectancy locally was also reflected in the garrison's regulations for the care and feeding of horses. Penalties were prescribed for mortalities of new arrivals at intervals of three, six, and nine months and rewards for those lasting more than a year. Penalties were subsequently extended out to three years, with rewards being bestowed for each year of life after that. Conditions in Fuzhou were so bad that officials were making annual supplementary purchases of "big horses" ranging the pasture complexes beyond Zhangjiakou.[104] In some southern cases, however, incentives, punishments, and extra purchases were not enough to surmount deep-rooted ecological problems. "Toxic grasses," for example, killed off enough horses in some Yunnan banner

The Nature of Imperial Pastoralism in Southern Inner Mongolia 149

pastures that they were soon converted to agriculture. Seventy-two percent of Hangzhou's vast pasturage tracts were converted in 1769 and 50 percent of the remainder in 1782 as herds were cut. Such mortal conditions form the empirical context of views such as the Yongzheng emperor's.[105] Ecological diversity thus obstructed imperial spatial and identity constructs. By sapping soldier-equine interactions, ecology knocked Manchu and Hanjun cavalry out of the saddle in south China more effectively than armed Han resistance had done.

Managing either fields or pastures outside of their normal constructs was particularly complicated. It was hard just keeping track of cultivators and their produce beyond the passes and, so, beyond the China proper's highly developed system of agricultural surveillance. This problem tended to erode Han steppe agriculture's utility to the state. A 1733 investigation into the condition of Han fields in the jurisdiction of the Pastoral Chakar Right Wing reveals some of these problems. Manchu officers found that 36 percent (1,365 households) of the 3,745 Han households engaged in cultivation were unregistered in violation of statute. Seventy-two percent (2,714 households) were illicitly harboring women and children, who had been there for six years although their residence in Mongol areas was strictly prohibited to avoid "incidents." There were also crimes of theft and campfires that could start ethnic and grassland conflagrations. The supervising Zhangjiakou magistrate could not even verify his figures for fields or cultivators.[106]

State supervision was also vital to ensure the integrity of pastures, which in practice meant keeping Mongols and Han apart. In 1730 the Yongzheng emperor had decreed investigations to ensure this separation, because Han migrant agriculture in and around Mongol herds would "hem in pastoral areas." An ensuing 1732 inspection in the Pastoral Chakhar Bordered Blue Banner area, for example, unearthed "a large number" of Han cultivators working fifteen thousand *mu* of land producing six hundred *shi* of glutinous millet and buckwheat annually. Investigators determined that these activities were constricting herding areas and inhibiting breeding. Concluding that "there is no benefit should commoners be permitted to live intermixed with Mongols," the investigators recommended all Han be returned to their places of origin in China proper.[107] By the mid–eighteenth century this formulation was being cited as a justification for active prevention of Han cultivation activities in the vicinity of Mongol pastures, because land clearance would "put pressure on the Mongols' pastoral herding of livestock." Pastoral Chakhar officers were formally tasked with ensuring pastures would remain Han-free, but problems persisted in the Bordered Blue pastures that precluded such absolute solutions. A 1739 report on the regional problem concluded that itinerant Han cultivators who had become economically dependent on pastureland they had worked to arablize should be allowed to remain and pay rent to Mongol banners. However, they would be kept firmly within clear-cut boundaries to preserve Mongol military virtues and pastoral livelihood.[108]

Putting this formulation another way, the proximity and scale of Han cultivation could create serious and potentially irreversible environmental damage to herd areas. This problem is exemplified by a 1747 proposal to expand the boundaries of *Taipusi* horse herds that had become hemmed in between Han cultivation to the south and Pastoral Chakhar lands to the north. Both wolves and bandits had begun ravaging the horses since the inception of Han cultivation, which had probably disrupted carnivore habitats and attracted human predators.[109] No later than 1732 the dynasty, in an ironic reversal, was actually trying to maintain "border ramparts," outliers of the Great Wall, to keep Han trespassers out of Mongolia. Green standard troops were expected to effect patrols and repairs. Some ramparts had broken down that year to permit infiltration by a train of twenty-seven donkeys and nineteen Han. Such were the Han cultivators that officials feared would "harm the interests of the Mongols' pastoral livelihood."[110]

Han cultivation not only increased the potentially criminal human population of the locality, but also may have been more destructive of animal habitat in clearing land for both fields and barriers than the comparatively casual form of Mongol cultivation. Indeed, this may be a reason why Mongols did not practice intensive cultivation in the first place. Comparatively radical ecological alteration, for good or bad, may also have been part of what was meant by the term "Han-style cultivation" (Ma: *nikarame usin tari[ngge]*), which occasionally appears in Manchu documents.[111] It is also important to recognize that, like its modern analogs elsewhere, Han-style cultivation restricted and effectively precluded the mobility vital to herding populations.[112] So Han-style cultivation outside its "native" Hanspace ecosystems required considerable administration, such as the 1747 pasture shifts involving thousands of horses.

Han cultivation also began to complicate, narrow, and, in some instances, preclude options for the provision of Mongol relief. A proposal from Chakhar Plain Yellow Superintendant Ušiba to provide his banner's impoverished Mongol households with glutinous millet seed and unused banner pasture lands to till was firmly rejected by central officials as a threat to Mongol pastoral identity. The official deliberation of the proposal categorically asserted that "the Chahar Mongols all require good grasslands and water in order to live by herding horses and livestock in a way not comparable to Han commoners who live by cultivating fields." The rejection assumed that Mongol cultivation would eventually be handed over to more efficient and enthusiastic Han farmer tenants, a common contemporary practice, legal or not. This had already happened to some Tümed fields five years earlier. Officials were certain these poor Mongols, who had no livestock, would also "abandon their old ways of herding" as their pastures came under pressure "because they have been ceded to Han who have been recruited and brought in to cultivate them."[113]

In rejecting Ušiba's proposal Beijing authorities probably had in mind previous incidents of unauthorized introductions of Han cultivators into Mongol farming areas by local officials. Once such incident had occurred in 1727 among Mongols who had shifted to agriculture after their livestock was devastated by "large-scale epidemics and depredations of tigers." Another had happened in 1745 among Chakhar Plain Red Banner troops without livestock living on lands unfit for herding. They had permitted their fields to go to seed and finally resorted to Han farmers.[114] General decline in state promotion of Mongol agriculture was already visible in 1725, when a request was made to discontinue grain levies on the Pastoral Chakhar, who "were quite unaccustomed" to cultivation. Some of their lands had never even been planted because of unseasonably early frosts.[115]

Mid–eighteenth-century pastures were not well equipped administratively to control these new environmental relations. Enforcement to reconvert illicit plots to pastureland and return their residents to China proper carried out in 1750 found little evidence of outright violation. It did, however, reveal that Mongol banner records had failed to properly register about twenty-two hundred hectares and twenty-four hundred Han residents. Such discrepancies led one investigator to conclude that non-Mongol replacements were needed because "Mongols would make muddled inquiries and carelessly compile registers."[116] Mongol identity was administratively incompatible with Han identity.

As fundamental as it was, land was not the only resource that required extensive interethnic administrative management as Han migration increased. For all its problems, cultivation was an essentially sedentary activity that was easier to control than access to more portable resources such as fish, wood, or salt. These resources tended to create disruptively rapid influxes of many Han from the south in search of sustenance or profit.

152   *Across Forest, Steppe, and Mountain*

Just two lakes in the Kheshigten Banner area of the Juu Uda League, for example, annually drew more than one thousand itinerant Han peddlers and merchants, who arrived driving carts to haul the fish away for sale on both sides of the Great Wall. These activities were inadvertently discovered by an antirustling patrol in 1742. Although fishing was technically prohibited, local officials had not actively enforced the regulations. Moreover, Zhili Governor General Sun Jiagan, serving from 1738 to 1741, had effectively legalized the fishing under questionable circumstances during his last year in office. Sun painted a picture of destitute Han in search of food who would nevertheless somehow be able to pay local "bannermen" rent for fishing access, which he claimed could be seasonally controlled by special troop patrols. Within a year resident Mongols were complaining about "disruptive" commercial fishing by "over one thousand" Han. Many were hard drinking gamblers who illegally stayed the winter to ice fish, when no Zhili troops were on patrol. The state duly restored prohibition, with regular patrols empowered to arrest fish peddlers and their accomplices, both Han and Mongol, and confiscate any fish.[117]

Fish could be a critical resource for Mongols in times of dearth, as they were in 1716 in the Ordos region, which had endured a not unusual combination of several years of drought, seasoned with a devastating *dzud*-like snowstorm. These natural disasters synergistically eliminated the major sources of food on the Qing steppe, leaving "no harvest in the fields," livestock "devastated," and local Mongols "without means of subsistence." Fortunately, the discovery of eight lakes filled with thousands of carp and catfish provided more than seventy-seven hundred fish to two thousand distressed locals.[118]

Extensive timber tracts in the mountains running north and west from Guihua to the Urad banner in the Ulaanchab league were attracting at least ten times the number of Han involved in fishing. More than ten thousand from Shanxi and Shaanxi were belatedly discovered cutting in the Muna range in 1734. Investigators estimated the delegation of enforcing timber prohibitions to unreliable elements had resulted in more than twenty-five years of neglect. Reenforcement captured more than thirty thousand logs.[119] A chronology of Muna timber prohibition may have begun around 1708–09, but other mountain forests, such as those north of Shahukou and in the Daqing range, had never been off limits and were being legally cut as early as 1699. This suggests no express prohibition on timbering beyond the passes before the turn of the century. Evidence from the Juu Uda League far to the east shows

Mongol logging from 1707 at the request of the Baarin and Ongni'ud banners. Objections from the nearby Kheshigten Banner, whose "livelihood depended on these trees," persuaded the dynasty to divide the timber between the three banners.[120]

Selective enforcement of timber prohibition proved unsustainable in many of these cases. Muna, for example, was subjected to ongoing illicit timbering with official connivance from authorities in Shanxi. By 1759 the Qianlong emperor acknowledged that merchant cutting taxed by the state for the benefit of locals was preferable to unenforceable prohibition that resulted only in smuggling. Relying primarily on private interests, however, was a questionable method that had already failed in 1733 in the Daqing region, where smuggling to avoid taxes was rife. Moreover, by 1760 more than three hundred households of more than one thousand Han cultivators were belatedly discovered by officials to have cleared thirty thousand *qing* (about two hundred thousand hectares) in fifteen Daqing valleys. A 1761 proposal to tax these cultivators, and remit some of the revenue to Mongols, echoes the throne's 1759 pragmatism. Timber resources were further compromised in the wake of massive state construction projects. Suiyuan was built in 1739 and Beijing's Yuanming Yuan and Chengde's Potala Temple (*Putuozongcheng miao*) between 1768 and 1774, although expanded urbanization at Han-Mongol trade centers such as Dolon Nuur was also becoming a factor around 1761.[121]

Such mid-Qianlong operations were probably the beginning of authorized large-scale deforestation in Inner Mongolia. Significant merchant cutting, the bulk of which was probably illegal and therefore incalculable, predated state logging by around fifty years. Although there were certainly Mongols involved, the main demand for this wood, including that cut by banners for profit between 1707 and 1717, came from China proper. Even ostensibly Mongolian projects at Suiyuan and Chengde were explicitly intended to maintain an imperial borderland for the security and prosperity of those resident south of the Great Wall.

A north-south conflict of interest could manifest itself within officialdom, whose administrative interests were in part determined by environmental relations between their respective populations and resources. A sixteen-year deliberation between Inner Mongolian, Zhili, and Beijing officials over access to alkali deposits in and around five lakes in the Pastoral Chakhar cattle and sheep pastures reveals complicated interdependencies that did not conform to administrative, or even species, boundaries.

Like milk, salt is a nutritional prerequisite for both humans and animals because, among other functions, it regulates osmotic pressure in cells vital to the transfer of nutrients and wastes. For livestock in particular it also may assist in the digestion of forage. Moreover, humans and animals not only need salt, they like it. Livestock are so attracted to salt that it can be distributed to control their movements across rangeland.[122]

The imperial state was, of course, well aware of the attractions of salt, especially for revenue purposes, and Han merchants likewise found salt equally compelling for economic reasons.[123] Salt's role as a general necessity of life, along with its consequent significance for state revenue and private profit, not only linked herders, merchants, bureaucrats, and livestock, but it could just as easily set them at odds. Indeed, a large part of the imperial enterprise was to mediate such potentially divisive interests. In this sense, empire was a set of environmental relations requiring ongoing maintenance.

Humans, moreover, extracted salt from deposits existing only in certain locales. Access to salt was thus afforded by a combination of interactions between humans, animals, and geologic terrain, which became the subject of regional concern from 1741–56. Sun Jiagan again was chafing under steppe resource restrictions, this time on access to five salt lakes in the Kododo region of the Plain Blue Banner pastures.

Access to the lakes, which local Mongol herders and some Han cultivators along the frontier had been using without restrictions, had been granted to licensed salt merchants during the Kangxi reign. The *Neiwufu* banned salt extraction, apparently for everyone, by the end of the Yongzheng reign in response to the default of its chief Han merchant tax farmer on his revenue quota. At this point, the *Neiwufu* decided that grass was the area's main asset and concluded that there "was no better place for [exclusive] livestock breeding" than Kododo. By 1741 Zhili Governor-General Sun, a former supervisor of Shanxi's salt administration in 1734–35, spoke up for salt. He had already requested Shaanxi and Shanxi officials be ordered to locate salt sources beyond the passes, arguing that "not a single Mongol" was commercially exploiting them. He now contended that the ban "left the natural bounty of heaven and earth forsaken in a useless place" to the detriment of resident Mongols and Han. Probably around the same time, the governor-general was also proposing to turn over tens of thousands of arable *qing* right in the middle of the imperial herding complexes. This immense tract stretched along roughly two-thirds of Koubei San Ting's northeast-southwest axis from Kaiping to Xinghe. Han farmers would be recruited to convert it to agriculture for

The Nature of Imperial Pastoralism in Southern Inner Mongolia 155

support of Manchu garrisons of ten thousand men. Sun envisioned a "paradise" (*letu*) that would permit Han cultivators and banner herders to live in harmonious, prosperous proximity while providing the basis for further agrarian expansion. Although it seems Sun's scheme was not realized, he did succeed in restoring local access to salt for personal use and even commercial sale south of the passes. The ban on certified commercial extraction, however, remained in putative force.[124]

In 1741 two views of the Kododo lakes had been articulated, split along ethnic lines. From the Inner Asian perspective, Kododo was a pastoral idyll that precluded commercial salt extraction associated mainly, but not exclusively, with Han merchants. From the Han perspective it was an undeveloped backwater salvageable only through salt extraction. Such Han views could be expressed in stark nativist terms, such as those employed by Sun Jiagan, in the initial draft of his 1741 proposal to legalize fishing. Sun's casual reference to the Juu Uda League's Kheshigten banner Mongols as "barbarians" (*yiren*) drew a reprimand from the Qianlong emperor, who castigated Sun for his "grave error." The emperor asserted that the term "barbarian" was reserved for the Zunghars, not for dynastic servants, and wondered "if the inner *jasag* are called barbarians, by what term will the Zunghars be called!" Sun Jiagan's "careless" words equating the inner *jasag* with Zunghars "would chill their hearts." Sun had to rewrite his memorial for public promulgation, and the officially published version, with its references to "bannermen" and "Kheshigten," now appears as a model of dynastic multiculturalism.[125]

Two years later, Inner Asian and Han perspectives were put to the test in Kododo, as in Kheshigten, to demonstrate the practical incompatibility of the terms "limit" and "access" under transfrontier multiethnic conditions. Both local Mongols, mostly state herders, and Han were extracting salt as frozen bricks of alkali soil in winter and as boiled lake water in summer and fall. The Mongols also rented out carts and extraction services at great profit. Operations continued, without regard for Sun's nuanced prohibition, until "several hundred" diggers were active in the area in 1742, months after the governor-general had left his post. These extractors were mainly Han from Zhili, which had forsaken any prohibition however nominally qualified.[126]

Giohoto, superintendant of the cattle herds and sheep flocks of the three upper banners, was the most vocal among officials who wanted a total ban on salt in favor of grass. In 1742 he asserted that Han had come in unsustainable droves, setting off interethnic incidents. They also ruined excellent pastures by building shelters and cutting grass and trees daily for fuel, especially to "boil" alkali-impregnated soil on the spot. Beijing officials, torn between their desire to discourage Han migration and their recognition that an absolute ban was impractical, effectively temporized.[127]

A 1745 patrol report submitted by *Lifanyuan* official Zengfu reopened the issue by asserting that the area's soil was too saturated with alkali to support grasslands. He requested that the old Kangxi licensing system of merchant extraction be resumed for the benefit of both Han and Mongols. Further central deliberation of this report finally noted the critical relationship between grass and salt for a pastoral environment. Livestock, especially camels, required alkali salt. Camels, who require about eight times more salt than sheep or cattle, rely on nearly a kilogram per week of salt for their superior water-retaining capacity. So, assumptions of some memorialists to the contrary, livestock did not live by grass alone, and this necessitated further deliberations. A 1746 reconnoiter of the area interviewed local pastoral Mongols who clearly stated that they used dunes and willow stands that dotted the region for shelter from harsh winter weather. They also affirmed that regulated salt extraction, which began in 1709, had ruined grasslands and forests.[128] This testimony elicited some anthropocentric responses even from local banner officers such as Plain Blue Banner Superintendant Shuwangju. He argued in 1748 that "the Mongol steppe was too vast" to prohibit access. Moreover, salt, like wood cut by Han in Kheshigten or salt extracted in the Khuuchid banner area, was "a daily necessity for the people from the capital and provinces" that would also provide a livelihood for locals.[129]

People driven by economic necessity within an immense expanse assembled a set of relations that rendered state agency ineffectual. Formal prohibition of Han agrarian clearance in the same year technically remained in nominal force until 1795.[130]

The *Lifanyuan*'s decision to maintain a qualified ban allowing some residential extraction, limited to about forty *jin* per person for personal use, while preventing deforestation that was destroying pastures, was quickly undermined. Huise, Giohoto's successor, reported that state herds in the Shangdu River region were endangered by more than two hundred carts hauling about 160 to 170 *jin* to Dushikou. Incidents included theft of Mongol personal property livestock. An estimated one thousand Han were also digging saline soil around the ruins of the old Yuan capital of Kaiping itself. Patrols caught few if

The Nature of Imperial Pastoralism in Southern Inner Mongolia 157

any diggers but found ample evidence of unauthorized commercial extraction of sufficient scale to adversely affect state and private herds. Prohibition was tightened, but residential access was continued.[131]

Six years later in 1755 Shuwangwu's successor, Jaocang, made another appeal for prohibition repeal, claiming that local Mongols considered Han merchant extraction profitable because they could rent out carts and oxen and supply firewood. He also reasserted the area was too saline and barren for herding. Huise's opposition resulted in a joint inquiry by representatives of both sides.[132] They found decisive evidence from local Mongols that Han salt extraction caused social disruption, pasture degradation, and erosive deforestation, in which "trees were cut and burned to such an extent that mountains were deforested, ruining our grasslands." With the cessation of commercial extraction for several years, however, "forests gradually reestablished themselves." This testimony persuaded the Grand Council itself in 1756 to restrict unconditionally mass Han incursion to protect Mongol grass by restricting access to Mongol salt.[133]

GUIHUA: HANSPACE ON THE STEPPE

The alkali deliberations of 1741–56 reveal explicit stresses on environmental relations that transcended ecosystems and cultures ostensibly kept in their respective places by the Great Wall and its attendant administrative structures. In fact, however, Qing state administrative structures were not simply trying to maintain a certain form of sustainable relations between Han and Mongols under distinct pastoral or agrarian conditions, but imperial borderland relations across an ecotone. Had the Great Wall or provinces or leagues or subprefectures or banners actually delineated the environmental boundaries of the area, such relations would have been relatively self-sustaining. At least management would have been much less complicated. As it was, maintaining an imperial borderland in the Inner Mongolian grasslands necessitated a sixteen-year deliberation just to decide the status of a few salt lakes.[134]

These deliberations were only a very small part of the immense adaptations the Qing state had to undergo to maintain its networked order in Inner Mongolia. This order centered on provisions for the breeding of several hundred thousand head of state livestock alone and the livelihoods of an estimated more than two million people during the eighteenth century. Imperial relations, however, made it impossible to isolate this large and interdependent group from the even larger masses to the south. From an administrative perspective, there was an irresistible imperative to maximize bureaucratic efficiency under existing technological and material constraints by making the empire's environmental diversity as monoculturally legible as possible.

The effects of these dual pressures of Han migration and imperial administration may be most visible in eighteenth-century Inner Mongolia's most urbanized space, the regional administrative hub of Guihua. A report from 1734 estimated forty to fifty thousand Han residents cultivating fields and running pawnshops and bordellos "in every village and hamlet" in the vicinity. These activities included "daily occurrences" of banditry, quarrels, and gambling among the Han commoners. These Han, many of them former camp followers from the Zunghar campaigns, became intermixed with Mongols from various banners "so that when an incident occurs, both Mongol and Han are involved."[135]

A 1750 report by Jungfoboo deplored the degraded state of the local Tümed Mongols. The arrival of Han commoners had set off "a struggle for commercial profit and the cultivation of fields over a long period, so that Han customs infiltrated among our people that could not be overcome." "Wasteful competition" had "deceived" these Tümed, who were totally dependent on grain, "into striving in all matters to emulate the ways of the Han of the interior" to their ruin. He advocated a set of Tümed social reforms prefaced by an exhortation to "follow the old ways ... living frugally" and separately from Han who "bring their dependents here and build houses, open stores, trade, and cultivate fields." For once "Han customs of the interior ... become a fixed way of life for Mongols, ... poverty inevitably results ... to the detriment of all state affairs."[136]

These reports display steppe environmental relations in the midst of an unprecedented transformation that Qing imperial pastoralism had simultaneously resisted, abetted, and ultimately could not control. Even the 1734 imposition of China proper's *baojia* household registration system on both Tümed and Han residents of Guihua proved ineffective[137] The Tümed were clearly adapting in a manner corrosive for imperial pastoralism, and the core of the problem, at least in Jungfoboo's view, was that Mongols were becoming Han. Similar concerns over Han commercial "contamination" (Ma: *icembi*) were also expressed in 1748 about an unauthorized influx of thousands more Shandong peasants fleeing from drought into areas of mixed Han-Mongol residence in Bagou. Bagou

The Nature of Imperial Pastoralism in Southern Inner Mongolia 159

already hosted more than 117,600 "old" Han, some of whom were probably the cultivators who clashed with local Kharachin Mongols during Sun Jiagan's tenure a decade earlier. While taking measures to keep both populations apart, including adopting Sun's old proposal to appoint an official to oversee interethnic affairs, the state acquiesced to the incursion.[138]

Jungfoboo's and similar Inner accounts reflect some of the same concerns expressed by the throne over the "contamination" of Manchus by Han customs noted in Chapter 2. Mongolian identity, however was threatened by unanticipated Han migration beyond the passes while Manchu identity was threatened by deliberate Manchu "migration" to China proper. The Mongolian transformation was, moreover, made possible in large measure not by preexisting relations in China proper, but by a space amenable to Han urban-agrarian reconstitution that occluded or entirely precluded pastoral relationships. The Inner Mongolian ecotone proved too adaptable to act as the solid ground of imperial pastoralism and its banner Mongol identity. The environmental relations constituting other spaces of areas such as southwestern Yunnan, however, were far less congenial for the construction of an imperial borderland.

Notes

1 Na Risen, "Guanyu Taipusi Qi shengtai jianshe," 291–93.
2 See, for example, Di Cosmo, "Ancient Inner Asian Nomads," 1092–1126.
3 Elverskog, *Our Great Qing*, 21. Note also evidence from Manchu sources that the Qing court modified the league system; Oyunbilig, "Guanyu Qingdai nei zha-sa-ke Menggu meng," 62–75.
4 Banner Mongols were also called the "Unified Mongol Tribes of the Marches" (*waifan Menggu tongbu*), *Jiaqing chongxiu yitongzhi*, 33:26, 449. Eighteenth-century Manchu and nineteenth-century Chinese sources employed the term "inner *jasag*" (Ma: *dorgi jasak se*) or paired the terms "inner and outer *jasag*" (*nei zha-sa-ke* and *wai zha-sa-ke*); MWLF, QL 2/11/3 [03-0171-0360-009]; *Huidian shili* (GX), 10:980b, 989a, 1173a; Zhang Mu, *Menggu youmu ji*, 1, 141.
5 Fu Ge, "Jiubai," 37.
6 Zhao Zhiheng, ed., *Neimenggu tongshi, disan juan*, 3:7.
7 For Lingdan Khan, see, Yi-du-he-xi-ge et al., *Menggu minzu tongshi, disi juan*, 4:5–28; Li, "State-building Before 1644," 55–56. For an account of various Mongol revolts, see Zhao Zhiheng, ed., *Neimenggu tongshi, disan juan*, 3:8–20.
8 I have mainly relied on Zhao Yuntian, *Qingdai zhili bianchui de shuniu* for the *Lifanyuan*. Other important studies include Zhao Yuntian, "Qing zhi Mingguo guanli Menggu," 208–11; Ning, "The Li-fan Yuan in the Early Ch'ing Dynasty"; Legrand, *L'administration dans la domination Sino-Mandchoue en Mongolie Qala-a*.

160 *Across Forest, Steppe, and Mountain*

9 Heuschert, "Legal Pluralism," 313–14. For overviews of Qing Mongol law and its major compilations, see Oljeitogtoqu, "Qingchao dui Menggu de lifa gaisu," 348-70; Dalizhabu, "'Menggu lüeli'," 1–10.

10 Zhao Zhiheng, ed., *Neimenggu tongshi, disan juan*, 3:3–4; Perdue, *China Marches West*, 175–76; Lu Minghui, *Qingdai Menggu shi*, 20–21; Yi-du-he-xi-ge, *Menggu minzu tongshi, disi juan*, 4:123; Zhang Mu, *Menggu youmu ji*, 148. Many of the Chinese works give unsupported and differing figures for the total number of banners in 1691 or at an unspecified date.

11 *Qianlongchao neifu chaoben*, 92; *Da Qing huidian* (QL), 619: 741–42. There is some confusion in secondary sources over the number of Khalkha banners and their chronology. This is probably because there are eighty-three northern Khalkha banners, as well as two "Khalkha" banners of an unrelated group resident south of the desert (*monan zhi ka-er-ka*) and a third "Khalkha" banner in Qinghai; *Da Qing huidian shili* (JQ), 637:2397. One Qing source that lists a number of such potential confusions is Fu Ge, "Tongming Menggu bu," 33.

12 *Huidian* (KX), 728:7029. It has been argued that the league system was only fully developed after the consolidation of Mongol banner pastures; Oyunbilig, "Meng de chuxing," 76–77.

13 *Da Qing huidian* (QL), 619:735b; *Qianlong chao neifu chaoben*, 48–49.

14 *Da Qing huidian* (KX), 728:7049. For an example from Mongolia proper, see Oka,"Shindai shiryō ni mieru Mongoru no saigai," 54.

15 Gu Yanwu, *Yuan chaoben ri zhi lu*, 834–45.

16 *Manbun rōtō*, 1:456; *QSL*,TC 8/6/24, 2:249a.

17 *QSL*, TC 8/11/10, 2:276a–77b. For some important context for and analysis of this meeting, see Dalizhabu, "Qing chu nei zha-sa-ke qi de jianli wenti," 261–62. I am grateful to Professor Bao Meihua for her assistance with the transliteration of "Šongqor."

18 *Da Qing huidian shili* (GX), 10:1247b–48a.

19 Zhang Mu, *Menggu youmu ji*, 374–78, 264–65.

20 MWLF, YZ 10/12/17 [03-0173-1031-012].

21 See, for example, an October 1679 report that "recently, those crossing the border to plunder are all poor people without any means of subsistence who have been defeated by Galdan and fled here," *QSL*, KX 18/8/27, 4:1063a–b. See also, *QSL* KX 16/12/25, 4:903b; Perdue, *China Marches West*, 139.

22 *QSL*, KX 22/9/15, 5:151a–b. This entry is dated 1683, the same year that 1682–83 statutes limiting the size of Zunghar delegations appear in *Da Qing huidian* (KX), 728:7076.

23 Dalizhabu, "Qingdai Baqi Chakhar kao," 7:287–305; Wei Yuan, *Shengwu ji*,1:97; Fu Ge, "Menggu," 31; *Qingshigao*, 14:4173.

24 *Da Qing huidian* (GX), 668a; MWLF, YZ 13/11/19 [03-174-1544-011.2]. For an overview of the state herding system, see Li Sanmou, "Qingdai beibu bianjiang de guan muchang," *Zhongguo bianjiang shi yanjiu*, 1 (1999): 69–77.

25 Ba-yin-mu-ren, *Menggu Shouyi Yanjiu*, 69–75.

26 *Da Qing huidian* (GX), 871a, 857b; *Da Qing huidian shili* (GX), 11: 889b, 890a–b, 893a.

The Nature of Imperial Pastoralism in Southern Inner Mongolia 161

27 *Da Qing huidian shili* (GX), 11:893b-894b; MWLF, QL 15/7/4 [03-171-0374-008], QL 15/7/4 [03-171-0374-009]. Shunzhi-era lashing penalties for shortfalls are listed in the Kangxi and Yongzheng editions of the *Huidian*, but are not present in *Da Qing huidian shili* (JQ), which generally omits *Taipusi* Shunzhi statutes; *Da Qing huidian* (KX), 730:7625-26; *Da Qing huidian* (YZ), 789:15,319-20. Both the Manchu documents cited herein, however, attest to the ongoing employment of the whip on herders of the lowest rank.

28 There is some uncertainty regarding the precise date these quotas were fixed. *Da Qing huidian shili* (GX) states that the Shangdu/Dabsun Nuur quota of 210,000 head was fixed in 1705 and the Dariganga quota of one hundred thousand head was fixed in 1717; 12:1013b. A 1743 pasture report states both quotas were fixed in 1705; MWLF, QL 8/11/4 [03-175-1560-004]. Another report dated 1741 refers to Dariganga's set number of eighty flocks, a regulation figure not mentioned in the statues; MWLF, QL 6/10/5 [03-172-0673-001].

29 MWLF, QL 19/9/6 [03-172-0687-002]. Estimates of 1.2 percent and 5 percent both exclude the outlying, and probably inaccurate, figures for Dariganga in QL 4/10/6. The truth probably lies in between them, although likely closer to 5 percent.

30 MWLF, QL 1/8/7 [03-171-0358-010]. Statutory quotas do not accurately reflect the actual number of livestock that could be grazing in a herd area. The 1730 mare herd camel population in the report, for example, averages 270 head per herd, well over the 1707 statutory range of between one and two hundred head.

31 Xiao et al., "Sensitivity of Inner Mongolia Grasslands to Climate Change," 643; Committee on Scholarly Communication with the People's Republic of China, ed., *Grasslands and Grassland Sciences*, 11, 17; Brown et al., *Sustainable Development*, 27. For a summary of grassland study in China, see Le Kang et al., "Grassland Ecosystems in China," 997–1008.

32 Goulden et al., "The Geology, Climate and Ecology of Mongolia," 91; Xu Ke, *Qingbai leichao*, 1:46.

33 Committee on Scholarly Communication, *Grasslands and Grassland Sciences*, 11; Brown et al., *Sustainable Development*, 29–30; Goulden, "The Geology, Climate and Ecology of Mongolia," 93.

34 Sternberg et al., "Pressurised Pastoralism," 365.

35 Sternberg et al., "Pressurised Pastoralism," 365, 371; Sun Quanzhu, "Neimenggu ziran huanjing de yanbian," 3–4; Goulden, "The Geology, Climate and Ecology of Mongolia," 91.

36 Wang Yejian and Huang Yingjue, "Qingdai Zhongguo qihou bianqian," 5, 8–9. The Little Ice Age as a *globally synchronous* period of anomalous cold climate has been called into question; Folland et al., eds., *Climate Change 2001*, 133–36. Evidence, however, that China in general, including Inner Mongolia, underwent a marked cooling period, which the literature generally terms "the Little Ice Age," continues to emerge; see, for example, Yongming Han et al., "Atmospheric Cu and Pb Deposition," 172–73.

37 A number of complex problems and exceptions qualify any absolute assertion of the validity of either nonequilibrium or steady state rangeland models;

162 Across Forest, Steppe, and Mountain

Fernandez-Gimenez and Allen-Diaz, "Testing a Non-equilibrium Model of Rangeland," 871–85.

38 Wang Zhigang, "Central Inner Mongolia," 88; Committee on Scholarly Communication, *Grasslands and Grassland Sciences*, 188–89. For some representative Chinese views, which tend to focus on anthropogenic factors, see Da Lintai, "Zhidu yu zhengce," 176–215, Lin Wenping and Gao Minjie, "Neimenggu caoyuan shengtai huifu," 32–35. For a view critical of Chinese perspectives, see Williams, *Beyond Great Walls*, 41–44.

39 The Manchu unit of measure *urgun* (or *urhun*) is roughly equal to 0.5 of a traditional Chinese inch (*cun*), which in the Qing was the equivalent of about 1.75 centimeters (0.69 inches). Thus the length of the grass was approximately 5.25–7 centimeters (2.07–2.76 inches). MWLF, QL 13/i.c. 7/13 [03-171-0372–005]. Such reports, whose basic format appears standardized, also emphasized the necessity for rainwater to soak thoroughly into the ground; MWLF, QL 9/5/25 [03-172-0676-001], QL 12/5/27 [03-172-0680-001], QL 17/5/27 [03-171-0378-007].

40 For an overview of the relations between Inner Mongolian climate and natural disaster during the Qing, see Yu Zhiyong, "Qingdai Neimenggu diqu de ziran zaihai," 35–40.

41 MWLF, QL 14/3/28 [03-0172-0682-005].

42 For studies of disaster relief mainly focused on China proper, see Will, *Bureaucracy and Famine*; Li, *Fighting Famine*; Li Xiangjun, *Qingdai huangzheng yanjiu*; He Zhiqing, ed., *Zhongguo gudai zaihai*; Cao Shuji, ed., *Tianzu you shen*. Literature on natural disasters in Qing China is reviewed in Zhu Hu, "Ershi shiji Qingdai zaihuang," 104–19.

43 MWLF, YZ 11/6/3 [03-0173-1034-007], 11/6/26 [03-0172-0598-003], 11/8/28 [03-0173-1032-021]. One *shi*, the standard Chinese measure for grain volume, is roughly equal to 2.8 bushels or one hectoliter.

44 Will, *Bureaucracy and Famine*, 129. Of course, state relief also had to adapt to environmental variation in China proper; ibid., 129–30.

45 Dunstan, "Heirs of Yu the Great," 523; Will, *Bureaucracy and Famine*, 5–6; *Da Qing Huidian shili* (GX), 10:1229a. The high Qing state assumed new, direct responsibilities for relief that had previously been in local purview; Li, *Fighting Famine*, 222.

46 *Da Qing Huidian shili* (GX), 10:1229a. Compare an almost verbatim version in *Menggu lüli*, 2:11.

47 MWLF, YZ 11/6/3 [03-0173-1034-007], 11/6/26 [03-0172-0598-003]. The precedent cases cited in the *Da Qing huidian shili* (GX) contain only one instance of state provision of livestock, again from penalty holdings; 10:1231a. Yu Zhiyong, "Qingdai Neimenggu xibu diqu de huangzheng," 32–36, asserts the Qing state did provide livestock directly but cites no specific cases.

48 *Kangxichao Manwen zhupi*, #2784, 1103.

49 MWLF, YZ 12/4/20 [03-173-1039-003].

50 MWLF, YZ 10/12/? [03-211-4595-003]. This document makes provisions for five sheep and one ox per household. Another document provided single males with one "large" head of livestock and five sheep; MWLF, YZ 10/10/13 [03-173-1028-018].

The Nature of Imperial Pastoralism in Southern Inner Mongolia 163

51 For imperial flock statistics, see MWLF, QL 4/10/6 [03-0171-0362-012].

52 Representative documents include MWLF, QL 19/9/6 [03-0172-0687-002] and QL 28/7/9 [03-0180-2038-021]. One of the heroes of the 1732 battle of Erdene Juu, Tseren, was awarded two thousand head of horses, one thousand head of cattle, and five thousand sheep from state herds to replace the losses he had suffered from Zunghar depredations while on campaign for the Qing; *Pingding Zhun-ge-er fanglue*, 1:534–35.

53 MWLF, YZ 12/4/20 12/4/20 [03-173-1039-003]. See also the brief entry on the operation in *QSL*, YZ 12/4/29, 8:791b. Such detailed Manchu archival documents refute assertions that the Qing state, for various reasons, could not extend effective aid for steppe disaster relief; Yu Zhiyong, Neimenggu xibu diqu de huangzheng," 36; Oka, "Shindai shiryō ni mieru Mongoru no saigai," 47–48.

54 MWLF, QL 14/9/12 [03-0171-0373-009]; 17/3/24 [03-0171-0378-003].

55 Cited in Oka, "Shindai shiryō ni mieru Mongoru no saigai," 60.

56 Will, *Bureaucracy and Famine*, p. 27; Marks, "It Never Used to Snow," 435; MWLF, QL 17/3/24 [03-0171-0378-003]; Dunstan, "Heirs of Yu," 521–22. The necessity of, in some cases, annual disbursement of substantial percentages of grain stocks simply to prevent spoilage may have regularly depleted stocks in normal times; R. Bin Wong, "Foundations of Success, 1650–1735," 33–34. A closely spaced series of disasters was probably the biggest check on a relief strategy depending on ever-normal granaries; Dunstan, "Heirs of Yu," 527.

57 A similar erosion is also visible in the "blurring" of Mongol into Han law, which "does not seem to have been intentional," toward the end of the eighteenth century; Heuschert, "Legal Pluralism," 317.

58 MWLF, QL 28/7/9 [03-0180-2038-021].

59 *Da Qing huidian* (YZ), 788:14893; *Da Qing huidian* (GX), 668b, 857b. Allowances varied across species and herds, 10 percent mortality permissible among the *Taipusi* gelding herds, 5 percent among the three-banner horse and camel herds, 13 percent among the *Qifengsi*'s cattle herds, and 10 percent among its flocks. These variations may have been concessions to livestock diversity within shifting ecological conditions of the pastures.

60 MWLF, QL 15/7/4 [03-0171-0374-009], QL 20/4/18 [03-0172-0688-001].

61 MWLF, QL 9/8/3 [03-0171-0367-006]; QL 15/7/4 [03-0171-0374-008].

62 MWLF, QL 9/8/3 [03-0171-0367-006]. According to *Da Qing huidian shili* (JQ) the appointment of personnel from the capital was technically suspended by a 1723 edict, but the QL 9/8/3 document clearly shows in greater detail that the practice continued into the 1740s; 694:3750-51.

63 *Taipusi* "herding officials and troops," who were posted as pasture guards, "are all Chakhar," a reference that may include the lowest level herders themselves; *Da Qing huidian* (GX), 668b. For Chakhar herder deployment at the Three Upper Banner pastures, Shangdu/Dabsun Nuur and Dariganga, see MWLF, QL 11/8/11 [03-0172-0678-002], YZ 12/5/27 [03-0171-0356-005] and *Koubei Santing zhi*, 104b, respectively.

64 MWLF YZ 10/5/16 [03-0173-1031-001], 10/7/1 [03-0173-1028-010], 10/7/1 [03-0173-1028-011].

164   *Across Forest, Steppe, and Mountain*

65 *QSL*, QL 6/7/24, 10:1117b-18a. In this entry "inner" is "*neidi*" and "outer" "*waidi*." The emperor's statement is one indication that the Khalkha outer *jasag* were effectively less subject to Qing command than the inner *jasag*, who were geographically much closer central administrative centers. Proximity may explain differences in the effectiveness of Qing relief regimes for both areas. Inner and outer regimes are outlined in Joseph Fletcher, "Ch'ing Inner Asia *c.* 1800," 48–58. For an overview of the Qing pastoral order among the Khalkha, see Sh. Natsagdorj, "The Economic Basis of Feudalism," 265–81.

66 Jiang Yongjiang, "Lun Qingdai monan Menggu diqu," 33–35.

67 Walker, *The Conquest of Ainu Lands*, 85–87.

68 MWLF, YZ 10/10/12 [03-0173-1031-005].

69 Perdue, *China Marches West*, 254–55.

70 MWLF, YZ 10/12/? [03-211-4595-003]. The document is damaged, so full details are lacking.

71 MWLF, QL 5/1/25 [03-173-1056-003]; Zhang Mu, *Menggu youmu ji*, 379–82. These Torghuts were one of a small number of groups that remained behind in Xinjiang, Qinghai, and Gansu when most of their *aimag* migrated to Russia around 1630, then famously returned to Qing territory in 1771; Zhang Mu, *Menggu youmu ji*, 377–78; Ma Ruheng and Ma Dazheng, *Piaolue yiyu de minzu*, 44; He Qiutao, *Shuofang beisheng*, 16:642b.

72 MWLF, QL 4/6/16 [03-173-1054-003]. For livestock prices, see YZ 12/8/26 [03-0173-1039-005].

73 The Zunghars were certainly aware of the importance of diversifying their environmental relations on the steppe, especially in terms of the promotion of agriculture; Cai Jiayi, Zhun-ge-er de nongye," 53–68.

74 MWLF, QL 1/1/4 [03-171-0359-001.1]. Milk consumption is ideal for dry steppe conditions since the metabolization of such fat-rich foods produces water; Rinchingiin, "Mongolian Dairy Products," 84.

75 MWLF, QL 1/1/4 [03–171–0359–001.1]. Similar practices of weaning and preservation continue today, as does the frequent milking of mares, whose small udders continue to produce more milk than is often required by foals in their later stages of development; Rinchingiin, "Mongolian Dairy Products," 71, 74. The precise nature of *kūru* is unclear, but it may be *agarts*, sour milk curds, or *aragoul*, a fermented *agarts* by-product; ibid., 82–83.

76 MWLF, QL 12/1/22 [03-0173-1082-001], QL 12/2/6 [03-0173-1082-002].

77 MWLF, YZ 10/10/19 [03-171-0294-004].

78 MWLF, QL 1/1/4 [03-171-0359-001.1].

79 *Da Qing huidian* (YZ), 789: 15,327; MWLF, YZ 9/8/8 [03-171-0352-003]. These proportions certainly did not remain invariably constant everywhere at all times. A disproportionate expansion of both types of herds at Shangdu/Dabsun Nuur in 1738 resulted in 174 mare and thirty gelding herds with a population ratio of 3.4:1 (assuming the same stud proportion as in the *Taipusi* herds), for example, but this was unusually low for the period; MWLF, QL 3/4/11 [03-171-0361-003].

The Nature of Imperial Pastoralism in Southern Inner Mongolia 165

80 *Da Qing huidian* (GX), 668a; MWLF, QL 3/3/23 [03-171-0208-004].

81 MWLF, QL 12/7/4 [03-0172-0680-002].

82 MWLF, QL 14/3/28 [03-0172-0682-005].

83 Zhao Yi, "Menggu shi lao," 16. The Qianlong emperor similarly equated Mongol "dairy products" (*rubing*) with "grain" (*liang*); "Passing through the Mongol Tribes," *Qing Gaozong yuzhi shi* 1:289b. Eighteenth-century Han observers also viewed milk products as "grain" among Tibetan pastoralists; Zhou Ailian, *Xizang jiyou*, 115.

84 MWLF, QL 26/9/5 [03-0179-1893-025], 26/9/15 [03-0179-1894-013].

85 MWLF, QL 1/12/11 [03-174-1481-001].

86 *Qing Gaozong yuzhi shi* 1:153a.

87 Qing emperors were indeed receiving Mongol dairy tribute, in addition to actual livestock, of "sour fermented cakes [*kūru*], milk, butter, koumiss, etc."; MWLF, QL 14/10/19 [03-171-0373-011]. Koumiss in particular formed substantial parts of the Khorchin and Ordos banner tributes from 1674, although later reduced to token amounts; *Da Qing huidian shili* (GX), 10:1188a,b; *Da Qing huidian* (GX), 858a.

88 One representative example that views agriculture as progressive is Zhang Yongjiang, "Liangshi xuqiu," 30–42. A representative critical view of agriculture's environmental effects is Yun Heyi, "Qingdai yilai Neimenggu daliang kaiken tudi," 8–11. For a current evaluation linking grassland degradation to agriculture, see Da-lin-tai, "Zhidu yu zhengce," 176–92. For a more comprehensive view, see Chen Shan, "Inner Asian Grassland Degradation."

89 See, for example, Cheng Chongde, "Qingdai qianqi dui Menggu de fengjin zhengce," 26–31; Sun Zhe, "Qing Qianqi Menggu diqu de renkou,' 41–50; Reardon-Anderson, *Reluctant Pioneers* 37–45, 48–65; Yu Tongyuan and Wang Laigang, "Qingdai zhong-yuan renkou bei yi," 327–40; Zhu-sa, 18–20 18-20 *shiji chu dongbu Neimenggu nonggeng*.

90 *Koubei San Ting zhi*, 1b.

91 Serruys, "Chinese in Southern Mongolia," 41–44.

92 *QSL*, KX 51/5/18, 6:478a.

93 Calculations based on figures in Li Xiangjun, *Qingdai huangzheng yanjiu*, 123–47.

94 MWLF, QL 11/4/12 [03-170-0059-001]. For Shanxi's disaster figures that year, see Li Xiangjun, *Qingdai huangzheng yanjiu*, 165.

95 For an administrative chronology of these subprefectures, see, Niu Pinghan, *Qingdai zhengqu yan'ge zongbiao*, 15–16, 52. Regional administrative boundaries are so complicated that locales like Guihua have been mapped as part of both Shanxi and Inner Mongolia; Tan Qixiang, ed., *Zhongguo lishi ditu ji*, 7, 20, 58. See also point #16 in the bilingual unpaginated "compiling principles" sections.

96 *Qing Gaozong yuzhi shi* 14:282a–b.

97 Zhang Yongjiang, *Qindai fanbu yanjiu*, 260–315; Yu Tongyuan and bei yi, "Qingdai zhongyuan renkou," 330.

98 Zhang Yongjiang, "Lun Qingdai monan Menggu Diqu," 29–40.

166   *Across Forest, Steppe, and Mountain*

99 For an analysis of Han agricultural migration under late Qing conditions, see Su De, "Guanyu Qingmo Neimenggu xibu," 434–48.

100 Liu et al., "The Origin of Remnant Forest Stands," 139, 148–49, 150.

101 MWLF, QL 5/1/29 [03-175-1553-019]. These thirteen companies were assigned to lama herders.

102 Gao, "The Retreat of the Horses," 110–11; *Hangzhou Baqi zhu fangying zhilue,* 170.

103 *Fuzhou zhufang zhi,* 644–45, 669; Yan Gao, "The Retreat of the Horses," 113; *Hangzhou Baqi zhu fangying zhilue,* 160; *Zhu Yue Baqi zhi,* 290–91. Niu Guanjie estimates that there were about two hundred thousand head under banner and Green Standard management in the eighteenth century, but his figures for Kangxi and Yongzheng era Guangzhou, for example, overestimate the garrison's three thousand head by 100 and 200 percent, respectively; "Qingdai mazheng chu tan," 58.

104 *Fuzhou zhufang zhi,* 645–46, 669. Supplementary purchases were also made in Sichuan, but these horses, while more acclimated to south China conditions, were generally too small for warfare.

105 Yan Gao, "The Retreat of the Horses," 110–11; *Hangzhou Baqi zhu fangying zhilue,* 170–71.

106 *Yongzhengchao Manwen zhupi,* #4212, 2:2172–74.

107 *QSL,* YZ 8/9/29, 8:311a-b; MWLF, YZ 10/10/2 [03-0173-1027-010]; YZ 10/10/19 [03-0173-1027-009]. The reported yield seems too low for the area under cultivation.

108 MWLF, QL 12/2/6 [03-0173-1082-002]; QL 4/2/14 [03-0173-1054-001]. The 1747 deliberation cited a similar formulation from "the seventh year of the Yongzheng emperor (1729) as a precedent; MWLF, QL 12/2/6 [03-0173-1082-002].

109 MWLF, QL 12/7/4 [03-0172-0680-002].

110 MWLF, YZ 10/10/19 [03-171-0318-011].

111 See, for example, MWLF, YZ 10/10/2 [03-0173-1027-010].

112 Contemporary problems rooted in conflicts between pastoral and agricultural "cultures" continue to contribute to pastoral degradation in the IMAR; E. Erdenijab, "An Economic Assessment," 191–92; for a study of the significance of mobility in contemporary Mongolia, see B. Erdenebaatar, "Socioeconomic Aspects."

113 MWLF, QL 12/2/6 [03-0173-1082-002]; 7/3/26 [03-0172-0463-001]. For Han-Mongol collusion in illicit cultivation, see, for example, MWLF, YZ 11/8/23 [03-0174-1489-002 and-003].

114 MWLF, YZ 11/8/28 [03-0173-1032-021]; QL 14/4/13 [03-0172-0620-005]. In a 1742 report on Han cultivators in Guihua Shanxi Governor Ka-er-ji-shan mentioned 1691 as the date when the Qing state began to promote Mongol agriculture. He did add, however, that Mongols "continued to rely on grasslands for livestock breeding"; *Qingdai zhouzhe huibian,* QL 7/10/15, 69–70.

115 *Yongzhengchao Manwen zhupi,* #2214, 1:1,233–34.

116 MWLF, QL 15/4/28 [03-0173-1089-02], 15/6/14 [03-0172-0621-003].

The Nature of Imperial Pastoralism in Southern Inner Mongolia 167

117 MWLF, QL 7/12/8 [03-0172-0909-004], 8/1/8 [03-0172-0910-001]. Sun's "original" memorial can be found in Sun Jiagan, *Sun Wending Gong zoushu*, 1:383–87. See also note 125.

118 *Kangxichao Manwen zhupi*, #2784, 1101–03. Forests similarly functioned as reserve food sources for agrarian societies in times of crisis; Marks, *China: Its Environment and History*, 253–54.

119 MWLF, YZ 12/11/3 [03-0172-0902-006], 12/12/11 [03-0172-0902-006], 13/6/24 [03-0172-0754-005], 13/7/? [03-0172-0754-006].

120 *Kangxichao Manwen zhupi*, #2960, 1173; *QSL* KX 38/4/19, 5:1043a–b. The 1699 deliberations refute assertions that the early Qing "strictly prohibited tree-cutting and especially prohibited commoners from China proper from logging." This view misinterprets a terse Chinese version of 1717 deliberations, which are more fully extant in Manchu; Yi-du-he-xi-ge, *Menggu minzu tongshi, disi juan*; 4:272; *Qianlongchao neifu chaoben*, 65.

121 MWLF, YZ 11/12/7 [03-0172-0469-002], QL 26/3/7 [03-0179-1868-015]; *Qianlongchao shangyu dang*, 3:523b, 544b. For a study of Muna forestry in the succeeding Qianlong period, see Huang Zhiguo, "Cong fengjin dao kaijin," 90–94.

122 Schwennesen, "Using Salt for Livestock," 43; Launchbaugh and Howery, "Understanding Landscape Use Patterns of Livestock," 105.

123 See, for example, Tao-Chang Chiang, "The Salt Trade," 197–219; Kwan Man Bun, *The Salt Merchants of Tianjin*, 29–49.

124 Sun Jiagan, *Sun Wending Gong zoushu*, 1: 217–21, 319–26, 367–71; MWLF, QL 7/5/8 [03-0172-0711-001]. Sun's third memorial cited here is summarized in *QSL*, QL 5/11/29, 10:916a as well as in the QL 7/5/8 Manchu document.

125 *QSL* QL 6/3/24, 10:1005a; Sun Jiagan *Sun Wending Gong zoushu*, 1:383–87.

126 MWLF, QL 7/5/8 [03-0172-0711-001], 10/10/18 [03-0172-0712-001], 10/11/4 [03-0172-0711-002], 11/i.c.3/1 [03-0172-0913-001].

127 MWLF, QL 7/5/8 [03-0172-0711-001], 7/5/21 [03-0172-0711-002].

128 MWLF, QL 10/10/18 [03-0172-0712-001]; 10/11/4 [03-0172-0711-002], 11/i.c.3/1 [03-0172-0913-001]; FAO, *A Manual for the Primary Animal Health Care Worker*, 183. There seem to be some gaps in the documentary record, but the issue clearly remained unresolved by 1745.

129 MWLF, QL 13/11/6 [03-0172-0713-001].

130 Yu Tongyuan and Wang Laigang, "Qingdai zhongyuan renkou bei yi," 329.

131 MWLF, QL 14/7/7 [03-0175-1565-008].

132 MWLF, QL 20/1/24 [03-0172-0715-001]; QL 21/6/23 [03-0176-1599-001].

133 MWLF, QL 21/6/23 [03-0176-1599-001], QL 21/7/22 [03-0176-1603-022], QL 21/8/4 [03-0176-1604-030]. Timbering continues to adversely affect pastoral practices in contemporary Mongolia; Erdenebaatar, "Socio-economic Aspects," 87.

134 Interethnic conflict over salt lakes was not unique to the Qing. For a similar incident from the 1920s, see Henry Serruys, "Five Documents," 338–53.

168 Across Forest, Steppe, and Mountain

135 MWLF, YZ 12/11/15 [03-0173-1040-002]. For overviews of Guihua urban development and administration, see Wu-yun-ger-ri-le, *Shiba zhi ershi shiji chu Neimenggu chengzhen yanjiu*, 17–19, 52–57; Jin Hai et al., *Qingdai Menggu zhi*, 177–81, 282; Zhao Zhiheng, *Neimenggu tongshi, disan juan*, 3:138–42. For recent studies of urban-rural interactions in Mongolia, see Bruun and Narangoa, eds., *Mongols from Country to City*.

136 MWLF, QL 15/10/25 [03-0173-1089-004].

137 MWLF, YZ 12/11/29 [03-0173-1163-007.2].

138 MWLF, QL 13/2/20 [03-0170-0061-002]; Sun Jiagan, *Sun Wending Gong zoushu*, 1: 329–24. The figure of 117,600, in addition to another 10,400-plus new arrivals, submitted by local officials in the Manchu report seems more precise, than the "two to three hundred thousand-plus" Han reportedly engaged in agricultural clearance in Bagou according to *QSL*, QL 12/12/3, 12:972b–73a.

4

The Nature of Imperial Indigenism in Southwestern Yunnan

In 1769, Zhou Yu ended his diary account of the disastrous 1766–69 Qing Myanmar campaigns with a revealing gripe: "I have seen Myanmar, and it is nothing more than a southwestern tribe. Its people are neither brave nor vigorous, their weapons dull. They fall far short of Chinese troops and preserved themselves only because of rugged terrain and virulent malaria."[1] The Qianlong emperor, who presided over the Myanmar campaigns, concurred, admitting in a 1780 audience with another military chronicler that "Myanmar has awful conditions. Human beings cannot compete with Nature. It is very pitiful to see that our crack soldiers and elite generals died of deadly diseases for nothing. So [I am] determined never to have a war again [with Myanmar]."[2]

The borderland that Qing China had been fighting to maintain in southwestern Yunnan against its regional imperial rival, Myanmar's Konbaung Dynasty (1752–1885), was indeed constrained by a combination of cultural and ecological factors so unmalleable that state elites viewed them almost as a conspiracy against Qing rule. The diversity along the Qing empire's southwestern fringes was resistant to centralized domination by virtue of nature and culture, forcing state power to resort to less sustainable adaptations. Culture-nature interconnections were complicated by ties between human bodies, mosquitoes, and haematozoa (blood parasites). Their precise relations were not simply obscured, but were to a critical extent invisible, except as a pervasive regional disease environment of "miasma" (*zhangqi*).

Southwestern interweaving of culture and ecology was much less subject to state manipulation than those tying people to forage or to livestock. The Qing adaptation, consequently, was more anthropocentric, relying heavily on culture, generally mediated through native chieftainships, to transform indigenous peoples into proper subjects. Even the region's basic set of relations, highland swidden agriculture, was less adaptable to imperial arablist practices of lowland cultivation.

So southwestern Yunnan was a borderland radically different from its northern counterparts in Manchuria and Mongolia, the home territories of the Qing core elites. The embodiments of these latter borderlands were quite acclimated to them, and this facilitated the Qing imposition of imperial pastoralism or imperial foraging. Neither embodiment, however, was sufficiently conditioned for the extremes of the empire's mountainous southwestern fringes. Even a Han agrarian identity, which had proved so adaptable to conditions across forest, steppe, and alluvial plain, had difficulty finding a foothold in these precipitous highlands and diseased lowlands. All three of the empire's primary ethnic identities were united by their mutual vulnerability to the disease environment of southwestern Yunnan, which precluded standard imperial adaptations for administratively significant Manchu, Mongol, or Han residence. Dynastic control over the region was correspondingly weaker than in Mongolian or Manchurian borderlands despite southwestern Yunnan's much smaller size. Nevertheless, its strategic importance both as gateway to the area's considerable mineral wealth, which attracted large numbers of Han migrants, and as conduit between Qing and Konbaung territory made the borderland decisive for regional stability.[3]

Differential resistance structured these critical southwestern borderland interactions. The state's interpretation of the effects of malaria in monolithic "racial" terms reinforced ethnic identities. Distinctions between vulnerable Han newcomers and acclimated indigenous "tribal" (*yi*) peoples were spatially expressed as the ethnic administrative areas contrived for separate control. Organizational distinction between particular ethnicities interconnected with particular ecologies, rather than simply between different "cultures" alone, was characteristic of Qing borderland policy in general. The disease-attenuated Qing southwestern order took the administrative form of an unstable "imperial indigenism" of chieftainships as the dynasty's compromise with southwestern Yunnan's nexus of malarial nature and indigenous culture.

Of course, the Qing southwestern borderland was not simply a product of relations between humans, mosquitoes, and haematozoa, but these were integral to the regional order of imperial indigenism.

The Nature of Imperial Indigenism in Southwestern Yunnan 171

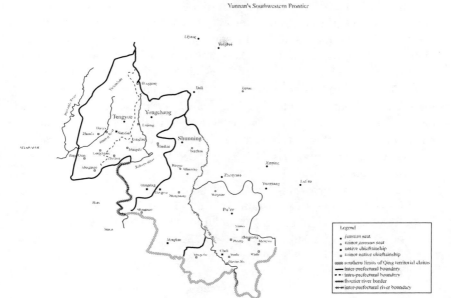

MAP 5: Yunnan's Southwestern Frontier

The following chapter will present this argument in greater detail with an initial focus on the "civilized," or chieftainship, "tribal" as the dynasty's idealized political embodiment of its southwestern borderland. The effects of distinct environmental forms of differential resistance, cultivation, and disease informing this identity and its spatial expression will then be examined under the stress of Qing rivalry with Myanmar. Overall, "chieftainship tribal" identity was a necessary, but problematic, imperial adaptation to the region's malaria conditions, which, while not immutable, were not subject to effective alteration or control.

THE TERRAIN OF NATIVE CHIEFTAINSHIPS

It is certainly possible to understand the space created by the intersection of Han and indigenous cultures as a "middle ground" constructed by both and dominated by neither. Nevertheless, as the Qing also "constructed their frontier institutions around Chinese and Manchu susceptibility to tropical disease," ecological factors substantially conditioned these cultural relationships.[4] Consideration of connections between malaria and ethnic identity in Qing Yunnan expands the two-dimensional representation of Han-indigenous relations as a cultural product to include biological processes such as differential resistance. Residence in southwestern Yunnan meant intimate involvement in the life cycles of both mosquitoes and haematozoa with malaria a common result. The most spatially significant human adaptive response produced chieftainships. In this way the disease environment created political as well as biological boundaries that complicated borderland construction of imperial indigenism.

Pertinent and forbidding ecological boundaries commence amid the river systems that cut through Yunnan's mountains. These make up about 84 percent of a province that is part of larger geographical systems such as the Greater Mekong Subregion and the Southeast Asian massif. They extend millions of square kilometers beyond the boundaries of any single state past or present. Wide divergences in elevation, ranging from well under one hundred to well over six thousand meters, can occur over comparatively short distances covering tropical to frigid zones. The province is also a meeting point for monsoon systems from both the Pacific and Indian oceans. These widely varying conditions permit year-round malaria transmission at lower altitudes, generally below fifteen hundred meters and south of $25°$ N, while usually, but not always, precluding it at higher elevations.[5] The resulting ecological diversity created many environmental obstacles, especially disease, to a direct, sustained dynastic presence. The Qing solution was a reliance on native chieftainships despite the problems they caused.[6]

These problems were numerous and complex but generally stemmed from the considerable indigenous autonomy enjoyed by these "native chieftainships" as well as by free-range "wild tribals" (*yeyi*). In large degree, these Qing administrative terms were another variation on the traditional imperial binary of "civilized" (*shu*) and "savage" (*sheng*), or, as in the discourse of smallpox, "raw" and "cooked." Yet differences between wild and chieftainship peoples were often indistinct and even imaginary, as some officials recognized. Liu Bin, a provincial private secretary in the 1710s, wrote that in Yongchang and Shunning prefectures there was no practical difference between wild and chieftainship groups. Both were actually subject to the dynasty "in name only" because they resided in areas such as Gengma where dynastic "law did not reach." One frustrated Yun-Gui governor-general in 1766 even recommended

The Nature of Imperial Indigenism in Southwestern Yunnan   173

that "civilized" chieftainship subjects shave their heads to resemble Han subjects, to distinguish them from their wild counterparts.[7]

Another Yun-Gui governor-general, Belin, summarized dynastic administrators' more conventional views more than a generation later in his discussion of a 1770 "wild people" incursion of Kawa and their collusion with resident "Luohei." Belin said that "wild" stockade settlements "appointed their own chiefs" and were so "widely scattered and loosely tied" that they "could not keep order among ... the violent." Groups, such as the Luohei raiding southern Shunning in 1800, who "had no chiefs and, moreover, were not subjects of Myanmar" were also wild in Qing eyes.[8] Imperial indigenism was a domesticating response to these wild conditions.

Qing descriptions support arguments by E. R. Leach in his classic study of the peoples of the "highland Burma" border region. Leach held that centralized *gumsa* and "anarchic" *gumlao* forms of indigenous political organization among Kachin hill peoples alternated in unstable fashion. Yunnan officials wished to deal exclusively with chieftainship "polities," locally called *muong* (*meng*), run either by *gumsa* Kachin or by valley-dwelling, paddy-cultivating Shan or "Tai."[9] Leach unveiled a bewildering degree of fluidity between these various political and ethnic distinctions, particularly among the Kachin. He concluded that a given group's *gumsa* or *gumlao* (in Qing terms, civilized or wild) affiliations were "not necessarily ascertainable in the realm of empirical facts."[10] The Qing state's political mechanism to eliminate this uncertainty was official confirmation of a Shan *saohpa* (Burmese: *sawbwa*) chieftain's succession. Ethnically ambiguous chieftainships nevertheless remained susceptible to internecine strife or external infiltration by "wild" elements that actually confirmed convictions such as Liu Bin's.[11]

Gumsa and Shan chieftainships were to operate as the spatial fulcrum of an ethnic administrative middle ground. They would balance Han-dominated areas of Yunnan proper and the exclusive abodes of wholly autonomous, or "wild," groups beyond the farthest claims of Qing territory. As in Thongchai Winichakul's conceptualization of Siam's prenational space, chieftainships in southwestern Yunnan constituted an intermediary "inner frontier" of attenuated state authority between a direct state presence on one side and a vacuum of state authority on the other.[12] At various times during the Qing, the southwestern border *junxian* prefectures of Shunning, Pu'er, and Yongchang, along with the latter's important subprefecture of Tengyue (only established in 1820), fluctuated between these three conditions.[13]

174 *Across Forest, Steppe, and Mountain*

Chieftainships were exceptional from the onset of Qing rule, when they were permitted to "temporarily follow their old customs until the region was stabilized." Only gradually would they be "made aware of orthodoxy and slowly compelled to a respectful compliance with the new system" to effect the adoption of "norms and ethics identical" with China proper's.[14] This assimilation process, however, was qualified by security concerns. As provincial military official Zhou Huafeng explained, "China's having native chieftains is like a residence having a fence. If the fence is not secure, then the residence will not be peaceful" and subject to incursion by other indigenous peoples or Myanmar invasion. He also admitted that "the reason that native chieftainships along the border ... all accept our institutions and pay our taxes and labor services without becoming disaffected is because of our state's bountiful favor and virtue and because we dare not recklessly interfere with foreign customs."[15] Such remarks indicate that chieftainships resembled allies more than subjects and were treated accordingly by officials. Human agency and ecological conditions necessitated compromise for the intermittent Qing control of inner frontier chieftainships, which were tied to an unstable concept of indigenous identity as the only option to embody a dynastic presence in an otherwise forbidding disease environment.

Malaria was, in contemporary terms of eighteenth- and nineteenth-century Yunnan, an immutable reality that did not arrest but did structure and constrain human action. The following examination of interaction between disease and human agency takes select environmental conditions into active historical account without allowing them to dictate human actions. Specifically, mosquitoes and haematozoa have contributed to the spatial and ethnic formation of Yunnan's imperial borderlands even as these borderlands were formed by interactions of the region's indigenous peoples, Qing administrators, and Han settlers. Indeed, spatial and identity formations arising from human interaction with disease environments were restricted neither to western Yunnan nor to the Qing empire between the seventeenth and nineteenth centuries.

DISEASE: SOME COMPARATIVE CONSIDERATIONS

Concepts of "biopower" or "biosociality" are some of the more influential approaches to the study of the formation of "health identities," that is, the production of human social diversity based on perceptions of variation in the physical condition of human bodies. It has recently been suggested, however, that the central concern of these approaches with

The Nature of Imperial Indigenism in Southwestern Yunnan   175

identity formation in relatively narrow terms of bodily health may obscure other elements that create health inequalities, including political, economic, and technological factors.[16] Nevertheless, common to all these elements is a focus on human action that effectively excludes nonhuman factors often included as a matter of course in environmental studies. "From an ecological perspective, disease does not exist as a thing in and of itself," but is rather "a process triggered by interaction between a host and an environmental insult, most often a pathogenic organism ... Disease is one possible outcome of the relationship between the host and the potential pathogen." Disease is a relationship involving humans but is not limited to them. The concept of adaptation is central to the analysis of such relations as disease ecology, which views health and disease as measures of the efficacy of human management of "cultural and biological resources [to] adapt to their environments."[17]

Some results of these adaptations are spatial and ethnic. Both malaria and yellow fever, for example, were critical for empire and state formation, as well as that of Creole identity, in the Greater Caribbean. As argued by John Robert McNeill, "differential resistance" enabled acclimated locals to protract defense long enough for more susceptible outside invaders to succumb to disease over a few months of regional military operations. This difference was critical for the persistence of the Spanish empire. It relied heavily on local recruits to hold out against much stronger imperial rivals through the eighteenth century, with yellow fever as "a crucial part of Spain's imperial defense." These diseases gave similar support to subsequent revolutionary movements by acclimated Creoles against further imperial domination.[18]

As McNeill recognizes, humans and ecology entered into distinctive relations to form these historical effects. Yet he goes on to assert that "the disease environment of the Caribbean was a cultural artifact" that would not have existed without the human initiated slave trade that brought both yellow fever and malaria to the New World.[19] Although hardly a deliberate construct and with many of its elements entirely beyond contemporary human calculation, this disease environment was indeed partly the inadvertent creation of human beings. In significant contrast, southwestern Yunnan's disease environment was not an anthropogenic product. It was formed from environmental ties over an extended period that included humans, but was not initiated or substantially directed by them. Imperial indigenism, or the formation of space embodied in chieftainship ethnicity, more closely resembles a cultural artifact, which emerged from these ties. This artifact, however, was not monocultural. Human diversity related differently to regional ecology, resulting in the relative autonomy enjoyed by many indigenous peoples. The core of such autonomy, as Qing authorities recognized, was inextricable from this same ecology.

Disease environments did not always ensure indigenous autonomy in Qing lands, particularly in the period of dynastic subordination to western colonialism. Ignorance of epidemiological factors such as animal vectors could translate into a racialized anthropocentric origination theory for diseases like plague. Subjective western responses to China's "filthy" living conditions and social hygienic deficiencies informed Treaty Port space. The resulting Han identity was a Chinese version of a wider pattern of ethnic interpretations of disease environments under western-influenced colonialism, also visible in the Tokugawa state's vaccination of Ainu for smallpox.[20]

Smallpox was one of the most important diseases on the steppe and accordingly contributed to the formation of space and ethnicity in the Qing northern borderlands. It could mortally devastate indigenous populations and even played a "critical" role in the Qing defeat of the Zunghars.[21] Smallpox, however, conditioned disease environmental relations that were not colonial in the same racially polarized way as in Treaty Ports, and that did not promote indigenous autonomy. These effects were more equitably, if still hierarchically, expressed in Muran, as a venery space that enabled social interaction between people "who had not had smallpox" and metropolitan officials from China proper. Potentially susceptible Mongols from throughout Inner Asia were expressly allowed in this way to attend the Qianlong emperor's 1752 birthday celebrations at Muran.[22]

Inner Asian, like Native American and Ainu, vulnerability was directly related to contrasting environments. Like all epidemic diseases smallpox, usually in the strain of *variola major*, is transmitted by highly evolved microbes. These organisms depend directly and exclusively on vulnerable humans, ideally in large numbers, for reproduction presenting as mass outbreaks that either kill or immunize their hosts. Microbes then wait for the next human reproductive cycle to propagate again. This interdependency of microbe and human reproductive cycles is directly related, so that the more humans there are, the more opportunities for microbe reproduction there will be. Sparsely populated regions like Inner Asia, where conditions that formed pastoral and foraging practices limited the number of people, presented far fewer opportunities for smallpox microbe reproduction. Transhumance, unlike sedentary agriculture and urbanization, also inhibited epidemics by both minimizing the

The Nature of Imperial Indigenism in Southwestern Yunnan   177

accumulation of human waste in living spaces and by limiting the prolonged face-to-face contact through which the disease generally spreads. Once settled, however, people become more vulnerable, often, as in the case of seven Liaodong banner villages in the eighteenth and nineteenth centuries, in direct proportion to their numbers. Overall, a number of social and ecological factors influence microbe and host, both of which may exhibit consequent change over a range of time scales from seasonal to evolutionary, that condition epidemics historically. Thus, an outbreak of "Qing" smallpox would not necessarily involve a microbe strain of the same virulence as a "Ming" outbreak.[23] Some of these factors also contribute to the development of differential resistance.

As Chia-feng Chang explains in detail, Qing authorities carefully regulated interactions between groups with differential resistance. Immunized, mainly Han carriers resident south of the Great Wall posed a threat to those Mongols and Manchus who came from populations resident to the north who had never been adequately exposed to acquire sufficient immunization. There was, of course, not such a neat divide in practice. Some indigenous peoples of the lower SAH, for example, would not venture even as far south as Ilan Hala in Jilin to present their pelt tribute in epidemic years such as 1825. Even before the Qing conquest diplomatic activities, including audiences, sable tribute, and embassies, could be hindered by the participation of individuals who had not yet been infected. The Manchus accordingly made a further distinction between people north of the Great Wall who had survived smallpox, and were therefore immune ("cooked bodies"; *shu shen*), and those who had not yet contracted it ("raw bodies"; *sheng shen*). Hong Taiji cited the vulnerability of his own raw body to avoid an audience in 1638 during an outbreak in his realm.[24]

Already in the 1650s smallpox had become associated with "contamination" from Han people in an urban environment. In culturally relativist terms, it was a "Han" disease. Such perceptions not only helped to reinforce human difference but also began to label postconquest populations in terms of their residence north or south of the Great Wall regardless of any other factors uniting a group across this boundary. So, for example, a 1726 regulation on hunting parties referred to susceptible Chakhar Mongols as those who "had not broken out in smallpox" (*wei chudou*). It made separate provision for their variolation to permit them to mix with "the banner people of China proper," a general reference including Manchus and Mongols.[25] This is one example of intraethnic division arising from Inner Asian diaspora south of the Great Wall that

178   *Across Forest, Steppe, and Mountain*

blended with more cultural influences, disparagingly generalized as "Han contamination," to produce distinctions between borderland and diasporic Manchus.

Like smallpox, malaria could certainly act as an obstacle to human settlement, as it did in much of Lingnan mainly before the Ming, to inhibit Han settlement of the region. Although different from epidemic diseases such as smallpox in terms of vectors and other characteristics, malaria and its disease environment could also reinforce or even help create spatial and ethnic distinctions, as it apparently did in the subtropical foothills of the Nepali Tarai. The Tarai, "virtually synonymous with malaria," was inhabited by the Tharu, "popularly believed to be immune" to this disease environment. Immunity partly conferred ethnic distinction, especially from more susceptible Indian settlers fleeing various natural disasters, on the Tharu.[26]

A broadly similar dynamic seems to have structured relations between Yunnan areas of indigenous and Han residence. In the process, an intraethnic distinction between peoples in and beyond chieftainships formed, based in part on differential resistance. The imperative for the imposition of chieftainship identity on some indigenous peoples was largely rooted in the susceptibility of Han populations to malaria. This precluded the dynasty's normal *junxian* incorporation of southwestern space and so required relatively immune and cooperative intermediaries. The resulting native chieftainships were not wholly imperial cultural constructs, but rather imperial adaptations to preexisting regional environmental relations informed by both nature and culture. This network of imperial indigenism did not integrate well with an emerging imperial arablism.

CULTIVATING BORDERLAND

When Cai Yurong took up his post as Yun(nan)-Gui(zhou) governor-general in 1682, he was faced with the task of restoring order to a distant province that had been in revolt against the central government since 1673. There were fugitives and bandits to be caught, weapons to be confiscated, infrastructure to be repaired and administrative expenses to be met. Yunnan's real problem, however, was organic. In his memorial proposing "Ten Measures for Providing for Yunnan" in the wake of the Three Feudatories Rebellion, Cai located the fundamental problem within "the empire's natural order." Yunnan was saddled with "an abundance of mountains" and hobbled with "a scarcity of fields." Its food supply

The Nature of Imperial Indigenism in Southwestern Yunnan   179

was so constrained in consequence that "a year's harvest can only just provide for the necessities of that year." There was no surplus left to set aside for military emergency or natural disaster, nor were there any viable water or land routes along which supplies from neighboring provinces could be easily brought in.[27] Yunnan was just not natural Hanspace.

The province was also hostile terrain for the usual sort of terraforming to which Han cultivators would normally resort to turn wilderness into paddy. Cai summarized the dynamic relations between disease, population, terrain, and riziculture when he reported that Yunnan's malarial conditions caused high mortality rates to make "wastelands difficult to develop." So "not much rice is produced among its myriad mountains."[28] Provincial authorities would spend the eighteenth century trying to domesticate these relations in service of an imperial indigenism.

One of Cai's immediate and influential solutions was literally to dig beneath the surface of the problem to tap Yunnan's mineral wealth. Reiterating that there was "not much tax revenue" to be found in the province's "mountain clusters and bamboo thickets," Cai proposed a number of mining incentives. So, although Yunnan was "distant and isolated," it did have the advantage of producing "the five metals," especially copper and lead for coinage, which were "not as difficult to appropriate as in other provinces."[29] In this way, underground produce would be used to substitute for provincial revenues unobtainable on the surface.

Unfortunately, mining again exhumed the food problem. At the most basic production level, mining inhibited any agriculture in its immediate vicinity due to the toxic materials produced through mineral extraction and processing. However, mining's stimulation of commercial activity also both increased population and demand for food.[30] By the mid–seventeenth century Cai Yurong's successors were complaining about the high cost of rice directly linked to large populations that were not only concentrated around provincial urban centers, but around mines as well. Yun-Gui governor-general Zhang Yunsui made an indirect reference to the problem in 1748 when he reported that provincial rice prices had been highest in Zhaotong and Dongchuan prefectures, centers of the mining industry, before the opening of the Jinsha River route to the Sichuan traffic. In 1765, Yun-Gui governor-general Liu Zao was overtly seeking to alleviate the high cost of rice in the province's towns and "places where many people congregate at copper and lead mines." Both provincial officials were deeply engaged in an ongoing search for rice sources in and beyond the province. Significantly, Zhang briefly alluded to an important provincial element missing from Cai Yurong's previous summary of Yunnan's natural predicament. He noted that Yunnan was "quite different from other provinces" in that local "tribal peoples" engaged in "slash and burn agriculture" that mostly produced buckwheat at a reasonable price, but "not in great quantities."[31] From an imperial arablist position under pressure, this sort of indigenous cultivation was an unacceptable waste of space.

Mining and food production were intimately related through the eighteenth century in Yunnan, which experienced a large influx of Han immigrants, estimated to have quadrupled the province's population from 5 to 20 million between 1700 and 1850. They were attracted mainly by the region's mineral wealth, which included gems, silver, and other precious metals. However, more mundane metals, primarily copper but also lead, zinc, and tin, were the real basis of provincial urban and commercial development during this period. Copper mining was geographically centered in northeastern Yunnan, particularly in the prefecture of Dongchuan, which by 1746 was producing two-thirds of the province's copper. This wealth kept Qing Yunnan's population expansion and urbanization centered in the east.[32] Western, and especially southwestern, Yunnan remained on the sidelines of the province's mineral-based economic leap forward during the eighteenth century.

The ground gained, however, was far from solid as copper extraction was undermined in the nineteenth century by rising production costs. Food and fuel were especially expensive and in short supply in Yunnan's core development regions. Food was already a critical factor in the mid–eighteenth century. The province's copper mines were generally located in the mountains far from urban commercial areas, so it was necessary to import large amounts of food at great expense to feed the many laborers on site. As food prices began to rise and ore veins petered out or ran too deeply, mining became prohibitively expensive and production dropped off as people abandoned it for other livelihoods.[33]

The insupportably high food and fuel costs linked to the province's major commercial activity and source of revenue foreshadowed the economic and ecological crisis that Yunnan would fall into by the nineteenth century. The formula for this dual crisis, however, went well beyond the apparently straightforward linkage between input costs of food and fuel that exceeded output profits from copper in some official calculations.[34] As originally adumbrated by Cai Yurong, the process of dynastic borderland construction that the Qing pursued in Yunnan was actually a complex coordination of many environmental elements to work plots

The Nature of Imperial Indigenism in Southwestern Yunnan 181

unpropitious for riziculture but full of buried treasure crammed amid crowded peaks laced with disease.

Dynastic authorities would have to respond by cultivating plants and people suitable to the province's environmental conditions that could also be subjected to sufficient administrative control. The tension between Yunnan's diversity and the state's standardizing imperatives narrowed Qing options and required concessions. Reduced to its most basic essentials, the Qing cultivation of the Yunnan borderland was rooted in mining, swidden agriculture, and native chieftainships. As Cai Yurong and other administrators realized, while mining was the best way to incorporate Yunnan into the empire, it remained critically dependent on food and fuel that were locally scarce. Although this deficiency was fitfully offset by expensive imports from other provinces, a more stable solution appeared to be an increase in Yunnan's arable land, which required securing mountainous and malarial areas for arablism. Ideally, security would be provided by chieftainships, swiddening by "shack" people. The deliberations of governors-general Cai, Zhang, and Liu contain references to many of these crucial elements. Their interrelations require further clarification in order to delineate more precisely the boundaries of dynastic borderland cultivation as an adaptation to Yunnan's disease environment.

Swiddening and indigenous settlement, as chieftainships or otherwise, were in many respects interdependent. Writing around 1680 Liu Kun, who had served as a provincial official, described agriculture in Yunnan's chieftainships as "slash and burn. Barley, wheat, oats, buckwheat, and beans were obtained by the plow from high mountains and lofty ranges of narrow paths and dangerous slopes." He distinguished these conditions from the "arable flats and wet fields" where paddy rice was grown by "Yi and Han" lowlanders in the province's center and southeast.[35] There was certainly more than one way to plant a field in Yunnan, and each was often ethnically distinctive in varying degrees, but there were also differences within a single planting regimen that had profound environmental consequences.

Despite the connotations of its more common denomination as "slash and burn," swidden agriculture can be quite sustainable when properly practiced. It is much less ecologically debilitating than the arablist extremes pursued by Han farmers. Recent research has shown that "the swidden cultivator's goal is not to destroy forest, but to obtain a continuous harvest of cultigens while managing the succession toward a new forest of high diversity." The work of Yin Shaoting in particular has demonstrated that southwestern swiddening is a viable adaptation to ecologies rich in sylvan resources and low in population. Yin explains that indigenous farmers did not indiscriminately slash and burn. Instead, they made provisions for sustained use of their resources, conserving forests to maintain shade around villages and conserving water. Land use was collectively regulated, and rotation was practiced. Even stumps were carefully kept alive, and some groups practiced reforestation to deliberately facilitate soil regeneration. These techniques synergistically combined to prevent serious soil erosion that is a common effect of both intensive, Han sedentary agriculture and the comparatively casual swiddening used by shack people to clear mountainous regions in China proper.[36]

Strictly speaking, "shack people" were actually made up of diverse itinerant groups, which could include Hakka, for example. Depending on time and location, the ethnic composition of a given wave of shack people was not necessarily all "Han." Yet in Yunnan's case the cultural, and agricultural, practices of the migrant flood inundating southwestern China from the eighteenth into the nineteenth century were generally characterized in ethnic Chinese terms of various sorts from Jiangxi, Hunan, and Sichuan. Intermixed with them, however, were also "Miao" from Guizhou and Liangguang.[37]

Although the precise proportions of ethnicities remain invisible, the erosive effects of the hillside cultivation pursued by the eighteenth- and nineteenth-century Yunnan migrants as a whole are apparent, as in the lower Yangzi delta highlands, the paradigmatic ground of largely Han shack people activity. Anne Osborne cites some pertinent examples from this region: "In the west of Huzhou, the various mountains extend far into inaccessible gullies and lonely precipices ... [The soil] is not suitable for millet or rice. In the past there were none who farmed it." Sometime around the mid-1790s a group of people finally appeared who wanted to sow the area. These "shack people" came from Wenzhou in Zhejiang to "plant sweet potatoes and peanuts." By the 1830s officials were decrying their ecological effects. "The shack people's reclamation of mountains and planting of crops" was "harmful to agriculture" because it caused hillside erosion that eventually "silted up waterways" downstream.[38] In environmental terms, the sort of unsustainable cultivation that went on at both ends of the empire was "Han-style," regardless of the actual ethnicity or nominal designations of its practitioners.

There appear in some cases, nevertheless, to have been critical ethnic distinctions. Southeastern Yunnan's "Miao" migrants may have taken up

The Nature of Imperial Indigenism in Southwestern Yunnan 183

particular, disease-determined niches within the larger mountainscape then being opened to cultivation. In Kaihua prefecture forming part of Yunnan's southeastern border with Vietnam, "Miao moved to dwell in the cliffs and bamboo stands ... scattered along the malarial border area."[39] This is evidence from beyond the southwestern core of Yunnan of the larger disease environment's structuralizing effects on provincial migration and agricultural development patterns. Differential resistance let Miao cultivators break ground, possibly Han-style, in places where Han farmers themselves could not.

These Miao had a choice between Han-style and indigenous swiddening, with critical implications for Yunnan's basic ecological and political structure. Han-style swiddening would have caused rapid deforestation that would eliminate arable land on the mountainside within a few years and erode more downstream later. Farmers would have to move on, pursuing an ultimately rootless existence that prevented any territorial consolidation. Indigenous-style swiddening, in contrast, protected tree cover to preserve soil for long-term residence around which imperial indigenist chieftainships could form.

Swiddening was a critical dimension of indigenous ethnic identity for adaptation to regional ecological conditions. The dynamics of the "region" in this instance extend well beyond Yunnan and other subsections controlled at various times by various states. This dense cluster of highlands of lands and peoples at altitudes above three hundred meters or so stretches across Southeast Asia to northeastern India. James C. Scott has recently explored this transnational territory of "Zomia," also known to geographers as the Southeast Asian Mainland Massif. He has found it a haven of "self-governing" hill peoples whose every expression from kinship to cultivation manifests opposition to state control in general and "the precocious Han-Chinese state" in particular. Scott conceives of this opposition as a series of deliberate political "adaptations designed to evade both state capture and state formation" as a response of "nonstate peoples to a world of states that are, at once, attractive and threatening." He even accords upland crops a role in indigenous resistance, arguing that roots and tubers are especially "appropriation-proof" against centralizing state tax collectors. They can, for example, be left in the ground for up to two years after ripening. Would-be confiscators are thus denied the easy access afforded them by conventional granaries full of already processed revenue in kind. Cultivators in Burma in the 1980s and in Ireland in the early nineteenth century liked potatoes partly because they were not cost-effective for the state to root out.[40]

Moreover, swiddening of New World hillside crops such as potatoes as well as Old World cultivars such as taro is quite compatible with Zomia's forested conditions. Yunnan abounded in obstacles to wet rice cultivation, the preferred ground of the Chinese imperial dynastic order. Even when rice was regionally cultivated throughout the Yun-Gui plateau, it was overwhelmingly of the glutinous variety rather than those long-grained types preferentially grown and consumed in China proper. Glutinous rice was more suited to the wide fluctuations in temperature and rainfall characteristic of this region, part of what has been called the "glutinous rice zone" of continental Southeast Asia. The simple techniques required to cultivate glutinous rice also were more suitable for the preservation of the forests that constituted the most critical resource for long-term indigenous subsistence. Politically, glutinous rice, because of the greater difficulties in processing, transportation, and storage, made the staple a "potato-like" medium of taxation. Qing authorities repeatedly and unsuccessfully tried to force indigenous farmers to switch to more accessible standard Chinese varieties. Moreover, imperial troops, as the main regional beneficiaries of state taxation in kind, preferred nonglutinous varieties.[41]

The importance of forest for general subsistence throughout the region was a main motivation for even lowland rice cultivators such as the Shan to engage in reforestation. A single village stand, properly managed, could sustainably provide for inhabitants for around a century without recourse to clear-cutting.[42] In locales such as southwestern Yunnan, rice cultivation in general remained viable largely because it was glutinous; that is, riziculture was not intensively practiced at the imperial Chinese scale. Deforestation was thereby minimized and catastrophic erosion avoided. One recent study has correlated an upsurge in provincial ecological problems with land clearance and related resource exploitation, arising from Han migration, especially in the nineteenth century.[43] It is likely that the combination of sustainable swidden and glutinous cultivation, along with limitations of the regional disease environment, constrained indigenous population growth. So migration alleviated the primary pressure existing in densely populated China proper for more intensive forms of cultivation and the space in which to conduct them.

Shack people practiced perhaps the least sustainable form of Han intensive cultivation in Yunnan, an activity that even affected more conventional Han agriculture. Anne Osborne has described how the land-hungry migrants of her study brought "new techniques and crops which would exploit" agriculturally marginal slopes "through a

The Nature of Imperial Indigenism in Southwestern Yunnan 185

distinctive adaptation to the highland environment." Unfortunately, this adaptation relied on ephemeral forms of shifting cultivation, causing deforestation and erosion that "threatened the stability of the [existing] agricultural ecosystem". Moreover, shack people's maintenance of their constituent environmental relations led to "a downward spiral of reclamation, abandonment and new reclamation which threatened agricultural and social stability" both in the marginal hills and in the lowland cores.[44] This Han-style swiddening, far less sophisticated and sustainable than the "slash and burn" practices of hill peoples in the southwest, was a product of new relations between cultivators and new world crops that created a new identity, shack people, that the state found difficult to incorporate.

The ecological effects of the development of shack people identity threatened to erode the agrarian basis of the more established Han identity in parts of China proper. Liu Min's study argues that this threat to the empire's main grain production areas was the primary reason for state control of shack people in the lower Yangzi.[45] Much of Yunnan, however, had not yet made the transition into fully developed arablism, and its attendant Han peasant embodiment was in commensurate flux. Although major cultivation had begun with the first wave of Han migrants in the preceding Yuan-Ming period, fields were largely restricted to valleys. It was only with the second wave during the Qing, surging roughly between 1775 and 1825, that hillsides came under widespread cultivation.[46] Consequently, shack people's activities, focused on "virgin" hillsides, were initially more disruptive to indigenous swiddening in the mountains than to conventional Han settlers working the lands well below.

A starkly instructive contrast between Han and indigenous land use in Yunnan comes from an 1845 account of Han settlers' intensive cultivation of mushrooms on hillsides they occupied in Yongbei and Dayao. The traditional approach of indigenous Lisu and others was simply to gather mushrooms produced from natural timber falls. The Han way was to "fell large trees an armful in diameter ... pare off their top branches and chisel twenty to thirty holes in their trunks." Then the holes would be stuffed with "fine ash ... and a small quantity of a mixture containing the powder of the ground stipes of old mushrooms ... and cold rice gruel." After covering the logs with foliage to provide sufficient shade, a small crop of a few dozen mushrooms would spring up in one to two years, with a large crop of thousands in four to five years, to form a "red mountain" (*hongshan*). The trunks, however, rotted within a decade or so, leaving the mountains entirely denuded. The consequent soil erosion

186   *Across Forest, Steppe, and Mountain*

made further production impossible, including indigenous swiddening and foraging activities. Christian Daniels has argued such processes had the ethnohistoric consequences of either assimilating indigenous peoples to Han practices or forcing them to migrate over considerable distances.[47]

Statements from Qing officials themselves occasionally confirm their entertainment of notions of a deliberate assimilationist agenda teleologically realized through arablist and related mechanisms. These ideals would not have normally included the Han-style swiddening of shack people, considered a pernicious nuisance by some officials in China proper. Local Yunnan officials, however, seemed enthusiastic about any agrarian conversion of their ground by Han of any sort at the expense of what they saw as inferior indigenous agriculture. This sort of arablist opportunism would rebound against state-sponsored fields in the nineteenth century.

Many attitudes of the Qing and other states in the southwest were, and are, rooted in a conviction that it is effectively a space with a negligible degree of order, that it has had virtually no significance as a distinct cultural or natural region before the arrival of the state, and that it is essentially primordial. This impression was probably reinforced in Yunnan during the late dynastic period by periodic incursions "wild people" (*yeren*). They occasionally appear in Ming and Qing chronicles mainly as undesirable intruders from the *Yerenshan* (Wild People Mountains) in northwestern Tengyue. These groups have been identified as the Kachin branch of the official PRC ethnic minority of the Jingpo. So they were not synonymous with multiethnic successor groups of "wild tribals," who may have begun the introduction of Kachin *gumlao* practices that later periodically appear among these successors. Records indicate that this "race" (*zhongren*), clad in tree bark, fur, and bone circlets, had originally lived beyond Yunnan "unrestrained by headmen." They began no later than the Ming Wanli period (1573–1620) to gradually intermix with inner frontier groups.[48] Resulting conglomerations of Kachin and Shan decentralized and centralized political cultures persisted into the twentieth century.[49] "Civilized" elements were not absorbing "wild" elements, and the ensuing expression of any *gumlao* ethnic identity caused only further administrative confusion because it was not "racially" restricted. Instead it became the characteristic political culture of various contemporary indigenous peoples such as the Lahu, Lisu, and Mang.

During the Qianlong reign, "wild tribals" was a term attached to the Lisu during their incursions from the interstices of southwestern chieftainships into Lijiang, Dali, and Yongchang as well as to the Mang during their eastward incursions into Pu'er and Shunning. In the succeeding Jiaqing

The Nature of Imperial Indigenism in Southwestern Yunnan 187

reign, the Luohei's activities in gaps between chieftainships and *junxian* jurisdictions in southern Shunning and Pu'er triggered three major uprisings between 1796 and 1814.[50] Belin's encounters with the Luohei and Kawa during his 1804–14 governor-generalship informed his observation that the malarial conditions of their zones made assault with anything but chieftainship auxiliaries impossible. The Luohei "lairs" he mapped out on both sides of the Lancang stretch of the Mekong River boundary between Shunning and Pu'er, however, were well within the inner frontier chieftainships supposed to keep the wild at bay.[51] Imperial indigenist space was also hosting wild infestations that would leave Yunnan proper exposed.

Consequently, the Qing had to cultivate a particular type of political ground within this disease environment, in the more centralized forms of Kachin *gumsa* and Shan organizations, but state efforts did not blossom into a stable borderland. Even the centralized chieftainships were unacceptably disruptive, in the view of some officials, precisely because they had hereditary or "feudal" (*fengjian*) rulers. Hereditary succession made bloody, divisive succession struggles inevitable and obstructed the removal of established chiefs by any means short of war.[52]

Chronic conflict was a main rationale for campaigns, peaking in the Yongzheng reign, to replace native chieftainships with central state administrations (*gaitu guiliu*). Perhaps the most radical Qing attempt to expand Yunnan proper, along with similar expansions in Guizhou and Sichuan, this conversion effort was led by the famous Qing official and imperial confidant Ortai as governor-general of Yun-Gui. His deployment of more than one hundred thousand troops in a series of bloody and controversial conversion operations against what he called "the frontier's great scourge" can easily give the impression that Ortai wanted to eradicate indigenous rule throughout southwestern China.[53]

In practice, Yunnan's disease environment helped to preclude such extremes, as some limited statistics suggest. Out of an estimated 220 native chieftainships abolished during the Yongzheng reign, only seventeen were located in Yunnan and only four in southwestern prefectures, which were otherwise untouched by Yongzheng conversion operations. Ortai himself had explicitly put chieftainships west of the Mekong ("Lancang") River, namely, those in Shunning and probably southern Yongchang, effectively out of conversion bounds before operations started in 1726. The southwesternmost two of the four converted chieftainships, located in what would become Tengyue, were even restored in 1771. Conversion operations

188 *Across Forest, Steppe, and Mountain*

in Yunnan and elsewhere in southwestern China were extremely limited in terms of full abolition, although local powers were generally curtailed.[54]

Whatever their limits, conversion operations attracted the relatively boundless support of local arablization advocates such as provincial administration commissioner for Yun-Gui, Chang Deshou. Chang complained in 1726 that only 30 to 40 percent of Yun-Gui's arable land, including mountainous terrain, lay in *junxian* jurisdictions. The remaining 60 to 70 percent was controlled by chieftains who "don't know how to coordinate things." The chieftains, ruling "Yi people who know nothing of cultivation," were nominally subject to minimal, largely indifferent, and entirely indirect supervision from subprovincial *junxian* officials. Others denigrated indigenous peoples as generally unfit to manage all their rich natural resources, from minerals to timber.[55]

Chang's was only one expression of the rather conventionally dim Han official view of indigenous agriculture, which was quite dismissive of its efforts, especially in terms of scale. From the perspective of the imperial Chinese state these practices were not legitimately "agricultural" in the same sense as Han cultivation because swiddening failed to maximize exploitation of arable land. Wang Lüjie's exaggerated accusation that indigenous peoples in Guizhou's "Miao frontier" had "excellent fields, but did not know how to plow and possessed extraordinary resources but did not use them" must be read in this context. In 1732, Huguang's Provincial Military Commander (*tidu*) Yue Chaolong exaggerated in similar spirit that "places ripe for agricultural clearance are extremely numerous, but the hill country is comparatively vast. The Miao lack the power to fully exploit the land for cultivation (*bianzhong*) and so abandon it entirely, something deeply to be regretted." Radical agricultural clearance on a sufficiently enhanced scale was proposed in the wake of the Yongzheng chieftainship conversion operations. Ortai wanted to secure them in part by "clearing brush and burning out mountains and marshes, which are all long-term plans of prime urgency for frontier provinces." Furthermore, isolated enclaves of fewer than three households, "whether Han commoner or tribal" would be relocated closer together to form more administratively legible *baojia* units. This tactic would effectively narrow the range of environmental relations, and ultimately ethnic identities, permissible under a comparatively full-blown imperial arablist regime.[56]

Such a regime for the transformation of land and people seems to have been successfully implemented in Yunnan's Zhaotong prefecture, a main center of Yongzheng conversion operations. According to Yun-Gui Governor-General Gao Qizhuo, there was "a kind of indigene" in Zhaotong

The Nature of Imperial Indigenism in Southwestern Yunnan   189

of the civilized [shu] Miao sort, who hitherto did not much cultivate paddy rice. All of them were ordered to form tenant households to pay taxes and supply food [presumably thorough paddy cultivation]. These people were diligent in cultivation and their nature was quite honest and open. Now they can no longer be classed as Yi households and can properly augment cultivation.[57]

This "civilizing" of the Zhaotong Yi was the ethnic outcome of an arablist process that Gao had envisioned during his tenure. He began with a relatively limited notion in 1724–25. Greater state direction of local salt mines would "steadily transform and rectify" restive indigenous peoples scattered across the Yuanjiang, Zhenyuan and Pu'er prefectural border region "until this nesting place for wild bandits can be changed over time into *neidi* [i.e., Yunnan proper, or Hanspace]."[58] This process, however, was merely an adjunct to the larger arablist dream with which Gao concluded his deliberations that can stand for the Qing state's own ideal agenda for the proper conduct of environmental relations in the southwest:

In the native fields of Weiyuan, Pu'er, and the Mekong region there is to be found a richness that far surpasses the core regions of Yunnan province. Their mountaintops abound in water and their grains ripen twice annually. Yet forsaken lands are extremely vast generally because the indigenous tribals are few and so unable to fully exploit the land for cultivation. Moreover, the disturbances of wild bandits preclude a peaceful existence from year to year.

If these native fields are completely opened up, there will not only be a sufficiency of supply for military rations, but the area can be transformed into a paradise [letu]. There are yet places where departments and districts can be established, but there are currently very few households, and the malaria [yanzhang] of the riverbanks is not yet dissipated. So there is no question of haste; plans should be made gradually.

I, in conjunction with Yunnan Governor Yang Mingshi, have ordered local officials of the various locales to advise the tribals in their jurisdictions to engage in widespread cultivation. I have also ordered them to induce people from other places who sincerely wish to do so to come here and clear lands for cultivation. I therefore request, in accordance with regulations established in 1723, that dry fields so cleared not be taxed for a decade. As the density of human habitation steadily flourishes, the mists and miasmas will dissipate on their own; as the residents increase, banditry will be quelled commensurately.[59]

Indigenous peoples, friendly or not, and disease constitute the two main obstacles to arablization, and therefore incorporation, of Yunnan as a Hanspace *letu*. Gao's solution was the intensification of relations apparently based on increasing the population of Han-style agriculturalists, but that ultimately relied on an ecological abundance of water, rich soil, and the right climate to ensure a firm foundation

190 *Across Forest, Steppe, and Mountain*

for this paradise. However, variation in disease and cultivation inhibited incorporation of Yunnan borderlands via the concentrated multiplication of Han agrarian identity. Plans such as Gao's notwithstanding, indigenous peoples like the "wild bandits" of 1724 and indigenous disease continued, separately and jointly, to maintain a diversity that the imperial order could not fully amalgamate within its arablist agenda. Like swiddening, malaria staked out boundaries that the Qing state found difficult to cross without local assistance organized under a regime of imperial indigenism.

MALARIA: AN ENDEMIC ARBITER OF BORDERLAND SPACE

It is not always possible to link *zhangqi* and related terms to malaria over centuries throughout China. Yet it is also unwarranted to read every such reference as a Han cultural construct of an impenetrable miasma of febrile diseases pervading Chinese records.[60] Cultural reification and essentialization of disease often ignores more complex ecological dimensions. Malaria can, for example, cause an immune system to "go into overdrive in its attempts to kill the [blood] parasites." The host is left vulnerable to other febrile diseases such as blackwater fever, a lethal complication arising from falciparum malarial infection likely related to an autoimmune response.[61] Other implausible suspects for *zhangqi*, such as lymphatic filariasis, are asymptomatic in most people infected and appear only years later in a minority of cases. The main issue is not how many diseases vectors transmit, but which diseases so transmitted are pertinent to the inquiry.[62]

An environmental analysis must consider the combination of ecological and cultural factors, including climate, elevation, water, haematozoa, mosquitoes, human physiology, social relations, and printed materials interacting to form *zhangqi*. Scale, however, qualifies these elements. It is not necessary here to demonstrate that every manifestation of *zhangqi* across hundreds of years and square kilometers was malarial. It is simply sufficient to show that the disease environment centered in southwestern Yunnan during the Qing was primarily malarial, especially in terms of mortality rates, for the development of a borderland imperial indigenism. It is inarguable that a number of social, political, and economic factors contributed to the construction of the Qing regional order. Yet it is equally clear that specific environmental factors, such as malaria, limited this enterprise considerably. Dynastic officials themselves noted quite explicitly the administrative constraints created by disease, which

The Nature of Imperial Indigenism in Southwestern Yunnan 191

blocked the advance of Han *junxian* jurisdictions to perpetuate native chieftainship rule.

Qing authorities grudgingly admitted the indispensability of chieftainships, usually with the justification that "these chieftains are not just a source of distress, but are actually our fence without which there would be no stability." Ortai himself did not seek the eradication of all chieftainship officers, especially low-ranking ones, under all circumstances. He even acknowledged in 1727 "that in pacifying the Yi, one must use Sinified (*hanhua*) Yi to govern them in their own fashion." A critical reason for this limited conversion from local to central rule was the conviction that environmental conditions in key locales made long-term residence impossible for Han Chinese, or indeed for any nonindigenous personnel. Officials used equally conventional terms to describe conditions in Tengyue's chieftainship territory: "Regular officials cannot be put there because it is a land of malaria." Ortai even confirmed that "the Ming's former division of the area into native- and central government-controlled zones originally arose from the new frontier's malarial (*yanzhang*) climate, to which Chinese officials were not accustomed."[63]

Zhang, a southern Chinese term, and *nüe*, its northern Chinese counterpart, can both refer to a variety of febrile diseases, with the specific illnesses determined by context. *Yanzhang* was doubtless used in such a general sense in formulating the highest degree of military life exile under Qing law: sentence "to an insalubrious" (*yanzhang*) region of Yunnan, Guizhou, Guangxi, or Guangdong. By 1772 penal officials had decided that imposing such a sentence on serious offenders was excessively unwieldy, in part because of the patchy fact that "not every department and district" within these four provinces "was insalubrious." But earlier applications of this statute make clear that before 1772, exile to an insalubrious region was intended to be literally a "near-death" sentence, carried out by the febrile diseases present. In 1770, for example, a Qing deserter from the Myanmar campaigns was explicitly exiled to Yunnan's Pu'er prefecture, where "*yanzhang* was most severe."[64]

Before 1936, it was impossible to confirm that the term *yanzhang* and its variants such as *zhangqi*, appearing in many southwestern accounts (including Ortai's), generally referred to malaria. An epidemiology of malaria did not emerge until 1880, when it was demonstrated that the hematozoan *Plasmodium*, a parasite found in blood, caused the disease. It took another twenty years before researchers understood that the parasites were being transmitted to humans via the female mosquito of the genus *Anopheles*. Not until thirty-five years later, in 1935–36, was malaria scientifically confirmed endemic to Yunnan, as well as Guizhou. Appalled at the casualties that a disease identified by southwestern provincials as *zhangqi* was causing among his troops during anticommunist operations, Chiang Kai-shek dispatched a team to investigate. The team determined that *zhangqi* was, in the vast majority of cases, falciparum malaria, which caused more deaths in Yunnan than all other diseases combined.[65]

Such lethally intimate experience with regional ecological conditions more than 160 years previously had already compelled officers of Qing banner units operating on the Yunnan-Myanmar border to make more specific distinctions. Their Manchu reports generally blamed *ehe sukdun*, "foul vapors," literally *mala aria*, that pervaded the region for causing a range of illness among the troops. Yet one 1769 report characterized *ehe sukdun* as a distinct disease, stating that "although there has been no outbreak of "foul vapors," there have been general outbreaks of dysentery (Ma: *hefeliyenere*), malaria (Ma: *indehen*), and chills and fever (Ma: *shahūrun halhūn*)." This report must qualify absolute equation of malaria with miasmatic terms, but also imprecisely considers symptoms as a distinct disease. It may likewise obscure outbreaks of cerebral malaria as "a fever that works within and an external chill," often accompanied by "dizziness and raving," leaving some "unable to speak at all."[66]

Southwestern Yunnan's main malarial vector, the mosquito *Anopheles minimus*, plays host to the blood parasite *Plasomdium falciparum* in the process of the insect's reproductive cycle. Female mosquitoes generally need a blood to initiate their own egg production, and they can transmit *P. falciparum* as they feed over the few weeks of their lifespan. Once injected into a human body, *P. falciparum* infects the liver to begin its own reproductive cycle. The parasites develop, then enter the bloodstream to multiply and cause symptoms that include chills, fever, and sweating and lead to other complications. *P. falciparum*'s capacity for infecting thousands of blood cells in only a few days renders it the most virulent form of the disease, which includes three other strains transmitted by *Anopheles*, the species *P. vivax*, *P. malariae*, and *P. ovale*. The cycle is complete when *An. minimus* feeds on infected humans, who then host sexually mature parasites that move to breed asexual offspring within the gut of the mosquito. In untreated humans, cerebral malaria can develop to afflict the brain, inducing mental problems. It is the most common lethal form of malarial infection of the central nervous system. Its range of

The Nature of Imperial Indigenism in Southwestern Yunnan   193

symptoms culminate in coma accompanied by fever with a mortality rate of 25 to 50 percent, which occurs within one to three days in untreated cases. Even those in recovery can suffer acute psychoses and other "post-malaria neurological syndromes."[67]

So "malaria" is in substantial measure a reification of complex inter-connections that appear as a particular range of febrile diseases in humans. It is, thus, more accurate to speak of a malarial, or even more precisely a *P. falciparum*, disease environment in southwestern Yunnan. Accounts that stress the imprecise nature of *zhangqi* tend to construct malaria in essentialized terms that obscure the diversity of these relations and their multiple effects on human physiology. It is true that malarial relations were hardly the only ones constituting western Yunnan's larger disease environment. Yunnan also contains several subareas of "enzootic foci," breeding grounds for plague bacilli transmitted to humans mainly through fleas on animal hosts, especially rodents. However, the muddle made of these distinctions and relations by premodern Chinese culture, which could distinguish between *zhangqi* as a climate condition and outbreaks of "plague" (*yi*) as omens, can be exaggerated, if not dismissed.[68]

Yunnan's malarial disease environment is further complicated by the diversity and adaptability of mosquitoes themselves. *An. minimus* is just one of many species indigenous to southwestern China, but it is the main vector for malarial haematozoa across Southeast Asia, including south-western China.[69] *An. minimus* nevertheless remains so taxonomically muddled that it is currently impossible to identify all members of what specialists call the "Minimus Complex," which definitely includes two mainland Southeast Asian malarial species, *An. miminus* A and C. Further complicating factors include each species' varying rate of malarial transmission, their different abilities to acclimate to control measures, etc. These are all related to geographical differences in the highly adaptable complex that is apparently scattered from eastern India to Taiwan. The preference of the complex for ideal breeding conditions near slowly running clear water with partially shaded grassy margins commonly found among foothills can leave *An. miminus* vulnerable to both human intervention and ecological fluctuation, particularly deforestation. However, the presence of breeding populations in urban areas in Vietnam and India suggests that *An. miminus* can flourish within a considerable range of conditions, so anthropogenic change has not always been hostile to it. British India's large-scale irrigation projects notoriously replicated malarial disease environments, with a subsequent increase in human mortality rates among previously uninfected populations. In like manner, another *P. falciparum* vector, *Anopheles gambiae*, took advantage of a series of British dam projects in Egypt that increased its breeding habitat and, lifted by airplanes, spread it well beyond its normal two-mile range. Cross-border contact with Myanmar, including migrant labor, has also proliferated *P. falciparum* in southwestern Yunnan. Other recent findings from southern Yunnan confirm that certain anthropogenic changes, such as irrigation and construction of potable water channels near dwellings, can actually expand *An. miminus* habitat.[70]

Confusion over the precise biology and ecology of the Minimus Complex has been an obstacle to public health measures throughout its range. The complexity of the complex continues to ensure that Yunnan remains one of the only two provinces in China where the disease environment for falciparum malaria persists. Malaria is endemic primarily among minority peoples in mountain and forested areas in the province's southern and southwestern extremities.[71] In sum, *Anopheles'* marked predilection for human blood (its "anthropophilic" tendency) as a vital component of its reproductive cycle is the basis for the human-mosquito relationship that in turn transmits *P. falciparum* to form a human-haematozoon relationship. Both sets of relations are conditioned by the larger environmental context of southwestern Yunnan.

Accounts from 1679 and 1935–36 present strong evidence that these environmental dynamics in southwestern Yunnan constituted a malarial disease environment where the regional version of *zhangqi* was primarily, if not exclusively, falciparum malaria and its related conditions. The seventeenth-century Manchu report, moreover, proves that a single indiscriminate term such as *zhangqi* or *ehe sukdun* was not always used to slur over the range of diseases that afflicted dynastic personnel in the area. The multilingual documentation of the Qing is one way to transcend the limitations of the Han record and of monocultural linguistic arguments about the inconsistency of *zhangqi*. The state could make finer, if still problematic, nosological distinctions.

Other important distinctions also emerge from these reports. The Nationalist medical team believed that malaria had originally reached Yunnan from the south and west. They also found that locals in both provinces believed themselves to be more immune to malaria than outsiders. Although not expressing skepticism about that belief in their published report, the team did put it in the same category as popular notions that eels, toads, or butterflies were carriers.[72]

The Nature of Imperial Indigenism in Southwestern Yunnan   195

These beliefs had emerged from a long Chinese struggle with malaria that can be traced back to at least the third century BCE. Remedies had a similarly long history, perhaps best summarized in the Guizhou proverb "Don't get up early, don't eat too much, and don't bathe." Limited eating and drinking was also a general prescription for malaria and related illness among troops fighting Myanmar. Local officials were said to "dwell in the mountains" to avoid the disease. Both Han and indigenous peoples even came to consider opium smoking a prophylactic during the nineteenth century. Indeed, by this time, malaria, opium, and indigenous ethnicity had become conflated in the term *manyan*, a two-character word that could mean either the miasmas (*yan*) considered characteristic of regions of southwestern indigenous (*man*) habitation, or the opium "smoke" (*yan*) drifting into China from foreign (*man*) sources.[73] All these measures probably reflect a general shift from palliative to preventive treatments of malaria in initial response to the geographic and regnal transition from the Northern to the Southern Sung dynasties. As the empire expanded south of the Yangzi, it had to confront the new and more virulent malarial strains present in central and south China. Northern Chinese were believed to be particularly "unaccustomed" to the "malarial wildernesses of the south," but by the Ming-Qing period, the disease was centered in Yunnan.[74]

Racist interpretations of the effects of differential resistance to tropical disease between colonized peoples and Euro-American colonizers were mainstays of imperialist discourse. These effects, which could leave one group untouched while devastating the other, proved to colonizers lacking in concepts of immunology that there was "a profound biological difference between them and non-Europeans."[75] Yet its pedigree does not necessarily render this idea exclusively western or even entirely inaccurate. Malaria did present as differential resistance between indigenous peoples and newcomers to southwestern China, although along genetic, rather than ethnic or "racial," lines. Sickle-cell anemia and thalassemia are examples of genetic disorders from Africa and China, respectively, that affect globin protein chains of hemoglobin. These conditions are characteristic of certain populations and are thought to be hereditary adaptations to resist malaria. Such abnormal hemoglobins are more common in southern than northern China. One 1987 national study of nine hundred thousand subjects found that Yunnan's rate of 6.06 percent was roughly fifteen times the concentration of such disorders in the next largest rate of 0.41 percent, found in both Xinjiang and Fujian. These hemoglobin genetic disorders are one of the human traits arising from southwestern Yunnan's disease environment that conferred a greater resistance, if by no means total immunity, on indigenous peoples.[76] Hemoglobin genetic disorders are a human response to southwestern Yunnan's disease environment.

Swidden agriculture may have helped to produce this environment by making malaria endemic. Frank B. Livingstone's classic anthropological study of this connection in West Africa indicated that the employment of iron tools for swiddening effectively increased the breeding ground for *Anopheles gambiae*, the regional falciparum malaria vector. Swiddening increased the density of human populations and reduced shaded areas avoided by the insects to expand the blood supply and space available for *A. gambiae*'s reproduction. Incidence of the defensive human genetic adaptation of sickle-cell anemia increased in response. Livingstone also showed a lower incidence of malaria and genetic adaptations among foragers who do not practice swiddening and who, therefore, had not accidentally built a disease environment in response to local ecology. One 1932 study found *A. gambiae* numbers actually increased when a forest was cut down and dropped during subsequent reforestation. Similar environmental dynamics may also have been operative in southwestern Yunnan. The affinity of certain *Anopheles* species for environments transformed by humans would help explain the persistence of regional malarial ties despite the radical terraforming by Han cultivation.[77]

In sum, observations by Qing subjects and Nationalist citizens regarding the superior resistance of southwestern provincials to the most lethal form of malaria endemic to the region has a basis in current scientific understanding. A 1943 study of the disease in Mangshi confirmed a much higher incidence of chronic malaria among Chinese than among indigenous residents. Of course, it is necessary to qualify observations that tend to overgeneralize in racial terms and so can easily give the false impression that Han residence in southwestern Yunnan's malarial disease environment was impossible in all circumstances. Some accounts note the particular susceptibility of "migrants" (*liuyu*). Yet, in at least one instance, Ortai demonstrated his own understanding that resistance to malaria was not so determined and thus did not constitute an immutable distinction between Han and local peoples. In 1726, responding to fears that a proposed site of walled construction in Yuanjiang prefecture might be malarial, he pointed out that Yuanjiang had been under *junxian*, and, so, Han, control since 1660. Over time, "both gentry and commoners" had become "acclimated" (*xiguan*) to the disease.[78]

The Nature of Imperial Indigenism in Southwestern Yunnan 197

Casualty lists from the Myanmar campaign reports strongly suggest differential resistance among multiethnic soldiery, although varying external conditions experienced by different units doubtless played a role as well. The possible 1769 outbreak of cerebral malaria previously referred to, for example, affected all troops. However, it was said to have "devastated" Solon-Ewenki and Oirad troops from Manchuria whereas regular "Manchu" troops, probably from garrisons in China proper, and Han Green standard men were comparatively less afflicted. The report concluded that "the Solon and Oirad are unsuited to local environmental conditions [Ma: *muke boihon de acharakū*], and they simply cannot stand the heat. Since they still don't know how to control their eating and drinking, many die in consequence."[79]

"Many" could range among highs such as the 48.5 percent mortality suffered by a detachment of 307 Orochun troops from northern Manchuria serving in the borderland in 1670 after hostilities formally ended or the crippling 83 percent visited on a detachment of 2,008 "hunting Solon" the same year. These "deaths from illness" (Ma: *nimeku aku oho*) were in stark contrast to deaths from wounds, about 0.006 percent in the Orochun unit's case. Although the precise causes are unspecific in these cases, the overall context of reports on Inner Asian casualties mainly relates them to febrile disease in general and *indehen* in particular. Of course, Han troops were far from immune. One late 1769 report stated that the "quite extreme" malarial season that year had lasted through the winter, sparing only about thirteen thousand out of an original thirty thousand green standard and one thousand Manchu troops, a mortality rate of 42 percent. The men were withdrawn to higher ground, leaving lowlands for chieftainships to garrison. Such hard and fast numbers doubtless informed general impressions, such as that expressed by Liu Kun no later than 1680, that malarial conditions along Yunnan's rivers could inflict a 90 percent mortality rate on garrisons within a year, leaving only debilitated survivors. This estimate proved accurate nearly ninety years later in 1766–67 as a Qing garrison stationed in the Menggen chieftainship endured an 80 percent mortality rate, with an additional 10 percent ill. An imperial edict rejected these rates as "not credible" and insisted they were from combat. By 1770, however, the Qianlong emperor himself was advocating reliance on chieftainship auxiliary garrisons to replace regular troops who could not stand the region's "foul" conditions.[80]

Such experiences formed part of the working assumptions of Qing southwestern administrators that indigenous peoples were more

198 *Across Forest, Steppe, and Mountain*

resistant to malaria than Han Chinese, Mongols, or Manchus. The Qianlong emperor was sufficiently concerned about the disease environment's anticipated effects on his forces moving into Myanmar that he sent magic charms against miasma to be distributed throughout the army.[81] As a result of the interaction between these ecological and cultural elements, malaria fundamentally conditioned the adaptive response of differentially immune administrative space in Yunnan. Accounts generally characterized Yongchang chieftainships, for example, as areas of intense malaria, in contrast to *junxian* districts such as Yongping notably free of the disease. One account is quite explicit about connections between terrain, chieftainships, and malarial conditions, stating that "the climate in chieftainship areas is generally insalubrious, with conditions in the flatlands being much worse than those in the mountains." The fifteen *muong* in the Lin'an prefectural jurisdiction; ten in Pu'er; Shunning's Gengma and Mengmeng; Yongchang's Mengding, Lujiang, Wandian, and Denggeng; and Tengyue's Mangshi, Zhefang, Mengmao, and Longchuan chieftainships were "all famous malarial (*yanzhang*) areas," through which anyone from "the interior" (*neidi*) would be afraid to traverse in summer.[82] Table 9 lists areas recorded as unambiguously, if not uniformly, malarial. Native chieftainships predominate.

These dangerous paths also restricted Qing forays into the outer frontier, as demonstrated by the Qing military reports during the Myanmar campaigns, as well as prevented units from maintaining the inner frontier garrisons established in their wake. Another Manchu military report from 1769 concerns the shift of garrison troops from chieftainship areas of Zhefang, Zhanda, and Longchuan "in the season when foul vapors rose" in early February to areas in Tengyue that remained unaffected. Still another report reveals that locals considered malarial conditions in 1769 to be much less severe than in previous years, permitting shifts to relatively nearby areas that would otherwise have been insalubrious. Nevertheless, even in such a comparatively mild year, certain areas, such as Mangshi and Zhefang that were singled out in this report, remained off-limits and still required troop rotations.[83]

The regional disease environment affected both active military operations and passive garrison duties. Malaria figured prominently in Yun-Gui Governor-General Yin-ji-shan's reconstruction proposal in the wake of the costly Pu('er)-Si(mao)-Yuan(jiang)-Xin(ping) uprising that rocked northern Pu'er and central Yuanjiang prefectures from 1732 to 1735 in response to oppressive postconversion conditions. Conversion and its

The Nature of Imperial Indigenism in Southwestern Yunnan 199

TABLE 9 *Malarial Locales in Qing Southwestern Yunnan*

Prefecture/ Subunit[a]	Source	Prefecture/ Subunit	Source
Pu'er	*QDSX*, QL 35/4/2, 3:260	Yongchang	TS, 3:2131a
Weiyuan NC	CLSSS, 8:448	Denggeng NC	*QBLC*, 1:45
Mengwu NC	CLSSS, 8:450	Huju Guan	*QDSX*, QL 35/2/4, 3:255
Mozhe	CLSSS, 8:450	Tengyue	*YZHZ*, YZ 5/3/12, 9:237
Wude NC	CLSSS, 8:449	Longchuan NC	*QBLC*, 1:46
Youle NC	CLSSS, 8:447	Lujiang NC	*YCFZ*, 29b
Zhengdong NC	CLSSS, 8:449	Mangshi NC	*YCFZ*, 29b
Ganlan Ba	DLZ, 11:101	Mengding NC	*QBLC*, 1:45
		Mengmao NC	*QBLC*, 1:46
Shunning	TS, 3:2131a	Nandian NC	*YCFZ*, 198a
Mianning	*JDSY*, JQ 17/7/8, 17:260a	Wandian NC	*DYZC*, 11:453
Bingye	*JDSY*, JQ 17/7/8, 17:260a	Zhanda NC	MWLF, QL 34/3/12 [03-183-2349-003]
Yunzhou	*JDSY*, JQ 17/7/8, 17:260a	Zhefang NC	*YCFZ*, 29b
Gengma NC	*QBLC*, 1:45		
Menglian NC	*QBLC*, 1:45		
Mengmeng NC	*QBLC*, 1:45		

Notes: [a] Subprefectural units are indented under their controlling prefectures.
NC = Native chieftainship at some time during the Qing.
Source Key:
CLSSS: Gao Qizhuo, Chouzhuo Lukuishan shanhou shu
DLZ: Ni Tui, Dianyun linian zhuan
DYZC: Daoguang Yunnan zhi chao
JDSY: Jiaqing Daoguang shangyu
QDSX: Qingdai dang'an shiliao xuanbian
QBLC: Qingbai leichao
TS: Ni Tui, Tuguan shuo
YCFZ: Yongchang fuzhi
YZHZ: Yongzhengchao Hanwen zhupi

immediate violent aftermath were substantially impelled by a struggle to control the tea hills that provided the area's main source of income. There had also been state attempts to systematically exploit salt mines in the region, which were abandoned in 1729 because of the mines' remote and

200   *Across Forest, Steppe, and Mountain*

malarial locales, in favor of a limited and meager tax on indigenous producers.[84] Indigenous peoples and disease prevented full Chinese incorporation of the region as conflict continued over control of its special resources.

The abortive uprising three years later necessitated shifts in local garrisons to bring them closer to prefectural cores, but this also meant their withdrawal from the main tea and salt regions. To this end a garrison was redeployed from Youle to Simao seventy kilometers to the north to reduce its isolation from main administrative centers. The disease environment, however, was also a critical factor. Malaria in Youle was so "extreme" and its soil and water so "foul" that the majority of troops stationed there died, and the remainder were so debilitated that "it was difficult to employ them to keep the area suppressed." The proposed site in Simao for redeployment was, in contrast, on high ground with fresh air and good soil and water. Another garrison was shifted from malarial Weiyuan to Zhenyuan for similar reasons. Yin-ji-shan actually considered virtually the whole region of Pu'er prefecture east of the Mekong and south of Simao to be so vast, mountainous, and malarial that "it is impossible to station troops anywhere ... So if native headmen [*tumu*] are not ordered to control their individual locales ... the region will be difficult to keep quiet." He still paradoxically asserted this would not roll conversion back to indigenous rule since "the natives can still be controlled by headmen, who in turn remain under the supervision of regular officials. So there will be no barren hill, remote border or dangerously malarial area that is not under some authority and restraint."[85]

Such posturing aside, malaria was plainly a determining factor in the deployment of frontier garrisons and could determine their ethnic composition as well. Indigenous garrisons figure prominently during the Jiaqing and Daoguang reigns when militia from various chieftainships occupied posts in malarial areas that troops from Yunnan proper could not man.

As Ortai opined, however, native chieftainships themselves were administrative spaces substantially filled by the variable effects of malaria on different human populations. In fact, malaria was the only reason that the native chieftain system should have been preserved in southwestern Yunnan, in the view of Ni Tui. His experience as a private secretary and local historian active in Yunnan between 1716 and 1737 prompted him to join the general calls for chieftainship conversion in the early eighteenth century. His opposition to chieftainships was strong enough for him to outline a plan whereby hereditary chieftains could be eliminated "within twenty years" through natural attrition from illness or punishment for revolt. Nevertheless, Ni made an exception to this otherwise absolute eradication program for chieftainships "bordering on Myanmar," namely, those that formed the inner frontiers of Yongchang, Shunning, and Pu'er prefectures. He acknowledged that "in particularly isolated areas where malaria is especially intense, it would be difficult to establish a regular officialdom unfamiliar with the lay of the land. Malaria would also be unavoidable when deploying garrison troops." This statement may have included some malarial zones in southeastern prefectures such as Kaihua, where the disease had also afflicted regular troops.[86]

Unambiguous examples of malaria's deleterious effects on Qing personnel are abundant in the record of the dynasty's transfrontier military operations, making it possible to sketch malarial boundaries that subdivided prefectures. Rivers, which included rich breeding grounds for Yunnan's primary malarial vector, *An. minimus*, generally constituted the main geographic divisions between Han *junxian* and indigenous chieftainship jurisdictions. Three of southwestern Yunnan's rivers, the Salween, the Mekong, and the Binlang, formed such divisions as they flowed through Tengyue, Yongchang, Shunning, and Pu'er. The Binlang River marked the area's western boundary, which roughly conformed to the "eight passes" (*ba guan*) established in 1594 in the wake of a prior Ming-Myanmar conflict.[87] The Qing suspended its operations in the river's lower reaches against "wild tribals" and Han bandits, under the renegade Zhang Fuguo, "beyond the [*junxian*] border" in chieftainship territory because of the oncoming malarial season. Little more than a decade later, points along the Binlang delineated the outer limits of Tengyue's defenses, manned by indigenous militia resistant to the disease.[88]

Commensurate restrictions on administrative operational space can be seen in the rest of Yongchang, as well as in Shunning and, to a lesser extent, in Pu'er. Prefectural boundary rivers to the south and east functioned like the Binlang. Malaria existed "all along the upper and lower" reaches of the Salween River west of Yongchang's provincial seat. The Wandian native chieftainship, on the Salween about sixty kilometers south of Yongchang's prefectural seat, had "many malarial areas that could not be approached." Farther to the southeast in central Shunning, malarial conditions and Zhang Fuguo's 1812 raids into Gengma and Mengmeng necessitated the deployment of indigenous auxiliaries in Mianning subprefecture, which lay on a tributary of the Salween around thirty kilometers west of the Mekong.[89]

Mianning, converted from a native chieftainship into part of Yunnan proper in 1746, had at least twenty strategic locales within its confines that "government troops were unable to garrison" because of the disease. Within two months, Qing troops were withdrawn from the nearby chieftainship zones as the seasonal "malaria beyond the *junxian* boundary (*bianwai*) became extreme."[90] Patchy Mianning, at the southern fringes of Yunnan proper but well inside its disease environment, remained incompletely incorporated. Malarial conditions complicated the defense of the subprefecture, which continued to rely on locals for its viability.

Malaria in the chieftainships also inhibited the projection of Qing power beyond them. During the initial stages of the Myanmar campaigns in 1766, Yun-Gui Governor-General Liu Cao expressed reservations about crossing the Mekong River during the malaria season. He described his objective as "beyond the frontier of Pu'er," in the restive Sipsongpanna (Xi-shuang-ban-na) region of the Cheli chieftainship in the prefecture's southwestern corner. His worries earned him a rebuke from the throne, which asserted that Liu was not very familiar with border conditions if he thought the disease ubiquitously virulent. He was warned not to use malaria as a pretext for inaction. Yet at least one contemporary account of the campaign asserts that the Mekong's branches in southern Pu'er were ridden with malaria. Strategic passes such as that of Puteng then had to be garrisoned with auxiliaries or seasonal deployments when the malarial season subsided. Furthermore, routine Manchu reports from 1793–94 confirm that regular patrols of "tribal officers and troops" (Ma: aiman i hafan cooha) through Pu'er's Simao and Mekong ("Jiulong") river areas could be conducted only "at times when malaria (Ma: *ehe sukdun*) subsides."[91]

A series of reports from 1766–67 makes it clear that fighting in the borderland's disease environment with the assistance of indigenous auxiliaries "who could stand malaria" limited operations in Myanmar during the malarial peak seasons in spring and summer. It also precluded garrisoning of strategic areas just across the border as well as along the Mekong, here a prefectural boundary wholly within Qing territory between Pu'er and Shunning. Disease deeply marked subsequent dynastic policies, which frankly rejected military intervention in the face of borderland malarial conditions.[92]

The disease was certainly a major obstacle to the Qing advance. As the campaign progressed and losses from illness mounted, central authorities in Beijing adopted a more cautious tone. By the end of the campaign in

The Nature of Imperial Indigenism in Southwestern Yunnan 203

1769, troops were being ordered to move along high ground to avoid malaria-infested areas. The throne's decision was a concession to conditions produced by the effects of different elevations on the distribution of malaria, which in turn made Qing reliance on auxiliaries essential. Locals had already informed Qing troops in 1681 during closing operations of the Three Feudatories campaign nearly a century earlier that "foul vapors" could be avoided by constructing dwellings on mountaintops. These conditions were "the reason as the army advanced it had to simultaneously deploy native auxiliaries because they were thoroughly familiar with the mountain passes and able to stand malaria."[93]

When the Qing army was moving westward through Yongchang toward its jumping-off point at Longling, it crossed the Salween into "a land that was a chieftainship frontier zone already sweltering with malaria." Marching farther west toward Tengyue, the army moved into the "refreshing alpine climate" of Longling, considered the gateway to Myanmar. Little more than thirty kilometers south of Longling, the troops again encountered "particularly sweltering malaria" as they marched through chieftainship territory in Mangshi, which like all local chieftainships was ridden with the disease.[94] Malarial patchiness hampered these operations.

The postwar order established by the Qing in the wake of its defeats by Myanmar was also deeply affected by the presence of malaria and by official perceptions of the disease's seasonal fluctuations. The main administrative innovation, the trade embargo against Myanmar that lasted from 1770 through 1789, was no exception. The more than three thousand Green Standard Army troops earmarked to help enforce the embargo were deployed quite selectively beyond their *junxian* bases, despite initial imperial ambitions. Patrols in frontier zones were envisioned only for the fall and winter trading season, when malaria subsided. For the rest of the year, the troops would be pulled back to garrisons within the healthier fringes of *junxian* administration.[95]

One such fallback location was Longling, which had been converted to a subprefecture in 1770 to better accommodate its new six hundred–strong garrison. These men were to guard a virtually unimpeded route from Myanmar into Yunnan whose loss could cut Tengyue off from the rest of the province. The subprefecture was viable in part because of its elevation, which kept it relatively free of malaria. Officials explicitly emphasized another critical factor. Longling, whose mountainous terrain was unsuited to agriculture, was so dependent on food supplies from nearby Mangshi that "Longling would not exist without Mangshi."[96]

204   *Across Forest, Steppe, and Mountain*

Similar dependencies are implied in Gao Qizhuo's deliberations on the supply of proposed garrisons for the restive Lukuishan region in the mid-1720s. After calling Weiyuan a "malarial extremity of the frontier," Gao proposed that its rice production areas, along with those of Yuanjiang and Pu'er, be used to feed troops stationed to maintain order in Lukuishan.[97] Differences in cultivation practices previously referenced may be latent factors in this arrangement, but records demonstrate that Qing officials needed malaria-free mountainous terrain to establish direct *junxian* control. This control also required active cooperation of the native chieftainships situated in malarial and arable reaches of the inner frontier. Southwestern Hanspace was, in this way, literally dependent on imperial indigenism and kept patchy by the regional disease environment.

The dynasty soon had evidence that its assumptions about the seasonal and ethnic limits to local mobility imposed by malaria were not entirely accurate. There was an incursion of dozens of hungry "wild tribals" into the Menglian native chieftainship in May 1774 just after the malaria season commenced. The return of a Han emissary to Yunnan from Myanmar at what was regarded as the height of the malaria season in the summer of 1778 prompted the Acting Governor-General of Yun-Gui to observe that the disease had not rendered the frontier entirely impassable. Despite the emperor's personal vermilion endorsement of this "correct statement," he decreed that no further transborder contacts were possible until the malarial season ended in winter. It is as difficult to explain this example of the Qianlong era's central indifference to local experience as it is to account for the Kangxi emperor's conviction, expressed to an approving courtier in 1717, that malaria had been eliminated from Yunnan except for "a bit" in Yuanjiang prefecture.[98] Some of the confusion over when the disease could be contracted is attributable to the habits of *An. minimus* itself, which did not hibernate in winter and so could spread malaria year-round. Some studies find that the malaria transmission season can vary from nine to twelve months in Yunnan. There were two peak seasons, however – from May to June and, with higher rates of infection, from October to November – that were found in 1949 to correspond to increases in the *An. minimus* population.[99]

These seasons roughly coincide with some Myanmar campaign military reports associating disease outbreaks with a wide range of temperature fluctuations and precipitation. One report asserted that the "region's insalubrious environmental conditions" (Ma: *ba na i muke boihon ehe*) were stimulated by random and sudden shifts in temperature. Cooler periods, which could include frost, effectively stopped major outbreaks,

The Nature of Imperial Indigenism in Southwestern Yunnan 205

while sweltering rainy periods promoted them.[100] Mosquito lifecycles were similarly influenced, and it is possible that the broods of 1717 and 1778 were minimized by cooler conditions that, therefore, radically reduced malaria cases in those years. Furthermore, seasonal fluctuation in outbreaks and disease-free zones, both well attested to in the record, problematize current explanations that attribute outbreaks to "miasmas" produced by the "inherently toxic" nature of regional flora and fauna.[101]

Whatever the reason for periodic anomalies, provincial administrators were quite conscious that in fringe areas, such as Longling and Mianning, they depended on a number of ecological and ethnic factors to maintain an orderly division between chieftainships and the provincial zone of sovereignty. This does not mean that nominal conversion to *junxian* administration was obstructed throughout the southwest by ethnic diversity or disease. Malaria did not stop the conversion of chieftainships in Guizhou, where it was also rife in southwestern prefectures amid the valleys of the Pan River. Many such conversions, as in Xingyi's Zhenfeng department, however, seem to have been superficial. Even after its 1727 reorganization, Zhenfeng was regarded as a fiercely Miao and malarial area into the nineteenth century.[102]

The environmental complexity of southwestern Qing empire in practice is perhaps most legible in a lengthy 1768 lament from the Grand Minister Consultant for the Myanmar campaign, Šuhede, and Yun-Gui Governor-General Oning. Their list of woes that beset Qing operations midway between the dynasty's second and third forays into the disputed frontier began with the sobering calculation that the ten thousand Manchu and thirty thousand Han troops involved required more than one hundred thousand horses. These figures alone posed insuperable logistic obstacles in a province where "mountains are numerous and roads long" and so narrow that "two people could not walk abreast" in many places. It would take mounted troops months to cross this terrain, only to arrive "unfit" for combat. Horses, as well as men, also had to subsist on the same expensive rations because Yongchang, the main Qing base, "lacked fodder" and so "used rice instead." A year's worth of rice for the horses alone would have exhausted the entirety of the provincial stocks, then estimated at 350,000 to 360,000 *shi*. The additional food for the troops, about 144,000 *shi* more, could not be efficiently transported in over precipitous roads that were said to be even worse outside the inner frontier. In any case, there were no porters available beyond the Lujiang River and south of Nandian, which were all under chieftainships whose people had been driven out or into hiding

206 *Across Forest, Steppe, and Mountain*

by "years" of military action. These chieftainships were, moreover, "all" located in malarial areas, whose noninfectious season was "extremely brief." The authors admitted that they had as yet no viable plan to deal with these conditions.[103]

Šuhede and Oning approached despair because there was no fully developed imperial arablist infrastructure for the production and transport of the right kind of staple to feed the dynasty's oryzivorous vanguard of elite "Manchu" cavalry and their Han cobelligerents, all saddled with a huge herd of horses laboriously bred in distant steppe pastures that would have to munch pricey rice while clopping over precipitous and malarial terrain only remotely accessible through the cooperation of differentially resistant chieftainship "tribals" restive in their imperially prefabricated identities. I have found no better example of the environmentally networked convolutions required of a Qing fence that could ensconce such awesomely radiant borderland forests, steppe, and mountains.

YUNNAN'S UNSTABLE COMPROMISE WITH NATURE AND CULTURE

Malaria was a major constituent of the fundamental structure through which Qing imperial agency operated in frontier Yunnan. The ecological conditions created by the disease functioned to keep Han and indigenous peoples physically separate. This separation in turn made the native chieftainship system of imperial indigenism an integral component of dynastic control of the province – even though the presence of considerable numbers of largely unsupervised "tribals" certainly limited and could undermine dynastic control as well. Chieftainship identity in southwestern Yunnan can be understood as a product of the dynastic order's political compromise with malaria. It was the instability of this compromise, embodied in the often merely nominal distinction between wild and chieftainship "tribal," that constantly threatened to disrupt the relations of imperial indigenism.

After the conclusion of the Myanmar campaigns, the erosion of the inner frontier began in the form of wild migration, which grew more destabilizing during the first decades of the nineteenth century. One major migration of "wild tribals" during the Qing occurred in 1770, when they "began to gradually move inside the passes and so increased in number that they could not be expelled." Another wave also may have occurred in 1789.[104] These two dates, furthermore, mark the full span of the

The Nature of Imperial Indigenism in Southwestern Yunnan 207

postwar trade embargo, which appears to have been only nominally enforced until its 1790 termination. Major wild migration can be directly connected with the consolidation and decline of this postwar order.[105]

In 1769, when hostilities with Myanmar had ended, the Qing state permitted indigenous groups from beyond the nominal pale of the Binlang River to settle around the mountainous terrain just inside Qing territory. This reward, bestowed on "wild tribals" who had served the dynasty's allied native chieftainships as grain porters during the war, was intended as protection from Konbaung reprisals. Further unauthorized settlements soon followed. Some were probably driven by transfrontier social ties, and others were certainly propelled by periodic famine, especially during the Jiaqing reign. In fact, social ties and hunger appear to have been mutually reinforcing factors, as "wild tribals within the river [i.e., east of the Binlang] colluded with those beyond the river [i.e. west of the Binlang] every time famine arrived." Social ties, if not famine, were certainly a factor in the trans-Mekong indigenous contacts along the Pu'er-Shunning boundary that Qing officials sought to regulate with transit certificates in the 1720s. The newcomers from across the Binlang had initially caused no serious conflicts. Apparently the wild settlers "cleared hills for subsistence and seldom came down" from them, while the old "Han and Dai" residents tended to occupy and cultivate the flatlands, so that the two groups "have no mutual contact." The mounting Jiaqing era incidents that occurred when these wild settlers "came down from the hills to raid" may have been caused by poor swiddening that exhausted the hillside soils.[106] Generally speaking, wild migration appears intimately connected with shifts in food supply, and this migration, in turn, blurred the fragile distinctions between wild and chieftainship groups as environmental relations also broke down.

The dynastic response to this perennial problem was to continue its predecessors' reliance on indigenous auxiliaries to maintain an inner frontier zone as Yunnan proper's buffer against wild incursion. However, native chieftainships, the primary units of imperial indigenism, were based on political forms and ethnic identities that were too unstable to exert firm control over southwestern Yunnan's diversity on behalf of the Qing. Chieftainships did not block indigenous fraternization with Myanmar or the proliferation of wild *gumlao* stockades. They did not even reliably construct unambiguously "civilized tribal" identities that could serve as conduits for the consistent and confident assertion of dynastic power in the region. Indeed, chieftainships were so unsuited to these basic tasks that some provincial officials wished to replace them entirely with *junxian* subprefectures, districts, and departments.

Conversion of all native chieftainships in Yunnan to imperial arablist administration nevertheless remained an unfulfilled official wish, because despite their considerable and even destabilizing shortcomings as instruments of Qing rule, chieftainships did fulfill a critical need. They could fitfully mobilize numbers of indigenous bodies in the service of the dynasty to go where no Han could go for long. In noting the critical role played by auxiliaries in securing malarial areas during the advance into Myanmar, one official stressed that it was imperative to "win the hearts" of these auxiliaries, who were all "civilized tribals" (*shuyi*), so that they could act as "the vanguard for the regular army. Lose them and bandit incursions will result."[107]

The strategic need to construct and maintain "civilized tribal" identities is why the Qing state seriously pursued ideological policies as alternatives to brute administrative conversion. The general intent of such policies, particularly the "educational transformation" (*jiaohua*) of southwestern peoples advocated by officials such as Ortai, Cai Yurong, and Chen Hongmou, was to gradually produce more stable chieftainship identities rather than take the drastic and impractical step of eliminating tribal identities altogether through conversion.[108] Differential resistance to malaria underlay such identity (re)construction projects because of the disease's ethnic significance for the long-term occupation of strategic border territory. Yunnan's borderland order of imperial indigenism was thus embodied in a "chieftainship tribal" identity, as Ortai noted.

Indigenous ethnicity in this way became linked with malarial areas, not simply, or even primarily, because of Han prejudice, but because of differential resistance between these two ethnic groups, broadly construed. This is not to argue that Han prejudice was entirely irrelevant to state connections between place and "race," but it is to assert that such prejudice was not the only or most important factor. Perceptions of this differential resistance should be analytically distinguished from its demonstrable and discernible biological effects that made material contributions to the construction of imperial indigenist space and identity.

These constructs were, of course, also partly the product of official wishful thinking that, as Liu Bin observed, uncritically maintained an absolute distinction between chieftainship and wild groups. Such cultural responses to the disease environment formed the basis for connections that were not wholly subject to state control, as was continuously

The Nature of Imperial Indigenism in Southwestern Yunnan 209

demonstrated. Officials' rhetorical assertions that particular groups were chieftainships did not prevent these groups from colluding with Myanmar, raiding Yunnan proper, failing to grow "proper" rice, or even being physically indistinguishable from their wild counterparts. Qing garrisons might ensure greater conformity by chieftainships to dynastic expectations, but malaria's effect on troops and officials made this stabilizing presence biologically impossible to maintain on an effective scale. There were also practical administrative and gustatory difficulties with glutinous rice cultivation. Although many of these problems seem tied mainly to human agency, the underlying basis for the exercise of most of this agency to either abet or resist Qing power was also ecological. The disease remained a fundamental check on the formation of a congenial "tribal" identity, and by extension a dynastically manageable borderland, even as it necessitated such a formation. Southwestern Yunnan's environmental network inhibited its dynastic disposition to a far greater extent than in either Manchuria or Mongolia. This inhibition was mainly due to the region's "nature" as primarily manifested in its mountainous and malarial disease environment. Regional networks could be used within certain limits, but never fully controlled by any group at the time, because these networks' full range was not sufficiently comprehended by anyone.

Malaria is particularly significant in this borderland comparative perspective precisely because it included elements that dynastic authorities either did not perceive as relevant, like *Anopheles*, or simply did not perceive at all, like *Plasmodium*. The inability to identify particular insects and microbes as relational elements key for the construction of its mountainous southwestern borderland contrasts starkly with the acute Qing awareness of the critical roles played by livestock on the steppe, forage in the forest, and game beyond the Great Wall. The dynasty was left to rely on much more narrowly anthropocentric modes of adaptation, namely, the native chieftainship "system," rather than the more consciously comprehensive structures like imperial foraging or imperial pastoralism.

Swidden agriculture along with forest foraging under generally mountainous conditions was the actual "Zomian" counterpart to Manchurian hunting and gathering and Mongol herding. It is a testimony to the imperial Chinese state's indifference to Zomia's fundamental environmental relation that no "imperial swiddening" emerged. Perhaps "Zomi-culture" would be an appropriately distinctive neologism, but "imperial Zomi-culture" must wistfully remain a Qing might-have-been,

Across Forest, Steppe, and Mountain

never really implemented or even seriously contemplated. The dynasty's inability to grasp Zomi-culture in anything but human terms accounts in considerable measure for the ongoing contradictions in the Qing process of imperial borderland formation in southwestern Yunnan. Here conditions were often indiscriminately essentialized as "savage," or "miasma-(*zhangqi*) ridden," among similar pejorative terms.

The contradictory demands created by malaria along the southwestern edges of the Qing empire substantially conditioned the formation, maintenance, and limits of provincial administrative space in ethnic terms. The result was an official compromise in the form of native chieftainships acting as the dynasty's fickle pickets between the subjects of Yunnan proper and the "wilds" of the outer frontier. Yet this contestable division of provincial space was not entirely the product of conflicting human ambition, for behind the clamor of its indigenous and imperial creators rises the relentless whine of mosquitoes.

Notes

1 Zhou Yu, "Cong zheng Miandian riji," 8:786. For accounts of the Myanmar campaigns, see Zhuang Jifa, "Qing Gaozong shidai de Zhong Mian guanxi," 11–37; Zhuang Jifa, *Qing Gaozong shi quan wu gong*, Chapter 6; Dai Yingcong, "A Disguised Defeat," 145–89.

2 Quoted in Dai Yingcong, "A Disguised Defeat"; 182–83.

3 Pasquet, "Entre Chine et Birmanie," 57–59.

4 Giersch, "'A Motley Throng'," 72; White, *The Middle Ground*, 50–53; Giersch, "Qing China's Reluctant Subjects," 29.

5 Zhou Shunwu, *China Provincial Geography*, 384–86; Xu and Liu, "The Challenges of Malaria Elimination," 1–4. A number of distinctions regarding various species of malarial mosquitoes can be made in terms of range and elevation. Generally speaking *Anopheles minimus* is the main, but not the only, vector south of $25°$ N below elevations of fifteen hundred meters. *Anopheles sinensis* is the main vector above this elevation and scattered more thinly over roughly the same region. Still other species are vectors to the north and east of these locales; Dong Xueshu, "Yunnan sheng de chuannüe meijie," 144–47.

6 For general accounts of the Qing native chieftain system, see You Zhong, *Zhongguo xinan gudai minzu*, 362–68; Herman, "Empire in the Southwest," 50–52; Gong Yin, *Zhongguo tusi zhidu*, 110–12; Ma Ruheng and Ma Dazheng, eds., *Qingdai de bianjiang zhengce*, 34–36, 382–406.

7 Liu Bin, "Yongchang tusi lun," 3:2131b–32a; *QSL*, QL 31/5/28, 18:375b. For an example of official acknowledgement of the limited utility of the chieftainship-wild distinction, see Ni Tui, "Tuguan shuo," 3:2131a. Such distinctive hairstyles did emerge prior to the 1850s. Subsequently, as a result of postuprising revisions in ethnic policy, the heads of all Miao were ordered shaved; Xu Jiagan, *Miaojiang wenjian lu*, 214.

The Nature of Imperial Indigenism in Southwestern Yunnan 211

8 Belin, "Jin Yunnan zhongren tushuo," 13:13.6a–b; *Shunning fuzhi*, 1:508–9. The Kawa (now the PRC minority Wa), allies of the Luohei (now the PRC minority Wa) described as wild in 1770, were doubtlessly from the "savage" (*sheng*) branch that "plundered" rather than the "civilized" (*shu*) branch that "protected routes"; *Yongchang fuzhi*, 333a.

9 Tai ("Dai" in Chinese) is a dialect group that includes "Thai" but is not synonymous with it.

10 Leach, *Political Systems*, 286. Leach shows that locals could consider themselves both Kachin (Jingpo) and Shan for generations or shift between the two (1–2, 61). Note also his comments on the necessity for a historicist revision of functionalist anthropology (282–83).

11 Leach, *Political Systems*, 56–57, 204; Thant, *The Making of Modern Burma*, 24; Gong Yin, *Tusi zhidu*, 121–24. Leach's influential views have been subjected to considerable criticism over the past fifty years; François Robinne and Mandy Sadan, eds., *Social Dynamics in the Highlands of Southeast Asia*. However, James C. Scott has affirmed his analysis, especially of *gumlao* state resistance; Scott, *The Art of Not Being Governed*, 213–16.

12 Winichakul, *Siam Mapped*, 74–77. Different concepts of inner and outer frontiers have been briefly discussed in studies of the Han city as it exists in both core and periphery; Skinner, "The Hierarchy of Local Systems," 318–19; Gaubatz, *Beyond the Great Wall*, 24–25. Relevant issues of frontier urbanization also inform Liu Jingchun's *Qingdai huangtu gaoyuan diqu*. For some important preliminary connections between boundaries and ethnic groups, see Teng, *Taiwan's Imagined Geography*, 120–21; Shepherd, *Statecraft and Political Economy*, 190–91.

13 For chronologies of the respective establishments of these administrative units, see, Niu Pinghan, *Qingdai zhengqu yan'ge zongbiao*, 386 (Shunning), 392 (Tengyue), 389–90 (Pu'er), 395 (Yongchang).

14 Wang Hongzuo, "Diannan shi yishu," 8:386.

15 Zhou Huafeng, "Shang zongdu Yongchang shiyi tiaoyi," 13:10.12a–b.

16 Whyte, "Health Identities and Subjectivities," 13.

17 Brown and Inhorn, "Disease, Ecology and Human Behavior," 190, 191. For an overview of past human-disease relations informed by relevant interdisciplinary approaches, see Newson, "A Historical-Ecological Perspective on Epidemic Disease."

18 McNeill, *Mosquito Empires*, 4–5.

19 McNeill, *Mosquito Empires*, 6.

20 See, for example, Benedict, *Bubonic Plague*, 169; Rogaski, *Hygienic Modernity*, 9; Walker, "The Early Modern Japanese State and Ainu Vaccinations," 121–60.

21 Perdue, *China Marches West*, 46–48.

22 *Qing Gaozong yuzhi shi* 4:74a. Also note Qianlong's preface to "Bishu Shanzhuang bai yunshi" [One hundred verses from the Imperial Retreat to Avoid the Heat] in *Rehe zhi*, 2:840–41.

23 Newson, "A Historical-Ecological Perspective on Epidemic Disease'; "Smallpox Fact Sheet/Smallpox Disease Overview"; Campbell and Lee, "Mortality and Household," 316, 318.

24 *Qingdai Sanxing Fu Dutong Yamen Man Han wen dang'an yibian*, #74, 204–05; Chang, "Disease and Its Impact on Politics, Diplomacy and the Military," 177–97; *Chongde san nian Manwen dang'an*, 88, 99, 113–14. Chang demonstrates through numerous examples Hong Taiji's concerns about small pox. For an account of smallpox devastations among Tümed Mongols during the Ming, see Fisher, "Smallpox, Salesmen and Sectarians," 4–8.

25 Tan Qian, *Bei you lu*, 355; *Qianlongchao neifu chaoben 'Lifan yuan zeli,'* 27. Han urbanization created small pox threats to indigenous peoples even in "Mongol" steppe zones south of the Great Wall like the Qinghai-Gansu border, where the "most fearful" outbreak occurred among "an extraordinary number" of three hundred Ordos Mongols involved in logistical operations in Xining during the Khoshot uprising in 1723–24; Nian Gengyao, *Nian Gengyao Man Han zouzhe*, 103.

26 Marks, "Geography Is Not Destiny," 13–17; Guneratne, "Modernization, the State, and the Construction of a Tharu Identity," 753–54.

27 Cai Yurong, "Chou Dian shi shu," 8:433.

28 Cai Yurong, "Chou Dian shi shu," 8:436.

29 Cai Yurong, "Chou Dian shi shu," 8:429.

30 See citations in Duan Wei and Li Jun, "Qingdai yimin yu Yunnan shengtai," 264–65.

31 *QSL*, QL 13/3/"end of month," 13:104a–05a, QL 13/11/ "end of month," 18:252a.

32 Li Zhongqing, *Zhongguo xinan bianjiang de shehui jingji*, 153–54, 269, 296; *Daoguang Yunnan zhi chao*, 11:525, 527.

33 Li Zhongqing, *Zhongguo xinan bianjiang de shehui jingji*, 282. Miners' demands were, of course, only one source of rising food prices. For a contemporary summary of causes, see *QSL* QL 38/i.c. 3/30, 20:510b–11b.

34 For an analysis of the socioeconomic constraints on agrarian expansion in Yunnan, see Lee, "Food Supply and Population," 738–41.

35 Liu Kun, *Nanzhong za shuo*, 11:355. Liu Kun and Zhang Yunsui use converse terms for "swiddening"; *dao geng huo zhong* and *huo zhong dao geng*, respectively. For spatial distribution of crops, see Xu Junfeng, "Qingdai Yunnan liangshi zuowu," 86–87. For an important analysis of the effects of highland and lowland basin (*bazi*) ecology on Yunnan's social and historical dynamics, see Ma, "The Zhaozhou *Bazi* Society in Yunnan," 131–55.

36 Xu and Wilkes, "State Simplifications of Land-Use," 544; Yin Shaoting, *People and Forests*, 79–82, 98–99; Osborne, "Highlands and Lowlands" Daniels, "Environmental Degradation, Part II," 3–6.

37 Li Zhongqing, *Zhongguo xinan bianjiang de shehui jingji*, 107–11; Averill, "The Shed People and the Opening of the Yangzi Highlands," 87–88; Liu Lingping, Qingdai Diandong diqu yimin kaifa," 235.

38 Osborne, "The Local Politics of Land Reclamation," 4–5, 24.

39 *Weiyuan tingzhi*, 3.50a, 373. Cited in Liu Lingping, "Diandong diqu yimin kaifa," 235.

40 Scott, *The Art of Not Being Governed*, ix–x, 9, 190–207. For the conceptualization of Zomia, see van Schendel, "Geographies of Knowing, Geographies

The Nature of Imperial Indigenism in Southwestern Yunnan   213

of Ignorance," 647–68. My comments about Zomia here are restricted primarily to Yunnan in general and its southwestern zone in particular.

41 Sakamoto, "Glutinous-Endosperm Starch Food," 215–31; Luo Kanglong, "Lun Ming Qing yilai tongyi shuizhi de tuixing," 294–97; Xu Junfeng, "Qingdai Yunnan liangshi zuowu," 86.

42 Yin Shaoting, *People and Forests*, 420–21. Daniels, "Environmental Degradation, Part II," 5.

43 Duan Wei and Li Jun, "Qingdai yimin yu Yunnan Shengtai." Reforestation was not entirely ethnically determined, and officials could prescribe hillside reforestation by Han cultivators as part of more general programs for provincial development; Cai Yurong, "Chou Dian shi shu," 8:436.

44 Osborne, "The Local Politics of Land Reclamation," 4, 6, 39.

45 Liu Min, "Lun Qingdai Pengmin huji wenti," 22.

46 Li Zhongqing, *Zhongguo xinan bianjiang de shehui jingji*, 100–101, 185.

47 Cited in Daniels, "Environmental Degradation, Part I," 9. Takeuchi Fusaji has also studied the violent consequences arising from radical Han agrarian transformation of this swidden environment; "'Kaifa yu fengjin.' Daniels, citing Takeuchi's work on the uprising, calls for "more attention to the ethnic side of the history of environmental degradation in China" (10).

48 You Zhong, *Zhongguo Xinan gudai minzu*, 381–85. Less frequently *yeren*, as a synonym for *yeyi* (wild tribal), was also applied to other indigenous peoples like the Lisu, who could also be called the "red-haired wild people" (*chifa yeren*); Zhang Yunsui "Zhang Yunsui zougao," 8:709.

49 Leach, *Political Systems*, 35–36.

50 *Qingdai dang'an shiliao xuanbian*, QL 13/3/13, 2:468–70; *Donghua lu*, QL 31/1/18, 7:391b–92b; Belin, "Yunnan zhongren tushuo," 13:13.6a–b. Although related *QSL* entries (18:284b, 285b) omit the terms, Belin employs "wild people" and "wild tribals" interchangably. The Lisu were itinerant and considered "the most ferocious among the tribals" in Tengyue, *Tengyue tingzhi*, 247b–48a. Zhang Yunsui made a distinction between "civilized" Lisu who cultivated and "savage" types who hunted because they knew nothing of farming; *Qingdai dang'an shiliao xuanbian*, QL 7/2/17, 2:466–68. "Mang" was a reference to Myanmar peoples, some of whom settled in China and intermixed with the Dai during the Qing; You Zhong, *Zhongguo Xinan gudai minzu*, 388–89; *Daoguang Yunnan zhi*, 11:526.

51 Belin, "Yunnan zhongren tushuo," 13:13.6a.

52 Leach, *Political Systems*, 289; Ni Tui. "Tuguan shuo," 3:2131a.

53 *Yongzhengchao Hanwen zhupi*, YZ 4/9/19, 8:115a–16a. For accounts of conversion operations during the Yongzheng reign, see Li Shiyu, *Qingdai tusi zhidu lunkao*, 33–36. For a study of Ortai's operations, see Smith, "Ch'ing Policy."

54 Li Shiyu, *Qingdai tusi zhidu lunkao*, 59, 102, 207, 212–13; *Qingshigao*, 34:10,230; 47:14,205. The corresponding unsupported entries in Gong Yin, erroneously lists 1769 as the date of restoration; *Zhongguo tusi zhidu*, 650, 652. Li cites the date given in *Yongchang fuzhi*, 198b.

55 *Yongzhengchao Hanwen zhupi*, YZ 4/7/26, 7:776a; Wang Lüjie, "Gaitu guiliu shuo," 11: 6,687–88.

56 Wang Lüjie, "Gaitu guiliu shuo," 11: 6,687–88; *Yongzhengchao Hanwen zhupi*, YZ 10/1/28, 21:771a; YZ 9/8/1, 20:984a; YZ 4/8/6, 7:852a.

57 Gao Qizhuo, "Weiyuan fu Zhao banli kaiken shu," 8:454.

58 Gao Qizhuo, "Chouzhuo Lukuishan shanhou shu," 8:445.

59 Gao Qizhuo, "Chouzhuo Lukuishan shanhou shu," 8:446–47.

60 See, for example, Zhang Wen, "Diyu pianjian yu zuqun zhishi," 68–69. Even Zhou Qiong's outstanding work, which accepts the specialist consensus on malaria, problematically asserts that science has only identified the vectors, not all the diseases they carry; Zhou Qiong, *Qingdai Yunnan zhangqi*, 24–25.

61 Riley, "Malaria and the Human Immune System"; Gutiérrez, "Blackwater Fever," 245. For a review of the *zhangqi* literature in Chinese, see Zhou Qiong, *Qingdai Yunnan zhangqi*, 5–28. The range of current scientific literature on malaria in a global context is well-represented in *Malaria Journal*.

62 Centers for Disease Control and Prevention, "Lymphatic Filariasis Fact Sheet."

63 *Yongchang fuzhi*, 48a; *Tengyue tingzhi*, 151a, *Yongzhengchao Hanwen zhupi*, YZ 5/3/12, 9:237a–b; *Qingshigao*, 34:10,231. Smith provides important context for Ortai's 1727 statement; "Ch'ing Policy," 139–43.

64 Fan Jiawei, "Liuchao shiqi renkou qianyi," 34; Obringer, "A Song Innovation in Pharmacotherapy," 201; *Da Qing huidian shili* (GX), 9.228b–30a; *Qingdai dang'an shiliao xuanbian*, QL 35/4/2, 3:260–61.

65 Busvine, *Disease Transmission by Insects*," 15–22; Yao et al., "Studies on the So-Called *Changch'i*: Part I," 737; Yao et al., "Studies on the So-Called *Changch'i*: Part II," 1818, 1828. For a bibliography of articles published between 1936 and 1994 showing that historical terms like *zhangqi* refer specifically to malaria, see Fan Jiawei, "Liuchao shiqi renkou qianyi," 35n. Nüe remains a more controversial term; Fan Jiawei, "Han Tang shiqi nüebing yu nüegui," 2–4.

66 MWLF, QL 34/9/11 [03-183-2356-008].

67 National Institutes of Health, "Malaria," 3, 8; "Report SEAR/WPR Biregional Meeting on Control of Malaria," 9; Newton and Warrell, "Neurological Manifestations of Falciparum Malaria," 695–97; "Malaria."

68 Benedict, *Bubonic Plague*, 18, 20–21. As Benedict notes, *yi* is not a precise term in the modern medical sense and so cannot usually be unambiguously identified as bubonic or pneumonic plague prior to the mid–nineteenth century, but historical accounts of masses of rats and bodily swellings can help to make a reasonably certain determination (8).

69 Garros et al., "Minimus Complex," *Tropical Medicine and International Health*, 11.1 (Jan. 2006): 102, 109.

70 Garros et al., "Minimus Complex," 102–05; Donnelly et al., "Malaria and Urbanization in Sub-Saharan Africa," 1–5; Watts, "British Development Policies and Malaria," 141–81; Liu Meide et al., "Analysis of the Relationship between Density and Dominance of *Anopheles minimus*," 1009; Mitchell, *Rule of Experts*, 2–23; Xu and Liu, "Border Malaria in Yunnan, China," 456–59.

The Nature of Imperial Indigenism in Southwestern Yunnan 215

71 For a recent comparative study of cases in Yunnan and Hainan, see Lin et al., "Spatial and temporal distribution of falciparum malaria," 1–9.

72 Yao et al., "Studies on the So-Called *Changch'i*: Part I," 730; ibid., "Studies on the So-Called *Changch'i*: Part II," 1816n, 1818.

73 Xu Jiagan, *Miaojiang wenjian lu*, 160; Zhang Hong, *Diannan xin yu*, 11:394, 395; MWLF, QL 34/9/11 [03-183-2356-008]; Gongzhong dang, falü dalei, jinyan, DG 20/1/18.

74 Miyashita Saburō, "Malaria (*yao*) in Chinese Medicine 103; *Qingshigao*, 31:9402; Gong Shengsheng, "2000 nianlai Zhongguo zhangbing fenbu," 312.

75 Curtin, "The Environment Beyond Europe," 133–38.

76 Centers for Disease Control and Prevention, "Human Factors and Malaria"; Clegg and Weatherall, "Thalassemia and Malaria," 278–80; Zeng and Huang, "Disorders of Haemoglobin in China," 579–81; Luo, "Medical Genetics in China," 254.

77 Livingstone, "Anthropological Implications of Sickle Cell Gene Distribution in West Africa," 553–55. Livingstone's work made a central contribution to the confirmation of the relationship between malaria and sickle-cell anemia, and has also been viewed as a classic demonstration of the interdependency of nature and culture.

78 Yao et al., "Some Epidemiological Factors of Malaria in Mangshih," 198–200; *Yongzhengchao Hanwen zhupi*, YZ 4/3/20, 7:15a; Zhang Hong, *Diannan xin yu*, 11:393. Yuanjiang was noted as a particularly virulent place for malaria for thirty years spanning the Tongzhi and Guangxu reigns; Yao et al., "Studies on the So-Called *Changch'i*: Part II," 1816.

79 MWLF, QL 34/9/11 [03-183-2356-008]. The "Oirad," or "Ūlet" in the original Manchu text, are probably one or more Zunghar groups relocated to Manchuria; Janhunen, *Manchuria: An Ethnic History*, 110–13.

80 MWLF, QL 35/1/5 [03-184-2394-023], 34/8/27 [03-183-2329-006]; 34/12/25 [03-184-2393-011]; Liu Kun, *Nanzhong za shuo*, 11:358; QSL QL 32/4/22, 18:628b–29a, QL 34/11/18, 19:338a–b, QL 34/12/11 19:362a–b. Inner Asian differential resistance can also be seen in the QL 34/12/25 report distinguishing between three detachments of Solon-Ewenki and Orochun soldiers' deaths from illness "within the passes" (*furdan i dolo*) and "beyond the passes" (*furdan i tule*). These terms likely refer to Yunnan's inner and outer frontiers, respectively. If so, deaths from "illness" caused 99 percent of all casualties suffered by troops of these detachments, and 89.5 percent of these deaths occurred in the outer frontier. Deaths from illness overall reduced total manpower in these detachments by 62 percent, from 3,380 to 1,259. While the "hunting Solon" detachment of this group lost 1,549 of its 2,008 men to illness beyond the passes and 120 within them, the group's Orochun unit of three hundred, which lost 50 percent of its strength to disease overall, reported almost equal losses within and beyond the passes. Another report later in the same month of January 1770 shows illness to have inflicted mortalities of 35 percent among four detachments of "New Manchu Sibe," Oirad Mongol and regular Manchu troops, with 63 percent of the losses incurred in the outer frontier; MWLF QL 35/1/5 [03-184-2394-023].

216 *Across Forest, Steppe, and Mountain*

81 MWLF, QL 32/11/23 [03-182-2254-026], 32/12/5 [03-182-2254-037]. For an insightful discussion of Qing approaches to "magic and war" in the context of the Jinchuan conflicts, see Waley-Cohen, *The Culture of War in China*, 57–61. "Awei" (*Ferula assa foetida*) resin, a traditional Chinese medicine, was belatedly sent in from Guangdong in 1769 with little practical, but some psychological, effect on the troops; *QSL*, QL 34/6/15, 19:168a.

82 *Yongchang fuzhi*, 29a–b; Xu Ke, *Qingbai leichao*, 1:45–46. Xu Ke's work also mentions the "border subdistricts" of Menglian, Shangxia Meng, Yunmeng, and Jiaodong, which generally lay in southern Shunning.

83 Belin, "Yunnan zhongren tushuo," 13:13.6a; MWLF, QL 34/3/12 [03-183-2349-041], 34/7/13 [03-183-2354-004]. For a recent study of the malaria's effects on the campaign using Chinese sources, see Zhang Yuan, "Qian lun zhangli dui Qianlong sanci zheng Mian zhanyi de yingxiang" 62–70.

84 Yin-ji-shan, "Chouzhuo Pu-Si-Yuan-Xin shanhou shiyi"; You Zhong, *Yunnan minzu shi*, 565–66.

85 Yin-ji-shan, "Pu-Si-Yuan-Xin shanhou shiyi," 8:447–49. "Headmen" of nominal authority were retained in some postconversion areas that a range of local conditions, including malarial ones, precluded from full *junxian* conversion; Li Shiyu, *Qingdai tusi zhidu lunkao*, 109, 186–87.

86 Ni Tui, "Tuguan shuo," 3:2131a; *Kaihua fuzhi*, 273.

87 *Xu Yunnan tongzhi gao*, 5:3,969. By the time of the Qing Myanmar campaigns, the passes had lost any strategic value they might once have possessed, for they could be easily bypassed; Wang Chang, "Zheng Mian jilüe," 21:17.17b. Malaria also complicated dynastic control of the eight passes region by forcing regular Ming garrisons to abandon their posts to auxiliaries; Wu Zhongyao, "Tengyue ting guan ai lun," 470b.

88 *Jiaqing Daoguang liang chao shangyu*, JQ 17/4/6, 17:119a–b; Hu Qirong, "Diaobao tushuo," 5:3973–74. Attempts were made from the late 1930s through the 1940s to determine precisely which species of *Anopheles* was responsible for the transmission of malaria. The most plausible theory was that *An. minimus*, with its pronounced taste for human rather than animal blood, was the main vector of infection; Yao et al., "Some Epidemiological Factors of Malaria in Mangshih." One 1940 investigation found that *An. minimus* was found primarily along river margins, streams with grassy edges, and drainage channels; Robertson, "Malaria in Western Yunnan," 70.

89 *Yongchang fuzhi*, 29a; *Daoguang Yunnan zhi*, 11:453; *QSL*, JQ 17/3/8, 31:441a–42a; *Jiaqing Daoguang liang chao shangyu*, JQ 17/7/8, 17:260a.

90 Gong Yin, *Zhongguo tusi zhidu*, 553; *Jiaqing Daoguang shangyu*, JQ 17/7/8, 17:260a, JQ 17/5/8, 17:155b. The concept of *bianwai* locales as malarial by definition is supported by a 1769 decree that confidently asserted Yunnan's malaria "does not cross beyond *bianwai* locales." The Qianlong emperor issued this rebuke in response to Yun-Gui Governor-General Ming-de's explanation that the onset of the fall malaria season had delayed copper shipments to China proper mints. The emperor reasoned that transport routes all ran through Yunnan's heartland, where there could be no malaria; *Qianlongchao shangyu*, QL 34/10/14, 5:916b–17a.

The Nature of Imperial Indigenism in Southwestern Yunnan 217

91 *QSL*, QL 31/2/22, 18:315a-16a, QL 31/3/9, 18:329a–b, QL 33/8/19, 18:1073a–b; Zhou Yuli, "Tiao chen zheng Mian shi yi shu," 3:2162b–63a; MWLF, QL 58/10/25 [03-195-3453-036], 59/11/18 [03-195-3491-001].

92 Shiyu yanjiu suo, ed., *Ming Qing shiliao*, QL 31/8/6, 2:1302–05, QL 32/6/13, 2:1339–41, QL 32/9/6, 2:1354–55, QL 47/6/29, 2:1439–41.

93 Dai, "A Disguised Defeat," 158–59, 169, 171; *QSL*, QL 34/7/7, 19:193a–b; Dzengšeo, *The Diary of a Manchu Soldier*, 60–61, 94; Zhou Yuli, "Tiao chen zheng Mian shi yi shu," 3:2162a.

94 Zhou Yu, "Cong zheng Miandian riji," 782; *Yongchang fuzhi*, 29b. Longling was certainly not free of the disease, and malaria there was described as "particularly extreme"; *Daoguang Yunnan zhi*, 11:608.

95 *Qianlongchao shangyu*, QL 35/5/25, 6:179b-80b; *QSL*, QL 35/2/25, 19:422b–24b.

96 *QSL*, QL 35/2/25, 19:422a–24b; QL 36/6/4, 19.868b–69b; Niu Pinghan, *Qingdai zhengqu yan'ge zongbiao*, 386; Zhao Jinsheng, "Longling jiangyu xu," 13:14.1b.

97 Gao Qizhuo, "Chouzhuo Lukuishan shanhou shu," 8:445. Lukui was located on the northern section of the border between Yuangjiang and Lin'an prefectures.

98 *Gongzhong dang Qianlongchao*, QL 39/4/12, 35:290a–92a *Qingdai dang'an shiliao*, QL 43/6/1, 3:332–33; *Qianlongchao shangyu*, QL 43/6/3, 9:108b; *Kangxi qiju zhu*, 3:2,383.

99 Zhou Zu-jie, "The Malaria Situation in the People's Republic of China," 931; Chow and Balfour, "The Natural Infection and Seasonal Prevalence of Anopheles Mosquitoes," 409–10, 412. Seasonal variance is common to malarial conditions; Roca-Feltrer et al., "A Simple Method for Defining Malaria Seasonality," *Malaria Journal*, 8.276 (2009): 1–14.

100 MWLF, QL 34/8/27 [03-183-2329-006], 34/11/7 [03-183-2341-016].

101 For such a "toxicological" explanation, see Zhou Qiong, *Qingdai Yunnan zhangqi*, 37–40. For an example of the influence of seasonal outbreaks and disease-free zones during those times on troop deployments, see MWLF, QL 34/3/12 [03-183-2349-043]. For indications that "miasma" in Taiwan was substantially malarial, see Liu, "Han Migration and the Settlement of Taiwan," 196–98.

102 Ai Bida, *Qiannan shilue*, 184, 222, 232–34; Yao et al., "Studies on the So-Called *Changch'i*: Part I," 728; Luo Raodian, *Qiannan zhifang jilue*, 291–92; Tan Qixiang, *Zhongguo lishi ditu ji*, 50.

103 *QSL*, QL 33/4/19, 18: 930b–32b.

104 *Belin*, "Yunnan zhongren tushuo," 13:13.6b; Zhang Yingtai, "Tengyue Nandian ying xiujian chengdan bei ji," 13:13.8b; Ilibu, "Tengyue *Liji* tan bei wen," 13:13.10a–b.

105 *Qingdai dang'an shiliao xuanbian*, QL 43/1/11, 3:323–25; Dai Yingcong, "A Disguised Defeat"; 172, 175.

106 Zhou Shu, "Tengyue bianfang ji," 300b; Gao Qizhuo, "Chouzhuo Lukuishan shanhou shu," 8:446.

107 Zhou Yuli, "Tiao chen zheng Mian shi yi shu," 3:2163a.

108 Rowe, "Education and Empire in Southwest China"; Herman, "Empire in the Southwest," 58–60; Smith, "Ch'ing Policy," 147–44; Li Shiyu, *Qingdai tusi zhidu lunkao*, 86–89. It should be noted that such educational schemes could also be part of general provincial reconstruction programs for both Han and indigenous residents, like that proposed by Cai Yurong in the wake of the Three Feudatories Rebellion; Cai Yurong, "Chou Dian shi shu," 8:426, 427, 437.

5

Borderland Hanspace in the Nineteenth Century

When considering the quantity of *qi* circulating in the cosmos, there was, after the Ming Jiajing reign [1522–66], a decline in the virtue of relations between ruler and subject, risings of bandits and rebels everywhere, great sufferings among the populace, and unrest on the frontiers. Could it not be said that there was a blockage in the [circulation of the] cosmos at this time? ... The great peace of the cosmos today and the favor enjoyed by all surpass that of the Ming dynasty, as is commonly understood by even the smallest child ... The cosmos takes benevolence as its core and covering and supporting all without partiality as its measure. Thus, if virtue is located near and at the core, so the empire gathers round near and at the core; if it is located afar and at the periphery, the empire gathers round afar and at the periphery. As Confucius has said, "thus, those of great virtue must receive the mandate," and since there have been kings and emperors, this calculus has been the same.[1]

In this Qing version of *qi* mechanics penned by the Yongzheng emperor in *Dayi juemi lu*, an ethnic Han dynasty falls victim to the same cosmic process that brought the Mongol regime down in Ming Taizu's version, quoted in Chapter 2. Both these royal expressions of accommodationist and dissident Hanspace acknowledge the centrality of *qi* in the dynastic life cycle. The geographic location of *qi*, however, remains, typically, in ethnic dispute. For Ming Taizu, *qi* wanes or waxes in the Hanspace core. For the Yongzheng emperor *qi*'s positional significance shifts between Han center and non-Han periphery. Despite these genuine differences, both the Han and Manchu regimes seek a steady state that will "virtuously" impose human hierarchy on environmental heterarchy. Yet once there is a substantial conviction that the resulting hierarchical constructs are wholly organic, once its own mimesis of nature is accepted as natural,

220   *Across Forest, Steppe, and Mountain*

the state's relation to heterarchical diversity begins to break down. State assertions become correspondingly less authoritative as its contrivances multiply to prevent or simply deny inevitable and often uncongenial change rather than adapt to it.

Something of this conviction, amnesia, and delusion seems to have hardened around the dawn of the nineteenth century. At this time imperial arablism was radiating across borderlands whose regional orders were no longer able to manageably contain it, regardless of how many local ordinances or imperial decrees were stubbornly issued. Environmental scholarship in China generally tends to concur and often portrays the century in grim, nearly Malthusian terms. Whatever economic development that occurred led to a combination of destabilizing population increase and ecological degradation.[2]

Western studies tend to be more qualified, but may be equally explicit, as in the assertion that "the 1810s were a watershed that marked the beginning of intensified Malthusian pressures" in the Liaoning community of Daoyi tun. It is, however, necessary to qualify the role of Han migration in this process of the "environmental degradation" of "frontier regions," especially in its acute nineteenth-century form. Kenneth Pomeranz has perceptively noted that although this degradation may have been related to eighteenth-century Han expansionism, it did not manifest uniformly across the empire as the inevitable consequence of Han population pressure. Lee and Campbell's study of demographic change in eighteenth-century Liaoning, for example, identifies climate change as one likely origin of price rises associated with periods of high mortality. Wang and Huang, correlating several major studies of Chinese climate trends with the most common Qing disasters, found greater frequency of drought and flood during the cooler nineteenth century than in the warmer eighteenth century. Li Bozhong has argued that a rapid climate change from dry to wet conditions associated with a nineteenth-century cooling trend had a devastating effect on Jiangnan rice production during the Daoguang period (1821–50). This contributed to the ensuring "Daoguang depression" (*Daoguang xiaotiao*). David D. Zhang and his associates have made a more detailed climatological argument that links state instability over the last millennium to similar cold phases rather than to population growth.[3]

The Qing's nineteenth-century environmental crisis was unquestionably grave, particularly in the north and northwest macroregions. This period also marks the high point in the state's unprecedented

Borderland Hanspace in the Nineteenth Century

promotion of imperial arablism in borderland areas when temperatures were at a low point.[4] A striking statistical example of this emerges from the spread of cultivated area in Fengtian, in comparison to the provinces of China proper, from the benchmark year of 1724 to 1887. During the succeeding five comparison years of 1753, 1812, 1851, 1873, and 1887, Fengtian's expansion rate was the highest by far at 434, 3,688, 1,984, and 4,907 percent, respectively, of the 1724 baseline figure. Even in the relatively "restrained" year of 1753, the province with the next highest expansion rate, Sichuan, managed only 213 percent, and twelve out of eighteen provinces ranged from 94 to 112 percent. In Fengtian's peak year of 1887, its 4,907 percent growth rate was almost forty times that of the empire's average growth rate of 126 percent.[5]

The following chapter will examine comparatively some of the nineteenth-century developments in the seventeenth- and eighteenth-century adaptations of imperial foraging, imperial pastoralism, and imperial indignenism within this burgeoning imperial arablist context. Although by no means comprehensive, this examination will attempt to locate where "virtue," or sustainable adaptation to new conditions, lay within the vast Qing mandate.

THE CORE VIRTUE AND ITS CONTRADICTIONS: IMPERIAL ARABLISM

Han numbers, estimated to have doubled from a rough minimum of 150 million around 1700 to more than 300 million by the 1780s to 1790s, were not the empire's only population increases. Others also benefiting in terms of reproductive sprawl include various New World plants, *Anopheles minimus*, and *Plasmodium falciparum*. Some of these species were intended, some accidental, beneficiaries of their connections with Han humanity, with cultivated cereals in general being the prerequisite copartner in arablist radiation. Some research on preindustrial agrarian populations in both China and Europe actually indicates broadly interconnected seasonal patterns in human and crop reproductive cycles. These plants grew beyond merely forming "part of the natural environment for human beings," as Han "humans and their activities [became] ... part of the environment for plants." It was not simply an increase in the Han population that created various environmental pressures, but an intensification of connections between Han and, especially, their primary cultivars (traditionally acknowledged as the *wugu* or the "five grains").

This is why particular sorts of soil subject to particular climate conditions were the primary limiting factor for preindustrial expansion. Livestock numbers beyond the passes, as detailed in Chapter 3, also increased. A less anthropocentric perspective sees interdependencies between "both humans and the animals and plants on which they depend for a livelihood ... as fellow participants in the *same* world, a world that is at once social and natural."[6]

Such terrain is effectively unexplored in prevailing socioeconomic analyses of Qing China. Interpretations have focused on human population increase as, conventionally, the source of nineteenth-century systemic dysfunction or, more recently, as indicative of a preindustrial "East Asian miracle" of development. Some western scholars are questioning this convention as the monocause of dynastic decline, while most scholars working in China adhere to it, even in explicitly ecological approaches.[7] Whether emphasizing eighteenth-century gains or nineteenth-century losses, both arguments generally proceed from people, as producers and consumers, alone. Answers to questions concerning the changes in area and species of plant cover, for example, might not only help to undermine or bolster conventional wisdom, but also transform the nature of its terms of "success" and "decline."[8] Analyses more fully informed by environmental perspectives could constructively confront the visible dynastic contradictions. Currently, it is difficult to integrate overt signs of "ecological problems, ... challenges to the rural social order" and weak state control with equally explicit "evidence of commercial growth," urbanization, and enhanced state capacities "that reflect more positive possibilities."[9]

Compare, for example, the competition for land in areas such as Muran that initially created ecological problems for Inner Asian hunter-foragers and economic opportunities for Han cultivators, but eventually hurt both. The Qianlong emperor observes in "What I Saw" that land clearance for agriculture and Han settlement had been conducted at the expense of foraging space to restrict battue hunting to reserves such as Muran over a thirty-year period from 1729 to 1759. Poaching of preserve resources dates from before this time, and pressure on Muran is evident from the inception of the Yongzheng reign. As early as 1723 there was a request submitted to the throne to permit cultivation of some fertile Muran fields to produce reserves for price control of grain in Beijing.[10]

By the early nineteenth century there was a marked decline in the preserve, which had been subjected for decades to Mongol and Han

Borderland Hanspace in the Nineteenth Century

incursion that caused deforestation and declines in game. The Jiaqing emperor complained that game was almost nowhere to be found in Muran for four years from 1802 to 1805, despite the fact that no imperial hunts had been conducted for ten years. The emperor held that only a reimposition of discipline on lax preserve guards had stopped timber and game poaching to restore hunting conditions in 1806. By 1810, however, quarry was again scarce, and the emperor renewed his condemnation of guards whose carelessness had permitted both Han and Mongols to poach animals and wood. Problems with guards may have been related to a corresponding decline in human resources. The emperor had voiced complaints in 1808 about the poor battue equestrianship of Mongol hunters, who were unable to understand the Manchu and Mongol commands of their lords and officers. His order to employ only hunters who could perform mounted archery and "understand Mongol and Manchu well" is indicative of the intimate and fraying ties between culture and nature so critical for sustainable venery.[11]

The breaking of these bonds is even visible in the interchanges between the emperor and his Manchu subjects. There is little evidence of the Qianlong emperor's poetic references to the "close relations" and "intimacy" between Manchu and Mongol hunters in the Jiaqing emperor's own 1807 public declaration of the enduring value of the preserve. His *"Muran i ejebun"* (*Mu-lan ji*; Record of Muran), carved in stone on one of the preserve's steles, displays his filial adherence to the onerous duty of conducting the annual autumn hunt for purposes of Mongol pacification. Further indications of alienation come from Belin's memorial of gratitude for the emperor's gift of a copy of the *Muran i Ejebun*. Belin laments that his patron must hunt in Muran to "carry out the pacification of distant tribes each year, thus willingly abstaining from ease and bearing woes." He makes no reference to the ritual's value for military training.[12] At this time, thirteen years before its termination, Manchu and Han discourses seem to be converging on the "Sinified" consensus that the hunt is simply an unpleasant task mainly to keep the Mongols in line. It is possible that the emperor's disenchantment peaked around the same time game became too hard to track down in 1810.

Perhaps not entirely coincidentally, 1810 was also the year that Han trading posts were found operating along the hunting reserve's northern perimeter to commodify deer antlers and other forage filched from Muran. Ginseng, used as a sort of currency to pay off banner guards for illicit access as early as 1726, was the key resource for these transactions.

224   *Across Forest, Steppe, and Mountain*

The emergence of these posts was probably linked to another massive wave of more than one hundred thousand Han migrants moving through the region in 1808 on their way to clear fields in the Juu Uda League. Declining trends continued with the termination of imperial hunts in 1821. An epitaph on the hunt both fitting and revealing may be found in an 1823 regulation. Soldiers are ordered to expel any "Han commoners" trying to establish "shops and market places" or "Mongol nobles seeking recruits for unauthorized land reclamation" within thirty *li* of the preserve's perimeter. Official requests for the reserve's agricultural conversion were being granted by the 1860s in belated acknowledgement of the ongoing agrarian infiltration during the intervening decades. One observer in 1940, scratching the surface of deeper twenty-first-century concerns over mineral extraction, summarized the unsustainable effects of Han agrarian resource concentration since the late Qing: "Wherever Han go, the forests are first cut down, then the land plowed and sown. In the process the stone of the mountains is exposed, soil is washed away, and the surface of the land becomes more dried out each year until finally there is the desolation like that today."[13] By the mid–eighteenth century, Han masses, abetted by Mongols, had begun excluding Inner Asian elites from Muran through excess accumulation of local resources for arablist purposes at the expense of venery ones. By the nineteenth century the ground had been cut from under both arablism and venery.

The environmental link between Inner Asian venery elites and Han arablist masses was brittlely forged from a limited resource, arable land, neither inexhaustible nor even easily renewable. Mark Elvin has characterized Han core agricultural practices as "the reduction of biomass in order to be able to control the use of what remains."[14] This remainder, however problematic its production, could be manipulated for the immediate benefit of varied constituencies. The group best positioned to take advantage of the fruits of this remnant was not, over time, the multiethnic dynastic elite or its Inner Asian subjects, but the Han masses.

Under such conditions, the almost centripetal pull that agro-urbanized assimilation exerted against the other embodiments of dynastic borderland space, so apparent even by the seventeenth century and so imposing in the nineteenth, is unsurprising. Jungfoboo's 1750 observations about the dangerous alacrity with which Guihua's Tümed Mongols embraced Han urban and agrarian culture is one example. The dynasty's imposition of an agrarian identity on the SAH Warka in the 1670s is another. In the hostile disease environment of southwestern Yunnan, indigenous peoples in Mangshi were incorporated into the Qing garrison system as provisioners for troops in Longling in the 1770s. A Han observer in the 1600s could already note that "during the past 300 years of steady steeping in Han customs those native chieftains resident in and around [Yunnan] towns are indistinguishable from Han."[15] Gao Qizhuo's "civilized" Zhaotong "Miao" affirms the continuity of this process into the eighteenth century. Conversion to a comparatively monolithic form of empire-wide environmental relations was becoming an imperative, despite recent accounts of some sort of "agro-pastoral integration."[16]

Indeed, given its real ecological limitations, imperial arablism was expanding to the point of dysfunctional disharmony. This is particularly visible in the work done on a key strategy for the production and maintenance of arable land, water control. The most dramatic, and indeed paradigmatic, nineteenth-century example is, of course, the crisis of the Yellow River–Grand Canal hydraulic control system. The crisis culminated in the monumental shift of the river's course in the mid-1850s that would terminate the network. An important study of the Yellow River administration concluded that this shift "signaled neither dynastic decline nor an irresistible natural cycle, but the administrative, technological, and economic limits of the late imperial state." This state had maintained a huge infrastructure to confine the river's course for the preceding two hundred years.[17]

The conventional emphasis, however, on the corruption or efficiency of hydraulic statecraft fails to consider the possibility that the "successful" control of the river over this period was a main reason for the system's mid–nineteenth-century collapse. A study on the role of water control in the transformation of Yunnan borderland to more "interiorized" (neidihua) agrarian practices suggests just such a dynamic. It effectively argues that subsequent problems with silting and related environmental problems are symptomatic of such "successful" development and incorporation.[18] The Yellow River's increasing siltation, abrupt floods, and random flows were all products of sustained human intervention to concentrate water in an unsustainable fashion, manifested administratively as escalating and corrupting financial costs. Effects of corruption or efficiency must be qualified by critical consideration of the questionable equilibrium assumption that humans could always control the river to cope with its response to the effective imposition of that control. These dynamics, in and beyond Hanspace, are signature characteristics of systematic imperial arablist overdevelopment, not simply of corruption or dynastic decline.

In many respects, the entire Qing water control enterprise can be viewed as an inadvertent "feasibility study" to determine how much complexity the state's hydraulic system could impose before it collapsed under its own water weight. The dynamic networked behavior of humans and rivers, rather than simply humans alone, is relevant when considering the contradictions of hydraulic statecraft.

Water control disharmony also surfaces in the Dongting lake area. The process begins with effective state-sponsored dike infrastructure construction programs, followed by unauthorized private local initiatives that radically expand arable land while also undermining vital drainage routes. The resulting period of economic expansion increases the local population and draws immigrants until all the land is overoccupied and resource conflicts break out to undermine the whole system. Signs of unsustainablity are unambiguous from the end of the eighteenth century as "the ecology of the Yangzi River and Dongting Lake region [became] increasingly precarious."[19] Disharmonious ecological change that exceeds human expectations is not limited to the Qing, as shown in a study of land reclamation in Republican-era Hangzhou Bay. The substantial tracts of newly arable land deposited by the Qiantang River were dependent for their "very existence" on "unpredictable" river currents. The random emergence and submergence of this land made it impossible to stably cultivate or tax. Qing officials experienced similar problems with marshlands "fluctuating from time to time," emerging and submerging at random.[20]

This "cycle of growth and decline" understood in terms of nonequilibrium disharmony dynamics effectively concentrates resources to create an intense, destabilizing efflorescence. Human concentration of land and water resources results in a drastic increase in human population and triggers commensurate ecological changes, such as silting. The resulting synergy creates much more precipitous and disruptive change than would occur without the initial concentration. In effect, without timely adaptations, the more successful the concentration, the bigger the pile-up of instabilities resulting in a more drastic collapse of existing networks. This is not, exactly, a Malthusian process in which human reproduction eventually exceeds agrarian carrying capacity. Instead, carrying capacity is exhausted through networks that intensify it unsustainably. The end result is more people and less acreage than before, not more people and the same amount of arable land.

These brief glimpses of water control from Hunan, Zhejiang, and the Yellow River reveal the dynamics of disharmony at work in China proper

Borderland Hanspace in the Nineteenth Century 227

to create destablizing counterpressures similar to those at work in borderlands under different environmental regimes subject to Han agrarian migration. Warning signs regarding the unsustainability of arablist practice both within and beyond China proper are either ignored or misinterpreted to continue to accommodate the expansion of fields to the point of overload. Elvin has insightfully summarized the period of "3,000 thousand years of unsustainable growth" in China. He observes that "if numerous details are ignored, it is possible to say that the long term trend of basic exploitation of the environment was toward maximal 'arablization' for cereal cultivation as opposed to" herding or foraging from "non-farm" food sources in forests and wetlands. Elvin sees this paradox that protracts unsustainable cultivation as possible only because of a combination of technical adaptations and straightforward expansion into areas not yet subject to Chinese-style agriculture. The "single most important factor" in his view is "the social structure of power," which makes the "key decisions" that control "what happens to the environment."[21]

This conception of "arablization," important as it is to my study, nevertheless tends to emphasize human action as solely decisive even as it stresses the ecological limitations on that human action. In the Qing case, this emphasis obscures a wider significance of the critical role played by arable, but not yet arablized, regions. Such places largely lay in the empire's "forsaken" non-Han borderlands, where environmental relations had already been subject to alternative forms of dynastic organization. Han arablism in China proper had resorted to expedients from stripping hillsides with New World crops to siphoning off lakes through dams, but these tactics alone could not fill the strategic need for more farmland. So it is hardly coincidental that the eighteenth century saw both the unprecedented doubling of the Han population and the equally peerless consolidation of Qing authority across vast, and fertile, areas of Inner Asia.

Although each initially reinforced the other, serious contradictions between the orders in the borderlands and China proper became acute in the nineteenth century. The Qing elite's "social structure of power" found it increasingly hard to implement "key decisions" in its own long-term interests, despite, and sometimes because of, the short-term efficacy of those same key decisions. Its central role in the crisis of the Middle Kingdom notwithstanding, Han population problems did not spawn such mortal contradictions to empire. High population was, instead, one of many products of interrelations between China proper and its borderlands embodying these contradictions. Throughout these borderlands,

228 *Across Forest, Steppe, and Mountain*

state attempts to arrest change by imposing greater uniformity, rather than by adapting to diversity, exhibit similar destabilizing contradictions not entirely attributable to Han population pressure, or purely human interrelations, alone.

VIRTUE UNDER PRESSURE AT THE PERIPHERIES: MANCHURIA'S SAH BASIN

As Chapter 3 shows, Qing state-sponsored conversion of central and northern basin peoples to a more uniformly agrarian set of environmental relations manifested contradictions driven by Russian, rather than by Han, incursions in the seventeenth century. By the nineteenth century, however, the Manchu dynasty was being pressed from both sides seeking to exploit northeastern resources.

Han pressure came largely from the south, via Fengtian, as the prominent Manchu official Nayančeng averred in 1804. By this time, the Qing had come to consider Jilin and Heilongjiang the last preserves of an unspoiled Manchu identity, which elsewhere had succumbed to Han "contamination" during years of banner garrison duty in China. Nayančeng argued to maintain an ethnically pristine Manchuria through the ban on Han migration beyond Fengtian to stop the degradation of one of the empire's most important human resources, Manchu soldiers:

The banner people of the three eastern provinces [Manchuria] take bow and horse as their essential tasks. They daily practice with diligence in hunting animals so that their military strength reaches the utmost level of power and skill. To set Han among them would certainly result in the contamination of their customs, which would steadily flow away into weakness. Now the troops of Heilongjiang are superior to those of Jilin, as are those of Jilin in comparison to those of Fengtian. This is clear, visible evidence that strength of arms does not lie in commercial relations.[22]

Here is the official conviction concerning the formative links between ecology and ethnic identity that produce a unique northeastern human resource that must be kept in a steady state of preservation. In terms of the moral geography laid out by the Yongzheng emperor in *Dayi juemi lu*, virtue lies at the northeastern periphery. Nayančeng warns of a Han civilian commercial threat to Manchu military skill that will, implicitly, leave the empire exposed to Russian encroachment, again the northeast's primary security concern.

Nayančeng's views can appear as part of a larger contemporary discourse of "the purity of place, people, and production" that expressed a

Borderland Hanspace in the Nineteenth Century 229

dynastic policy in the first half of the nineteenth century to maintain certain environmental relations critical to Inner Asian venery identity under increasing market pressures.[23] In a very direct sense, here rather belatedly realized by Nayančeng, game had been producing people. This production process had been going on long before the transformative rise of a global market, which nevertheless did dramatically deplete Inner Asian forage and Inner Asian "purity."

As the century progressed, Russian imperialism exerted a more direct pressure that, like Han commerce, also threatened the stability of foraging relations, but through yet another mobilization of indigenous peoples. Senior Heilongjiang officials and the throne deliberated the temporary suspension of pelt tribute in 1855–56, for example, to make preparations to organize indigenous foraging peoples and the hunting banners against anticipated Russian incursions into the SAH basin. Widely dispersed Orochen and Birar sable tributaries were singled out in particular for enhanced control through "division into households" once they had been "brought in" from areas adjoining the Russian frontier. This was part of a deliberate and traditional strategy to "clear the wilds" (qing ye) to both deny an incursion resources and remove fragile subjects "as a defense against" Russian "inducements and incitements." Ultimately rejected partly because of mobilization's effects on hunting livelihoods, the proposal's deliberation briefly recapitulates many of the concerns and rationales of the first Qing-Romanov conflict of the late seventeenth century.[24]

Over the intervening span of two hundred years, imperial forager identity was plainly still in the uneven process of being formed in critical regions of the empire's northeastern borderlands. Pelt tribute itself would be decreed out of existence across the empire in 1887. By the latter half of the nineteenth century, however, local conditions were no longer as amenable to drastic intervention as they had been in the latter half of the seventeenth century, and indigenous peoples could not be so casually relocated.[25] Without alerting the Russians, the Qing could not effect immediate, large-scale adaptation to these new conditions, produced in part by its own constructions.

The ecology of imperial foraging itself, particularly its patchy quality, further complicated dynastic adaptation. As a 1910 proposal to convert some resource enclave space in Butha Ula to banner cultivation explained, the raw materials of tribute such as

> pine nuts and cones ... are not produced on every tree of every mountain. Wind and insects harm their flowers; rain and drought blight their fruits, all making for a scant harvest. Honey naturally cannot be made in places other than those near

230   *Across Forest, Steppe, and Mountain*

mountains and close to rivers where people seldom tread. Rivers that produce *hua* fish lie in shady spots deep in the mountains. Hence the broad spaces allotted to tribute mountains.

Experience over time had demonstrated that even authorized land clearance for cultivation under such conditions seriously degraded a region's foraging capacity. Every "*li* of waste" cleared made it "necessary to abandon ten *li* of mountains" to accommodate the humans and domesticates whose residence generally resulted in deforestation. There had been "ongoing" shifting cultivation of "abandoning this patch and clearing that patch." A decree three years before this proposal had already affirmed that "steady" land clearance in the vicinity of the Butha Ula and Mergen settlements was eliminating the region's wildlife, including sable. This unintentional 1910 experiment to determine the compatibility of arablism and foraging within a resource enclave had made it "more difficult to obtain forage now than in former days." The proposal concluded that without prompt state intervention, "barren hills will appear and difficulties of later days will be even more unimaginable."[26] Significantly, dynastically sanctioned Han agrarian practices, rather than dynastically prohibited Han bodies, destroyed this foraging space.

A century earlier in 1810 Jilin authorities were asserting the necessity of restricting Han migrants into Bedune on the Inner Mongolian border. They wanted to protect both the Manchu "root occupation" of cultivation, and nearby foraging enclaves whose mountain produce contributed to the honey and pine nut quotas. Supernumerary urban Manchus had been dispatched from Beijing several times during the Qianlong reign between 1744 and 1769 to work fields in Bedune and several other nearby regions to ensure the preservation of "pure and honest" Manchu customs. Manchu agricultural roots were actually shallow. A 1763 proposal to transfer East Turkestani Muslims adept in irrigation to educate drought-beleaguered Solon-Ewenki foragers in the Hulun Buir steppe hit a rock bottom rejection by the emperor's own senior advisors. The Grand Council asserted that if the hunters devoted themselves exclusively to agriculture, "their basic skills will be lost over time to the detriment of the frontier . . . [Therefore,] order them to practice hunting as before." For some, hacking such a frontier out of Xinjiang, Myanmar, and Tibet "depended solely on the nimble, robust" Solon-Ewenki troops.[27]

Such concerns were subsiding by 1810. Several thousand Han agrarian households from Zhili, Shandong, and neighboring Inner Mongolia swamped Bedune. This raised fears of deforestation and foraging habitat degradation as well as displacement of Manchu cultivators. Among state

Borderland Hanspace in the Nineteenth Century   231

measures to restrict further incursion, however, was a concession – the addition of a regular *junxian* subprefectural magistrate in Bedune to manage Han migrants now too numerous to be expelled. Outposts around foraging enclaves and prohibition of Han tenancy in Manchu fields were among the measures proposed to save what was to be a purely Manchu arablist and foraging preserve.[28]

Patchy compromises also underlay the proposal to consolidate a more regulated borderland space. Mountains were to be "protected and rent and revenue collected without scrimping the hunters' duties while simultaneously making full provision for their livelihood." A preliminary survey was conducted to determine foraging and arable boundaries on the basis of red pine distribution. Butha Ula's flat and thinly forested Sihe River area, where unauthorized activity was already underway, was marked for agricultural clearance. The enclave's northeastern mountainous Huolun River region, thickly covered with red pine, was restrictively reserved for foraging. Nevertheless, a request for farming this area's arable subsections, "where tree cover is light around the bases of the mountains," would be entertained to aid "surplus population without a livelihood to clear land for taxable cultivation." Despite the proposal's intentions to promote indigenous hunting interests, it reveals a susceptibility to qualities of ecotones and patchiness that continued to abet the expansion of arablism and, inadvertently, Hanspace.[29]

It is significant that any pines were left to be surveyed by this time, given the testimony engraved on a boundary marker on the tributary enclave's northern perimeter. "Commoners" were said to be in league with guards who had already "cut down no less than 30–40,000 red pines that produce tribute." The marker's southern counterpart provided a more detailed chronology of the preliminary deforestation phase of arablist penetration. This was spearheaded by Han settlers, sometimes with state countenance or indigenous collusion. Jilin's administrators had indeed already requested that, in light of "ill-omened" harvests," some of Butha Ula's hills be fired during the Xianfeng reign. Further relaxation of state restrictions on land clearance in 1870 had resulted in the "cutting of wood everywhere in the mountains and plowing every foot of ground." Both steles, probably erected no earlier than the 1880s, reiterated prohibitions that reserved tribute mountain enclave resources explicitly for state hunter-gatherers out of "respect for the ritual objects of the court and in all matters of foraging in the wilderness." Trespass "obscured distinctions between public and private and negated those between household and state." Both poaching and further agricultural clearance were accordingly banned. Another stele on "tribute rivers" designated certain areas as "tribute foraging regions in perpetuity."[30]

As the 1910 survey that relied on red pines suggests, this prohibition must have been enforced to some effect around the turn of the century to arrest deforestation. As the steles make clear, this enforcement was justified in large measure to maintain dynastic prestige and authority in the Qing home territory. This may account for the ban's apparent efficacy. Whatever its precise motives, the Qing state could still occasionally and with great reservation seek an accommodation between foraging and farming reminiscent of more rigorous eighteenth-century policies, despite nineteenth-century imperialist pressure.

Such accommodation, however limited, was far easier to reach with Hanspace farming, which permitted comparatively more ecological connections, than with the Hanspace commerce that was Nayančeng's primary concern. Mid–eighteenth-century Heilongjiang had already become endangered in the view of *Hubu* inspector Shurungga, who successfully urged a ban on Han-run wine and teashops in the territory in 1742. Shurungga had understood the region's "upright" bannermen to be self-reliantly free from commerce. When sent to look them over, however, he discovered "some people of no account" who actually bought food and clothing and even wasted money in shops. Shurngga stressed that Heilongjiang's multiethnic population of "New Manchus, Solon, Dagur and Bargut" required regulations unnecessary to impose on Han core areas to safeguard these peoples' "venerable practices of working the land and hunting."[31]

Shurungga's report provides an explicit articulation of the more general concerns expressed more than sixty years later by Nayančeng. He clarifies Nayančeng's allusions to the corrosive effects of Han consumption practices on borderland Manchu environmental relations often vaguely formulated as "Han contamination." The Han-built environments of tea houses and wine shops were still few in Shurungga's time. Yet they could already transform indigenous peoples from autonomous consumer-producers into dependent, unproductive customers by terminating sustained networked interaction with plants and animals. Indigenous peoples are thus shifted from more diverse relations to a comparative monoculture of human interaction. Han contamination here is a process of alienation rather than one of mere acculturation or assimilation. Similar dynamics are implicit in reports from Inner Mongolia in the latter half of the 1730s that express concern over the disruptive effects of

Borderland Hanspace in the Nineteenth Century 233

Han merchant sales of alcohol on traditional Mongol practices.[32] As in instances discussed in Chapters 2 and 3, Han "pollution" of Inner Asia was primarily agro-urban.

The ultimate source of this pollution was the Qing unification of Inner Asia and China proper, which gave Han migrants unprecedented access to fields north of the passes. The general Qing response in Manchuria was to actively culture the nature of imperial foraging, which nevertheless, as Shurungga's report demonstrates, could not be contrived by humans alone. Foraging enclaves and their microclimates functioned as preserves for the interdependency of unique northeastern biodiversity, such as ginseng, and unique borderland Manchu identities that included New Manchus, Solon-Ewenki, Dargur, and Bargut. Some Warka refused to lose their quarry along with their old identities. Sable pelts still counted even when they were discarded as actual forage. The evaluation of stalkers of stork and pheasant was tied directly to their prey's elusiveness. Banner groups were compelled to choose between maintaining ties with cultivated crops or wild foxes, with distinct hybridizing implications for each alternative.

Such implications, however, are often obscured, within rather blithe and idealized formulations such as Nayančeng's, and even Shurunnga's, that hide the complex and contradictory processes by which Qing borderland orders were achieved and maintained. In the seventeenth century, the northerly reaches of the SAH basin were inhabited by peoples whose lifestyle Manchu officers could denigrate as that of "wild beasts and birds," whose loyalty Šarhūda could question and whose character the Kangxi emperor could impugn as "actually savage."

By the nineteenth century, a distinct spatial hierarchy had emerged, whose ethnic apex was occupied by the descendants of these very same dubious, itinerant savages. Manchuria became commensurately subdivided under varying degrees of preservation, with rank determined by physical proximity to the agro-urban Han of China proper. In short and ironically, the more northern the more Manchu. It is difficult to imagine Hong Taiji could have anticipated the results of the spatial and ethnic shifts Qing consolidation of boreal power had engendered. People who needed to be "taken prisoner with fine words" explaining their ethnic affinities with the Qing in 1634 would constitute the empire's most exemplary, and rarest, Manchus 170 years later.

Human resource scarcity was a direct consequence of the dynasty's effective borderland construction in response to seventeenth-century Russian incursion. Borderland was subsequently consolidated through the expanded arablization of southern Manchuria concurrent with the further development of imperial foraging throughout. However, nineteenth-century officials such as Nayančeng were realizing the adverse consequences of this success for the basis of imperial security, Manchu venery. This was certainly an "environmental crisis" for the empire's non-Han elite as well as for many indigenous peoples in the region. It was simultaneously, however, indicative of an environmental development toward "maximal arablization" for the Han masses, as well as for their requisite domesticated flora and fauna. Such paradoxes go unacknowledged by work that praises dynastic "resource protection" policy for conversion of "wilderness" to farmland as well as its, hardly comparable, commitment to forest protection.[33]

VIRTUE UNDER PRESSURE AT THE PERIPHERIES: SOUTH-CENTRAL INNER MONGOLIA

Imperial pastoralism in south-central Inner Mongolian was undergoing similar crisis and development in the nineteenth century as Russian incursion reemerged and multiple environmental disasters mounted in northern China. Writing in 1879–80, the famous scholar official Zhang Zhidong's solution to both problems was the enhanced arablization of Mongols and grasslands. His views reflected wider contemporary trends throughout the empire's northern borderlands. In contrast to its past practices of attempting to balance the needs of both farmers and herders, the state would shift to full support for cultivation for primarily strategic reasons. In this way, the Qing state and its burgeoning Han population became mutually enhancing causes of regional environmental change during this period. The scale of these synergistic relations, however, was made possible only by the Inner Mongolian ecotone's hospitality to arablism.

Zhang memorialized in 1879 that drought was a major problem in Zhili. The province by that time had been stricken for several years, but deliberations for large-scale water control projects, "which should have been initiated in the north," had been going on intermittently since the Yuan dynasty. Zhang said implementation had been obstructed because "the terrain, water quality, soil content and custom are not at all suitable for wet rice cultivation." Furthermore, the requisite major undertakings such as dredging were "difficult to begin and easy to abandon" as had already happened in the Yongzheng reign. Although he suggested some forms of immediate relief, such as well-digging, Zhang, nevertheless, felt that given the unpredictability of both ecological conditions and human response to them, a more comprehensive solution for Zhili, as well as other afflicted northern provinces, was necessary. He wanted deliberation on "how to reduce and consolidate hunting and herd areas to expand agriculture." Such expansion of both banner and commoner agricultural colonies along the northern borders of Zhili and Shanxi "to effect an inexhaustible supply of grain" was already underway. He also wanted to "find ways to extract" the "produce of hills and marshes in all provinces north and south" to feed "innumerable" itinerants.[34]

Zhang Zhidong's memorial reveals the overconnection of interdependencies developed in order to overconcentrate arable resources. Some of the limits of dynastic adaptation in maintaining the equilibrium of this overconcentration in the face of diversity-driven pressures are also apparent. Environmental relations north and south of the Yangzi were sufficiently different to preclude the ideal arablist adaptation, namely, large-scale water control to irrigate paddies. Attempts to maintain a relatively monolithic agricultural regime on an imperial scale required constant management, as had been recognized by Mongol, Han, and Manchu dynasties alike. Their common solution, however, would amass arable resources, in an increasingly precarious manner, to mainly benefit the Han masses.

The resulting harvest of leftover agrarian biomass was still vulnerable to many factors beyond state control, especially weather. Moreover, overconcentration's destabilizing effects became potentially more catastrophic over time as arablization successfully intensified. Zhang Zhidong's solution might solve water problems, but only in some areas and only temporarily. Further dependency relations between people and resources would be established in the process that might preserve and even expand arable land and farmers. Greater disruption, however, would eventually result as wells ran dry or state maintenance faltered or water conflicts broke out to undermine the larger dependency network initially made possible by well digging. By making an additional, expedient connection to ground water, dependency on a resource is created that will probably not be self-sustaining, especially if bad weather persists and human effort does not. Human agency *alone* could not maintain these connections.

Moreover, full implementation of Zhang's program involved the clearance for cultivation of both Mongolian pastoral and foraging spaces to overtly promote one set of environmental relations at the expense of others. From the perspective of imperial pastoralism this would degrade

236 *Across Forest, Steppe, and Mountain*

both natural and human resources, as opponents of Han migration such as Giohoto recognized. It would also expand imperial arablism by multiplying and strengthening its connections with the Inner Mongolian ecotone. The results, like those of well-digging, would be not be self-sustaining and could be inherently disruptive. Resources, such as wood, fish, and salt, would be exhausted as agrarian connections expanded that might render the ecotone less flexible, or even unfit for reversion to pastoralism under altered circumstances. There would also be an expanded state obligation to manage human conflict over these increasingly scarce resources that would also add more interethnic tension to the cost of imperial arablist development.

Other interethnic conflicts were already being generated by new Russian expansion across China's northern frontier. Zhang's representative response was, again, imperial arablist, although in a relatively more qualified manner that acknowledged the importance of imperial pastoralism. He requested that "retrained forces" (*lianbing*) be raised and made fit for service from among Chakhar Mongols and "banner people" in the vicinity of Suiyuan and the nearby Chakhar lands to resist the Russians. He laid a particular emphasis on their deployment in "military pastoral colonies" (*tunmu*), a variation on the more traditional "military agricultural colonies" (*tuntian*) usually manned by regular troops. This form of organization, however, which was intended to provide for Mongol pastoral livelihoods, nevertheless required recruits to be specially trained because of the "ignorant character of Mongols."[35] The details of Zhang's critique of this character reveal familiar disharmonies resonant in human responses to ecological cycles.

Zhang said that the seasonally lush abundance of the steppe grasslands in spring and summer lulled conventional Mongol herders into a false sense of security. Herders would let their "livestock multiply in inexhaustible numbers" until "ice and snow covered the wilds" when, "since they know nothing of stores," all began to starve. Zhang held that this poor conduct of environmental relations accounted for "the recent feebleness of the Mongols" to resist invasion. He proposed a "genuine consolidation of the frontiers" through a coordinated plan "for the storage of grass against the winter" to ensure proper livestock breeding. More straightforward measures "to promote agricultural work and soil fertility to enrich livelihoods" would also be taken, including the sowing of grains "in the many arable places" that ripened in summer to avoid the early regional frosts that afflicted fall harvests. Most importantly, existing "unauthorized" cultivation of vast fertile tracts in the

Borderland Hanspace in the Nineteenth Century 237

Chakhar hunting preserves would be regularized as military agricultural colonies, which had long been advocated. It was especially necessary to tax this unauthorized cultivation, previously exempt because of its location in Mongol territory. It was also critical to establish a state presence that would serve to control the "bad people" (youmin) and "corrupt practices" (liubi) produced by "unauthorized clearance for cultivation" (siken).[36]

For Zhang, human resources were underdeveloped in both imperial pastoral and arablist terms. The solution was a greater interconnection between the two practices to strengthen dynastic control of the Mongolian borderland. Although ties to livestock clearly remained a critical component of the steppe borderland construct, Mongols were supposedly not conducting them properly to avoid famine and consequent degradation of borderland security. Zhang's conceptualization exemplifies the theme of orchestration of relations between identity and ecology central to Qing borderland construction policies.

Zhang's view of proper conduct involved an enhanced arablization of herding through the stockpiling of fodder, the livestock equivalent of grain. Further augmentation along these lines would be implemented through direct arablization of pastoral space as military agricultural colonies to ensure improved food security, probably through weather-resistant grain storage. Finally, appropriate arablization would not only increase food resources for security purposes, but it would also enable the state to systematically inhibit the formation of "bad," or destabilizing, Han youmin identities (literally "green bristle grass people" or "weed people"). These weed people were also produced through agricultural relations, but ones that were conducted, like those of shack people, without state oversight. Unfortunately, state intervention was substantially impeded by bureaucratic myopia to adverse "ecological effects" that "crossed administrative boundaries."[37] In this and other respects, the framework of state control had become too narrow and precarious to contain these effects or to accommodate the alternative Han agrarian identities that were grassroots adaptive responses to diversity and change within China proper.

Of course, Zhang's proposals were based on trends that had long been present north of the passes. However, as demonstrated by the rank presence of weed people, arablization was often not authorized or fully supported by dynastic authorities. Even legitimate activities were generally limited by counterbalancing concerns to preserve an imperial pastoral banner Mongol identity and were accordingly restricted in scale.

Examples include the eight-year "temporary" accommodation of Torgut Beile Lubsang Darja's two hundred refugee households in 1733 that permitted them access to winter fodder stores south of the passes; the establishment of *junxian* subprefectures just beyond the Great Wall from 1723 to 1741 intended to control Han agriculture and mediate interethnic disputes; and, perhaps most problematically, the general disaster relief aid in the form of grain and silver about which the Qianlong emperor expressed such conflicting concerns in his 1741 edict.

The eighteenth-century Qing state could actively retard or even roll back imperial arablism for the express purpose of preserving herding areas. One such example occurred in 1732 in the Chakar Bordered Blue Banner areas when authorities repatriated large numbers of industrious Han cultivators working thousands of *mu* of glutinous millet and buckwheat. The state's limitation of arablism is also exemplified that same year in its express concern to maintain border ramparts to bar illicit cultivators from infiltrating Mongolian grasslands. In the same spirit, Chakhar Plain Yellow Banner Superintendant Ušiba's 1747 request to permit his impoverished households to cultivate unused pastures was rejected for fear that they would ultimately be replaced by Han farmers.

Of course, the overall efficacy of these measures was limited, and ongoing accommodation to a series of arablist faits accomplis was often necessary. State accommodation is visible in belated attempts to register the more than one hundred thousand Shandong migrants cultivating beyond the passes who suddenly came to the attention of central authorities in 1720. The inadequacy of such accommodation is equally apparent in revelations from surveys of legitimate Han fields in 1732–33 and 1750 revealing the local state's inability to keep accurate population or cultivation records, overlooking thousands of people and hectares in the process.

Nevertheless, the clearly discernible tension between imperial pastoralism and imperial arablism, arising from a substantial state commitment to both, remains distinctive of eighteenth-century borderland relations. By Zhang Zhidong's time, however, the state's ability and incentive to conduct them separately had shifted to a relatively unambiguous and active promotion of imperial arablism regardless of other considerations. The origins of this shift are discernible in state regulatory practices from at least the 1720s. Unauthorized Han settlement for clearance could be provisionally legitimated if it was of longstanding, generated rent for Mongol proprietors, and did not continue. State acquiescence became precedent through a case of Han cultivation in the forward Gorlos Banner

Borderland Hanspace in the Nineteenth Century   239

around the turn of the century in 1799–1800. The resulting Changchun subprefecture institutionalized the residence of previously unauthorized Han tenants, whose numbers blithely continued to rise beyond official quotas. The ruling allowed Han to rent land from Mongols and was subsequently cited in other cases as regulations developed in recognition of Mongol elites' ongoing recruitment of Han cultivators.[38]

Manifestations of state-sponsored arablist expansions have been recognized as an "interiorization" or a "growth without change" that transplanted institutions and practices previously established in China proper.[39] Such formulations tend toward a relatively exclusive and teleological focus on the Hanspace arabalist dimensions of the analysis that downplays pastoral resistance, commitments to pastoral accommodation, and the complex dynamics of environmental relations. The Qing state's "vulgar" arablism, which sought to turn everyone into (Han) farmers and everywhere into (Han) cropland, was a nineteenth-century, rather than perennial, phenomenon driven by state responses to both Han demographic and imperialist military pressure.

Furthermore, the dynastic shift to unrestricted promotion of imperial arablism was also a consequence of the success of imperial pastoralism in certain critical respects, disaster relief chief among them. Such relief, heavily reliant on silver-driven grain markets and extensive water transport infrastructure, was an unwarranted extrapolation of Jiangnan conditions made plausible by the Qing unification of Inner Asia and China proper.[40] The "ignorant" Mongol attitudes Zhang decried as fundamental to their "recent feebleness" thus embody the Qianlong emperor's 1741 worries about the ethnically debilitating effects of grain and silver relief. This tendency was only encouraged by the systematic establishment of an ever-normal granary system throughout southern Inner Mongolia initiated in the early eighteenth century. The system was functional in Guihua, Rehe, the Khorchin banners, and many other places by 1718. As of 1784, it had reserves of more than 440,000 *shi*, comparable to low-end figures for Shanxi in 1721 or Sichuan in 1731, but was not really comparable to contemporary China proper civilian grain holdings, which averaged around 2.5 million *shi*. Even Fengtian and Urumqi held about 790,000 shi and 600,000 *shi*, respectively.[41]

Furthermore, as some economic reform problems in present-day Mongolia suggest, any practices reducing the seasonal mobility of pastoralists tend to undermine sustainable herding. A problematic legacy of reduced mobility has been particularly acute in the IMAR. As one herder in Mongolia concisely explained, "if we stay in one place, the livestock stops getting fat."[42] Qing state policies that encouraged Mongol - sedentarization, fixing boundaries, promoting intensive agriculture, and creating relief dependencies, all worked to reduce pastoral mobility and sustainability.

In sum, by the nineteenth century, the dynasty could not host both imperial pastoralism and imperial arablism in its Inner Mongolian borderland. In 1908 Prince Güngsangnorbu, the prominent late Qing Kharachin reformer, expressed this dilemma in straightforward terms still pertinent to today's IMAR:

> For over the past hundred years wilderness clearance for cultivation has steadily expanded and the old customs have steadily changed. Consequently, two sorts of practices have developed over time. One is the resolute protection of herding areas, which fears that as soon as land for cultivation is cleared, the inevitable result will be the abandonment of the old [ways] in pursuit of new [ones], with many inconveniences. The other is there should be prolonged clearance for cultivation to effect habituation to agriculture and disdain for further herding activities.[43]

In a fundamental sense, disharmony arose because imperial arablism's primary long-term form of adaptation, to both success and failure, was spatial expansion related to human population increase. This is not to say that herding did not require equally large or even larger spaces. Arablism, however, was better at concentrating resources more rapidly and intensively. One reason is because the production of meat and milk required more interconnections, especially with animals, sustained over a longer time period than grain production required. To a large degree this is simply a distinction between consumption at different levels of the food chain, but one with critical environmental effects.

It is likely that much of the recent environmental degradation has actually arisen not from pastoral practices in isolation, but in dynamic relation to the expansion of cultivation over the last fifty years or so. Officials have generally attributed this condition to overstocking and overgrazing that has been estimated as high as 35.6 percent of IMAR grasslands. During this period, some of the most fertile land has been transferred from pastoralists to cultivators. In turn, larger concentrations of livestock, whose overall population is now roughly that of the 1920s, have been moved to substandard range land under conditions of decreased mobility. Many of these same dynamics connecting arablization to steppe desertification are also prominent in the later decades of the nineteenth century. State encouragement

Borderland Hanspace in the Nineteenth Century 241

of Han agriculture to "fill the borders" (*shibian*) in response to over-population, imperialist pressure, and Mongol elite blandishments combined at this time with ecologies that were already cool, dry, and very fragile.[44]

Grassland fragility seems linked to a combination of unfavorable climate and an unbalanced expansion in Han arablization rather than simple, and exclusively Mongol, overgrazing. Large herding populations, however, remain subject to catastrophic loss that stockpiling does little to avoid. Pastoralism in Mongolia proper was nearly shattered by the "winter of white death" in 2009. Temperatures dropping to minus 50°C and blizzards that buried grass killed off 10 million, about 20 percent, of the country's livestock despite anticipatory provisions including the stockpiling of fodder. Some authorities in Mongolia, a country of 2.6 million people (about a third of whom are pastoralists and half of whom are to some degree dependent on pastoralism), have stated that this disaster has simply exposed the endemic unsustainability of attempting to pasture 44 million animals, a figure one considers "far beyond Mongolia's natural capacity." Consequently, there have been contrasting calls. Some want to shift the national economy away from its dependency on herding to dependency on Mongolia's relatively unexploited mineral wealth. Others want to hold to the pastoralism "identified with the country's very spirit," arguing that "Mongolia without herders is unimaginable."[45]

VIRTUE UNDER PRESSURE AT THE PERIPHERIES: SOUTHWESTERN YUNNAN

In contrast to its integration of people and ecologies in the constitution of the empire's Manchurian and Mongolian borderlands, southwestern Yunnan's unusual conditions obstructed commensurate Qing state access to human and natural resources. It is suggestive that unrest in northern areas was quite limited once the state had established a foundation for imperial pastoralism and imperial foraging. Southwestern Yunnan by comparison remained profoundly unstable even in the eighteenth century.[46] Regional instability was directly embodied in multiethnic rebels, but state control was critically hobbled by a disease environment that made it difficult for the dynasty to supervise local resource access. Instead, the state was always excessively dependent on indigenous humans for this access, and its presence was correspondingly weak from the outset.

By the mid–nineteenth century, however, state control had completely deteriorated into the eighteen-year Panthay Rebellion (1856–73), which brought the western half of Yunnan under the state of Pingnan. Although the precise causes of the rebellion remain in dispute, its preliminary stages were characterized by intense interethnic strife. Large influxes of recent Han settlers, supported by the local Qing state, clashed with more numerous resident Hui, culminating in the "Kunming Massacre" of 1856. Conflict, which ultimately drew in indigenous peoples as well, seems to have been generally centered on access to agricultural, trading, and mining resources.[47]

Some important Chinese scholarship on the ecological effects of agriculture in Yunnan has suggested that the cultivation of New World crops, especially maize and potatoes, was instrumental for increasing food production. The ensuing hillside farming altered the province's cropping structure. However, deforestation and erosion grew to undercut, and even reverse, previous gains during the nineteenth century. Signs of this reversal are visible as early as the 1750s when considerable tracts of cultivated land began to drop out of taxation registers due to environmental problems of various sorts. Preliminary and partial statistics indicate that eighteenth-century losses had quadrupled just between 1803 and 1827. There are further indications that new land clearance did not make up these losses, resulting in a provincial net decrease in total arable land.[48]

Shack people cultivation of New World crops, however, was not the only form of agriculture pursued in Yunnan during this period. In contrast, indigenous swidden agriculture sustainably prioritized forest preservation over increasing yields or acreage. Numerous steles engraved with protection regulations erected by Yi villages anxious to defend their forested grounds from Han axes attest to active indigenous resistance against Han swiddening. These steles, which primarily date from the high tide of provincial migration from the mid–eighteenth to the mid–nineteenth centuries, demonstrate in stone the dramatic differences and conflicts between the two culturally and ecologically distinct swiddening styles.[49]

If indigenous cultivation is ignored, it can appear that farming in essence, rather than as a particular form of ethnically conditioned cultivation, was responsible for Yunnan's nineteenth-century agrarian crisis. Although, as some studies assert, the American crops involved may have contributed to erosion problems, the major factor, generally overlooked, is that Han cultivation was largely predicated on deforestation antithetical to traditional indigenous cultivation. In this case, it was neither

Borderland Hanspace in the Nineteenth Century 243

people nor plants alone, but a specific set of cultivation relations, which could also involve agriculturally Sinified indigenous peoples, that produced either barren or wooded highlands. During the nineteenth century a decisive shift toward a self-consuming Han style swiddening was evident throughout much of the province that probably resulted in an overall contraction in arable land. More attention to such ethnic distinctions would appropriately qualify overgeneralizations that "Qing dynasty ... ecological knowledge was deficient."[50]

Statecraft-minded officials like Bao Shichen understood sustainability problems associated with Han highland swiddening and offered provisions for "greener" modifications. Bao's idea was to prevent irreversible erosion, which casual practices, according to him, could effect in as few as three years. In response, he proposed dividing mountainous terrain into seven levels, of which the lower five would be burned off for cultivation. Then, in rotations of two-year intervals, root vegetables such as turnips would be initially planted to enhance the porosity of the soil while providing a harvest. The leaves would serve as fodder for pigs, which would, like the farmers, be accommodated in shacks. The manure of both humans and pigs would then be used to enhance the fertility of the soil until it could be planted with a wider variety of cultivars, including corn, millet, and, if fertility was particularly high, even cotton cash crops. The upper two intact fallow levels would act as catchments and reservoirs. Water could be channeled, exploiting existing slopes and gullies, in various directions to maintain "inexhaustibly" the fertility of the field levels below as they were cultivated in ascending order.[51]

Bao's provisions are, of course, provisional. The careful balance required to make Han shack swiddening sustainable in highlands with only "20 to 30 percent" soil cover hangs from a potentially destabilizing scale. The upper reaches of these regions, were, moreover entirely dependent on rainfall. Their designation, "fields that rely on heaven" (*kao tian tian*), is a Yunnan term that, unlike its Mongol variant, emphasized such plots' isolation from riverine irrigation.[52] Bao supplements this unpromising arablist intervention by adding manure, of which is "there is no lack" because there are "many shack people in the mountains" who should also bring "numerous" pigs and chickens. This substitution of excrement for wood nevertheless requires greater coordination between more creatures higher on the food chain than the eradicated wild plants, which needed no supervision to inhibit the erosion threatening to undermine the new efflorescent system.

244 *Across Forest, Steppe, and Mountain*

As with Zhang Zhidong's proposals for southern Mongolia, Bao's more generalized solutions are predicated on human impositions rather than adaptations. In modern terms of nonequilibrium ecology, these impositions may be understood as "regulat[ion of] natural variability and diversity (culturalization) in an attempt to obtain higher yield predictability and thus a lowered agricultural risk." The resulting "cultural landscape" increases, often inadvertently, for some species at others' expense. The range of permissible spatial variation upon which diversity depends is steeply reduced, mainly through various forms of agrarian clearance.[53]

The requisite standardization to render Han swiddening sustainable as a cultural, or perhaps more precisely "cultured," landscape remained unattainable during the Qing. The state did not even seem to have a uniform policy to legitimate a consistent Han swiddening identity across the empire. Instead it suppressed shack people in agriculturally developed eastern provinces of the lower Yangzi macroregion, especially Zhejiang and Anhui, while accommodating shack people in developing western provinces of the Yun-Gui macroregion, Yunnan in particular.[54] By 1836, for example, Liangjiang Governor-General Tao Zhu was being ordered to bar further expansion of shack people mainly in Anhui. He also had to return those already present to their places of origin because their "clearing mountains for cultivation harms agriculture and harbors the disloyal." Tao himself had complained several years earlier that the large-scale flooding in his jurisdiction was the result of "too much land clearance upstream" in provinces across several macroregions. "Sichuan, Shaanxi, Yunnan, and Guizhou," were infested with "unemployed wanderers everywhere cutting wood in the mountains and planting coarse grains, so that as soon as there is a storm, the soil washes away.[55] Zhejiang authorities even held maize, a shack people staple by the Jiaqing period, a primary accomplice in soil exhaustion and duly banned its cultivation in 1802. Anhui followed suit soon after. Although the opinion of many officials was mixed, by the nineteenth century the state had decided on an ultimately futile prohibition of Han swiddening in the lower Yangzi highlands to arrest security and ecological deterioration that had become increasingly apparent since the late eighteenth century.[56]

While Tao was attempting to drive shack people from his Yangzi jurisdictions, Yun-Gui Governor-General Ilibu spent part of the same year of 1836 trying to regularize the status of the more than forty-six thousand migrant households. Their first formal census in 1823 revealed

Borderland Hanspace in the Nineteenth Century 245

shack people to have moved in from Hunan, Hubei, Sichuan, Guizhou, and Liangguang to clear land in southeastern Yunnan's two southeastern boundary prefectures of Kaihua and Guangnan. Pu'er was also mentioned as a destination, but the prefecture had comparatively "few" migrants because of its distance and many "malarial locales." Although some of this large provincial influx had become regular tenants on existing farmlands, "many" of these households had "raised shacks, cut down trees and fired the hillsides in secluded and distant forested valleys." Kaihua's gazetteer states that half the prefecture, "with its many mountains," had been swiddened. These "migrant" (*liumin*) activities, which Ilibu did not associate with the explicit term "shack people," were nevertheless the basis of latter's distinct identity, which also had put down some roots in the cultivar-based "anarchy" of Zomia. Ilibu noted that the dispersed nature of these migrants precluded standard *baojia* household registration that was the norm in core regions. He also said that uneven soil conditions necessitated the scattered planting of "maize-type" (*baogu zhi lei*) cultivars and other "coarse grains" (*zaliang*) he found difficult to assess for taxation.[57] As with glutinous rice and tubers, maize, a major nineteenth-century Yunnan crop, was creating "potato-like" obstacles to regional legibility in the province's marginal soils.

Shack people and their coarse grains were at any rate welcome in Yunnan's mountains, even if they ignored Bao Shichen's provisions. The problems for state control that these migrants created did not turn provincial or central government officials against them as had generally been the contemporary case in the lower Yangzi highlands. Ilibu's joint deliberation with provincial governor He Xuan concerning registration of his new hillside swiddeners was a response to an 1836 imperial decree that said nothing about timbering or burning prohibitions, lack of riziculture, or scattered residence. Some security concerns were expressed to little effect. Ecological worries, especially those that could spread to other provinces and macroregions downstream, are entirely absent.

Stark contrasts between shack people policies in Yun-Gui and Liangjiang indicate an administrative disjuncture between provincial jurisdictions of serious environmental consequence transcending a regional administration or particular macroregion. Change across administrative boundaries explains many of the complications produced by new variants of Han arablist identity. Environmental diversity required regional flexibility in imperial arablist adaptations to fully incorporate the many patchy areas throughout the Han core. This interconnected diversity also

246   *Across Forest, Steppe, and Mountain*

qualifies analyses emphasizing "external" security and market factors driving migration over those related to the unsustainable agrarian practices of migrants themselves that trigger human shifts.[58]

Yunnan was no exception to the interdependency of security and ecological stability that so influenced "shack-hostile" policies in Liangjiang. The contraction of arablist space in Yunnan that had emerged long before these 1836 deliberations did little to enhance overall state control and probably was a major factor in undermining it as interethnic resource competition intensified. These dynamics suggest that Yunnan officials, unlike their more cautious Liangguang colleagues, may have been imprudent in their unrestrained encouragement of Han swiddening.

Prudence was advisable for the region because crisis often revealed that Qing state presence was limited in many areas of Yunnan, and, as provincial officials generally recognized, effectively absent for many purposes. The limits of Qing regional administration were particularly obvious in times of crisis such as the Panthay Rebellion. Limits were also manifest in more explicitly environmental terms in events such as the anti–poppy cultivation operations pursued as part of the state's larger crackdown on the opium traffic in the 1830s.

The opium traffic was an exemplary case of the critical necessity for state control of environmental, and not simply commercial, relations. Humans and poppies, from which opium was extracted, were particularly interdependent not only because of the drug's effects on human physiology, but also because of the poppy's inability to exist in a fully wild state independent of human cultivation.[59] The Qing state's limited supervision of southwestern Yunnan was exposed by senior provincial official admissions during the 1820s and 1830s. State prohibition pressure forced officials to admit that illicit poppy cultivation in isolated mountainous and chieftainship areas was effectively beyond their control. Yunnan Governor Ilibu flatly stated in 1828 that he could not directly oversee the eradication of poppy stands in the Gengma native chieftainship because the locale was too far from "Yunnan proper" (*neidi*) for provincial personnel to supervise directly. The operation was duly left to Gengma's indigenous authorities.[60] The delegation of such grave state responsibilities governing resource access to chieftainship proxies is indicative both of the limits of Qing state control and of the corresponding authority of local structures of indirect rule in the region.

More centralized native chieftainships of the *gumsa* and Shan types further undermined dynastic control by maintaining similar political ties

Borderland Hanspace in the Nineteenth Century   247

to the major Qing competitor for regional hegemony, the Konbaung. Some of the stimulating and inhibiting effects of this rivalry on the southwestern borderland were similar to those achieved by Konbaung Myanmar's northern counterpart, Romanov Russia.

Subversion of indigenous Qing subjects was one such effect. The immediate cause of the 1766–69 war itself concerned Qing and Konbaung wrangling over the territorial implications of indigenous allegiance.[61] The Konbaung court was able to split the allegiance of at least some Qing chieftainships, which in Myanmar's view formed the trans-Irawaddy and trans-Salween Shan States. The ambiguous relations maintained by native chieftainships with both powers enabled Myanmar to claim joint territorial sovereignty with the Qing. The Konbaung made such a claim regarding the Cheli native chieftainship in the wake of a major conflict from 1807 to 1808 in the area between Myanmar and the Siamese client state of Lanna (Chiangmai).[62]

Despite the throne's outraged declaration that a "fixed boundary" (*dingjie*) already existed that precluded any kind of joint jurisdiction between "the Celestial court and foreign tribals" in Cheli, Qing officials were quite aware of the divided loyalties of native chieftainships.[63] Some admitted that Gengma and "all dynastic chieftainships near Myanmar" maintained an "unofficial," if regular, political relationship with the Konbaung until at least the mid–eighteenth century. Such contacts remained an ongoing concern after the turn of the century. At that time Belin affirmed that a primary task of frontier defense was to prevent "collusion" between native chieftainships and either Myanmar or Lanna.[64] Transborder political ties incompatible with their status as dynastic client states could make chieftainships more a burden than a bulwark for the province.

One important spatial condition of the ambiguity of chieftainship allegiance was that southwestern provincial borders were operationally synonymous with *junxian* and not chieftainship boundaries. This distinction was occasionally, and inconsistently, expressed through the use of different terms for *junxian* boundaries (*bian* or *jiao*) and chieftainship boundaries (*jing*). The operational limits of direct dynastic control indicated by these terms explain why "Yunnan" chieftainships such as Menglian and Gengma could be considered "beyond the border" (*bianwai*) of the prefecture itself.[65]

Qing frontier policy reinforced this ethnic administrative divide by generally discouraging "reckless" official interference in chieftainships "along the border." These off-limits border polities included Gengma,

248   *Across Forest, Steppe, and Mountain*

Mengmian, Mengding, Zhefang, Longchuan, Mengmao, Menglian, and Ganya, as listed by Zhou Huafeng in his commentary discussed in Chapter 4. This was the rule even in extreme cases, as Yongchang Magistrate Wang Xuzai discovered in 1812 when he sent troops to the Mengding chieftainship in answer to an exaggerated distress call from a chief fearing a coup. The throne considered such events, real or not, to be internal affairs. Wang was reprimanded for his interference. Of course, if internal conflicts threatened to spill over into Yunnan proper, the throne would authorize intervention, as it did in 1818 in Gengma.[66]

Such state limitations, self-imposed and otherwise, qualify the nature of indigenous ethnic identity in relation to a more nominal, or even notional, "native chieftainship system" (*tusi zhidu*).[67] Checks on Qing authority to build chieftainships systematically, however, not only include decentralized indigenous resistance, and rival Southeast Asian polities, but also malarial mosquitoes and haematozoa within the larger disease environment. The unity of purpose and culture Scott finds among diverse Zomian peoples is questionable. Nevertheless, the recognition and further articulation of state limitations, especially before the mid-twentieth century, in the face of this same environmental variation is indisputable. This recognition must condition accounts of inner frontiers or *gumsa* and *gumlao* organizations, or, more recently, "native chieftainship zones" (*tusi dai*), to acknowledge that these constructs are to a significant degree provisional, reified, and sometimes delusional.[68] Their degree of dysfunction is substantially related to an inability or refusal to recognize ecological factors obscured by imperial and scholarly constructs.

The comparatively narrow cultural space occupied by recent and past analyses of chieftainships has yet to meaningfully include a broader ecological space that would help alleviate some of this dysfunction. Chieftainships actually oscillated over time within a range of manifestations. Their degree and type depended not only on the amount of power exerted by various human actors, but also by varying ecological inputs, including famine and disease, that were largely outside human control. So it is more accurate to speak of fluctuating chieftainship relations rather than of a concrete system. Nevertheless, Qing officials did exert themselves to maintain these relations in an organized, even systematic, fashion over time, as bureaucratic regulations attest.

These oscillations and some of their underlying environmental causes must also qualify both ideas of a "Confucian civilizing project" fueled by relentless Han imperial expansion and accounts of early modern state

Borderland Hanspace in the Nineteenth Century 249

projects of ethnic categorization to abet a Qing local colonialism.[69] No single condition of contraction, stasis, or expansion was the norm. So Qing imperial space periodically advanced, paused, or withdrew in response to shifts in local environmental relations often expressed in purely ethnic terms.

Persistent fluctuations or oscillations, viewed from the dynastic perspective as chronic instabilities, may nevertheless account for the eagerness of many Qing officials to replace their "system" with Han settlement. Even when it occurred under dubious or disruptive circumstances, a Han presence was seen as the best medium for local surveillance of the majority indigenous populace, which tended to collude with "wild [indigenous] bandits." This attitude may also help account for the active support of Han swiddening with little concern for its ecological implications visible in Ilibu's 1836 deliberations over how to adapt the *baojia* regime to shack people identity.

Just such a preference for settler over indigene was made in support of an 1831 decision to uphold Han claims in the Nandian native chieftainship. Officials hoped that by legitimating a Han presence, the Qing borderland would be solidified through a decreased dependency on indigenous peoples, whose nature one *junxian* memorialist held to be as inconstant as that "of dogs and sheep." This decision, however, was made in the context of infiltration of Nandian by elements of "wild tribals" and Han settlers who united to challenge indigenous authority.[70] An even more explicit process of immigrant Han acculturation to Yi identity was occurring in southern Sichuan around roughly the same time. Other evidence of Han ethnic instability is visible later in the century, when garrison troops sent to Pu'er from Guangdong and Guangxi began to mix with indigenous populations. They had become tribal *Guangren* by the twentieth century. Of course, there were also borderland inhabitants who defied any consistent ethnic characterization.[71]

As the Nandian example demonstrates, Han residence was not absolutely precluded in chieftainship territory by southwestern Yunnan's disease environment. Yet such residence remained conditional, limited, and even destabilizing for the ordering of a southwestern imperial borderland in the nineteenth century. The "natural" limits on this ordering not only include malaria, but also involve relatively fine distinctions between glutinous and nonglutinous riziculture as well as the sensitivity of forest slopes to different forms of swidden agriculture. Such constraints combined to obstruct the full realization of an arablist order of the sort

250   *Across Forest, Steppe, and Mountain*

contemplated by dynastic officials such as Gao Qizhuo. Indeed, just as it had in Cai Yurong's time, this mountainous disease environment's dynamics continued synergistically to impede, and even roll back, development of such a borderland-structured space to the end of the nineteenth century.

Events such as the Panthay Rebellion, and subsequent regional fragmentation that emerged in the early twentieth century, significantly disrupt the trajectory of regional integration informing some important modern historical analyses of the area.[72] It is really only in the light of post-1949 history that pre-Liberation Yunnan's rocky progress into a larger Han centralized polity can be continuously visualized. The impediments of human cultural diversity interacting with the province's disease environment formed a fundamental obstacle along this ostensible path, which Chiang Kai-shek's forces were bumping up against as late as the mid-1930s in Yunnan and Guizhou.

In southwestern Yunnan, the nineteenth-century Qing state seems to have reached an impasse. The ethnic composition of the Qing frontier zone had so changed that by 1799 parts of the Shunning native chieftainships of Menglian and Mengmeng had been taken over by wild Luohei and Kawa. Sometime later, officials believed Nandian, Tengyue's primary native chieftainship, to be abetting wild plunder operations. Even the forces of dynastic local administration were intimidated. To the throne's incredulous consternation, there were rumors of indigenous defiance, like the report of a "wild tribal" who might have cut the nose off a Qing squad leader without reprisal in 1817. Destabilizing incursions into provincial peripheries persisted into the 1820s.[73] Indirect rule through the *gumsa* unification appeared to be no great obstacle to the expansion of *gumlao*-style decentralization, a form of socioeconomic organization possibly better suited to dealing with intermittent famine conditions.

The deterioration of the inner frontier chieftainships of southwestern Yunnan's three prefectures continued unabated until 1825. At that time, Hu Qirong, in the penultimate year of his seven-year stint as Tengyue subprefectural magistrate, had resolved to take action. Hu memorialized that his subprefectural seat was "surrounded on all four sides by the stockades of wild tribals, which run straight through to the limits of the frontier in uncountable numbers." Only a single road, which still remained free of nearby wild stockades, connected the seat with Yunnan proper in Yongchang prefecture to the northeast. Lamenting such conditions, Hu revealed that there was no longer an

Borderland Hanspace in the Nineteenth Century

effective inner frontier zone: "Even the native chieftainships within the frontier cannot be defended. How can the inhabitants of Yunnan proper be protected?"[74]

Hu obtained permission to establish a western line of seventy-seven "strongpoints" (*diaobao*) manned by 624 chieftainship militia, backed up in a few strategic places by Han relief forces that could be stationed on nonmalarial high ground. The strongpoints were supposed to be self-supporting military agricultural colonies similar to those employed against the Miao in Hunan and against White Lotus sectarians in Sichuan and elsewhere. At least nine of Hu's blockhouses were constructed along the reaches of the Binlang River, some in explicitly malarial areas, which would now form the province's western extremity.[75]

Contrary to some statements in local gazetteers, this system did not function very effectively.[76] He Zikai, a contemporary of Hu, had opposed the strongpoints because they could not possibly cover the numerous passes connecting Yunnan proper with the border zones. During his operations against wild tribals as governor-general of Yun-Gui, Lin Zexu confirmed that invaders, who had taken twenty-six Han men and women, could simply bypass the strongpoints. In 1849 these raiders, "neither foreign subjects nor controlled by native chieftainships," were living "mixed together in mountain valleys in individual stockades that appoint their own headmen." There were still moving freely into Yunnan from the Yerenshan.[77]

The unrestricted movement of people through rugged, malarial terrain hindered Qing ability to secure Yunnan's southwestern frontier zones in 1849 as it had done in 1769. By 1899 disease environment dynamics were reasserting themselves to undermine imperial indigenism. A western observer at this time noted that "malaria is so prevalent" in five of ten chieftainships in southern Pu'er prefecture's Sipsongpanna region "that the Chinese will not dwell in them." Consequently, Chinese officials could "exercise no more than a nominal control over those districts. The actual *military* jurisdiction of the Chinese does not extend more than a few miles to the west or south of Sumao [Simao]." A Chinese official and some of his military escort had just died of the disease a few years before in 1897 while mediating a succession dispute in the Mengzhe chieftainship.[78]

Routine patrol reports from the early 1790s portray a much more harmonious society in the Simao and Jiulong stretch of the Mekong River region, with high-yield highland and lowland cultivation as well as mutually profitable commerce between Han settlers and indigenous peoples.[79]

252 *Across Forest, Steppe, and Mountain*

A century later, local disease conditions seem to have overcome whatever multiethnic harmony existed. Almost another half century after that, a local saying recorded in 1939 confirmed that Simao subprefecture in the middle of Pu'er still marked the ethnic boundary: "Go farther south and enter into another world."[80] Ethnic spatial distinctions, as part of the local disease environment, outlived the demise of the dynastic system itself.

THE LOCUS OF VIRTUE

Although the Qing dynasty did experience what many scholars see as a significant post-1860 "restoration" in certain respects, "it is undeniable that systemic failures within the Qing empire became manifest around the turn of the nineteenth century." China was "left behind by Europe in relative terms, and suffered "an intrinsic and absolute loss of capacity." This crisis emerged from "a perfect storm of three simultaneous problems: the external shock of the expanding west, a secular crisis caused by an accumulation of socio-economic difficulties over the long term and the more acute political dysfunctions associated with the familiar pattern of the dynastic cycle."[81]

The ecological metaphor is more appropriate to the empire's predicament than these three comparatively cultural articulations suggest. The Qing was, perhaps, not so much swamped by a secular socioeconomic crisis but inundated by an environmental one that washed away too much fertile land, the empire's keystone. Work currently done on empire-wide trends toward resource exhaustion is suggestive but remains preliminary. Yet there is a basic consensus that serious deforestation and related erosion fueled the century's environmental crisis.[82]

It is very difficult to find "virtuous" sustainable adaptations of any of the main Qing environmental networked regimes of imperial foraging, imperial pastoralism, imperial indigenism, or even imperial arablism during the nineteenth century comparable to the relative harmony they all enjoyed through most of the eighteenth century. In terms of Hanspace dissent, motley *qi* pollution waxes fully only in the nineteenth century. One common dependency underlying all four regimes across these times was their absolute reliance on fertile land that either was, or could usually be, arablized at varying scales. Fertile land's flexibility promoted diversity, but was also susceptible to agrarian encroachment that could destroy both trees and soil. This fundamental transimperial dependency on fertile land did not produce a mere population problem, but an imbalance between arable

Borderland Hanspace in the Nineteenth Century 253

land, people, and the identities formed from the intersection of the two. An open season on highland and borderland fields ensued, but the ratio of arable farmland per capita is nevertheless estimated to have fallen 43 percent between 1753 and 1812 to less than half an acre per person.[83]

This insufficiently bleak statistic, however, conveys the impression that there was no net decline in farmland, merely a scarcity that implicitly results from dynamic population increase. However, work on the effects of an absolute rollback in productive areas of Yunnan and the lower Yangzi highlands indicates there was a significant loss of previously arable land.[84] This is also true for parts of Inner Mongolia, particularly in the Ordos plateau region. Losses likewise occurred in adjacent areas of Shanxi and Shaanxi, as well as, most plainly, in the Hexi Corridor. There were problems in the eastern leagues too. One account based on a 1906 survey acknowledged that cultivation on alkaline soil could be pursued for only "several successive years" until neither grains nor grasses would grow in the exhausted ground.[85] Eighteenth-century attempts to increase arable land in Lingnan highlands during both the Yongzheng and Qianlong reigns may have also become unsustainable by the early nineteenth century.[86] Similar results of agrarian overreach are also visible today in the northeast's steadily eroding "black soil" (phaeozem, a humus-rich topsoil) region, originating in unrestricted arablization officially sanctioned from 1860 on. More recently, the black soil zone has contracted 27 percent since the 1950s from the synergistic effects of intensive human cultivation of a rich but fragile ecology naturally prone to erosion. Agrarian, not demographic, excess has eliminated both black soil and agriculture in some areas.[87]

The evidence, for and against a substantial agricultural rollback, is neither complete nor unambiguous. Contradictions abound, most starkly between evidence for an expanding population, a precipitous drop in acreage per capita, and a net increase in the empire's cultivated fields. The contradictions inherent in all such calculations based on incomplete and far from unimpeachable records are visible in Yen-chien Wang's analysis of land registered in 1753 and 1908. Wang concluded that "there was practically no change" in taxable acreage between these two periods, with the exception of Manchuria and Xinjiang, but speculated that as much as 80 percent of new fields could have gone unregistered from the mid–eighteenth century on. In contrast, Li Bozhong's more recent and more regionalized environmental study of the Jiangnan wet-rice heartland comes to the opposite conclusion that concealment "must have been low."[88] Hiding new cultivation in water-starved borderlands such as Xinjiang was not easy, as noted by Xinjiang military officer Qi Xizao in

254 *Across Forest, Steppe, and Mountain*

an 1851 response to accusations of concealment by Han cultivators. Qi asserted that any household clearing new land for cultivation would soon come into public conflict with other households over limited water resources. Neither could "spare the smallest drop of water, and it would come to a fight. It isn't like the situation in China proper."[89] Ecological realities kept locals honest and legible.

G. William Skinner's amusingly masterful 1987 exposé of gross errors and "mindless incompetence" in Sichuan's nineteenth-century population registers remains a fundamental check on demographic arguments for Qing historical change powered by vacuums such as acreage concealment. It is possible that what Skinner calls a similar "dialectical dynamic," which could distort decades of demographic data on the order of 6 million people, was also at work in registration of fields.[90] Here I can only briefly sketch an outline of what may be a similar agrarian dynamic from a more critical perspective taken on land registration, in a similar spirit if not in similar detail, within a wider context that includes borderland fields beyond core macroregions.

Some losses in arable land would have been absorbed by increases in wet rice productivity on existing Jiangnan fields, as argued by Li Bozhong, or by state action to alleviate a range of adverse conditions in Lingnan, as argued by Robert B. Marks. Rice imports from both Taiwan and Southeast Asia offset losses as well.[91] Conditions north of the Yangzi, however, were different. The onset of a colder mid–nineteenth century related to the Little Ice Age almost certainly created greater problems for the more fragile agricultural conditions in north China and beyond, where frantic clearance of poor soils was expanding. Furthermore, in contrast to effective adaptations to structural problems such as climate change by seasoned farmers in the south, cultivators in northern steppe and even on southwestern mountains appear to have been quite green.

By precise measures, loss of productive land was not reflected in the official record. Overall, state disaster relief to the more than nine thousand counties seriously affected by climate change from 1796 into the late 1840s was restricted to a lower percentage of these afflicted areas than in the eighteenth century, leaving more places to weather disasters by themselves and off the books.[92] Moreover, tax exemptions that were extended did not necessarily trickle down to revitalize ruined fields. As Pierre-Etienne Will has pointed out, "the taxpayer was not necessarily the farmer, the 'real' disaster victim." This was a major problem "in areas of high land concentration" because "landlords were not obliged to adjust rents to reflect a tax exemption." There were also practical disincentives for local administrators to apply tax relief for environmental disasters with precision. Officials would have had to recalculate levies separately for each plot affected to take into account differing levels of damage and distinctions between exempt grain-producing land and other nonexempt types.[93] In other words, tax exemption was a purely fiscal abstraction. Figures would not accurately reflect the actual condition of the exempted plots, which could be out of production. Yet these notional grounds could still "generate" incomes and revenues for state ledgers and landlords' pockets as tenants were pressed into lower subsistence rates on less productive land.[94]

There were other oversimplifying fiscal abstractions as well, such as the differences between the Qing statutory system of tax assessment and the one actually implemented. The statutory system's quota was based on a straightforward formula of land area taxed at variable rates based on a plot's level of productivity, which was influenced by various factors of soil quality, access to irrigation, etc. This often resulted, however, in administratively unwieldy assessments, such as the two hundred gradations of land, each taxed at a different rate, in highly ramified Jiangsu province. Many jurisdictions simplified assessment through the conversion of real multiple units of lower grade land into a single "virtual" unit of higher grade land. This practice conceals real acreage in overall Qing land statistics and includes reclaimed fields such as some in Shaanxi that produced an actual harvest only every five to ten years.[95] This amalgamation, which reflects the limitations of administrative legibility in some ways similar to the continued use of sable pelts as mere units of account, would obscure drops in land fertility.

The fiscal filters blurring state perceptions of local conditions were rendered even less transparent by the fact that land registers were not consistently and precisely updated for many reasons, and that provincial tax quotas were effectively fixed after 1750. As long as these quotas were met, there was no substantial incentive to revise the figures on which they were based through official inspection of the ground itself.[96] Many of Qing fiscal abstractions thus worked to "suppress temporal variation" and "homogenize spatial heterogeneity" so as to enhance "constancy and stability at the expense of variability and resilience." In this respect they resemble predispositions of present-day managerial structures in environmental and developmental policy.[97]

A memorial submitted to the throne around the time of the Yongzheng-Qianlong regnal transition provides an extensive commentary on how a number of social and administrative factors combined to distort state perceptions about the amount of land actually cleared for cultivation in China proper around this time. This memorial, written by Cao Yishi probably when he served in the censorate, outlines two major problems connected with "the extremely large amount of land now being cleared in various provinces." The first was counting already developed fields as newly cleared ones. This was a tactical response to excessive clearance quotas previously established by provincial officials on paper, which grossly overestimated the actual extent of as yet undeveloped provincial "wastelands." These "new" fields were then newly assessed, which simply increased the tax burden of farmers working what were really the same old fields as before. The other problem was, conversely, counting undeveloped wastelands as fully developed fields. Cultivation of marginal lands remaining uncleared along waterways and around mountain bases was often sustainable only for a few years before thin rocky soil gave out or boggy soil became inundated. Nevertheless, all reclamation of such areas was included in official figures, and revenues were fixed in state anticipation of recouping its initial investment in seed, livestock, and tax remissions from stable, fully productive fields. These commitments were incentives for provincial officials to conceal, through various reporting measures, the inevitable collapse of such reclamation schemes. Plots long gone to seed would be declared as productive, so that clearance "proceeds in name without any fields that have actually matured." Such "productive" lands thus inflated registers. Onsite surveys to determine what cleared land was viable for taxation and what should be written off were recommended. A 1740 memorial from Henan, however, suggests little change when it described similar problems. It concluded that provincial reclamation went on "in name only from the start," and any talk of revenue was just "empty phrases on paper."[98] Cao's memorial was probably penned around the time major scandals over false acreage reports emerged in 1735. One inquiry determined that only 127,400 *mu* out of 980,000 cleared was viable farmland for taxation. Likewise 1.3 million *mu* in Jiangnan were similarly written off.[99] Under such conditions, there is no reason to assume the predominance of dynamics for the concealment of new acreage over those for exaggerating the extent of new acreage and hiding loss of productive fields.

Finally, the statistics under discussion assume all productive land was worked by farmers, not herders or foragers, so only gains in grain, not losses in meat, milk, fish, or fungi, are accounted for. Moreover, the heads counted are all assumed to be agrarian. Were it possible to include these

Borderland Hanspace in the Nineteenth Century 257

other variables, as well as track related declines in ground cover and discount unsustainable cultivation, a more environmental accounting might reveal other net losses in both land and identity.

From an environmental, rather than a socioeconomic, perspective, it is perhaps more accurate, if still problematic, to say that arable land was the empire's limiting factor. In simple terms, Han-style swiddening and casual clearance destroyed arable land. Indigenous-style swiddening preserved it, as did indigenous forms of foraging and pastoralism. Their imperial counterparts were by no means inherently unsustainable, but were quite vulnerable to what appear to be intrinsic, almost "logical," excesses such as those that methodically toppled pines in Jiaqing-era Manchuria. Actively unsustainable practices in land use, rather than mere population growth, were the deeper roots of the nineteenth-century crisis. This is a Qing historical application of an environmental theory paradigm asserting that "the numbers of individuals present locally ... reflect the set of attributes of those individuals *and* the characteristics of the environment [emphasis added]. Numbers of individuals are not driving forces of the ecological process, but its effects." These individuals become a, derivative, effect only when their "density becomes excessive," but this density is not a Malthusian entity that determines its engendering relations with the surrounding ecology.[100]

Han arablism, the primary environmental relation configuring China proper and radiating well beyond it, had also developed into the realm's primary contradiction between culture and ecology by the nineteenth century. One of the empire's key adaptations to Han population growth was shack people's "cultivated deforestation." This adaptation rapidly exhausted fertile reserves that still existed even in the full-blown arablist Hanspace of China proper and eroded its developed areas as well. Like Inner Mongolia's naturally occurring limiting condition of rainfall, Han swiddening and arablist overconcentration of the sort contemplated by Zhang Zhidong anthropogenically converted fertile land into China proper's limiting factor.

In an unexpected way, such arablist radiation affirms some of Wang Fuzhi's most virulent convictions on the capacity of Hanspace's numinous natural defenses to cleanse this dragon's true lair of polluting ethnic diversity. Terrestrial *qi* works, in the form of agriculture, not only to obstruct foraging, herding, and even Zomi-culture within China proper, but had also, by the nineteenth century, expanded its circulation to erode these diverse practices in borderland areas. This enables the "re-Sinification" Wang saw in Guizhou to restore a proper Han habitat

258 *Across Forest, Steppe, and Mountain*

in places that had become geographically and, therefore, culturally isolated. It also allows this habitat to spread beyond traditional boundaries to approach an eradication of destabilizing diversity beyond it. Moreover, this view converges with accommodationists such as Hu Wei, and even the Yongzheng emperor himself, when they assert the civilizing effects over time on originally "barbarian" places such as Zhejiang, Hunan, Hubei, and Shanxi. A notable nineteenth-century accommodationist, Wei Yuan, validated these views. Wei asserted that Qing expansion into Khalkha territory spread *shengjiao*, mediated by tribute supervised under the *Lifanyuan*, beyond this forbidding "sea of sand" (*hanhai*), an obstacle that had even blocked the influence of Yu the Great. He also relied on a consequently more detailed (meta)spatial geography of the region to effect an expansion of Hanspace, arguing that the empire's northern dragon trunk actually lay beyond the Gobi in Uliastai.[101] Unfortunately in all its versions, monocultural Hanspace was materially limited. Failure to make the appropriate adaptations, such as a shift to sustainable swiddening, reconversion to pastureland, or reforestation, would indeed trigger "natural defenses" against any unsustainable monoculture.

The interdependencies of such networks exemplify the conditional relevance of the mainstay explanation of Han population growth to account for nineteenth-century declines. Problems of Qing demography further impair this explanation. Problems, nevertheless, remain difficult to address, because, as Li Bozhong has frankly acknowledged, although population figures may be too high, "it is not possible to obtain better ones, and so they are used here."[102] Much the same epitaph could be read over Qing acreage, but the more diverse environmental approaches of Li and Marks offer the possibility to transcend at least some of the real limitations of demographic and land statistics. So it may be said that the onset of nineteenth-century environmental crises reveals to anyone seeking the mandate that the locus of virtue had always lain in fertile ground bounded by neither core nor periphery, but by ecology.

Notes

1 Shanghai shudian chubanshe, ed., '*Dayi juemi lu' tan*, 134. I have translated *qishu* as "*qi* circulating in the cosmos," more conventionally rendered as "fate." The *Liji*: provides some context: "The celestial *qi* ascends and the mundane *qi* descends so that there is no circulation between the cosmic poles of heaven and earth. Winter develops in full from this blockage," *Liji zhuyi*, 210.

2 See, for example, Zhang Yanli, *Jia Dao shiqi de zaihuang*, 6–8.

Borderland Hanspace in the Nineteenth Century   259

3 Pomeranz, "How Exhausted an Earth?" 7, 9; Lee and Campbell, *Fate and Fortune*, 28–31, 44; Wang Yejian and Huang Yingjue, "Qingdai Zhongguo qihou bianqian," 3–18; Li Bozhong, "Shijiu shiji jiangnan de jingji xiaotiao"; Zhang et al., "Climate Change and War Frequency," 403–14. Han population increase was, also, not the sole cause of every arabalist success, which also depended on Chinese "customary practices"; Isett, "Village Regulation of Property."

4 The mid–nineteenth century, particularly because of the monumentally catastrophic shift of the Yellow River between 1852 and 1855, has been considered "the most critical period" of the ecological crisis faced by the "Huang-Yun" region of western Shandong and neighboring parts of Zhili and Henan; Pomeranz, *The Making of a Hinterland*, 128.

5 Calculations based on Liang Fangzhong, *Zhongguo lidai hukou, tiandi, tianfu tongji*, 383.

6 Ingold, "Growing Plants and Raising Animals," 22. For a discussion of human relations with plants in the context of larger timescales in "big history" as "co-evolutionary," see Christian, "The Case for 'Big History'," 231–34. For a pertinent case study from eighteenth-century China, Lee and Campbell, *Fate and Fortune*, 28–31.

7 See Pomeranz, *The Great Divergence*; Brenner and Isett, "England's Divergence from China's Yangzi Delta," 609–62; Lavely and Wong, "Revising the Malthusian Narrative," 714–48. Some larger contexts framing these debates are provided by Rowe, "Social Stability and Social Change," 474-80; Myers and Wang, "Economic Developments," 563–617, 626–45. For a representative view from Chinese language scholarship, see Young-tsu Wong, "'Tiandi zhi dao'," 87–114.

8 See, for example, Congbin Fu, "Potential Impacts of Human-Induced Land Cover Change on East Asia Monsoon," *Global and Planetary Change* 37 (2003): 219–29.

9 Lavely and Wong, "Revising the Malthusian Narrative," 739. More environmentally informed considerations are already reframing old debates; Parker, "Crisis and Catastrophe," 1053–79. Parker's revisions appropriately go well beyond employing ecological analyses simply as hermeneutic tropes or metaphors, as advocated by J. B. Shank in response: "Crisis: A Useful Category of Post-Social Scientific Historical Analysis," 1090–99.

10 *Qing Gaozong yuzhi shi*, 5:344a; *Yongzhengchao Manwen zhupi*, #500, 1:272.

11 *Da Qing huidian shili* (GX), 8:802a, 820b–21a; *QSL*, JQ 7/8/24, 29:372b.

12 Elliott and Ning, "The Qing Hunt at Mulan," 77–80; MWLF, JQ 13/3/26 [03-198-3739-010].

13 Han Guanghui and Zhao Yingmei, "Lun Qing chu yilai weichang diqu," 288–90; Zhao Zhen, "Qingdai saiwai weichang de ziyuan guanli," 149–54; Yu Tongyuan and Wang Laigang, "Qingdai zhongyuan renkou bei yi," 329; *Da Qing huidian shili* (GX), 8:802b, 821a–b; *Yongzhengchao Manwen zhupi*, #2317, 2:1293–94.

14 Elvin, "Three Thousand Years of Unsustainable Growth," 13.

15 Liu Kun, *Nanzhong za shuo*, 8:355.

260 *Across Forest, Steppe, and Mountain*

16 For a representative example of this view, which teleologically privileges Han arabalist development and ignores pastoralism, see Yu Tongyuan and Wang Laigang, "Qingdai zhongyuan renkou bei yi."

17 Dodgen, *Controlling the Dragon,* 146. Also note Dodgen's discussion of debates over the efficiency of the Jiaqing and Daoguang era statecraft (3–5, 145–46).

18 Zhou Qiong, "Qingdai Yunnan neidihua shengtai bianqian."

19 Perdue, "Official Goals and Local Interests," 747, 754, 756–57, 761, 763.

20 Schoppa, "State, Society, and Land Reclamation," 250–51; Huang Liuhong, *A Complete Book,* 217; Ya-er-tu, "Kan bao kai ken xu shi shu," 1:851a–52a; Tao Zhu, *Tao Wen Yi Gong (Zhu) ji,* 2:953–86.

21 Elvin, "Three Thousand Years of Unsustainable Growth," 10, 11.

22 *QSL,* JQ 9/2/11, 29:700b–701b. Long before in 1777 the Qianlong emperor was expressing concern that the proximity of Jilin to Fengtian's itinerant Han population endangered the former area as a reserve for borderland Manchu identity; *Qingdai Sanxing Fudutong Yamen Man Han wen dang'an xuanbian,* #4, 133–36.

23 Schelsinger, "Qing Invention of Nature," 24–25.

24 *Qingdai Zhong-E guanxi dang'an shiliao xuanbian,* 1:181.208–09, 1:183.210–11, 1:192.224–25.

25 *Da Qing huidian* (GX), 141a–b. *Qingdai Zhong-E guanxi dang'an shiliao xuanbian,* 1:183.210–11.

26 Pan Jinglong and Zhang Xuanru, eds., *Jilin gongpin,* XT 2/1/16, 25–27; *QSL,* GX 32/12/3, 59:511a. Such evidence of fragile cultivation conditions should qualify generalized statements that "Manchuria ... was particularly well-suited for agriculture"; Reardon-Anderson, *Reluctant Pioneers,* 11. "Manchuria" was actually quite patchy at best in this respect, as noted in Chapter 3.

27 *Huang Qing zouyi,* 3:1087–1104. The condition of Bedune and its environs as dual sites of Manchu agriculture and foraging is indicated by reports of ginseng poaching in 1733, when the town was also identified as a grain source for Khorchin relief; MWLF YZ 11/8/17 [03-172-0901-001], 11/7/1 [03-173-1032-016]. It is probably significant that the 1810 report does not mention ginseng in its discussion of forage despite deployment of outposts in ginseng fields around 1733.

28 *Huang Qing zouyi,* 3:1087–1104.

29 Pan Jinglong and Zhang Xuanru, eds., *Jilin gongpin,* XT 2/1/16, pp. 25–27. A perceived pastoral or foraging vacuum, sometimes arising from existing deforestation, seems to have regularly attracted agrarian interest. Heilongjiang lands around Hulan "formerly" foraged for ginseng and pearls did so in 1857, forests around Shengjing and Daqingshan pastures near Hohhot followed a year later and Jilin hunting grounds did likewise in 1861; *QSL,* XF 7/6/4, 43:567a–b, XF 8/6/24, 991b, XF 9/10/6, 44:347a–48b, TZ 7/8/24, 340b–41b.

30 *Da-sheng Wu-la difang xiangtu zhi,* 151–54. Some late Qing and early Mingguo gazetteers indicate that large-scale deforestation in a number of areas began in the Tongzhi reign; Li Li and Liang Mingwu, "Ming Qing shiqi dongbei diqu shengtai huanjing bianhua," 113–16.

31 MWLF, QL 7/4/25 [03-174-1495-002]; QL 7/5/6 [03-170-0055-009].

Borderland Hanspace in the Nineteenth Century   261

32 MWLF, QL 3/6/21 [03-172-0734-006], 4/2/14 [03-173-1054-001].

33 Ding Junna et al., "Lüelun Qingdai ziran ziyuan," 28–30.

34 Zhang Zhidong, *Zhang Zhidong quanshu*, 1:18b–20a.

35 Zhang Zhidong, *Zhang Zhidong quanshu*, 1:28b–29b.

36 Zhang Zhidong, *Zhang Zhidong quanshu*, 1:28b–29b.

37 Osborne, "The Politics of Land Reclamation," 37.

38 *Da Qing huidian shili* (GX), 8:1124b–29b; 1131b–32a. See also the overview in Yi-du-he-xi-ge, *Menggu minzu tongshi, disi juan*, 4:265–70, and a brief discussion of the Gorlos case in Zhao Zhiheng, *Nei Menggu tongshi*, 3:122. For an earlier 1727 case, which relies on decisions in 1712 and 1723–25 to institutionalize Han farmer residence north of the Jiangjia and Gubei passes, see QSL, YZ 5/2/23, 7:808b–09b. Such decisions, more ad hoc in the eighteen century but increasingly systematized in the nineteenth, were generally justified as alternatives to disruptive mass relocations of thousands of Han settlers; QSL JQ 11/7/14, 30:130a–31a, JQ 11/7/20, 30:137a–b, JQ 15/11/1, 31:175b–a.

39 Zhang Yongjiang, "Neidihua yu yitihua," 298–326"; Reardon-Anderson, *Reluctant Pioneers*, 7–8.

40 Such an extrapolation was even of limited application throughout China proper; Dunstan, "Heirs of Yu," 522.

41 Zhao Zhiheng, *Nei Menggu tongshi*, 3:107; Will and Wong, *Nourish the People*, 22, 531.

42 Fernandez-Gimenez, "The Role of Mongolian Pastoralists'," 1322; Humphrey and Sneath, "Introduction," 4–5; Mearns, "Decentralization, Rural Livelihoods and Pasture-Land Management," 140–41. Mearns observes that IMAR vegetation conditions are even worse than Mongolia's, "a clear demonstration of the importance of pastoral mobility for sustainable grassland management in dryland Inner Asia," (150). Fernandez-Gimenez provides evidence for a "universal conviction" among herders interviewed that private ownership of rangeland "would lead to disaster" by arbitrarily denying access to herds in distress from unpredictable ecological shifts, (1323).

43 Zhu Qiqian, *Dong San Sheng Mengwu gongdu huibian*, 31:355b. Cited in Su De, "Guanyu Qingmo Neimenggu xibu diqu de fangken," 437.

44 See the twentieth-century discussion in Sneath, *Changing Inner Mongolia*, 133–37. For the Qing period, see Xiao Ruiling et al., *Ming-Qing Nei Menggu xibu diqu kaifa*, 149–74.

45 Branigan, "Mongolia: How the Winter of 'White Death' Devastated Nomads' Way of Life."

46 Inner Mongolia's nineteenth-century uprisings were quite limited and ineffectual; Fletcher, "The Heyday of the Ch'ing Order," 352; Zhao Zhiheng, *Nei Menggu tongshi*, 3:285–305.

47 Atwill, "Blinkered Visions," 1085–86.

48 Zhou Qiong and Li Mei, "Qing zhong hou qi Yunnan shanqu nongye shengtai," 127–28.

49 For surveys of these steles' content, see Yan Shaomei and Zhang Xinchang, "Qingdai Yunnan Yizu diqu senlin shengtai baohu beike," 37–40; Shimizu Toru, "Yunnan nanbu de shengtai huanjing beike."

262 *Across Forest, Steppe, and Mountain*

50 Zhou Qiong and Li Mei, "Qing zhong hou qi Yunnan shanqu nongye shengtai,"126.

51 Bao Shichen, *Qimin si shu*, 173. For an introduction to his views on agriculture, see Rowe, "Bao Shichen."

52 Cao Shuqiao, "Diannan zazhi," 11:5983.

53 Hengeveld, "Biodiversity," 7.

54 The state targeted shack people in the Lower Yangzi for disruption of the empire's core agriculture and those in the Middle Yangzi for hindering water control; Leong, *Migration and Ethnicity*, 157, 171, 176–77.

55 *QSL*, DG 17/4/7, 37:590a–b; Tao Zhu, *Tao Wen Yi Gong (Zhu) ji*, 2:982. Tao may have pioneered a system of false reporting to obtain disaster relief tax remission that was subsequently regularized in the Lower Yangzi; Jones and Kuhn, "Dynastic Decline and the Roots of Rebellion," 130.

56 Osborne, "The Politics of Land Reclamation," 30–36; *Xi'an xianzhi*, 748–49; *Changhua xianzhi*, 133–34; Tao Zhu, *Tao Wen Yi Gong (Zhu) ji*, 2:2095–2102. For accounts of the highland soil erosion, including rocky desertification in Guizhou's karst peaks, linked to shack people's maize cultivation, see *Wucheng xianzhi*, 16:28b–29a; Leong, *Migration and Ethnicity*, 158–59; Han, "Maize Cultivation and Its Effect on Rocky Desertification,' 243–58. New World crops have been condemned and praised for both their impoverishing and enriching effects, respectively, on Zomian cultivators; Lan Yong, "Ming Qing Meizhou nongzuowu yinjin," 3–14; Pan Xianlin, "Gao chan nongzuowu chuanru," 60–64.

57 *Weiyuan tingzhi*, 371–81; *Kaihua fuzhi*, 68; DG 16/10/8, *QSL*, 472a–73a.

58 See, for example, Vermeer, "The Mountain Frontier in Late Imperial China," 300–29.

59 Merlin, *On the Trail of the Ancient Opium Poppy*, 53–54.

60 Neige, xingke tiben, weijin lei, DG 8/5/22, #10092 (tongben); Gongzhong dang, falü dalei, jinyan, DG 14/11/28; YPZZ, DG 18/12/18. For a general discussion of constraints on opium prohibition in Yunnan, see Bello, *Opium and the Limits of Empire*, Chapter 6.

61 Zhuang Jifa, *Qing Gaozong shi quan wu gong*, 284; Woodside, "The Ch'ien-lung Reign," 264, 267.

62 *Jiaqing Daoguang liang chao shangyu dang*, JQ 14/1/5, 14:8a–b. There is disagreement over the Konbaung state's degree of centralization, but its control of the Shan States along the Yunnan frontier was at best indirect; Koenig, *The Burmese Polity*, 17, 107, 220, 224–25; Leach, "The Frontiers of 'Burma'," 49–68.

63 *Jiaqing Daoguang liang chao shangyu dang*, JQ 14/1/5, 14:8a–b. The problem of dual tributary allegiance was not limited to the Yunnan borderlands. The Ryukyu Islands, for example, maintained tribute relations overtly with the Qing and covertly with the Tokugawa domain of Satsuma; Sakai, "The Ryukyu (Liu-Ch'iu) Islands as fief of Satsuma," 112–34. I am grateful to Rod Wilson for pointing out this similarity.

64 *Daoguang Yunnan zhi chao*, 11:527.

65 *Jiaqing Daoguang liang chao shangyu dang*, JQ 17/4/6, 17:119a–b; JQ 20/1/17, 20:27b; *Xu Yunnan tongzhi gao*, 5:3,979; *Yongchang fuzhi*, 438b;

Borderland Hanspace in the Nineteenth Century

Donghua lu, QL 31/1/18, 7:391b–92b; Gong Yin, *Zhongguo tusi zhidu*, 550–51; *Daoguang Yunnan zhi chao*, 11:528. One of Zhang Yunsui's memorials sited "the whole Lujiang region" "beyond the border" (*jiaowai*); *Qingdai dang'an shiliao congbian*, QL 13/6/11, 2:470–75.

66 *QSL*, 1986–87: JQ 17/4/2, 31:455a–b; *Shunning fuzhi*, 2:887–88. The Mengmian chieftainship was converted to Mianning subprefecture in 1746.

67 See, for example, Giersch, *Asian Borderlands*, 11. For a review of native chieftainship system studies in Chinese, see Jia Xiaofeng, "Ershi duo nian lai tusi zhidu yanjiu zongshu," 126–34.

68 For the concept of "native chieftainship zones," see Cheng Zhenming, *Qingdai tusi yanjiu*, 21–22.

69 For views stressing the dynamism of imperial Chinese expansion, see Harrell, ed., *Cultural Encounters*, 6–7; Hostetler, *Qing Colonial Enterprise*, 127, 136, 209.

70 Chuxiong Yizu wenhua yanjiusuo, ed., *Qingdai Wuding Yizu Nashi tusi*, DG 11.3.21, #4, 26–30.

71 *Chuxiong Yizu wenhua yanjiusuo*, ed., *Qingdai Wuding Yizu Nashi tusi*, DG 11/3/21, #4/26–30; Yan Deyi, "Pu Si yanbian," 29; Li Wenxun, *Zhongguo xinan bianjiang de shehui jingji*, 99–100; Giersch, "'A Motley Throng'," 85.

72 The integration narrative appears in serious works of both western and Chinese scholarship. See, for example, Li Zhongqing, *Zhongguo xinan bianjiang de shehui jingji*, 119–20; You Zhong, *Zhongguo xinan gudai minzu*, 465.

73 *Shunning fuzhi*, 1:482–85; He Zikai, "Tengyue bianwu," 14:4a–5a; *QSL*, JQ 22/12/9, 32:448b–49b; *Yongchang fuzhi*, 145b.

74 *Tengyue tingzhi*, 146a; *Xu Yunnan tongzhi gao*, 5:3971–72, 3978–79.

75 *Xu Yunnan tongzhi gao*, 5:3971–72, 3978–79; Hu Qirong, "Diaobao tushuo," 5:3973–74.

76 See, for example, *Tengyue tingzhi*, 92b.

77 He Zikai, "Tengyue bianwu," 14:4a–5a; Lin Zexu, *Lin Zexu ji*, 3.1156–59.

78 Carey, "A Trip to the Chinese Shan States," 380, 381; Yan Deyi, "Pu Si yanbian," 29.

79 MWLF, QL 58/10/25 [03-195-3453-036], 59/11/18 [03-195-3491-001].

80 Yan Deyi, "Pu Si yanbian," 29.

81 Rowe, *China's Last Empire*, 149–50.

82 For deforestation during the whole the imperial period, see Elvin, *The Retreat of the Elephants*. For the Qing, see, Vermeer, "Ch'ing Government Concerns," 203–48.

83 Rowe, *China's Last Empire*, 150. Over a longer period the decline may have been even more precipitous in north China, where there may have been a 70 percent drop from the mid–seventeenth to the mid–nineteenth centuries; Isett, "Village Regulation of Property," 126.

84 For evidence of a possible rollback in cultivation in the lower Yangzi highlands, see Liu Min, "Lun Qingdai pengmin huji wenti," 22–23.

85 Xiao Ruiling et al., *Ming-Qing Nei Menggu xibu diqu kaifa*, 167–82; Wang Han and Guo Pingruo, "Qingdai kenzhi zhengce," 91–92; Shinobu, "Historical Knowledge and the Response to Desertification," 199–212; Wu Luzhen,

264   *Across Forest, Steppe, and Mountain*

"*Dong si Menggu shiji,*" 221; Zhou Rong, "Kang, Qian shengshi de renkou pengzhang," 113, 114.

86 Some suggestive material dates the "near complete destruction" of the tigers' forested habitat by the early nineteenth century, with serious erosion visible in the twentieth century; Marks, "Commercialization without Capitalism," 70–75.

87 Fan Haoming et al., "Zhongguo Dongbei," 66–70; Yang Xulian et al., *Qingdai dongbei shi,* 440–50.

88 Wang, *Land Taxation in Imperial China,* 26–27; Li, "Changes in Climate, Land and Human Efforts," 478. Xinjiang was yet another place where it was reported that cases of abandoned waste previously cleared for agriculture were "numerous." This was attributed mainly to lack of water, although "the greater half" of the territory was not arable because of mountains, alkaline soil, and sand; *Dao, Xian, Tong, Guang sichao zouyi,* 3:962–68. In the vast Liaoning herding complex of Daling He, only thirty thousand *mu* out of an originally authorized agricultural clearance space of more than 123,000 *mu,* opened in the Jiaqing reign, was eventually found viable for cultivation after dust storms devastated the rest. Taxation was declared "canceled" for this lost acreage. The pasture, however, remained under arablist pressure into the succeeding Daoguang and Xianfeng reigns (3:1203–07). Cited in Vermeer, "Ch'ing Government Concerns," 217.

89 *Dao, Xian, Tong, Guang sichao zouyi,* 3:962–68. Cited and translated in Vermeer, "Ch'ing Government Concerns," 217.

90 Skinner, "Sichuan's Population Data in the Nineteenth Century," 11, 72.

91 Marks, "It Never Used to Snow"; Li, "Changes Climate, Land and Human Efforts"; Myers and Wang, "Economic Developments," 569.

92 Myers and Wang, "Economic Developments," 60.

93 Will, *Bureaucracy and Famine,* 241, 244.

94 Shangdong peasants in Yizhou during the 1660s, for example, were reported "too timid to ask for relief as long as they could make ends meet even barely." In another instance many damaged plots were not listed as requiring relief "because their owners had fled"; Huang Liuhong, *A Complete Book,* 164.

95 Wang, *Land Taxation in Imperial China,* pp. 32–33. For Shaanxi, see Vermeer, "Ch'ing Government Concerns," 236.

96 Wang, *Land Taxation in Imperial China,* 27–31.

97 Winterhalder, "Concepts in Historical Ecology," 39–40.

98 Cao Yishi, "Qing heshi kaiken dimu shu," 1.855b–56a; Ya-er-tu, ""Kan bao kai ken xu shi shu," 1:851a–52a. Vermeer, "Ch'ing Government Concerns," which translates portions of both memorials, can be read in some sections as an exposé of serious distortions in official reportage of acreage increases in China proper, especially Section VI.

99 Vermeer, "Ch'ing Government Concerns," 235.

100 Walter and Hengeveld, "The Structure of the Two Ecological Paradigms," 40–41. One paradigm is "the demographic paradigm," which considers dynamics within a population to the virtual exclusion of external ecological interactions. The other, "the autecological paradigm," takes these

interactions into dynamic, nonequilibrial account. A sophisticated example of the prevailing demographic paradigm in Chinese borderland history is Vermeer, "Population and Ecology."

101 Wei Yuan, *Shengwu ji*, 1:107; Wei Yuan, "Beigan kao," 6:3253–56. Wei's new layout also redraws Hanspace by moving imperial territory beyond its conventional northern water boundary, usually identified as the Yalu River.

102 Li, "Changes in Climate, Land and Human Efforts," 479.

6

Qing Environmentality

... more Chinese will come to our ancestral land, kick out the Mongolians, destroy the environment and plunder the mineral wealth ... This really is a three-dimensional attack on us by the Chinese: they have destroyed our land, polluted our air, and [are] now digging up what we have below ground. What we will be left with is a barren land uninhabitable to human beings.[1]

"Bayaguut, a Southern Mongolian cyber dissident," posted this grim assessment in May of 2011 in response to the death of a herding activist. The victim, Mergen, had been run over by a truck as he and fellow activists were attempting to block a coal transport caravan trespassing upon the pastures of the Right Ujumchin Banner. Five days after Mergen's death, another protestor, Yan Wenlong was killed by a forklift driver as he demonstrated against a coal mine operation in Xilinhot on May 15. The victims were both Mongols, the accused all Han Chinese. The confrontations and negotiations included burgeoning public protests, state prosecution of the perpetrators, and online calls to mark the day of Mergen's murder on May 10 as an annual "Herders' Rights Day." All are part of a legacy of the unintended consequences of the borderland environmental relations arising from the Qing unification of Inner Asia and China proper.

Mineral extraction and livestock herding north of the passes seem no more compatible now in the early twenty-first century than they appear to have been in the mid–eighteenth when Han alkali diggers were spoiling Mongol pasturelands in the Kododo lakes region. Then, as now, Inner Mongolia's resources both on and beneath the grasslands allow the formation of networks that quickly become mutually exclusive and ethnically polarizing. Then, as now, the state finds itself caught in the middle trying to balance the interests of both sides even as it also seeks to define the nature and limits of those same interests. Then, as now, the development of the Hanspace network comes, almost "naturally" or "inevitably," at the expense of the Mongol network, even as Han practices manifest as ecologically less sustainable and more disruptive. The result, then and now, is an existential threat that extends throughout China's borderlands across forest, steppe, and mountain to non-Han identities based on other environmental relations.

Of course, many things have changed, especially as Han activities have shifted to an industrial form. Such a profound transformation, however, has not altered basic human dependency on natural resources and has, in many respects, intensified it. This is most apparent in the increase in fossil fuel exploitation, exemplified in the above instances by the hundreds of coal pits currently envisioned by IMAR authorities. They plan to make their jurisdiction, now the PRC's largest coal-producing province, China's most important "energy base" (*nengyuan jidi*), an industrial *letu*.[2] The ongoing interdependency of humans and their ecologies forms a continuum from the past through to the present and into the future that endows environmental studies with a strong historical component.

This does not mean, however, that the same interdependencies simply progress in human-ordered fashion as time obligingly passes. Witness the emergence of a Han twentieth-century state that was hardly the anticipated or welcome progeny of its Manchu forebear. Moreover, new patches of uneven development emerged in the process of the Qing's Republican successor's pursuit of industrial modernization. This regime "abandoned" the traditional state's "most important task" of "underwriting of the ecological stability" in inland rural peripheries of north China left at the margins of new coastal urban core trends.[3]

Attempts to maintain such stability were predicated on questionable equilibrium assumptions, which persist even in fields such as conservation, up to the present.[4] One basic equilibrium commitment was rooted in centuries of state-society adherence to a particular form of intensive agriculture. Dependence on extensive water control and fertilizers required increasing, and increasingly complex, resource inputs to keep outputs high almost year-round without fallowing.[5] Ultimately, this "Han" agriculture nevertheless required still more uncultivated land to maintain its equilibrium.

So from the eighteenth century and far from the coast the radiation of a dominant arablist order beyond the confines of Hanspace became quite visible through the critical or enthusiastic eyes of Nayančeng, Giohoto, Zhang Zhidong, Ortai, Shurungga, Gao Qizhuo, Jungfoboo, Chang Deshou, Sun Jiagan, and Prince Güngsangnorbu or in the bewildered expressions on paper and stone of Warka and Yi. The dynasty's reactions to this trend are well represented by the diversity of opinion of these men who had all devoted their energies to assisting the Qing in its sustained attempt to rule across a wide range of peoples and ecologies. To this end, the state assembled a commensurate array of resources that, contrary to the intentions of the Qing elite that includes many of the names listed above, turned out to promote the reproductive and political interests of the empire's Han subjects. In terms consistent with those formulated in previous chapters, Qing fields grew decisively in imperial arablist terms at the expense of the other imperial environmental relations of venery, Zomi-culture, herding, and foraging.

Of course, swiddeners, foragers, and herders did not otherwise live in perfect harmony. Mongol pastoral practices in 1729, for example, so affected some Urianghai *otog* foraging in Uliastai that they had to be relocated far southward to undisrupted hunting grounds in Qiqihar. Conflict could also arise among groups engaged in the same activities. This set Hejen and Fiyaka against Solon-Ewenki and Dagur poachers who were chasing sable across the territorial boundaries of Jilin and Heilongjiang in 1731. Hunting Solon-Ewenki from Heilongjiang continued to poach sable in Jilin territory well into the Qianlong reign in violation of state regulations that seem partly intended to separate foraging areas in forests similar to the way pastures were separated in the steppe.[6] Such violations, possibly motivated by local resource exhaustion, could even be committed to fulfill pelt tribute obligations. As in the 1754 incident of Heilongjiang Hunting Solon-Ewenki's theft of 253 Jilin sable pelts, imperial foraging began to pay its tribute by plundering itself, a dramatic omen of a sustainability crisis.

Problems generated between or within Zomi-culture, herding, and foraging were nevertheless much smaller in scale and sprawl than those germinated by the more imposing success of arablism. This very success, however, was achieved in partially inadvertent terms that, as such, were insufficiently cognizant of the full range of contributing interdependencies. Domestic and foreign threats across all borderlands were critical factors for the agro-urban concentration of resources

Qing Environmentality 269

for purposes of enhanced security, even as they deforested the material basis for the nurturing of the empire's elite mounted soldiery. Some bannermen, such as Buhi, were worried by this continued contraction of venery space and its attendant identity. Others seemed unconcerned with the end of dismounted battue hunting in places such as Beijing. An 1801 banner request terminated the practice pursued since the dynasty's early years when "a fit habitat remained for birds and beasts" in the city's forested environs. Long years of agricultural clearance had left no fit habitat for wild animals and, so, none for serious military exercises.[7]

Things appear so grave for all the empire's main environmental relations by this time that sustainable swiddening, foraging, and pastoralism can seem deliberate choices "to remain outside state space."[8] This insight is applicable, however, mainly to those states that do not maintain their own substantial versions of herding or hunting and gathering or slashing and burning. Foraging or herding, and even swiddening, could all be encompassed within the Qing empire. Their orchestration in concert with Han agriculture was what made the empire distinctively Qing. This was less a choice than necessary adaptations to ecological conditions defining Manchurian forests, Mongolian steppe, Zomian mountains, or Beijing suburbs. All are strategies to "accommodate the spatial and temporal structure, intensity and unpredictability of environmental relations."[9]

These strategies employ "technologies of self and power" for "the creation of new subjects" recursively linked to their diverse ecologies in such a way as to replicate both within a stable imperial hierarchy.[10] Qing disaster management mechanisms, for example, reconstruct an "environmental subject." Thus is restored a politically stabilizing environmental relationship, imperial pastoralism, from which local people have become alienated through loss of livestock. This alienation can arise through human (raids) and/or ecological (*dzud*) agencies but is unlikely to return to a "steady state" if left to itself, and likely to continue if grain and silver substitutes are proffered as relief.

The proper formation or restoration of an environmental subjectivity in premodern terms, however, should internalize the conviction that what has been socially constructed is entirely natural. In modern terms, it should internalize the conviction that there is no nature but that which is socially constructed. The major difference between this premodern and modern "environmentality" is that the premodern enfolds the social within the natural, while the modern engulfs the natural within the social.

Across Forest, Steppe, and Mountain

So the twentieth-century socialist state declares human technology has rendered herding obsolete, *weather permitting*. Of course, the weather does not always permit, and in 2001 the *Taipusi* Banner of the Shili-yin Gool League repasturizes. So the eighteenth-century Qing state seeks to construct Mongol identity as solely and "naturally" dependent on livestock, *weather permitting*. Of course, the weather does not always permit, and in 1879 Zhang Zhidong wants banner Mongols to forsake herding for farming.

Neither instance is a purely mental exercise in which "men [*sic*] distance themselves from nature in order thus imaginatively to present it to themselves ... to determine how it is to be dominated."[11] In both instances subjects are formed through interaction with ecology and culture, although this is not always recognized or fully anticipated. So it is not "the human social condition" alone that "perpetually generates frontiers, dismantles them and generates new ones."[12] Although general cultural relations unquestionably inform historical spaces, these relations do not dictate their own terms of existence within an ecological vacuum. In fact, disruptive change is a sign that dictation has displaced an adaptive awareness along such marginal "cultural ecotones."

In the ideal Qing cases, banner Mongols are impervious to Zunghars and *dzud*; borderland Manchus can forage, farm, and bookkeep as needed; chieftainship tribals diligently work paddies to banish *ehe sukdun* for *junxian* administration. In all cases, proper relations to forest, steppe, and mountain are naturalized so that virtue is central everywhere and marginalized nowhere. Relations must be maintained with minimal supervision because of sheer ecological scale. Like its forest and mountain counterparts, even now the steppe "is simply too geographically dispersed and the underlying problems too complex for central officials to be aware of all the local nuances."[13] Environmentality becomes the prerequisite adaptation for human access to dynamic ecosystems.

The Qing state sought not to eliminate the diversity of adaptation throughout its borderland order, but to take all adaptations into its service as environmental subjects, produced through a structure of administrative control under conditions of both cultural and ecological change. The identity constructs of a Qing environmentality would be the agents who embodied a "Qingspace" triple-trunked dragon's true lair of Manchu forests, Mongol steppes and Zomian mountains from hide-bound Warka, free-range Chakhar, and *gumlao* ridden Kachin zones.

Qingspace was certainly not hermetically compartmentalized, as shown in deliberations as late as those in 1910 to arablize Butha Ula foraging zones, but it was integrated. The degree of this integration can serve as a measure of dynastic adaptation to the diversity of its dominions. By 1910, however, adaptation had long been eroding into impositions of *zhongbang* core uniformity. Han practices, rather than Han bodies, were being used in the Late Qing to mandate the same sort of "environmentality," or *zhengjiao* apparatus, throughout the empire.

Foraging could not perform the same service for a number of reasons, exposed in another exemplary 1910 incident from Manchuria. A local outbreak of plague had been triggered by a stampede of Han trappers who indiscriminately caught healthy and diseased marmots (*Marmota sibirica*) to meet market demands for imitation sable, which tripled the price of marmot pelts. These casual commercial foragers, unlike their more experienced and measured indigenous counterparts, had been unable to recognize and avoid infected animal vectors.[14] Proper foraging not only required a complex range of skills not readily acquired, but was also less responsive to mass market forces and relatively impervious to human intervention to increase supply in response to demand. Moreover, it could not simply be shifted to areas such as those throughout most of China proper that had been hunted out and deforested.

Foraging was much more conditioned by interconnections to the surrounding ecology than either herding or farming. It was far quicker and easier to cut down forests, foraging's limiting factor, than to grow them. Of course, as the Jiaqing emperor's pine nut and honey gatherers knew, it was possible in the short term to forage with an axe, but unsustainable beyond a brief span, as the emperor himself realized. In this representative case, the "logic" of imperial foraging had developed to an extreme that contradicted the ecological facts to the point where its own "enhanced" practice undermined it. Such logic almost certainly helped to create other shortfalls in foraging quotas of pheasants and storks.

Imperial foraging seems to be both the most flexible borderland environmental network because of its wider scope of possible action and also the most dependent on uncontrollable ecological shifts. The material results seem to have been a much lower surplus necessitating concentration over a much longer period of time. These limitations also imply foraging was the most sustainable, if the least predictable, set of imperial environmental relations under consideration. Foraging's comparative advantages under frigid northeastern conditions are apparent in the 1736–43 deliberations over Hulun Buir troop dispositions. On this ground Solon-Ewenki and Bargut hunters proved better able to keep themselves fed in extreme winter conditions than their agrarian Dagur comrades.

Adequate cultivation in more temperate woodlands, of course, was not impossible, as indigenous swiddening in the southwest demonstrates. However, cultivation that minimized deforestation had to work harder and, in an imperial arablist view, less efficiently, as Yun-Gui governors-general Cai Yurong and Gao Qizhuo both asserted. Some of this work is engraved on the forest protection steles erected during the period of growing Han agricultural pressure centering on the first half of the nineteenth century and scattered across areas of Yi settlement in Yunnan. Other parts of it are inked mainly on paper prescriptions, such as Bao Shichen's. Swiddening practiced by the Yi and other indigenous peoples appears to have been the most sustainable form of cultivation possible under sylvan conditions. Devastating extractions spawned by arablists such as the 1845 Han mushroom entrepreneurs in Yongbei and Dayao were taboo in Zomi-culture.

Nevertheless, by the nineteenth century, even imperial foraging had overconcentrated resources, symbolized by the barren pine stumps that so vexed the Jiaqing emperor. Zones of indigenous cultivation in the southwest had come under palpable pressure as well. Stress was legible in the fear expressed on an 1808 stele from what is now the Yi autonomous county of Jingdong in Pu'er prefecture: the "bitter toil of years gone by would be lost" to "shameless" timbering, burning off hillsides, fuel cutting, construction, and even herding.[15] Much of Yunnan, already under some form of cultivation, proved eminently convertible to Han-style agriculture in a way similar to that of the southern Inner Mongolian ecotone, and southern Manchuria's as well.

However, southwestern Yunnan's mosquitoes and blood parasites preferred fresh Han farmers to the livestock favored by Mongolian wolves, probably driven into putting further pressure on herders by arablist habitat destruction circa 1747. Settler susceptibility to the southwestern disease environment precluded a Han takeover of indigenous fields along the lines feared by northern officials deliberating in the same year over whether or not to provide seed grain and steppe plots for Mongol relief. Such differences were critical for the vulnerability of wide-open Mongolian pastures in comparison with Yunnan's coarse-grained highlands isolated by sweltering lowlands. On the contrary,

Qing Environmentality 273

differential resistance on the steppe would, if anything, favor Han settlers as smallpox crossed the passes with them to exploit "virgin" Mongolia.

Banner Mongol cultivators had repeatedly given ground to more skilled and persistent Han farmers in 1727, under pressure from tigers and disease, and in 1745, from what looks like plain despair. Again in contrast, southwestern Yunnan's pestiferous conditions may also have saved some of its forests from several decades of cutting by thousands of Han. Whole forests fell before the likes of the more than ten thousand Shanxi and Shaanxi migrants finally unearthed in the Muna range in 1734 or the concentrated descent of a mere one thousand Han cultivators who nevertheless managed to clear an estimated thirty thousand *qing* of woodland in Daqing by 1760.

As imposing as they seem to have been, Han farmers did not spread throughout Qing borderlands by themselves. They were firmly backed by their close allies the six domesticates and the five grains (both paid due tribute as primary Hanspace components by Wang Fuzhi). They were also abetted along the way by some opportunistic wolves and tigers, land-hungry, lake-thirsty Han governors-general such as Sun Jiagan, and, in the nineteenth century, directly by the Qing state, previously an equivocal partner. This was hardly the fruition of a Sinification plot laid in 1644 and systematically cultivated, but a process that developed organically and continues to do so beyond Qing purview in the form of other networked relations.

Like its Manchu predecessor, the Han state still attempts to orchestrate environmental relations in China proper and its adjacent borderlands, if under enormously altered circumstances. Malaria continues to pester the inhabitants of a less porous southwestern Yunnan, herds continue to roam the shrinking grasslands of Inner Mongolia, and a very few communities of Orochen, Dagur, Ewenki, and others continue to hunt and gather along the northern fringes of a truncated Chinese Manchuria.[16] There is, moreover, the beginning of another state rollback of steppe agriculture in favor of herding in deference to ecological realities denied for more than a century, even as a new challenge of industrial mineral extraction threatens to undermine the reemerging pastures. There has also been growing reforestation, if not yet a return to foraging.

Certainly borderland cultures and ecologies have not remained unchanged, especially judged by modern Han industrial, agrarian, and commercial practices, which exhibit their own resonances and

274 Across Forest, Steppe, and Mountain

transformations. Moreover, these complex relations continue to manifest elusive combinations of change and continuity. Yet complexity is by no means limited to the present. Its Qing version constituted a fundamental challenge to the organization and perpetuation of imperial relations unifying the immense diversity of China proper and its Inner Asian and Southeast Asian borderlands. The embodiments of these imperial spaces, Han farmers, banner Mongols, borderland Manchus, and chieftainship "tribals" naturally draw the attention of historians as the human manifestations of Qing imperial relations. The full view, however, should plainly range all across forest, steppe, and mountain.

Notes

1 "Mongolian Herder Brutally Killed by Chinese Coal Truck Driver."
2 "Mongolian Herder Brutally Killed"; "Energy Base Needed in Inner Mongolia."
3 Pomeranz, *Making of a Hinterland*, 275.
4 For a nonequilibrium reevaluation, see Zimmerer, "The Reworking of Conservation Geographies," 356–69.
5 For the distinction of Chinese agriculture in this regard, see Elvin, "Why Intensify?" 275, 295–96.
6 *Yongzhengchao Manwen zhupi*, #3872, 2:2037, #3461, 2:1837–38. Regulations proposed by Nigguta General Cangde to deal with the 1731 dispute in document #3872 appear as precedents cited to punish subsequent Hunting Solon-Ewenki trespass into Jilin for sable poaching in documents from the 1750s; *Lifanyuan Man-Meng wen tiben*, QL 19/7/16, 5:345–50, QL 23/7/25, 7:291–95. See also, *Qingdai E-lun-chun zu dang'an*, #26, 538, #27, 539.
7 *QSL*, JQ 6/ 10/13, 29:167b–68a, cited in Zhao, *Ziyuan, huangjing yu guojia quanli*, 57.
8 Scott, *Art of Not Being Governed*, 191.
9 Agrawal, *Greener Pastures*, 23.
10 Agrawal, "Environmentality," 166. My analysis here is a modification of insights in Agrawal's work on environmental subject formation under modern conditions of state-locality interaction enabled through new conceptual structures; Agrawal, *Environmentality*, 201–06.
11 Horkheimer and Adorno, *Dialectic of Enlightenment*, 39; Roberts, "Dialectic of Enlightenment," 68. Roberts's reading of the *Dialectic*'s critique of an "animal attempt to create instruments to master the outside" world's "chaotic" and "formless" condition accords well with some of the ideas of Geertz and Hale previously cited.
12 Crossley et al., eds., *Empire at the Margins*, 2–3.
13 Brown et al., *Sustainable Development in Western China*, 7.
14 Benedict, *Bubonic Plague*, 156.
15 Cited in Yan Shaomei and Zhang Xinchang, "Yizu diqu senlin shengtai," 38.

16 Some recent studies in the anthropological literature include He-qun, *Huanjing yu xiaoshu Minzu shengcai*; Ka-li-na, *Xunlu E-wen-ke ren*; Jiang Fan *Manzu shengtai yu minsu wenhua*; Wu-re-tao-ke-tao, "Mengguzu youmu jingji ji qi bianqian"; Yin Shaoting, *People and Forests*; Jianxiong Ma, *The Lahu Minority*. For an overview of current efforts to deal with Yunnan's disease environment, see Zheng Zuyou, Zhang Zaixing, and Yang Henglin, *Yunnan Nueji*.

Works Cited

ABBREVIATIONS

SZ: Shunzhi (r. 1644–61)
KX: Kangxi (r. 1662–1722)
YZ: Yongzheng (r. 1723–35)
QL: Qianlong (r. 1736–96)
JQ: Jiaqing (r. 1796–1820)
DG: Daoguang (r. 1821–50)
XF: Xianfeng (r. 1851–61)
TZ: Tongzhi (r. 1862–74)
GX: Guangxu (r. 1875–1907)
HJY: Heilongjiang jiangjun yamen dang'an
MWLF: Manwen lufu zouzhe
NFY: Ningguta fudutong yamen dang'an
QSL: *Qingshilu*

UNPUBLISHED ARCHIVAL SOURCES

Gongzhong dang, falü dalei, jinyan (Palace Memorial archive, legal category, opium prohibition). Daoguang period. Subject category of Chinese holdings in China's History Archive #1, Beijing, PRC.

Hei-tu dang (Archive of Lateral Administrative Communications). Subject category of Manchu holdings in the Liaoning Provincial Archives, Shenyang, PRC.

Heilongjiang jiangjun yamen dang'an (Archives of the Heilongjiang Military Governor's Office). Subject category of Manchu holdings in China's History Archive #1, Beijing, PRC.

Huke shishu (Routine memorial copy-books Board of Revenue). Subject category of Chinese holdings in China's History Archive #1, Beijing, PRC.

278 *Works Cited*

Manwen lufu zouzhe (Grand Council Manchu-language reference collection). Subject category of Manchu holdings in China's History Archive #1, Beijing, PRC.

Neige, xingke tiben, weijin lei (tongben/buben). (Grand Secretariat archive, routine memorials for the Office of Scrutiny of the Board of Punishments, prohibitions violations category [provincial/board memorial]). Subject category of archival holdings in China's History Archive #1.

Ningguta fudutong yamen dang'an (Ningguta Vice Commander-in-Chief's Office Archive). Subject category of Manchu holdings in China's History Archive #1, Beijing, PRC.

PUBLISHED SOURCES

Abramson, Marc S. *Ethnic Identity in Tang China*. Philadelphia: University of Pennsylvania Press, 2008.

Adelman, Jeremy and Stephen Aron. "From Borders to Empires, Nation-States and the Peoples in between in North American History." *American Historical Review* 104 (June 1999): 814–41.

Ai Bida. *Qiannan shilue* (Guizhou administrative primer). Guiyang: Guizhou renmin chubanshe. 1992.

Allsen, Thomas T. *The Royal Hunt in Eurasian History*. Philadelphia: University of Pennsylvania Press, 2006.

An Shuangcheng. "Qingchu zai Lafa dukou zhizao zhanchuan gaishu" (An overview of the construction of war boats at Lafa Ferry in the early Qing). *Lishi dang'an*, 2 (1995): 82–85.

Agrawal, Arun. *Greener Pastures Politics, Markets and Community Among a Migrant Pastoral People*. Durham: Duke University Press, 1998.

  "Environmentality: Community, Intimate Government, and the Making of Environmental Subjects in Kumaon, India." *Current Anthropology*, 46.2 (Apr. 2005): 161–90.

  Environmentality: Technologies of Government and the Making of Subjects. Durham: Duke University Press, 2005.

Asdal, Kristin. "The Problematic Nature of Nature: The Post-Constructivist Challenge to Environmental History." *History and Theory*, 42.4 (Dec. 2003): 60–74.

Atwill, David G. "Blinkered Visions: Islamic Identity, Hui Ethnicity and the Panthay Rebellion in Southwest China, 1856–1873." *Journal of Asian Studies* 62.3 (2003): 1079–1108.

Atwood, Christopher P. *Young Mongols and Vigilantes in Inner Mongolia's Interregnum Decades, 1911–1931*. Leiden: Brill, 2002.

Averill, Stephen C. "The Shed People and the Opening of the Yangzi Highlands." *Modern China*, 9.1 (Jan. 1983): 84–126.

Balée, William. "Historical Ecology: Premises and Postulates." In William Balée, ed. *Advances in Historical Ecology*. New York: Columbia University Press, 1998.

  "The Research Program of Historical Ecology." *Annual Review of Anthropology*, 35 (2006): 75–98.

Works Cited

Bao Maohong. "Environmental History in China." *Environment and History*, 10.4 (Nov. 2004): 475–99.

Bao Shichen. *Qimin si shu* (Four works for the people). In *Baoshi Chen quanji* (Bao Shichen's complete works). Hefei: Huangshan shushe, 1997.

(Qingding) Baqi tongzhi (Comprehensive annals of the Eight Banners, imperially ordained). Ji Yun et al., eds. 12 volumes. 1786. Reprint, Changchun: Jilin wenshi chubanshe, 2002.

Baqi tongzhi (Comprehensive annals of the Eight Banners). Ortai et al., ed. 1739. 8 volumes. Reprint, Changchun: Dongbei shifan daxue chubanshe, 1985.

Barfield, Thomas J. *The Perilous Frontier: Nomadic Empires and China 221 B.C. to A.D. 1757*. Oxford: Blackwell, 1989.

Barnard, Alan. "Hunter-Gatherers in History, Archaeology and Anthropology: Introductory Essay." In Alan Barnard, ed. *Hunter-Gatherers in History, Archaeology and Anthropology*. Oxford: Berg, 2004.

Baud, Michiel and Willem Van Schendel. "Toward a Comparative History of Borderlands." *Journal of World History*, 8.2 (Fall 1997): 211–42.

Ba-yin-mu-ren. *Menggu shouyi yanjiu* (Mongol veterinary studies). Liaoning: Liaoning minzu chubanshe, 2006.

Belin. "Jin Yunnan zhongren tushuo" (Presentation of an illustrated account of Yunnan's ethnicities). In Li Genyuan, comp. *Yongchang fu wenzheng* (Anthology of writings on Yongchang prefecture). Kunming: Teng chong li shi, 1941.

Bello, David A. *Opium and the Limits of Empire, Drug Prohibition in the Chinese Interior, 1729–1850*. Cambridge, MA: Harvard Council on East Asian Studies, 2005.

"To Go Where No Han Could Go for Long: Malaria and the Qing Construction of Ethnic Administrative Space in Frontier Yunnan." *Modern China*, 31.3 (July 2005): 283–317.

"The Cultured Nature of Imperial Foraging in Manchuria." *Late Imperial China*, 31.2 (Dec. 2010): 1–33.

"Environmental Issues in Pre-modern China." In Tim Wright, ed. *Oxford Bibliographies in Chinese Studies*. Oxford: Oxford University Press, 2014. www.oxfordbibliographies.com/obo/page/chinese-studies.

"Relieving Mongols of Their Pastoral Identity: The Environment of Disaster Management on the 18th Century Qing China Steppe." *Environmental History*, 19.3 (July 2014): 480–504.

Benedict, Carol. *Bubonic Plague in Nineteenth-Century China*. Stanford: Stanford University Press, 1996.

Bergholz, Fred W. *The Partition of the Steppe: The Struggle of the Russians, Manchus, and the Zunghar Mongols for Empire in Central Asia, 1619–1758*. New York: Peter Lang, 1993.

Bhabha, Homi K. *The Location of Culture*. London: Routledge, 1994.

Biersack, Aletta. "Introduction: From the 'New Ecology' to the New Ecologies." *American Anthropologist*, 101.1 (Mar. 1999): 5–18.

Bilik, Naran. "Culture, the Environment and Development in Inner Mongolia." In Caroline Humphrey and David Sneath, eds. *Culture and Environment in*

Works Cited

Inner Asia: Volume 2, Society and Culture. Cambridge: White Horse Press, 1996.

Bird-David, Nurit. "Beyond the 'Hunting and Gathering Mode of Subsistence': Culture-Sensitive Observations on the Nayaka and Other Modern Hunter-Gatherers." *Man*, 27.1 (Mar. 1992): 19–44.

Bishu Shanzhuang yanjiu huibian, ed. *Bishu Shanzhuang luncong* (Anthology on the imperial retreat to avoid the heat). Beijing: Zijin cheng chubanshe, 1986.

Black, Allison Harley. *Man and Nature in the Philosophical Thought of Wang Fuchih.* Seattle: University of Washington Press, 1989.

Blaut, James M. "Environmentalism and Eurocentrism." *Geographical Review*, 89.3 (July 1999): 391–408.

Bond, W. J. and J. E. Keeley. "Fire as Global 'Herbivore:' The Ecology and Evolution of Flammable Ecosystems." *Trends in Ecology and Evolution* (July 2005): 387–94.

Botkin, Daniel B. *Discordant Harmonies: A New Ecology for the Twenty-first Century.* Oxford: Oxford University Press, 1990.

Bourdieu, Pierre. *Outline of a Theory of Practice.* Cambridge: Cambridge University Press, 1988.

Branigan, Tania. "Mongolia: How the Winter of 'White Death' Devastated Nomads' Way of Life." *The Guardian*, 20 July 2010.

Bray, Francesca. *Biology and Biological Technology, Part 2: Agriculture.* In Joseph Needham, ed. *Science and Civilization in China*, volume 6, part 2. Cambridge: Cambridge University Press, 1984.

Brenner, Robert and Christopher Isett. "England's Divergence from China's Yangzi Delta: Property Relations, Microeconomics, and Patterns of Development." *Journal of Asian Studies*, 61.2 (May 2002): 609–62.

Brower, Daniel R. and Edward J. Lazzerini, eds. *Russia's Orient: Imperial Borderlands and Peoples, 1700–1917.* Bloomington: Indiana University Press, 1997.

Brown, Colin G., John W. Longworth, and Scott A. Waldron. *Sustainable Development in Western China: Managing People, Livestock and Grasslands in Pastoral Areas.* Cheltenham: Edward Elgar, 2008.

Brown, Peter J. and Marcia C. Inhorn. "Disease, Ecology and Human Behavior." In Thomas M. Johnson and Carolyn F. Sargent, eds. *Medical Anthropology: Contemporary Theory and Method.* New York: Greenwood Press, 1990.

Brubaker, Roger and Frederick Cooper. "Beyond 'Identity'." *Theory and Society*, 29.1 (Feb. 2000): 1–47.

Bruun, Ole. *Fengshui in China: Geomantic Divination between State Orthodoxy and Popular Religion.* Copenhagen: NIAS Press, 2003.

Bruun Ole and Li Narangoa eds. *Mongols from Country to City: Floating Boundaries, Pastoralism and City Life in the Mongol Lands.* Copenhagen: NIAS Press, 2006.

An Introduction to Feng Shui. Cambridge: Cambridge University Press, 2008.

Buskirk, Steven W., Ma Yiqing, Xu Li, and Jiang Zhaowen. "Winter Habitat Ecology of Sables (Martes Zibellina) in Relation to Forest Management in China." *Ecological Applications*, 6.1 (Feb. 1996): 318–25.

Works Cited

281

Busvine, James R. *Disease Transmission by Insects: Its Discovery and 90 Years of Effort to Prevent It*. Berlin: Springer-Verlag, 1993.

Cai Jiayi. Zhun-ge-er de nongye" (Zunghar agriculture). *Menggu shi yanjiu*, 1 (1985): 53–68.

Cai Yurong. "Chou Dian shi shu" (Ten measures for providing for Yunnan). In Fang Guoyu, ed. *Yunnan shiliao congkan* (Collectanea of Yunnan historical materials). Volume 8. Kunming: Yunnan Daxue chubanshe, 1998.

Campbell, Cameron and James Z. Lee. "Mortality and Household in Seven Liaodong Populations, 1749–1909." In Tommy Bengtsson, Cameron Campbell, James Z. Lee, eds. *Life Under Pressure: Mortality and Living Standards in Europe and Asia, 1700–1900*. Cambridge: Cambridge University Press, 2004.

Cao Shuqiao. "Diannan zazhi" (Yunnan miscellany). In Wang Xiqi, comp. *Xiao fang hu zhai yudi cong chao* (The little square vase studio geographical series). 16 volumes. 1877. Reprint, Taibei, Guangwen shuju, 1962.

Cao Ling. "Ming Qing Meizhou liangshi zuowu zhuanru Zhongguo yanjiu zhongshu" (A summary of the research on the introduction of American ceral crops into China in Ming and Qing dynasties [*sic*]). *Gujin nongye*, 2 (2004): 95–103.

Cao Shuji, ed. *Tianzu you shen: Ming-Qing yilai de ziran zaihai ji qi shehui yingdui jizhi* ('The father of husbandry's spiritual power: natural disasters and their social response mechanisms from the Ming-Qing period onwards). Shanghai: Shanghai jiaotong daxue chubanshe, 2007.

Cao Tingjian. *Cao Tingjian ji* (Cao Tingjian's collected works). Cong Peiyuan and Zhao Mingqi, eds. 2 volumes. Beijing: Zhonghua shuju, 1985.

Cao Yishi. "Qing heshi kaiken dimu shu" (Memorial requesting the verification of reclaimed acreage). In He Changling, ed. *Qing jingshi wenbian* (Collected writings on statecraft from the Qing dynasty). 3 volumes. 1826. Reprint, Beijing: Zhonghua Shuju, 1992.

Cao Zhihong and Wang Xiaoxia. "Ming Qing Shaan nan yimin kaifa zhuangtai xia de ren hu chongtu" (Human-tiger conflicts during migration and development of southern Shaanxi province in the Ming Qing period). *Ming Qing shi*, 1(2009): 11–17.

Carey, Fred W. "A Trip to the Chinese Shan States." *Geographical Journal*, 14.4 (Oct., 1899): 378–94.

Cartier, Carolyn. "Origins and Evolution of a Geographical Idea: The Macroregion in China." *Modern China*, 28.1 (Jan., 2002): 79–142.

Centers for Disease Control and Prevention. "Human Factors and Malaria." www.cdc.gov/malaria/about/biology/human_factors.html.

"Lymphatic Filariasis Fact Sheet." www.cdc.gov/parasites/lymphaticfilar iasis/.

Chakrabarty, Dipesh. "The Climate of History: Four Theses." *Critical Inquiry*, 35.2 (winter 2009): 197–222.

Chang, Chia-feng. "Disease and Its Impact on Politics, Diplomacy and the Military: The Case of Smallpox and the Manchus (1613–1795)." *Journal of the History of Medicine*, 57 (Apr. 2002): 177–97.

282 *Works Cited*

Chang, Michael G. *A Court on Horseback: Imperial Touring & the Construction of Qing Rule, 1680–1785*. Cambridge MA: Harvard University Asia Center, 2007.

Chiang, Tao-Chang. "The Salt Trade in Ch'ing China." *Modern Asian Studies*, 17.2 (1983): 197–219.

Changhua xianzhi (Gazetteer of Changhua district). Yu Shangling et al., comps. 3 volumes. 1823. Reprint, Taibei: Chengwen chubanshe, 1984.

Chappell, David A. "Ethnogenesis and Frontiers." *Journal of World History*, 4.2 (Fall 1993): 267–75.

Chavannes, Edouard. "Les deux plus anciens spécimens de la cartographie chinoise" (The two oldest specimens of Chinese cartography). *Bulletin de l'Ecole française d'Extrême-Orient*, 3.1 (1903): 214–47.

Chen Jian. *Huang Ming tongji* (Comprehensive accounts of the august Ming dynasty). Beijing: Zhonghua shuju, 2008.

"Lun *Shangjunshu* zhong de 'jingshen zhongnongzhuyi' jian tan Zhongguo fuojiao 'nongshen bing zhong de puqing Zhi" (On the spiritual physiocracy in Shang Yang's Works and in the History of Chinese Buddhism) *Hua'nan nongye daxue xuebao* (shehui kexue ban), 7.2 (2008): 99–104.

Chen Shan. "Inner Asian Grassland Degradation and Plant Transformation." In Caroline Humphrey and David Sneath, eds. *Culture and Environment in Inner Asia: Volume 1, The Pastoral Economy and the Environment*. Cambridge: White Horse Press, 1996.

Chen Song. "Lun Songdai shidafu jieceng falüe sixiang zhong de Fajia yinsu" (On legalist elements in legal thoughts of literati class in Song dynasty [*sic*]). *Zhongguo Zhengfa Daxue xuebao*, 5 (2009): 116–25.

Chen Zilong, ed. *Huang Ming jingshi wenbian* (Collected writings on statecraft from the Ming dynasty). 6 volumes. 1638. Reprint, Beijing: Zhonghua shuju, 1997.

Cheng Chongde. "Qingdai qianqi dui Menggu de fengjin zhengce yu renkou, kaifa ji shengtai huanjing de guanxi" (Mongol quarantine policy and relations of population, development and ecological environment in the early Qing). *Qingshi yanjiu*, 2 (1991): 26–31.

Cheng Zhenming. *Qingdai tusi yanjiu: yi zhong zhengzhi wenhua de lishi renleixue Guancha* (The Qing dynasty studies: One political culture historical anthropology observation [*sic*]). Beijing: Zhongguo shehui kexue chubanshe, 2008.

Chia Ning. "The Li-fan Yuan in the Early Ch'ing Dynasty." PhD diss., Johns Hopkins University, 1991.

"The Lifanyuan and the Inner Asian Rituals in the Early Qing (1644–1795)." *Late Imperial China*, 14.1 (June 1993): 60–92.

Ch'iu Chung-lin. "Xipi yu dongpi: Mingdai Menggu yu Liaodong diqu maopi zhi shuru" (Western and eastern furs: The import of furs from Mongolia and Manchuria during the Ming dynasty). *Danjiang shixue*, 20.3 (2009): 21–60.

Chongde san nian Manwen dang'an yibian (A compilation of translations from the Manchu archives in the third year of the Chongde reign). Li Yonghai and Liu Jingxian, eds. and trans. Shenyang: Liao Shen shushe, 1988.

Chŏson wangjo sillok (Veritable records of the Yi dynasty). 49 volumes. Seoul: Kuksa pyŏnch'an wiwŏnhoe, 1984.

Works Cited

Chow, C. Y. and M. C. Balfour. "The Natural Infection and Seasonal Prevalence of Anopheles Mosquitoes in Chefang and Vicinity, Yunnan-Burma Border." *Chinese Medical Journal*, 67.8 (1949): 405–13.

Christian, David. "The Case for 'Big History'." *Journal of World History*, 2.2 (Fall 1991): 223–38.

Chuxiong Yizu Wenhua Yanjiusuo, ed. *Qingdai Wuding Yizu Nashi tusi dangan shiliao jiaobian* (Edited compilation of Qing dynasty archival historical materials related to the Na line's Yi native chieftainship in Wuding Department). Beijing: Zhongyang minzu daxue chubanshe, 1993.

Clegg, John B. and David J. Weatherall. "Thalassemia and Malaria: New Insights into an Old Problem." *Proceedings of the American Association of Physicians*, 111.4 (July–Aug. 1999): 278–82.

Committee on Scholarly Communication with the People's Republic of China, ed. *Grasslands and Grassland Sciences in Northern China*. Washington, DC: National Academy Press, 1992.

Cong Peiyuan. *Dongbei sanbao jingji jianshi* (A Brief Economic History of the Three Northeastern Treasures). Beijing: Nongye chubanshe, 1989.

Cronon, William. *Changes in the Land: Indians, Colonists, and the Ecology of New England*. New York: Hill and Wang, 1983.

Crosby, Alfred W. *Ecological Imperialism: The Biological Expansion of Europe, 900–1900*. Cambridge: Cambridge University Press, 1986.

Crossley, Pamela Kyle. "Thinking about Ethnicity in Early Modern China." *Late Imperial China*, 11.1 (June 1990): 1–34.

Crossley, Pamela Kyle, Helen F. Siu, and Donald S. Sutton, eds. *Empire at the Margins: Culture, Ethnicity, and Frontier in Early Modern China*. Berkeley: University of California Press, 2006.

Crumley, Carole L. "The Ecology of Conquest: Contrasting Agropastoral and Agricultural Societies' Adaptation to Climatic Change." In Carole L. Crumley, ed. *Historical Ecology: A Multi-Dimensional Orientation*. Santa Fe: School of American Research Press, 1994.

Curtin, Philip D. "The Environment Beyond Europe and the European Theory of Empire." *Journal of World History*, 1.2 (Fall 1990): 131–50.

Da Lintai. "Zhidu yu zhengce de lishi yanbian dui Neimenggu caoyuan shengtai huanjing de yingxiang" (The impact of evolving institutions and policies on the grassland ecology of Inner Mongolia). *Zhongguo huanjing yu fazhan pinglun*. 3 (2007): 176–215.

Da Qing shi chao shengyu (Sacred edicts of the ten reigns of the great Qing). Zhao Zhiheng et al., eds. 20 volumes. Beijing: Beijing yanshan chubanshe, 1998.

(Da) Qing huidian (Guangxu) (Collected statutes of the great Qing, Guangxu edition). 1899. Reprinted, Beijing: Zhonghua shuju, 1991.

Da Qing huidian (Kangxi) (Collected statutes of the great Qing, Kangxi edition). In *Jindai Zhongguo shiliao congkan*, third series. 20 volumes. 1696. Reprinted, Taibei: Wenhai chubanshe, 1992.

Da Qing huidian (Qianlong) (Collected statutes of the great Qing, Qianlong edition). In *Wenyuan ge siku quan shu*. 20 volumes. 1768. Reprinted, Shanghai: Shanghai guji chubanshe, 2003.

Works Cited

Da Qing huidian (Yongzheng) (Collected statutes of the great Qing, Yongzheng edition). 30 volumes. 1734. Reprinted, Taibei: Wenhai chubanshe, 1995.

Da Qing huidian shili (Guangxu) (Collected Statutes and precedents of the great Qing, Guangxu edition). 1899. 12 volumes. Reprinted, Beijing: Zhonghua shuju, 1991.

Da Qing huidian shili (Jiaqing) (Collected statutes and precedents of the great Qing, Jiaqing edition). In *Jindai Zhongguo shiliao congkan*, third series. 80 volumes. 1822. Reprinted, Taibei: Wenhai chubanshe, 1991–92.

Da Qing huidian shili (Qianlong) (Collected statutes and precedents of the great Qing, Qianlong edition). 6 volumes. 1768. Reprinted, Shanghai: Shanghai guji chubanshe, 2003.

Dai Yi, ed. *Qingshi yanjiu yu Bishu Shanzhuang* (Qing studies and the imperial retreat to avoid the heat). Shenyang: Liaoning minzu chubanshe, 2005.

Dai Yingcong. "A Disguised Defeat: The Myanmar Campaign of the Qing Dynasty." *Modern Asian Studies*, 38.1, (2004): 145–89.

Dalizhabu. "Qingdai Baqi Chakhar kao" (A study of the Eight-Banner Chakhar in the Qing dynasty). In Yan Chongnian, ed. *Manxue yanjiu*, Volume 7. Beijing: Minzu chubanshe, 2002.

Qing chu nei zha-sa-ke qi de jianli wenti" (Problems with the establishment of the inner *jasags* in the early Qing). In Dalizhabu, *Ming Qing Menggu shi lungao* (Draft essays on Mongolian history in the Ming and Qing). Beijing: Minzu chubanshe, 2003.

"'Menggu lüeli' ji qi yu '*Lifanyuan Zeli* de guanxi" (The 'Mongol Precedents' and its relationship to the *Lifanyuan*). *Qingshi yanjiu*, 4 (Nov. 2003): 1–10.

Da-lin-tai. "Zhidu yu zhengce de lishi yanbian dui Neimenggu caoyuan shengtai huanjing de yingxiang" (The impact of evolving institutions and policies on the grassland ecology of Inner Mongolia). *Zhongguo huanjing yu fazhan pinglun*, 3 (2007): 176–92.

Daniels, Christian. "Environmental Degradation, Forest Protection and Ethnohistory in Yunnan: Part I: The Uprising by Swidden Agriculturalists in 1821." *Chinese Environmental History Newsletter*, 1.2 (Nov. 1994): 8–10.

"Environmental Degradation, Forest Protection and Ethno-history in Yunnan: Part II: Traditional Practices of Non-Han Swidden Cultivators for the Protection of Forests. *Chinese Environmental History Newsletter*, 2.1 (May 1995): 3–6.

Dao, Xian, Tong, Guang sichao zouyi (Memorials from the four reigns of Daoguang, Xianfeng, Tongzhi, and Guangxu). Wang Yunwu, comp. 12 volumes. Taibei: Shang wu yinshuguan, 1970.

Daoguang Yunnan zhi chao (Manuscript of the Daoguang reign's Yunnan gazetteer). Wang Song, comp. In Fang Guoyu, ed. *Yunnan shiliao congkan* (Collectanea of Yunnan historical materials). Volume 11. Kunming: Yunnan Daxue chubanshe, 1998.

Da-sheng Wu-la difang xiangtu zhi (Local gazetteer of the Butha Ula region). Quan Ming and En Qing comps. 1891. Reprint, Changchun: Jilin wenshi chubanshe, 1988.

Works Cited

Da-sheng Wu-la zhidian quanshu (Comprehensive annals of Butha Ula). Yun Sheng and Ying Xi, comps. 1884. Reprint, Changchun: Jilin wenshi chubanshe, 1988.

Da-wo-er ziliao ji (Collection of materials on the Dagur). *Da-wo-er ziliao ji* bianji weihui, et al., comps. Beijing: Minzu chubanshe, 2009.

De Mello, Margo. *Animals and Society: An Introduction to Human-Animal Studies*. New York: Columbia University Press, 2012.

Di Cosmo, Nicola. "Ancient Inner Asian Nomads: Their Economic Basis and Its Significance in Chinese History." *Journal of Asian Studies*, 53.4 (Nov. 1994): 1092–1126.

"Qing Colonial Administration in Inner Asia." *International History Review* 20.2 (June 1998): 287–309.

Diamond, Norma. "Defining the Miao: Ming, Qing and Contemporary Views." In Stevan Harrell, ed. *Cultural Encounters on China's Ethnic Frontiers*. Seattle: University of Washington Press, 1995.

Ding Guangling. *Qingchao qianqi liumin ancha zhengci yanjiu* (A study of refugee resettlement policy in the early Qing). Taibei: Wen shi zhe chubanshe, 2006.

Diao Shuren. "Shilun Kang Qian shiqi liumin chuguan yiken yu Dongbei qidi de bianhua" (On shifting land clearance by migrants beyond the passes and the transformation of northeastern banner lands in the Kangxi and Qianglong periods). *Shehui kexue zhanxian* (Dongbei lishi yu wenhua), 3 (1990): 224–30.

"Lun Qingdai dongbei liumin de liuxiang ji dui dongbei de kaifa" (On the flow of migrants into the Qing northeast and its exploitation) *Qingshi yanjiu*, 3 (1995): 30–36.

Dikötter, Frank. *The Discourse of Race in Modern China*. Stanford: Stanford University Press, 1992.

Ding Junna, Huang Lu, and Wang Lu. "Lüelun Qingdai ziran ziyuan de baohu yu liyong" (Discussion on natural resources protection and utilization in Qing dynasty [*sic*]). *Zhongguo huanjing guanli xueyuan xuebao*, 17.4 (Dec. 2007): 28–30.

Dodgen, Randall A. *Controlling the Dragon: Confucian Engineers and the Yellow River in Late Imperial China*. Honolulu: University of Hawai'i Press, 2001.

(Qing) *Donghua lu quan bian* (Complete Donghua annals). Wang Xianqian et al. comps. 25 volumes. Beijing: Xueyuan chubanshe, 2000.

Dong Xueshu. "Yunnan sheng de chuannüe meijie ji qi youguan de shengtai xixing" (The malaria vectors and their ecology in Yunnan Province). *Chinese Journal of Parasitic Disease Control*, 13.2 (June 2000): 144–47.

Donnelly M. J., P. J. McCall, C. Lengeler, I. Bates, U. D'Alessandro, G. Barnish, F. Konradsen, E. Klinkenberg, H. Townson, J. F. Trape, I. M. Hastings, and C. Mutero: "Malaria and Urbanization in Sub-Saharan Africa," *Malaria Journal*, 4.12 (2005): 1–5.

Du Jiaji. *Baqi yu Qingchao zhengzhi lungao* (The eight banners and Qing political Affairs). Beijing: Renmin Daxue chubanshe, 2008.

Du Weiyun. *Qingdai shixue yu shijia* (Qing historiography and historians). Taibei: Dongda tushu gongsi yinxing, 1991.

Duan Wei and Li Jun. "Qingdai yimin yu Yunnan shengtai weiji de zingcheng" (Qing migrants and the development of ecological crisis in Yunnan). In Yang

Works Cited

Weibing, ed. *Ming Qing yilai Yun Gui gaoyuan de huanjing yu shehui* (Environment and society on the Yun-Gui plateau since the Ming-Qing period). Shanghai: Dongfang Chuban Zhongxin, 2010.

Dunnell, Ruth W. and James A. Millward. "Introduction." In James A. Millward, Ruth W. Dunnell, Mark C. Elliott, and Phillippe Forêt, eds. *New Qing Imperial History: The Making of Inner Asian Empires at Qing Chengde.* London: RoutledgeCurzon, 2004.

Dunstan, Helen. "Heirs of Yu the Great: Flood Relief in 1740s China." *T'oung Pao,* 96 (2011): 471–542.

Duyvendak, J. J. L. *The Book of Lord Shang.* London: Arthur Probsthain, 1928.

Dzengšeo. *The Diary of a Manchu Soldier in Seventeenth-Century China: My Service in the Army by Dzengšeo.* Nicola di Cosmo, trans. New York: Routledge, 2006.

Edmonds, Richard L. "The Willow Palisade." *Annals of the Association of American Geographers,* 69:4 (Dec. 1979): 599–621.

Elliott, Mark C. "The Limits of Tartary." *The Journal of Asian Studies,* 59.3 (Aug. 2000): 603–46.

Elliott, Mark C. *The Manchu Way: the Eight Banners and Ethnic Identity in Late Imperial China.* Stanford: Stanford University Press, 2001.

"Ethnicity in the Qing Eight Banners." In Pamela Kyle Crossley, Helen F. Siu and Donald S. Sutton, eds. *Empire at the Margins: Culture, Ethnicity, and Frontier in Early Modern China.* Berkeley: University of California Press, 2001.

"The Manchu-language Archives of the Qing Dynasty and the Origins of the Palace Memorial System," *Late Imperial China,* 22.1 (June 2001): 1–70.

Elliott, Mark C., and Ning Chia. "The Qing Hunt at Mulan." In James A. Millward, Ruth W. Dunnell, Mark C. Elliott, and Phillippe Forêt, eds. *New Qing Imperial History: The Making of Inner Asian Empires at Qing Chengde.* New York: RoutledgeCurzon, 2004.

Elman, Benjamin A. *From Philosophy to Philology: Intellectual and Social Aspects of Change in Later Imperial China.* Cambridge, MA: Harvard Council on East Asian Studies, 1984.

A Cultural History of Civil Examinations in Late Imperial China. Berkeley: University of California Press, 2000.

Elverskog, Johan. *Our Great Qing: The Mongols, Buddhism and the State in Late Imperial China.* Honolulu: University of Hawai'i Press, 2006.

Johan Elverskog. "Wutai Shan, Qing Cosmopolitanism, and the Mongols." *Journal of the International Association of Tibetan Studies,* 6 (Dec. 2011): 243–74.

Elvin, Mark. "Three Thousand Years of Unsustainable Growth: China's Environment from Archaic Times to the Present." *East Asian History,* 6 (1993): 7–46.

The Retreat of the Elephants: an Environmental History of China. New Haven: Yale University Press, 2004.

"Why Intensify? The Outline of a Theory of the Institutional Causes Driving Long-Term Changes in Chinese Farming and the Consequent Modifications to the Environment." In Sverker Sörlin and Paul Warde, eds. *Nature's End: History and Environment.* Houndmills, Basingstoke: Palgrave Macmillan, 2009.

Works Cited

"Energy Base Needed in Inner Mongolia," *China Daily*, 01/02/08; www.chinada ily.com.cn/china/2008-01/02/content_6363042.htm.

Erdenebaatar, B. "Socio-Economic Aspects of the Pastoral Movement Patterns of Mongolian Herders." In Caroline Humphrey and David Sneath, eds. *Culture and Environment in Inner Asia: Volume 1, The Pastoral Economy and the Environment*. Cambridge: White Horse Press, 1996.

Erdenijab, E. "An Economic Assessment of Pasture Degradation." In Caroline Humphrey and David Sneath, eds. *Culture and Environment in Inner Asia: Volume 1, The Pastoral Economy and the Environment*. Cambridge: White Horse Press, 1996.

Etkind, Alexander. *Internal Colonization: Russia's Imperial Experience*. Cambridge: Cambridge University Press, 2011.

Fan, Fa-ti. "Nature and Nation in Chinese Political Thought: The National Essence Circle in Twentieth-Century China." In Lorraine Daston and Fernando Vidal, eds. *The Moral Authority of Nature*. Chicago: University of Chicago Press, 2004.

Fan Haoming, Cai Qiangguo, and Wang Hongshan. "Zhongguo dongbei heituqu turang qinshi huanjing," (Condition of soil erosion in phaeozem [*sic*] region of northeast China). *Shuitu baochi xuebao*, 18.2 (Apr. 2004): 66–70.

Fan Jiawei. "Han Tang shiqi nüebing yu nüegui" (Nüe disease and nüe spirits in the Han and Tang periods). Paper presented at conference on "The History of Disease," Institute of History and Philology, Academia Sinica, Taibei, Taiwan, June 2000.

Liuchao shiqi renkou qianyi yu Lingnan diqu zhangqi bing (Chang-ch'i disease and population migration in the Lingnan region during the six Dynasties). *Hanxue Yanjiu*, 16.1 (1998): 27–58.

Fang Kongzhao. *Quan bian lüe ji* (Records of strategies along the frontier). In Pan Zhe, Li Hongbin, and Sun Fangming, eds. *Qing ruguan qian shiliao xuanji, diyi ji* (Selected compilation of Qing pre-conquest historical materials, first series). Beijing: Zhongguo Renmin Daxue chubanshe, 1984.

Fang Shiji. *Longsha jilüe* (Frontier notes). In Shen Yunlong, ed. *Ming Qing shiliao huibian, chuji* (Compilation of Ming-Qing historical materials, first series). Taibei: Wenhai chubanshe, 1967.

Fernandez-Gimenez, Maria E. "The Role of Mongolian Pastoralists' Ecological Knowledge in Rangeland Management." *Ecological Applcations*, 10.5 (Oct. 2000): 1318–26.

Fernandez-Gimenez, Maria E. and Barbara Allen-Diaz. "Testing a Non-equilibrium Model of Rangeland Vegetation Dynamics in Mongolia." *Journal of Applied Ecology* 36 (1999): 871–85.

Field, Stephen L. "In Search of Dragons: The Folk Ecology of Fengshui." In N. J. Girardot, James Miller, and Liu Xiaogan, eds. *Daoism and Ecology: Ways within a Cosmic Landscape*. Cambridge, MA: Harvard University Press, 2001.

Fisher, Carney T. "Smallpox, Salesmen and Sectarians: Ming-Mongol Relations in the Jiajing Reign (1522–67)." *Ming Studies*, 25 (spring 1988): 1–23.

Fisher, R. H. *The Russian Fur Trade: 1550–1700*. Berkeley: University of California Press, 1943.

Works Cited

Fletcher, Joseph. "The Heyday of the Ch'ing Order in Mongolia, Sinkiang and Tibet." In John K. Fairbank, ed. *The Cambridge History of China, Volume 10, Part 1: Late Ch'ing, 1800–1911*. Cambridge: Cambridge University Press, 1978.

"Ch'ing Inner Asia *c.* 1800." In John K. Fairbank, ed. *The Cambridge History of China, Volume 10, Part 1: Late Ch'ing, 1800–1911*. Cambridge: Cambridge University Press, 1978.

Folland, C. K., T. R. Karl, J. R. Christy, R. A. Clarke, G. V. Gruza, J. Jouzel, M. E. Mann, J. Oerlemans, M. J. Salinger, and S.-W. Wang. "2001: Observed Climate Variability and Change." In J. T. Houghton,Y. Ding, D. J. Griggs, M. Noguer, P. J. van der Linden, X. Dai, K. Maskell, and C. A. Johnson, eds. *Climate Change 2001: The Scientific Basis. Contribution of Working Group I to the Third Assessment Report of the Intergovernmental Panel on Climate Change.* Cambridge: Cambridge University Press, 2001.

Food and Agriculture Organization of the United Nations. *A Manual for the Primary Animal Health Care Worker*. Rome: FAO, 1994. www.fao.org/docrep/to690e/to690eo9.htm#unit%2061:%20feeding%20and%20watering%20of%20camels, accessed 4/23/10.

Forêt, Phillippe. *Mapping Chengde: The Qing Landscape Enterprise*. Honolulu: University of Hawai'i Press, 2000.

Forsyth, James. *A History of the Peoples of Siberia: Russia's North Asian Colony, 1581–1990*. Cambridge: Cambridge University Press, 1992.

Fu Baichen. *Zhongguo lidai chaogong zhidu yanjiu* (Transdynastic study of China's tribute system). Changchun: Jilin renmin chubanshe, 2008.

Congbin Fu. "Potential Impacts of Human-induced Land Cover Change on East Asia Monsoon." *Global and Planetary Change*, 37 (2003): 219–29.

Fuge. "Jiubai" (The nine whites). In Fuge. *Tingyu cong tan* (Talks collected while listening to the rain). Beijing: Zhonghua shuju, 1997.

"Menggu" (Mongolia). In Fuge. *Tingyu cong tan* (Talks collected while listening to the rain). Beijing: Zhonghua shuju, 1997.

"Tongming Menggu bu" (Mongol tribes of the same name). In Fuge. *Tingyu cong tan* (Talks collected while listening to the rain). Beijing: Zhonghua shuju, 1997.

Fuzhou zhufang zhi (Gazetteer of the Fuzhou garrison). Xin Zhu, et al., comps. 1744. Reprint, Shenyang: Liaoning Daxue chubanshe, 1994.

Gao Qizhuo. "Chouzhuo Lukuishan shanhou shu" (Deliberation of Lukuishan's reconstruction). In Fang Guoyu, ed. *Yunnan shiliao congkan* (Collection of Yunnan historical materials). Volume 8. Kunming: Yunnan daxue chubanshe, 1998.

"Weiyuan fu Zhao banli kaiken shu" (Memorial for a deputation to Zhaotong for the management of agricultural clearance). In Fang Guoyu, ed. *Yunnan shiliao congkan* (Collection of Yunnan historical materials). Volume 8. Kunming: Yunnan daxue chubanshe, 1998.

Gao Shiqi. *Hucong dongxun rilu* (Diary of an eastern progress in the emperor's entourage). In Li Shutian, ed. *Changbai congshu, chuji* (Changbai collectanea, first series). 1684. Reprint, Changchun: Jilin wenshi chubanshe, 1986.

Gaozong. *Yuzhi shi wen shi quanji* (Imperial poetry and prose from the Ten Campaigns). La-ba-ping-cuo, Chen Jiajin, eds. Beijing: Zhongguo Zangxue chubanshe, 1993.

Works Cited

Garros, C., W. Van Bortel, H. D. Trung, M. Coosemans, and S. Manguin. "Review of the Minimus Complex of Anopheles, Main Malaria Vector in Southeast Asia: From Taxonomic Issues to Vector Control Strategies." *Tropical Medicine and International Health*, 11.1 (Jan. 2006): 102–14.

Gaubatz, Piper Rae. *Beyond the Great Wall, Urban Form and Transformation on the Chinese Frontiers*. Stanford: Stanford University Press, 1996.

Ge Quansheng, ed. *Qingdai zouzhe huibian: nongye, huanjing* (Compilation of Qing memorials: agriculture and environment). Beijing: Shangwu yinshuguan, 2005.

Geertz, Clifford. *The Interpretation of Cultures*. New York: Basic Books, 1973.

Giddens, Anthony. *The Constitution of Society*. Berkeley: University of California Press, 1984.

Giersch, C. Patterson. *Asian Borderlands: The Transformation of Qing China's Yunnan Frontier*. Cambridge MA: Harvard University Press, 2006.

"Qing China's Reluctant Subjects: Indigenous Communities and Empire along the Yunnan Frontier." PhD diss., Yale University, 1998.

"'A Motley Throng': Social Change on Southwest China's Early Modern Frontier, 1700–1880." *Journal of Asian Studies*, 60.1 (2001): 67–94.

Gladney, Dru C. *Dislocating China: Reflections on Muslims, Minorities, and Other Subaltern Subjects*. Chicago: University of Chicago Press, 2003.

Glebov, Sergey. "Siberian Middle Ground: Languages of Rule and Accommodation of the Siberian Frontier." In Ilia Gerasimov, Jan Kusber, and Alexander Semyonov, eds. *Empire Speaks Out: Languages of Rationalization and Self-Description in the Russian Empire*. Leiden: Brill, 2009.

Gong Shengsheng. "2000 nianlai Zhongguo zhangbing fenbu bianqian de chubu yanjiu" (A preliminary study on variations of the distribution of Zhang-disease for the past 2000 years in China). *Dili xuebao* 48.4 (1993): 304–16.

Gong Yin. *Zhongguo tusi zhidu* (China's native chieftain system). Kunming: Yunnan renmin chubanshe, 1992.

Gongzhong dang Qianlongchao zouzhe (Palace memorial archive, Qianlong court memorials). Guoli gugong bowuyuan, ed. 75 volumes. Taibei: Guoli gugong bowuyuan, 1982–88.

Gosz, James R. "Ecotone Hierarchies," *Ecological Applications*, 3.3 (Aug. 1993): 370–76.

Goulden, Clyde E., B. Nandintsetseg, and L. Ariuntsetseg. "The Geology, Climate and Ecology of Mongolia." In Paula L. W. Sabloff, ed. *Mapping Mongolia; Situating Mongolia in the World from Geologic Time to the Present*. Philadelphia: University of Pennsylvania Press, 2011.

Graham, A. C. "The Nung-chia 'School of the Tillers' and the Origins of Peasant Utopianism in China," *Bulletin of the School of Oriental and African Studies*, 42.1 (1979): 66–100.

Grishin, S. Yu. "The Boreal Forests of North-Eastern Eurasia." *Vegetatio*, 121.1/2, (Dec. 1995): 11–21.

Grove, Richard H. "Environmental History." In Peter Burke, ed. *New Perspectives on Historical Writing*. University Park: Pennsylvania State University Press, 2001.

Works Cited

Gu Yanwu. *Yuan chaoben ri zhi lu* (Original manuscript of the record of daily knowledge). Taibei: Minglun chubanshe, 1970.

Gu Zuyu. *Du shi fangyu jiyao* (Essentials of geography for reading history). Volume 11. Beijing: Zhonghua shuju, 2005.

Guan Jialu and Tong Yonggong. "Qingchao gong diao shang wu-lin zhidu de queli ji yanbian" (The establishment and transformation of the Qing court's system of rewarding pelt tribute with goods). *Lishi dang'an*, 3 (1986): 93–98.

Guan Jialu et al., eds. *Tiancong jiunian dang* (Archive of the Ninth Year of the Tiancong Reign). Tianjin: Tianjin guji chubanshe, 1987.

Gutiérrez, Yezid. "Blackwater Fever." In Yezid Gutiérrez. *Diagnostic Pathology of Parasitic Infections with Clinical Correlations*. Oxford: Oxford University Press, 2000.

Guneratne, Arjun. "Modernization, the State, and the Construction of a Tharu Identity in Nepal." *Journal of Asian Studies*, 57.3 (Aug. 1998): 749–73.

Guo Chengkang and Lin Tiejun. *Qingchao wenzi yu* (The Qing literary inquisitions). Beijing: Qunzhong chubanshe, 1990.

Guo Mengxiu. *Manwen wenxian gailun* (An introduction to historical records in Manchu). Beijing: Minzu chubanshe, 2004.

Guochao gong shi xubian. Qing Gui et al., comps. (Sequel compilation for the palace history of the dynasty). 2nd ed. Beijing: Beijing guji chubanshe, 2001.

Hale, Henry E. *Ethnic Politics: Separatism of States and Nations in Eurasia and the World*. Cambridge: Cambridge University Press, 2008.

Han Di. *Qingdai Baqi Suo-lon bu yanjiu* (Study of the Qing Eight-banner Solon tribes). Beijing: Zhongguo shehui kexue chubanshe, 2011.

Han Guanghui and Zhao Yingmei. "Lun Qing chu yilai weichang diqu ren di guanxi yanbian" (On the evolution of relations between people and land in the hunting preserves of the early Qing). In Dai Yi, ed. *Qingshi yanjiu yu Bishu Shanzhuang* (Qing studies and the imperial retreat to avoid the heat). Shenyang: Liaoning minzu chubanshe, 2005.

Han, Yongming, Zhangdong Jin, Junji Cao, Eric S. Posmentier, and Zhisheng An. "Atmospheric Cu and Pb Deposition and Transport in Lake Sediments in a Remote Mountain Area, Northern China." *Water, Air and Soil Pollution*, 179.1–4 (Feb. 2007): 167–81.

Hangzhou Baqi zhu fangying zhilue (Draft gazetteer of the Hangzhou Eight Banner garrison). Zhang Dachang et al., comps. 1893. Reprint, Shenyang: Liaoning Daxue chubanshe, 1994.

Haraway, Donna. "The Promises of Monsters: A Regenerative Politics for Inappropriate/d Others." In Lawrence Grossberg, Cary Nelson, and Paula A. Treichler, eds. *Cultural Studies*. New York: Routledge, 1992.

Harrell, Stevan. "Introduction: Civilizing Projects and the Reaction to Them." In Stevan Harrell, ed. *Cultural Encounters on China's Ethnic Frontiers*. Seattle: University of Washington Press, 1995.

Hayes, Jack Patrick. "Fire and Society in Modern China: Fire Disasters and Natural Landscapes in East Asian Environmental History" (1820–1965). *ASIANetwork Exchange* 20:1 (2012): 23–35.

Works Cited

He Changling, ed. *Qing jingshi wenbian* (Collected writings on statecraft from the Qing dynasty). 3 volumes. 1826. Reprint, Beijing: Zhonghua shuju, 1992.

He Pingli. *Xunshou yu fengchan: fengjian zhengzhi de wenhua jiuyi* (Imperial touring and cosmic ceremony: The cultural locus of the politics of feudalism). Jinan: Qi Lu shushe, 2003.

He Qiutao. *Shuofang beisheng* (History of the defense of the north). In Xu Lihua, ed. *Zhongguo shaoshu minzu guji jicheng* (Collection of old works on China's ethnic minorities). Volume 16. Chengdu: Sichuan minzu chubanshe, 2002.

He Zhiqing, ed. *Zhongguo gudai zaihai shi yanjiu* (Studies in the history of natural disasters in China's antiquity). Beijing: Zhongguo shehui kexue chubanshe, 2007.

He Zikai. "Tengyue bianwu deshi lun" (An evaluation of frontier matters in Tengyue). In Li Genyuan, comp. *Yongchang fu wenzheng* (Anthology of writings on Yongchang prefecture). Kunming: Teng chong li shi, 1941.

Rehe Zhi (Rehe gazetteer). He Shen, comp. 6 volumes. Taibei: Wenhai chubanshe, 1966.

Headland, Thomas N. "CA Forum on Theory in Anthropology: Revisionism in Ecological Anthropology [and Comments and Reply]." *Current Anthropology*, 38.4 9 (Aug.–Oct. 1997): 605–30.

Hedin, Sven. *Jehol: City of Emperors*. 1932. Reprint, Varanasi: Pilgrim's Publishing, 2000.

Henderson, John B. "Chinese Cosmographical Thought: The High Intellectual Tradition." In J. B. Harley and David Woodward, eds. *The History of Cartography, Volume 2, Book 2: Cartography in the Traditional East and Southeast Asian Societies*. Chicago: University of Chicago Press, 1994.

He-qun. *Huanjing yu xiaoshu minzu shengcai: E-lun-chun wenhua de bianqian* (Environment for the survival of an ethnic minority: Orochen people in China). Beijing: Shehui kexue wenxian chubanshe, 2006.

Herman, John E. "Empire in the Southwest: Early Qing Reforms to the Native Chieftain System." *Journal of Asian Studies*, 56.1 (1997): 47–74.

Hevia, James L. *Cherishing Men from Afar: Qing Guest Ritual and the Macartney Embassy of 1793*. Durham: Duke University Press, 1995.

Ho, Ping-Ti. "Early-Ripening Rice in Chinese History." *Economic History Review*, 9.2 (1956): 200–218.

Ho, Ping-ti. "In Defense of Sinicization: A Rebuttal of Evelyn Rawski's 'Reenvisioning the Qing." *Journal of Asian Studies*, 57.1 (1998): 123–55.

Holling, C. S. and Steven Sanderson. "Dynamics of Disharmony in Ecological and Social Systems." In Susan Hanna Carl Folke and Karl-Göran Mäler, eds. *Rights to Nature*. Washington, DC: Island Press, 1996.

Horkheimer, Max and Theodor Adorno. *Dialectic of Enlightenment*. John Cumming, trans. New York: Continuum, 1993.

Hostetler, Laura. *Qing Colonial Enterprise: Ethnography and Cartography in Early Modern China*. Chicago: University of Chicago Press, 2001.

Howell, David L. "Ainu Ethnicity and the Boundaries of the Early Modern Japanese State." *Past and Present*, 142 (Feb. 1994): 69–93.

Works Cited

Hsu, Shin-Yi. "The Cultural Ecology of the Locust Cult in Traditional China." *Annals of the Association of American Geographers*, 59.4 (Dec. 1969): 731–52.

Hu Han. *Hu Zhongzi ji* (Collected works of Hu Han). 1381. Harvard MA: Harvard Yenching Library. Microfilm.

Hu Huanyong. "Zhongguo renkou de fenbu, quhua he fazhan" (Population distribution, regionalization and prospects in China). *Acta Geographica Sinica*, 45.2 (June 1990): 139–45.

Hu Minghui. *Qingdai Menggu shi* (A history of Qing dynasty Mongolia). Tianjin: Tianjin guji chubanshe, 1990.

Hu Qirong. "Diaobao tushuo" (Illustrated gazetteer of the strongpoint line). In Wang Wenshao, comp. *Xu Yunnan tongzhi gao* (Draft of the comprehensive gazetteer of Yunnan). Taibei: Wenhai chubanshe, 1966.

Hu Wei. *Yugong chuizhi (A peep-hole view of the 'Tribute of Yu')*. Ed. Zou Yilin. Shanghai: Shanghai guji chubanshe, 2006.

Huang Liuhong. *A Complete Book Concerning Happiness and Benevolence, Fu hui quanshu: A Manual for Local Magistrates in Seventeenth-Century China*. Djang Chu, ed. and trans. Tucson: University of Arizona Press, 1984.

Huang Qing zouyi (Memorials from the Qing dynasty). Jiang Yasha, ed. 4 volumes. Beijing: Quanguo tushuguan wenxian suowei fuzhi zhongxin, 2004.

Huang Zhiguo. "Cong fengjin dao kaijin: Qing Qianlong shiqi dui Muna shan muchang de guanli" (From prohibition to lifting a ban: Administrating to [*sic*] the Muna woods during Qianlong period of the Qing dynasty). *Zhongyang Minzu Daxue Xuebao*, 36.2 (2009): 90–94.

Heuschert, Dorothea. "Legal Pluralism in the Qing Empire: Manchu Legislation for the Mongols." *International History Review*, 20.2 (June 1998): 310–24.

Hughes, Donald. "Three Dimensions of Environmental History," *Environment and History*, 14.3 (Aug. 2008): 319–30.

Humphrey, Caroline and David Sneath. "Introduction." In Caroline Humphrey and David Sneath, eds. *Culture and Environment in Inner Asia: Volume 1, The Pastoral Economy and the Environment*. Cambridge: White Horse Press, 1996.

Ilibu. "Tengyue *Liji* tan bei wen" (Text of Tengyue's *liji* altar stele). In Li Genyuan, comp. *Yongchang fu wenzheng* (Anthology of writings on Yongchang prefecture). Kunming: Teng chong Li shi, 1941.

Ingold, Tim. "Growing Plants and Raising Animals: An Anthropolgical Perspective on Domestication." In David R. Harris, ed. *The Origins and Spread of Agriculture and Pastoralism in Eurasia*. Washington, DC: Smithsonian Institution Press, 1996.

"Hunting and Gathering as Ways of Perceiving the Environment." In Roy Ellen and Katsuyoshi Fukui, eds. *Redefining Nature: Ecology, Culture and Domestication*. Oxford: Berg, 1996.

"Inner Mongolia Fights Rampant Locusts." *People's Daily Online*. July 1, 2008. http://english.people.com.cn/90001/90776/90882/6439887.html.

Isett, Christopher Mills. "Village Regulation of Property and the Social Basis for the Transformation of Qing Manchuria." *Late Imperial China*, 25.1 (June 2004): 124–86.

Works Cited

State, Peasant and Merchant in Qing Manchuria 1644–1862. Stanford: Stanford University Press, 2007.

Janhunen, Juha. *Manchuria: An Ethnic History*. Helsinki: Finno-Ugrian Society, 1996.

Jia Xiaofeng. "Ershi duo nian lai tusi zhidu yanjiu zongshu" (Summary of native chieftainship studies over the last twenty-odd years). *Zhongguo bianjiang shidi yanjiu*, 14.4 (Dec. 2004): 126–34.

Jiang Fan. *Manzu shengtai yu minsu wenhua* (Manchu ecology and folk culture). Beijing: Zhongguo shehui kexue chubanshe, 2004.

Jiang Zhushan. "Shengtai huanjing, rencang caiji yu guojia quanli" (Ecological environment, ginseng gathering and state power). In Wang Lihua, ed. *Zhongguo lishi shang de huanjing yu shehui* (Environment and society in Chinese history). Beijing: Sanlian shudian, 2007.

Jiaqing chongxiu yitongzhi (Jiaqing revision of the comprehensive gazeteer of the Qing). Mujangga et al., comps. 35 volumes. Beijing: Zhonghua shuju, 1986.

Jiaqing Daoguang liang chao shangyu dang, Jiaqing (Imperial edicts archive of the Jiaqing and Daoguang reigns, Jiaqing reign). Zhongguo diyi lishi dang'anguan, ed. 25 volumes. Guilin: Guangxi shifan daxue chubanshe, 2000.

Jilin tongzhi (Jilin gazetteer). Zhang Shun comp. 10 vols. 1891. Reprinted, Taibei: Wenhai chubanshe, 1965.

Jin Hai, Qi-mu-de-dao-er-ji, Hu Richa, and Ha-si-ba-gun. *Qingdai Menggu zhi* (Gazetteer of Qing Mongolia). Hohhot: Neimenggu renmin chubanshe, 2009.

Jinshu. (History of the Jin dynasty). 10 volumes. Beijing: Zhonghua shuju, 1974.

Jones, Susan Mann and Philip A. Kuhn. "Dynastic Decline and the Roots of Rebellion." In John K. Fairbank, ed. *The Cambridge History of China, Volume 10, Part 1: Late Ch'ing, 1800–1911*. Cambridge: Cambridge University Press, 1978.

Kaihua fuzhi. (Gazetteer of Kaihua Prefecture). Tang Dabin and Zhou Bing, comps. 1758 and 1828. Reprint, Lanzhou: Lanzhou daxue chubanshe, 2004.

Ka-li-na. Xunlu E-wen-ke ren wenhua yanjiu (A study of the culture of the Reindeer Evenki). Shenyang: Liaoning minzu chubanshe, 2006.

Le Kang, Xingguo Han, Zhibin Zhang, and Osbert Jianxin Sun. "Grassland Ecosystems in China: Review of Current Knowledge and Research Advancement." *Philosophical Transactions of the Royal Society B Biological Sciences* (June 2007): 997–1008.

Kangxichao Hanwen zhupi zouzhe huibian (The collected Chinese-language palace memorials of the Kangxi reign). Zhongguo diyi lishi dang'anguan, ed. 8 volumes. Beijing: Dang'an chubanshe, 1984–85.

Kangxichao Manwen zhupi zouzhe quan yi (Complete translation of the Kangxi court's Manchu palace memorials). Zhongguo diyi lishi dang'an guan, ed. and trans. Beijing: Zhongguo shehui kexue chubanshe, 1996.

Kangxi qiju zhu (Kangxi diaries). Zhongguo diyi lishi dang'anguan, ed. 3 volumes. Beijing: Zhonghua shuju, 1984.

Khodarkovsky, Michael. *Russia's Steppe Frontier: The Making of a Colonial Empire, 1500–1800*. Bloomington: Indiana University Press, 2002.

Works Cited

Kim, Seonmin. "Ginseng and Border Trespassing between Qing China and Chosôn Korea." *Late Imperial China*, 28.1 (June 2007): 33–61.

Koenig, William J. *The Burmese Polity, 1752–1819*. Ann Arbor: Michigan Papers on South and Southeast Asia, 1990.

Koren, Olga G., Vladimir V. Potenko, and Yuri N. Zhuravlev. "Inheritance and Variation of Allozomes in Panax Ginseng C.A. Meyer (Araliaceae)." *International Journal of Plant Science*, 164.1 (Jan. 2003): 189–95.

Koubei San Ting zhi (Gazeteer of the Three Sub-prefectures North of the Passes), comp. Huang Kerun. 1758. Reprinted, Taibei, Chengwen chubanshe, 1968.

Kwan Man Bun. *The The Salt Merchants of Tianjin: State-making and Civil Society in Late Imperial China*. Honolulu: University of Hawai'i Press, 2001.

Lan Yong. "Ming Qing Meizhou nongzuowu yinjin dui yaredai shandi jiegouxing pinkun xingcheng de yingxiang" (The effects of the introduction of American crops on the formation of structural poverty in the highland subtropics), *Nongye shi*, 4.20 (2001): 3–14.

Lantzeff, George V. and Richard A. Pierce. *Eastward to Empire: Exploration and Conquest on the Russian Open Frontier to 1750*. Montreal: McGill-Queens University Press, 1973.

Latour, Burno. *Reassembling the Social: An Introduction to Actor-Network Theory*. Oxford: Oxford University Press, 2005.

Lattimore, Owen. *Inner Asian Frontiers of China*. Boston: Beacon Press, 1962.

Launchbaugh, Karen L. and Larry D. Howery. "Understanding Landscape Use Patterns of Livestock as a Consequence of Foraging Behavior." *Rangeland Ecology & Management*, 58.2 (Mar. 2005): 99–108.

Lavely, William and R. Bin Wong. "Revising the Malthusian Narrative: The Comparative Study of Population Dynamics in Late Imperial China." *Journal of Asian Studies*, 57.3 (Aug. 1998): 714–48.

Leach, E. R. *Political Systems of Highland Burma: A Study of Kachin Social Structure*. Boston: Beacon Press, 1954.

"The Frontiers of 'Burma'." *Comparative Studies in Society and History*, 3.1 (1960): 49–68.

Ledonne, John P. *The Grand Strategy of the Russian Empire, 1650–1831*. Oxford: Oxford University Press, 2004.

Lee, James Z. "Food Supply and Population Growth in Southwest China, 1250–1850." *Journal of Asian Studies*, 41.4 (Aug. 1982): 711–46.

Lee, James Z. and Cameron Campbell. *Fate and Fortune in Rural China: Social Organization and Population Behavior in Liaoning, 1774–1873*. Cambridge: Cambridge University Press, 1997.

Lee, Robert H. G. *The Manchurian Frontier in Ch'ing History*. Cambridge, MA: Harvard University Press, 1970.

Legge, James, trans. *The Shoo King. Volume III of The Chinese Classics*. Revised ed. Taipei: Wen shi zhe chubanshe, 1971.

Legrand, Jacques. *L'administration dans la domination Sino-Mandchoue en Mongolie Qala-a: version mongole du Lifan Yuan Zeli* (The administration of Sino-Manchu rule in Khalkha Mongolia: The Mongol version of the *Lifanyuan Zeli*). Paris: Institut des hautes études chinoises, 1976.

Works Cited

Leong, Sow-Theng. *Migration and Ethnicity in Chinese History: Hakkas, Pengmin, and Their Neighbors.* Stanford: Stanford University Press, 1997.

Li Bozhong. "Changes in Climate, Land and Human Efforts: The Production of Wet-field Rice in Jiangnan during the Ming and Qing Dynasties." In Mark Elvin and Liu Ts'ui-jung, eds. *Sediments of Time: Environment and Society in Chinese History.* Cambridge: Cambridge University Press, 1998.

Shijiu shiji jiangnan de jingji xiaotiao yu qihou bianhua (Jiangnan's nineteenth century economic depression and climate change). In Wang Lihua, ed. *Zhongguo lishi shang de huanjing yu shehui (Environment and society in Chinese history).* Beijing: Sanlian shudian, 2007.

Li Dalong. "Quantong yi-Xia guan yu Zhongguo bianyu de xingcheng" (The traditional Barbarian-Han concept and the formation of China's borderlands). *Zhongguo bianjiang shidi yanjiu* 14.1 (Mar. 2004): 1–15.

Li Huazi. *Qingchao yu Chaoxian guanxi shi yanjiu: yi yuejing jiaoshe wei zhongxin* (A study of the history of Qing-Korean relations: From the perspective of negotiations over border trespass). Yanji: Yanbian Daxue chubanshe, 2006.

Li Li and Liang Mingwu. "Ming Qing shiqi dongbei diqu shengtai huanjing bianhua chutan" (Preliminary inquiry into environmental change in the northeast during the Ming-Qing period). *Xueshu yanjiu,* 10 (2009): 113–16.

Li, Lillian M. *Fighting Famine in North China: State, Market, and Environmental Decline, 1690s–1990s.* Stanford: Stanford University Press, 2007.

Li Sanmou. "Qingdai beibu bianjiang de guan muchang" (State pastures on the northern frontier during the Qing). *Zhongguo bianjiang shi yanjiu,* 1 (1999): 69–77.

Li Shiyu. *Qingdai tusi zhidu lunkao* (Studies of the Qing native chieftainship system). Beijing: Zhongguo shehui kexue chubanshe, 1998.

Li Zhongqing (James Z. Lee). *Zhongguo xinan bianjiang de shehui jingji: 1250–1850* (The political economy of a frontier: Southwest China, 1250–1850). Beijing: Renmin chubanshe, 2012.

Li Xiangjun. *Qingdai huangzheng yanjiu* (A study of the Qing dynasty's famine relief administration). Beijing: Zhongguo nongye chubanshe, 1995.

Li Xu. *Li Xu zouzhe* (Li Xu's memorials). Beijing: Zhonghua shuju, 1976.

Liang Fangzhong, ed. *Zhongguo lidai hukou, tiandi, tianfu tongji* (Chinese historical statistics on population, land and land taxation). Shanghai: Renmin Chubanshe, 1980.

Liaoshi (History of the Liao dynasty). 5 volumes. Beijing: Zhonghua shu ju, 1987.

Liaodong zhi (Jiajing) (Liaodong gazetteer, Jiajing edition). Bi Gong et al., comps. 1583. Reprint, Shanghai: Shanghai guji chubanshe, 1995–99.

Liji zhuyi (Annotated translation of the Record of Rites), Qian Miaojin ed. and trans. Hangzhou: Zhejiang guji chubanshe, 2007.

Lin, Hualiang Liang Lu, Linwei Tian, Shuisen Zhou, Haixia Wu, Yan Bi, Suzanne C. Ho, and Qiyong Liu. "Spatial and Temporal Distribution of Falciparum Malaria in China." *Malaria Journal,* 8.130 (2009): 1–9.

Lin Wenping and Gao Minjie. "Neimenggu caoyuan shengtai huifu de zhexue fenxi" (A philosophical analysis about grassland ecological restoration in Inner Mongolia). *Neimenggu shifan daxue xuebao* (zhexue shehui kexue ban) 36.3 (May 2007): 32–35.

296   *Works Cited*

Lin Zexu. *Lin Zexu ji: zougao* (Lin Zexu's collected works: Memorials). 3 volumes. Beijing: Zhonghua shuju, 1985.

Lishi wenxian bubian: Shiqi shiji Zhong-E guanxi wenjian xianyi (Historical document supplement: Select translations from seventeenth century documents on Sino-Russian relations). Hao Jianheng, general ed. and trans. Beijing: Shangwu yinshuguan, 1989.

Little, Paul E. "Environments and Environmentalisms in Anthropological Research: Facing a New Millennium." *Annual Review of Anthropology*, 28 (1999): 253–84.

Liu Bin. "Yongchang *tusi* lun" (On the native chieftainships of Yongchang). In He Changling, ed. *Qing jingshi wenbian* (Collected writings on statecraft from the Qing dynasty). 3 volumes. 1826. Reprint, Beijing: Zhonghua Shuju, 1992.

Liu Fengyun and Liu Wenpeng, eds., *Qingchao de guojia rentong: Xin Qingshi yanjiu yu zhengming* (The identity of the Qing state: The new Qing history research and debate). Beijing: Zhongguo renmin daxue chubanshe, 2010.

Liu, Hongyan Haiting Cui, Pengtao Yu, and Yongmei Huang. "The Origin of Remnant Forest Stands of *Pinus tabulaeformis* in Southeastern Inner Mongolia." *Plant Ecology*, 158.2 (Feb. 2002): 139–51.

Liu Jingchun. *Qingdai huangtu gaoyuan diqu chengzhen dili yanjiu* (Studies in the urban geography of the loess plateau region in the Qing period). Beijing: Zhonghua shuju, 2005.

Liu Jingxian, Guo Chengkang, and Liu Jianxin. "Qing Taizu shiqi de xin Manzhou wenti" (The New Manchu problem in the Qing Taizu period), *Lishi dang'an*, 4 (1981): 102–07, 116.

Liu Kun. *Nanzhong za shuo* (Various observations on Yunnan). In Fang Guoyu, ed. *Yunnan shiliao congkan* (Collectanea of Yunnan historical materials). Volume 11. Kunming: Yunnan Daxue chubanshe, 1998.

Liu Lingping. Qingdai Diandong diqu yimin kaifa yu juluo fazhang chutan (Preliminary study of migrant exploitation and settlement development in the eastern Yunnan region during the Qing dynasty). In Yang Weibing, ed. *Ming Qing yilai Yun Gui gaoyuan de huanjing yu shehui* (Environment and society on the Yun-Gui plateau from the Ming-Qing period). Shanghai: Dongfang chuban zhongxin, 2010.

Liu Meide, Wang Xuezhong, Zhao Tongyan, Du Zhunwei, Dong Yande, and Lu Baolin. "Analysis of the Relationship between Density and Dominance of *Anopheles minimus* (Diptera: Culicidae) with Environmental Parameters in Southern Yunnan Province, Peoples Republic of China." *Journal of Medical Entomology*, 45.6 (Nov. 2008): 1007–10.

Liu Min. "Lun Qingdai pengmin huji wenti" (Concerning the problem of shack people household registration in the Qing). *Zhongguo shehui jingji shi yanjiu*, 1 (Feb. 1983): 17–29.

Liu Shiyong. "Cong xuesi chong dao nüyuan chong: cong fengtu bing leixing yizhuang kan Taiwan xibu pingyuan zhi kaifa" (From Filaria to Plasmodium: A view of agricultural clearance in Taiwan's western plains from the perspective of the shift in the model of endemic disease). In Wang Lihua, ed. *Zhongguo lishi shang de huanjing yu shehui* (Environment and society in Chinese history). Beijing: Sanlian shudian, 2007.

Works Cited

Liu, Sky. "Contemporary Chinese Studies of Wang Fuzhi in Mainland China." *Dao: A Journal of Comparative Philosophy*, 3.2 (summer 2004): 307–30.

Liu Ts'ui-jung. "Han Migration and the Settlement of Taiwan: The Onset of Environmental Change." In Elvin and Liu, eds. *Sediments of Time: Environment and Society in Chinese History*. Cambridge: Cambridge University Press, 1998.

Liu Xiaomeng. "Mingmou Nüzhen shehui shizu zhidu de wajie." *Ming Qing Shi*, 5 (1996): 66–76.

Manzu cong buluo dao guojia de fazhan (The development of the Manchus from tribe to state). Shenyang: Liaoning minzu chubanshe, 2001.

Livingstone, Frank B. "Anthropological Implications of Sickle Cell Gene Distribution in West Africa." *American Anthropologist*, 60.3 (June 1958): 533–62.

Lockwood, Jeffrey A. et al. "Comparison of Grasshopper (Orthoptera: Acrididae) Ecology on the Grasslands of the Asian Steppe in Inner Mongolia and the Great Plains of North America," *Journal of Orthoptera Research*, 2 (Feb. 1994): 4–14.

Lombard-Salman, Claudine. *Un exemple d'acculturation Chinoise: La province du Gui Zhou au XVIIIe siècle* (An example of Chinese acculturation: The province of Guizhou in the eighteenth century). Paris: École Française D'Extrême-Orient, 1972.

Lu Minghui. *Qingdai Menggu shi* (History of Qing Mongolia). Tianjin: Tianjin guji chubanshe, 1990.

Lü Liuliang. *Lü Wancun wenji* (Lü Liuliang's prose works). Volume 2. Taibei: Taiwan shangwu shuguan, 1973.

Tiangai lou si shu yu lu (Notes on the four books from the Tiangai lou). In *Siku jinhui shu congkan* (Collectanea of books banned from the four treasuries and burned). Volume 1. Beijing: Beijing chubanshe, 1997–99.

Luo Hui-yuan. "Medical Genetics in China." *Journal of Medical Genetics*, 25 (1988): 253–57.

Luo Kanglong. "Lun Ming Qing yilai tongyi shuizhi de tuixing dui Baiyue zuqun chuantong gengzuo fangshi de yingxiang" (Regarding the influence of the implementation of unified taxation from the Ming and Qing dynasties on traditional cultivation practices of Baiyue ethnic groups). In Yang Weibing, ed. *Ming Qing yilai Yun Gui gaoyuan de huanjing yu shehui* (Environment and society on the Yun-Gui plateau from the Ming-Qing period). Shanghai: Dongfang Chuban Zhongxin, 2010.

Luo Raodian. *Qiannan zhifang jilue* (Summary of the main administrative aspects of Guizhou). Guiyang: Guizhou Renmin chubanshe, 1992.

Luo Wenhua. *Longpao yu jiasha: Qing gong zang zhuan fojiao wenhua kaocha* (Dragon robe and kaṣāya: an inquiry into Tibetan Buddhist culture at the Qing court). 2 volumes. Beijing: Zijin cheng chubanshe, 2005.

Ma Fengchen. "Manchu-Chinese Social and Economic Conflicts in the Early Ch'ing." In *Chinese Social History: Translations of Selected Studies*. E-tu Zen Sun and John De Francis, trans. Washington, DC: American Council of Learned Societies, 1956.

Ma, Jianxiong. *The Lahu Minority in Southwest China*. New York: Routledge, 2013.

Works Cited

"The Zhaozhou *Bazi* Society in Yunnan: Historical Process in the *Bazi* Basin Environmental System during the Ming Period (1368–1643)." In Ts'ui-jung Liu, ed. *Environmental History in East Asia*. New York: Routledge, 2014.

Ma Ruheng and Ma Dazheng, eds. *Qingdai de bianjiang zhengce* (Qing dynasty borderland policy). Beijing: Zhongguo shehui kexue chubanshe, 1994.

Piaolue yiyu de minzu 17 zhi 18 shiji de Tu-er-hu-te Menggu (A people's drift through exotic lands: the Torguds, 17th to 18th centuries). Beijing: Zhongguo shehui kexue chubanshe, 2003.

"Malaria." National Institute of Allergy and Infectious Diseases. www.niaid.nih .gov/topics/Malaria/Pages/lifecycle.aspx.

Malaria Journal. BioMed Central. 1999–2010. www.malariajournal.com/

Manbun rōtō (The Old Manchu Chronicles). Kanda Nobuo et al., eds. and trans. 7 volumes. Tōkyō: Tōyō Bunko, 1955–63.

Mancall, Mark. *Russia and China: Their Diplomatic Relations to 1728*. Cambridge MA: Harvard University Press, 1971.

Manchu Studies Group. www.manchustudiesgroup.org/.

Manzu lishi dang'an ziliao xuanji (Selected compilation of materials from Manchu historical archives). Zhongguo kexueyuan minzu yanjiusuo and Liaoning shaoshu minzu shehui lishi diaochazu, eds. and trans. Shenyang: n.p., 1963.

Marks, Robert B. "Commercialization without Capitalism: Processes of Environmental Change in South China, 1550–1850." *Environmental History*, 1.1 (Jan. 1996): 56–82.

"It Never Used to Snow: Climatic Variability and Harvest Yields in Late-Imperial South China, 1650–1850." In Mark Elvin and Liu Ts'ui-jung, eds. *Sediments of Time: Environment and Society in Chinese History*. Cambridge: Cambridge University Press, 1998.

Tigers, Rice, Silk, and Silt: Environment and Economy in Late Imperial South China. Cambridge: Cambridge University Press, 1998.

"Geography Is Not Destiny: Historical Contingency and the Making of the Pearl River Delta." In Abe Ken'ichi and James E. Nickum, eds. *Good Earths: Regional and Historical Insights into China's Environment*. Kyoto and Melbourne: Trans Pacific Press, 2009.

China: Its Environment and History. Lanham MD: Rowman and Littlefield, 2012.

Matsuura Shigeru. *Shinchō no Amūru seisaku to shōsū minzoku* (Qing policy toward the Amur district and minorities). Kyōto: Kyōto Daigaku gakujutsu shuppankai, 2006.

McNeill, John Robert. *Mosquito Empires: Ecology and War in the Greater Caribbean, 1620–1914*. Cambridge: Cambridge University Press, 2010.

Mearns, Robin. "Decentralization, Rural Livelihoods and Pasture-land Management in Post-Socialist Mongolia." *European Journal of Development Research*, 16.1 (spring 2004): 133–52.

Melikhov, G. V. "How the Feudal Rulers of the Ch'ing Empire Prepared Their Aggression against the Russian Settlements on the Amur in the 1680s." In S. L. Tikhvinsky, ed. *Chapters from the History of Russo-Chinese Relations, 17th–19th Centuries*. Vic Schneierson, trans. Moscow: Progress Publishers, 1982.

Works Cited

Menggu lüli, Huijiang zeli (Mongol statutes, Muslim frontier regulations). Zhongguo shehui kexue yuan Zhongguo bianjiang shidi yanjiu zhongxin, ed. Beijing: Quanguo tushuguan wenxian suowei fuzhi zhongxin, 1988.

Menzies, Nicholas K. *Forest & Land Management in Imperial China.* London: St. Martin's Press, 1994.

Merlin, Mark David. *On the Trail of the Ancient Opium Poppy.* Toronto: Associated University Presses, 1984.

Miller, Daniel and Dennis Sheehy. "The Relevance of Owen Lattimore's Writings for Nomadic Pastoralism Research and Development in Inner Asia." *Nomadic Peoples* 12.2 (2008): 103–15.

Mingshilu (Veritable records of the Ming dynasty). 133 volumes. Taibei: Zhongyang yanjiuyuan shiyu yanjiusuo, 1961–66.

Mitchell, Timothy. *Rule of Experts: Egypt, Techno-politics, Modernity.* Berkeley: University of California Press, 2002.

Miyashita Saburō. "Malaria (yao) in Chinese Medicine during the China and Yuan Periods." *Acta Asiatica,* 36 (1979): 90–112.

"Mongolian Herder Brutally Killed by Chinese Coal Truck Driver," 5/19/11, Southern Mongolian Human Rights Information Center, www.smhric.org/news_376.htm.

Moore-Gilbert, Bart. *Postcolonial Theory: Contexts, Practices, Politics.* London: Verso, 1997.

Murakoshi, Nobuo and Glenn T. Trewartha. "Land Utilization Maps of Manchuria." *Geographical Review,* 20.3 (July 1930): 480–93.

Myers Ramon, H. and Yeh-Chien Wang. "Economic Developments, 1644–1800." In Willard J. Peterson, ed. *The Cambridge History of China, Volume 9, Part 1: The Ch'ing Dynasty to 1800.* Cambridge: Cambridge University Press, 2002.

Na Risen. "Guanyu *Taipusi* Qi shengtai jianshe yu jiegou tiaozheng de jingyan yu sikao" (The ecological construction of the *Taipusi* Banner with regard to the experience and considerations of its structural adjustmen)]. *Beifang jingji,* 1 (2002): 291–93.

National Institutes of Health. "Malaria." NIH Publication no. 00-4715. Bethesda, MD: U.S. Dept. of Health and Human Services, National Institutes of Health, 2000.

Natsagdorj, Sh. "The Economic Basis of Feudalism in Mongolia," *Modern Asian Studies,* 1.3 (1967): 265–81.

Newson, Linda A. "A Historical-Ecological Perspective on Epidemic Disease." In William Balée, ed. *Advances in Historical Ecology.* New York: Columbia University, 1998.

"A Historical-Ecological Perspective on Epidemic Disease." In William Balée, ed. *Advances in Historical Ecology.* New York: Columbia University Press, 1998.

Newton, Charles R. J. C. and David A. Warrell. "Neurological Manifestations of Falciparum Malaria." *Annals of Neurology,* 43 (1998): 695–702.

Ni Tui. "Dianyun linian zhuan" (Annals of Yunnan) In Fang Guoyu, ed. Yunnan shiliao congkan (Collection of Yunnan historical materials). Volume 11. Kunming: Yunnan daxue chubanshe, 1998.

"Tuguan shuo" (Comments on native officials). In He Changling, ed. *Qing jingshi wenbian* (Collected writings on statecraft from the Qing dynasty). 3 volumes. 1826. Reprint, Beijing: Zhonghua Shuju, 1992.

Nian Gengyao. *Nian Gengyao Man Han zouzhe yibian* (Compilation of translations from the Manchu and Chinese language memorials of Nian Gengyao). Li Yonghai et al., eds. and trans. Tianjin: Tianjin guji chubanshe, 1995.

Ning, Chia. "The Lifanyuan and the Inner Asian Rituals in the Early Qing." *Late Imperial China*, 14.1 (June 1993): 60–92.

"The Li-fan Yuan in the Early Ch'ing Dynasty." PhD diss., Johns Hopkins University, 1991.

Niu Guanjie. "Qingdai mazheng chu tan" (Preliminary inquiry into the Qing horse administration). *Yanshan daxue xuebao* (zhexue, shehui kexue ban), 7.2 (May 2006): 57–63.

Niu Pinghan. *Qingdai zhengqu yan'ge zongbiao* (Summary tables of changes in Qing administrative regions). Beijing: Zhongguo ditu chubanshe, 1990.

Obringer, Frédéric. "A Song Innovation in Pharmacotherapy." In Elisabeth Hsu, ed. *Innovation in Chinese Medicine*. Cambridge: Cambridge University Press, 2001.

Oka, Hiroki. "Shindai shiryō ni mieru Mongoru no saigai ni kansuru jōhō ni tsuite" (Natural disasters in pre-modern archival sources of Mongolia). In Oka Hiroki, ed. *Mongoru no kankyō to hen'yō suru shakai* (Mongolian environments and transforming society). Sendai: Tōhoku daigaku tōhoku ajia kenkyū sentā, 2007.

Oljeitogtoqu. "Qingchao dui Menggu de lifa gaisu" (A brief account of the legislation for Mongols in the Qing dynasty). *Menggu shi yanjiu*, 7 (2004): 348–70.

Osborne, Anne. "The Local Politics of Land Reclamation in the Lower Yangzi Highlands." *Late Imperial China*, 15.1 (June 1994): 1–24.

"Highlands and Lowlands: Economic and Ecological Interactions in the Lower Yangzi Region under the Qing." In Elvin and Liu, eds. *Sediments of Time: Environment and Society in Chinese History*. Cambridge: Cambridge University Press, 1998.

Oyunbilig. "Guanyu Qingdai nei zha-sa-ke Menggu meng de chuxing" (Concerning early forms of the inner jasag leagues). In Oyunbilig, ed. *Manwen dang'an yu Qingdai bianjiang he minzu yanjiu* (Manchu archives and studies of Qing frontiers and ethnicities). Beijing: Shehui kexue wenxian chubanshe, 2013.

ed. *Manwen dang'an yu Qingdai bianjiang he minzu yanjiu* (Manchu archives and studies of Qing frontiers and ethnicities). Beijing: Shehui kexue wenxian chubanshe, 2013.

Pan Jinglong and Zhang Xuanru, eds. *Jilin gongpin* (Jilin tribute). Tianjin: Tianjin guji chubanshe, 1992.

Pan Xianlin. "Gao chan nongzuowu chuanru dui Dian, Chuan, Qian jiaojie diqu Yizu shehui de xingxiang" (The effects of the introduction of hi-yield crops on Yi society in the Yunnan, Sichuan, Guizhou frontier). *Sixiang zhanxian*, 5 (1997): 60–64.

Parfrey, Laura Wegener, Erika Barbero, Elyse Lasser, Micah Dunthorn, Debashish Bhattacharya, David J. Patterson, and Laura A. Katz. "Evaluating

Works Cited

Support for the Current Classification of Eukaryotic Diversity," *PLoS Genetics*, 2.12 (Dec. 2006): 2062–73.

Parker, Bradley J. "Towards an Understanding of Borderland Processes." *American Antiquity*, 71.1 (Jan. 2006): 77–100.

Parker, Geoffrey. "Crisis and Catastrophe: The Global Crisis of the Seventeenth Century Reconsidered." *American Historical Review* 113.4 (Oct. 2008): 1053–79.

Pasquet, Sylvie. "Entre Chine et Birmanie: Un mineur-diplomate au royaume de Hulu, 1743–1752" (première partie) (Between China and Burma: A minor emissary to the kingdom of Hulu, 1743–1752 [part one]). *Études Chinoises*, 8.1 (spring 1989): 41–68.

Peng Sunyi. *Shang zhong wenjian lu* (A record of things heard & seen amidst the mountains). In Pan Zhe, Li Hongbin, and Sun Fangming, eds. *Qing ruguan qian shiliao xuanji, disan ji* (Selected compilation of Qing pre-conquest historical materials, third series). Beijing: Zhongguo renmin daxue chubanshe, 1991.

Perdue, Peter C. "Official Goals and Local Interests: Water Control in the Dongting Lake Region during the Ming and Qing Periods." *Journal of Asian Studies*, 41.4 (Aug. 1982): 747–65.

Perdue, Peter C. *China Marches West: The Qing Conquest of Central Eurasia*. Cambridge MA: Harvard University Press, 2005.

Pingding Zhun-ge-er fanglue (Record of the pacification of the Zhughars). Fu-heng, comp. Beijing: Quanguo tushuguan wenxian suoyin fuzhi zhongxin, 1990.

Pomeranz, Kenneth. "How Exhausted an Earth? Some Thoughts on Qing (1644–1911) Environmental History." *Chinese Environmental History Newsletter*, 2.2 (Nov. 1995): 6–10.

The Making of a Hinterland: State, Society, and Economy in Inland North China, 1853–1937. Berkeley: University of California Press, 1993.

The Great Divergence: China, Europe and the Making of the Modern World Economy. Princeton: Princeton University Press, 2000.

Postone, Moishe, Edward LiPuma, and Craig Calhoun. "Introduction: Bourdieu and Social Theory." In Craig Calhoun, Edward LiPuma, and Moishe Postone, eds. *Bourdieu: Critical Perspectives*. Chicago: University of Chicago Press, 1993.

Power, Daniel and Naomi Standen, eds. *Frontiers in Question: Eurasian Borderlands, 700–1700*. London: Macmillan, 1999.

Qi Meiqin. *Qingdai Neiwufu* (The Qing imperial household department). Beijing: Zhongguo renmin daxue chubanshe, 1998.

"Guanyu Shengjing Neiwufu de sheli shijian wenti" (Concerning the problem of the time period of the establishment of the Shengjing imperial household department). *Qingshi yanjiu*, 3 (1995): 98–100.

Qianlongchao neifu chaoben 'Lifanyuan zeli' (Imperial household department draft of the *regulations of the Lifanyuan*, Qianlong edition). Zhao Yuntian, ed. Beijing: Zhongguo zangxue chubanshe, 2006.

Qianlongchao shangyu dang (Archive of imperial decrees from the Qianlong reign). Zhongguo Diyi Lishi Danganguan, ed. 8 volumes. Beijing: Dang'an chubanshe, 1991.

302 *Works Cited*

Qin Heping. "Yumi de zhongzhi ji dui Dai, Luoluo deng shandi minzu de yingxiang" (Corn cultivation and its influence on indigenous Yi and Lisu mountain ethnicities). In Yang Weibing, ed. *Ming Qing yilai Yun Gui gaoyuan de huanjing yu shehui* (Environment and society on the Yun-Gui plateau from the Ming-Qing period). Shanghai: Dongfang Chuban Zhongxin, 2010.

Qing Gaozong yuzhi shi (Imperial compilation of the poems of the Qianlong emperor of the Qing). Gugong Bowuyuan, ed. 19 volumes. Haikou: Hainan chubanshe, 2000.

Qing Shengzu yuzhi shi wen (Imperial compilation of the poems and prose of the Kangxi emperor of the Qing). Gugong Bowuyuan, ed. 6 volumes. Haikou: Hainan chubanshe, 2000.

Qingshigao (Draft official history of the Qing dynasty). 48 volumes. Beijing: Zhonghua Shuju, 1991.

Qingshilu (Veritable records of the Qing dynasty). 60 volumes. Beijing: Zhonghua shuju, 1985–87.

Qingchao qian Lifanyuan Man-Meng wen tiben (Routine memorials in Manchu and Mongolian from the early Qing Lifanyuan). Guan-bu-zha-bu and Wang Chihua, eds. 23 volumes. Hohhot: Neimenggu chubanshe and Neimenggu chuban jituan, 2010.

Qingchu neiguo shiyuan Manwen dang'an yi bian (Translated compilation of Manchu archives of the early Qing inner historical office). Zhongguo diyi lishi dang'anguan, ed. and trans. 3 volumes. Beijing: Guangming ribao chubanshe, 1989.

Qingdai dang'an shiliao congbian (Collectanea of Qing archival historical materials). Volume 14. Diyi lishi dang'anguan, ed. Beijing: Zhonghua shuju, 1990.

Qingdai dang'an shiliao xuanbian (Selected archival historical materials on the Qing dynasty). 4 volumes. Shanghai: Shanghai shudian chubanshe, 2010.

Qingdai E-lun-chun zu ManHan wen dang'an huibian (Compilation of Qing archives on the Orochon in Manchu and Chinese). Zhongguo diyi lishi dang'anguan and E-lun-chun minzu yanjiuhui eds. Beijing: Minzu chubanshe, 2001.

Qingdai Neige daku sanyi dang'an xuanbian: huangzhuang (Selected archives missing from the main vaults of the Qing Grand Secretariat: imperial manors). 2 volumes. Liaoning shehui kexue yuan lishi yanjiusuo, Dalian shi tushuguan wenxian yanjiu shi and Liaoning sheng minzu yanjiusuo lishi yanjiushi, et al., eds. and trans. Shenyang: Liaoning minzu chubanshe, 1988.

Qingdai Sanxing Fu Dutong Yamen Man Han wen dang'an yibian (Compilation of translations from the Sanxing Vice Commander-in-Chief's Office Manchu document archive). Liaoning sheng dang'anguan, ed. and trans. Shenyang: Liao Shen shushe, 1984.

Qingdai Sanxing Fu Dutong Yamen Man Han wen dang'an xuanbian (Qing Manchu archival selections in Chinese translation from the Sanxing Vice Commander-in-Chief's Office). Liaoning sheng Dang'an Guan, ed. and trans. Shenyang: Liaoning guji chubanshe, 1995.

Qingdai Zhong-E guanxi dang'an shiliao xuanbian: Xianfeng yuan nian zheng yue – Xianfeng ershiyi nian shier yue (Selections from the Qing Sino-Russian

Works Cited

relations archive: first year, first month of the Xianfeng reign to twenty-first year, twelfth month of the Xianfeng reign). Third series. Gugong Bowuyua andn Ming-Qing Dang'an Bu, eds. and trans. 3 volumes. Beijing: Zhonghua shuju, 1979.

Qingdai Zhong-E guanxi dang'an shiliao xuanbian: diyi bian, Shunzhi shi nian san yue – Kangxi wushiyi nian qi yue (Selections from the Qing Sino-Russian relations archive: first series, tenth year, third month of the Shunzhi reign to fifty-first year, seventh month of the Kangxi reign). Zhongguo diyi lishi dang'anguan, ed. and trans. 2 volumes. Beijing: Zhonghua shuju, 1981.

Rawski, Evelyn S. "Reenvisioning the Qing: The Significance of the Qing Period in Chinese History." *Journal of Asian Studies*, 55.4 (1996): 829–50.

Reardon-Anderson, James. *"Reluctant Pioneers: China's Expansion Northward, 1644–1937.* Stanford: Stanford University Press, 2005.

Ren Meie. *Zhongguo ziran dili gangyao* (Outline of China's natural geography). Beijing: Shangwu yinshuguan, 2009.

"Report SEAR/WPR Biregional Meeting on Control of Malaria." Manila: World Health Organization Regional Office for the Western Pacific, 2000.

Rhoades, Robert E. "Archaeological Use and Abuse of Ecological Concepts and Studies: The Ecotone Example." *American Antiquity*, 43.4 (Oct. 1978): 608–14.

Riley, Eleanor. "Malaria and the Human Immune System." Wellcome Trust Websites. http://malaria.wellcome.ac.uk/doc_WTD023881.html.

Rinchingiin, Indra. "Mongolian Dairy Products." *Mongolia Today; Science, Culture, Environment and Development* (2003): 68–85.

Ripley, Earle A., Wang Renzhong, and Zhu Tingcheng. "The Climate of the Songnen Plain, Northeast China." *International Journal of Ecology and Environmental Sciences*, 22.1 (Apr. 1996): 1–21.

Roberts, Julian. "Dialectic of Enlightenment." In Fred Rush, ed. *The Cambridge Companion to Critical Theory*. Cambridge: Cambridge University Press, 2004.

Robertson, R. Cecil. "Malaria in Western Yunnan with Reference to the China-Burma Highway." *Chinese Medical Journal* 57 (1940): 57–73.

Robinne, François and Mandy Sadan, eds. *Social Dynamics in the Highlands of Southeast Asia: Reconsidering Political Systems of Highland Burma by E.R. Leach*. Leiden: Brill, 2007.

Robson, James. *Power of Place: Religious Landscape of the Southern Sacred Peak (Nanyue 南嶽) in Medieval China*. Cambridge MA: Harvard University Asia Center, 2009.

Roca-Feltrer, Arantxa, Joanna R. M. Armstrong Schellenberg, Lucy Smith, and Ilona Carneiro. "A Simple Method for Defining Malaria Seasonality." *Malaria Journal*, 8.276 (2009): 1–14.

Rogaski, Ruth. *Hygienic Modernity: Meanings of Health and Disease in Treatyport China*. Berkeley: University of California Press, 2004.

Rohde, Klaus. *Nonequilibrium Ecology*. Cambridge: Cambridge University Press, 2005.

Roth Li, Gertraude. "State-building Before 1644." In Willard J. Peterson, ed. *The Cambridge History of China, Volume 9, Part 1: The Ch'ing Dynasty to 1800*. Cambridge: Cambridge University Press, 2002.

Works Cited

Rowe, William T. "Water Control and the Qing Political Process: The Fankou Dam Controversy, 1876–1883." *Modern China*, 14.4 (Oct. 1988): 353–87.

"Education and Empire in Southwest China: Ch'eng Hung-mou in Yunnan, 1733-38." In Benjamin Elman and Alexander Woodside, eds. *Education and Society in Late Imperial China, 1600–1900*. Berkeley: University of California Press, 1994.

"Social Stability and Social Change." In Willard J. Peterson, ed. *The Cambridge History of China, Volume 9, Part 1: The Ch'ing Dynasty to 1800*. Cambridge: Cambridge University Press, 2002.

China's Last Empire: The Great Qing. Cambridge, MA: Belknap Press of Harvard University Press, 2009.

"Bao Shichen: An Early Nineteenth-Century Chinese Agrarian Reformer." Paper delivered at the Yale Agrarian Studies Colloquium Series, Fall 2009–2010, Sept. 11, 2010 (www.yale.edu/agrarianstudies/colloqpapers/01rowe.pdf).

Basil Dmytryshyn, E. A. P. Crownhart-Vaughan, and Thomas Vaughan, eds. *Russia's Conquest of Siberia: A Documentary Record, 1558–1700*. Portland: Oregon Historical Society Press, 1985.

Sadao Sakamoto. "Glutinous-Endosperm Starch Food Culture Specific to Eastern and Southeastern Asia." In Roy Ellen and Katsuyoshi Fuki, eds. *Redefining Nature: Ecology, Culture and Domestication*. Oxford: Berg, 1996.

Sakai, Robert K. "The Ryukyu (Liu-Ch'iu) Islands as fief of Satsuma." In John K. Fairbank, ed. *The Chinese World Order*. Cambridge, MA: Harvard University Press, 1968.

Santangelo, Paolo. *"Collected Papers of the XXIX Congress of Chinese Studies: 10th to 15th September 1984, University of Tübingen."* Tübingen: University of Tübingen, 1988.

Schafer, Edward H. *Pacing the Void: T'ang Approaches to the Stars*. Berkeley: University of California Press, 1977.

Schlesinger, Jonathan. "The Qing Invention of Nature: Environment and Identity in Northeast China and Mongolia, 1750–1850." PhD diss., Harvard University, 2012.

Schoppa, R. Keith. "State, Society, and Land Reclamation on Hangzhou Bay during the Republican Period." *Modern China*, 23.2 (Apr. 1997): 246–71.

Schwennesen, E. P. "Using Salt for Livestock." In R. Gum, G. Ruyle, and R. Rice, eds. *Arizona Ranchers' Management Guide*. Tucson: University of Arizona, 1994.

Scoones, Ian. "New Ecology and the Social Sciences: What Prospects for a Fruitful Engagement?" *Annual Review of Anthropology*, 28 (1999): 479–507.

Scott, James C. *Seeing Like a State: How Certain Schemes to Improve the Human Condition Have Failed*. New Haven: Yale University Press, 1998.

The Art of Not Being Governed: An Anarchist History of Upland Southeast Asia. New Haven: Yale University Press, 2009.

Sebes, Joseph, S.J. *The Jesuits and the Sino-Russian Treaty of Nerchinsk*. Rome: Institutum Historicum S.I., 1961.

Serruys, Henry. "Chinese in Southern Mongolia during the Sixteenth Century." *Monumenta Serica*, 18 (1959): 1–95.

Works Cited

"Five Documents Regarding Salt Production in Ordos." *Bulletin of the School of Oriental and African Studies*, 40.2 (1977): 338–53.

Shangjunshu zhuyi (Annotated translation of the *Book of Lord Shang*). Gao Heng, ed. and trans. Beijing: Zhonghua shuju, 1974.

Shanghai shudian chubanshe, ed. *"Dayi juemi lu" tan* (Discussion of "the record of the great counsel to enlighten the deluded"). Shanghai: Shanghai shudian chubanshe, 1999.

Shank, J. B. "Crisis: A Useful Category of Post-Social Scientific Historical Analysis." *American Historical Review* 113.4 (Oct. 2008): 1090–99.

Shaw, David Gary. "Happy in Our Chains? Agency and Language in the Postmodern Age." *History and Theory*, 40.4 (Dec. 2001): 1–9.

Shepherd, John Robert. *Statecraft and Political Economy on the Taiwan Frontier, 1600–1800*. Stanford: Stanford University Press, 1993.

Shen Hao. *Dixue* (Terrestrial study). 1712. Reprint, Shanghai: Sao ye shanfang, 1910.

Shengjing shenwu dang'an shiliao (Historical materials from the Shengjing ginseng administration archives). Liaoning sheng dang'anguan, ed. and trans. Shenyang: Liaohai chubanshe, 2003.

Shimizu Toru. "Yunnan nanbu de shengtai huanjing beike" (Environmental steles from southern Yunnan). In Yang Weibing, ed. *Ming Qing yilai Yun Gui gaoyuan de huanjing yu shehui* (Environment and society on the Yun-Gui plateau from the Ming-Qing period). Shanghai: Dongfang huban zhongxin, 2010.

Shinobu Iguro. "Historical Knowledge and the Response to Desertification: A Study of Agricultural Water Supply Technology in Eighteenth-Century Northwestern China." In Ts'ui-jung Liu, ed. *Environmental History in East Asia*. New York: Routledge, 2014.

Shiqi shiji Shae qinlüe Heilongjiang liuyu shi ziliao (Historical materials on the 17th century Tsarist Russian invasion of the Heilong River basin). Liu Minsheng, Meng Xianzhang and Bu Ping, eds. Harbin: Heilongjiang jiaoyu chubanshe, 1992.

Shiyu yanjiu suo, ed. *Ming Qing shiliao, geng bian* (Historical materials from the Ming and Qing periods, volume 7). 2 volumes. 1960. Reprint, Beijing: Zhonghua Shuju, 1987.

Shukla, Himakshi. "Lactose Intolerance in Health and Disease." *Nutrition and Food Science*, 97.2 (1997): 66–70.

Shunning fuzhi (Gazetteer of Shunning Prefecture). Zhu Zhanke et al., comps. 2 volumes. 1904. Reprint, Taibei: Chengwen chubanshe, 1968.

Simonov, Eugene A. and Thomas D. Dahmer, eds. *Amur-Heilong River Basin Reader*. Hong Kong: Ecosystems, 2008.

Sin Yu. *Pukchŏngnok* (Record of a northern expedition). Sŏngnam: Han'guk Chŏngsin Munhwa Yŏn'guwŏn, 1980.

Skinner, G. William. "The Hierarchy of Local Systems." In G. William Skinner, ed. *The City in Late Imperial China*. Stanford: Stanford University Press, 1977.

"Sichuan's Population Data in the Nineteenth Century: Lessons from Disaggregated Data." *Late Imperial China*, 8.1 (June 1987): 1–79.

Works Cited

"Smallpox Fact Sheet/Smallpox Disease Overview." Centers for Disease Control and Prevention. www.bt.cdc.gov/agent/smallpox/overview/disease-facts.asp.

Smith, Kent Clarke. "Ch'ing Policy and the Development of Southwest China: Aspects of Ortai's Governor-Generalship, 1726–1731." PhD diss., Yale University, 1971.

Smith, Kidder, Peter K. Bol, Joseph A. Adler, and Don J. Wyatt, eds. *Sung Dynasty Uses of the I-Ching*. Princeton: Princeton University Press, 1990.

Smith, Kidder. "Sima Tan and the Invention of Daoism, 'Legalism,' *et cetera*," *Journal of Asian Studies*, 62.1 (Feb. 2003): 129–56.

Smith, Richard J. *Fathoming the Cosmos and Ordering the World: The Yijing and its Evolution in China*. Charlottesville: University of Virginia Press, 2008.

Sneath, David. *Changing Inner Mongolia: Pastoral Mongolian Society and the Chinese State*. Oxford: Oxford University Press, 2000.

The Headless State: Aristocratic Orders, Kinship Society, & Misrepresentations of Nomadic Inner Asia. New York: Columbia University Press, 2007.

Songben lidai dili zhizhang tu (Handbook of maps on historical geography, Song dynasty volume). Shanghai: Shanghai guji chubanshe, 1989.

Sörlin, Sverker and Paul Warde. "The Problem of Environmental History: A Re-reading of the Field." *Environmental History*, 12 (Jan. 2007): 107–30.

Soulé, Michael E. and Gary Lease, eds. *Reinventing Nature? Responses to Postmodern Deconstruction*. Washington, DC: Island Press, 1995.

Spence, Jonathan D. *Treason by the Book*. New York: Viking, 2001.

Steinberg, Ted. "Down to Earth: Nature, Agency, and Power in History." *American Historical Review*, 107.3 (June 2002): 798–820.

Sternberg, Troy, Nicholas Middleton, and David Thomas. "Pressurised Pastoralism in South Gobi, Mongolia: What Is the Role of Drought?" *Transactions of the Institute of British Geographers*, 34.3 (July 2009): 364–77.

Steward, Julian. *Theory of Culture Change: The Methodology of Multilinear Evolution* Urbana: University of Illinois Press, 1955.

Stiles, Daniel. "The Hunter-Gatherer Revisionist Debate." *Anthropology Today*, 8.2 (Apr. 1992): 13–17.

Stroud, Ellen. "Does Nature Always Matter? Following Dirt through History." *History and Theory*, 42 (Dec. 2003): 75–81.

Su De. "Guanyu Qingmo Neimenggu xibu diqu de fangken" (Concerning land clearance in the western Inner Mongolian region during the late Qing). *Menggu shi yanjiu*, 7 (Hohhot, 2003): 434–48.

Sun Jiagan. *Sun Wending Gong zoushu* (Sun Jiagan's collected memorials). 2 volumes. Taibei: Wenhai chubanshe, 1966.

Sun Quanzhu. "Neimenggu ziran huanjing de yanbian yu caoyuan de fazhan" (Evolution of Inner Mongolia's natural environment and the development of grassland). *Neimenggu caoye*, 2 (1992): 1–7.

Sun Xi and Zhang Weihua. *Qing qianqi Zhong-E guanxi* (Sino-Russian relations in the early Qing period). Jinan: Shangdong jiaoyu chubanshe, 1997.

Sun Zhe. "Qing qianqi Menggu diqu de renkou qianru ji Qing zhengfu de fengjin zhengce' (Migration into the Mongolian region and the quarantine policy of the Qing state in the early Qing period). *Qingshi yanjiu*, 2 (1998): 41–50.

Works Cited

Symons, Van Jay. *Ch'ing Ginseng Management: Ch'ing Monopolies in Microcosm.* Tempe: Center for Asian Studies, Arizona State University, 1981.

Takeuchi Fusaji. "'Kaifa yu fengjin:' Daoguang shiqi Qingchao dui Yun-Gui diqu minzu zhengce de qianxi" (Exploitation and quarantine: Preliminary analysis of ethnic policy in the Yun-Gui region during the Qing Daoguang period). In Yang Weibing, ed. *Ming Qing yilai Yun Gui gaoyuan de huanjing yu shehui* (Environment and society on the Yun-Gui plateau from the Ming-Qing period). Shanghai: Dongfang huban zhongxin, 2010.

Tan Qian. *Bei you lu* (Record of a journey to the north). Beijing: Zhonghua shuju, 2006.

Tan Qixiang, ed. *Zhongguo lishi ditu ji: diba ce, Qing shiqi* (The historical atlas of China, volume 8, the Qing period). Beijing: Ditu chubanshe, 1987.

Tang, Lina, Aixian Li, and Guofan Shao. "Landscape-level Forest Ecosystem Conservation on Changbai Mountain, China and North Korea (DPRK)." *Mountain Research and Development*, 31.2 (Apr. 2011): 169–75.

Tao Zhu. *Tao Wenyi Gong (Zhu)ji* (Tao Zhu's collected works). 8 volumes. Taibei: Wenhai chubanshe, 1968.

Teng, Emma. *Taiwan's Imagined Geography: Chinese Colonial Travel Writing and Pictures, 1683–1895.* Cambridge, MA: Harvard University Asia Center, 2004.

Tengyue tingzhi (Gazetteer of Tengyue Subprefecture). Chen Zonghai et al., comps. 1887. Reprint, Taibei: Chengwen chubanshe, 1967.

Thant, Myint-U. *The Making of Modern Burma.* Cambridge: Cambridge University Press, 2001.

Tillman, Hoyt Cleveland. "Proto-Nationalism in Twelfth-century China? The Case of Chen Liang." *Harvard Journal of Asiatic Studies*, 39.2 (Dec. 1979): 403–28.

Tong Yonggong. "Qingdai Shengjing Neiwufu liangzhuang gaishu" (Overview of Qing *Neiwufu* manors in Shengjing). In Tong Yonggong. *Manyuwen yu Manwen dang'an yanjiu* (Manchu and Manchu archival research). Shenyang: Liaoning minzu chubanshe, 2009.

"Qingdai Shengjing shang san qi bao-yi wenti buxu" (Supplementary material on the problem of the bondservants of the three superior banners in Qing Shengjing). In Tong Yonggong. *Manyuwen yu Manwen dang'an yanjiu* (Manchu and Manchu archival research). Shenyang: Liaoning minzu chubanshe, 2009.

"Qingdai Shengjing shenwu huodong shuyao" (Overview of operations of the Shengjing ginseng administration in the Qing period). In Tong Yonggong. *Manyuwen yu Manwen dang'an yanjiu* (Manchu and Manchu archival research). Shenyang: Liaoning minzu chubanshe, 2009.

"Shengjing *Neiwufu* de sheli ji yange" (The establishment and development of the Shengjing *Neiwufu*). In Tong Yonggong. *Manyuwen yu Manwen dang'an yanjiu* (Manchu and Manchu archival research). Shenyang: Liaoning minzu chubanshe, 2009.

Torbert, Preston M. *The Ch'ing Imperial Household Department.* Cambridge, MA: Harvard University Press, 1977.

Van Schendel, Willem. "Geographies of Knowing, Geographies of Ignorance: Jumping Scale in Southeast Asia," *Environment and Planning D: Society and Space*, 20.6 (2002): 647–68.

Works Cited

Vermeer, Eduard B. "The Mountain Frontier in Late Imperial China: Economic and Social Developments in the Bashan." *T'oung Pao*, 78.4–5 (1991): 300–329.

"Ch'ing Government Concerns with the Exploitation of New Farmland." In Léon Vandermeersch, ed. *La société civile face à l'Etat: dans les traditions chinoise, japonaise, coréenne et vietnamienne* (Paris: Ecole française d'Extrême-Orient, 1994): 203–48.

"Population and Ecology along the Frontier in Qing China." In Mark Elvin and Liu Ts'ui-jung, eds. *Sediments of Time: Environment and Society in Chinese History*. Cambridge: Cambridge University Press, 1998.

Wada Sei. "Natives of the Lower Reaches of the Amur River as Represented in Chinese Records." *Memoirs of the Research Department of the Tōyō Bunko*, 10 (1938): 41–102.

Wakeman, Frederic, Jr. *The Great Enterprise: The Manchu Reconstruction of Imperial Order in Seventeenth-Century China*. 2 volumes. Berkeley: University of California Press, 1985.

Waley-Cohen, Joanna. "The New Qing History." *Radical History Review*, 88 (winter 2004): 193–206.

The Culture of War in China: Empire and the Military under the Qing Dynasty. (London: I.B. Tauris, 2006),

Walker, Brett L. "The Early Modern Japanese State and Ainu Vaccinations: Redefining the Body Politic 1799–1868." *Past and Present*, 163 (May 1999): 121–60.

The Conquest of Ainu Lands: Ecology and Culture in Japanese Expansion, 1590–1800. Berkeley: University of California Press, 2001.

Walter, G. H. and R. Hengeveld. "The Structure of the Two Ecological Paradigms." *Acta Biotheoretica* 48.1 (Mar. 2000): 15–46.

Wang Chang. "Zheng Mian jilüe" (Notes on the Myanmar expedition). In Li Genyuan, comp. *Yongchang fu wenzheng* (Anthology of writings on Yongchang prefecture). Kunming: Teng chong li shi, 1941.

Wang, Yen-Chien. *Land Taxation in Imperial China, 1750–1911*. Cambridge MA: Harvard University Press, 1973.

Wang Chuihan. "Guoyu qishe yu Manzu de fazhan" (Shooting from horseback/speaking Manchu and the development of the Manchu ethnicity). In Wang Chuihan, *Qingshi xin kao* (New studies in Qing history). Shenyang: Liaoning Daxue chubanshe, 1990.

Wang Dehou. "Qingdai Sanxing difang maoyi shulun" (Overview of local trade in Qing dynasty Sanxing). *Shehui kexue zhanxian* (Dongbei lishi yu wenhua), 4 (1994): 177–83.

Wang Fuzhi. *Huangshu* (The yellow book). In Chuanshan quan shu bian ji wei yuan hui bian jiao, ed. *Chuanshan quanshu* (Complete works of Wang Fuzhi). Volume 12. Changsha: Yuelu shushe, 1988.

Du Tongjian Lun (On reading the *Tongjian*). In Chuanshan quan shu bian ji wei yuan hui bian jiao, ed. *Chuanshan quanshu* (Complete works of Wang Fuzhi). Volume 10. 2nd ed. Changsha: Yuelu chubanshe, 1996.

Song Lun (On the Song dynasty). Beijing: Zhonghua shuju, 2009.

Wang Han and Guo Pingruo. "Qingdai kenzhi zhengce yu Shaanbei Changcheng wai de shengtai huanjing" (The Qing dynasty reclamation policy and

Works Cited

ecological environment outside the Great Wall in north Shannxi). *Shixue yuekan*, 4 (2007): 86–93.

Wang Hongzuo. "Diannan shi yishu" (Ten deliberations on Yunnan). In Fang Guoyu, ed. *Yunnan shiliao congkan* (Collection of Yunnan historical materials). Volume 8. Kunming: Yunnan Daxue chubanshe, 1998.

Wang Jiange. "Qingdai Huabei de huangzai yu shehui kongzhi" (Locust plagues and social control in Qing north China). *Qingshi yanjiu*, 2 (2000): 100–107.

Wang Lüjie. "Gaitu guiliu shuo" (Comments on conversion). In Wang Xiqi, comp. *Xiao fang hu zhai yudi cong chao* (The little square vase studio geographical series). 16 volumes. 1877. Reprint, Taibei, Guangwen shuju, 1962.

Wang Peihuan and Zhao Degui. "Qingdai Sanxing cheng de boxing ji qi jingji tedian" (Growth and its economic characteristics in Qing Ilan Hala). *Shehui kexue zhanxian* (Dongbei lishi yu wenhua), 1 (1986): 197–202.

Wang Sizhi. "Bishu Shanzhuang de xingjian yu Suifu monan Menggu" (The construction of the imperial retreat to avoid the heat and the pacification of Mongols south of the desert). In Bishu Shanzhuang yanjiu huibian, ed. *Bishu Shanzhuang Luncong* (Anthology on the imperial retreat to avoid the heat). Beijing: Zijin cheng chubanshe, 1986.

Wang Yejian and Huang Yingjue. "Qingdai Zhongguo qihou bianqian, ziran zaihai yu liangjia de chubu kaocha" (Preliminary study of Qing climate change, natural disaster and grain prices). *Zhongguo jingji shi yanjiu*, 1 (1999): 3–18.

Wang Zhennian, "Fajia zhengzhi sixiang yanjiu ershi nian" (Twenty years of research on legalist political thought), *Shehui kexue zhanxian*, 6 (2002): 209–13.

Wang Zhigang. "Central Inner Mongolia." In Committee on Scholarly Communication with the People's Republic of China, ed. *Grasslands and Grassland Sciences in Northern China*. Washington, DC: National Academy Press, 1992.

Warde, Paul. "The Environmental History of Pre-Industrial Agriculture in Europe." In Sverker Sörlin and Paul Warde, eds. *Nature's End: History and Environment*. Houndmills, Basingstoke: Palgrave Macmillan, 2009.

Watts, Sheldon. British Development Policies and Malaria in India, 1897–c. 1929." *Past and Present*, 165 (Nov. 1999): 141–81.

Wei Yuan. "Beigan kao" (Study of the northern trunk). In Wang Xiqi, comp. *Xiao fang hu zhai yudi cong chao* (The little square vase studio geographical series). 16 volumes. 1877. Reprint, Taibei, Guangwen shuju, 1962.

"Dili gangmu xu" (Preface to an outline of terrestrial patterns). In Wei Yuan quanji bian ji wei yuan hui, ed. *Wei Yuan quanji* (Wei Yuan's complete works). 20 volumes. Changsha: Yuelu shushe, 2004.

"Zhi long cheng qi lun xu" (On the reception of *qi* in flatlands and highlands, preface). In Wei Yuan quanji bian ji wei yuan hui, ed. *Wei Yuan quanji* (Wei Yuan's complete works). 20 volumes. Changsha: Yuelu shushe, 2004.

Shengwu ji (Chronicle of imperial military campaigns). 2 volumes. Beijing: Zhonghua shuju, 1984.

(Daoguang) *Weiyuan tingzhi* (Gazetteer of Weiyuan sub-prefecture). Xie Tiren, comp. 1837. Reprint, Beijing: Beijing tushuguan chubanshe, 2005.

Works Cited

West, Paige. "Translation, Value and Space: Theorizing an Ethnographic and Engaged Environmental Anthropology." *American Anthropologist*, 107.4 (Dec. 2005): 632–42.

White, Richard. *The Middle Ground: Indians, Empires and Republics in the Great Lakes Region, 1650–1815*. Cambridge: Cambridge University Press, 1991.
"Creative Misunderstandings and New Understandings." *William and Mary Quarterly*, 63.1 (Jan. 2006): 9–14.

Whitehead, Neil N. "Ecological History and Historical Ecology: Diachronic Modeling versus Historical Explanation." In William Balée, ed. *Advances in Historical Ecology*. New York: Columbia University, 1998.

Whyte, Susan Reynolds. "Health Identities and Subjectivities: The Ethnographic Challenge." *Medical Anthropology Quarterly*, 23.1 (Mar. 2009): 6–15.

Wiens, Mi Chu. "Anti-Manchu Thought during the Early Qing." *Papers on China*, 22A (1969): 1–24.

Will, Pierre-Étienne. *Bureaucracy and Famine in Eighteenth-Century China*. Elborg Foster, trans. Stanford: Stanford University Press, 1990.

Will, Pierrre-Étienne and R. Bin Wong. *Nourish the People: The State Civilian Granary System in China, 1650–1850*. Ann Arbor: University of Michigan Center for Chinese Studies, 1991.

Williams, Dee Mack. *Beyond Great Walls: Environment, Identity and Development on the Chinese Grasslands of Inner Mongolia*. Stanford: Stanford University Press, 2002.

Wills, John E., Jr. "Maritime Asia, 1500–1800: The Interactive Emergence of European Domination." *American Historical Review*, 98.1 (Feb. 1993): 83–105.
Embassies and Illusions: Dutch and Portuguese Envoys to K'ang-his, 1666–1687. Cambridge MA: Harvard Council on East Asian Studies, 1984.

Winichakul, Thongchai. *Siam Mapped: A History of the Geo-body of a Nation*. Honolulu: University of Hawai'i Press, 1994.

Winterhalder, Bruce. "Concepts in Historical Ecology: The View from Evolutonary Ecology." In Carole L. Crumley, ed. *Historical Ecology: A Multi-Dimensional Orientation*. Santa Fe: School of American Research Press, 1994.

Witzenrath, Christoph. *Cossacks and the Russian Empire, 1598–1725 Manipulation, Rebellion and Expansion into Siberia*. New York: Routledge, 2007.

Wong, R. Bin. "Foundations of Success, 1650–1735." In Pierre-Étienne Will and R. Bin Wong, eds. *Nourish the People: The State Civilian Granary System in China, 1650–1850*. Ann Arbor: University of Michigan Center for Chinese Studies, 1991.

Woodside, Alexander. "The Ch'ien-lung Reign." In Willard J. Peterson, ed. *The Cambridge History of China, Volume 9, Part 1: The Ch'ing Dynasty to 1800*. Cambridge: Cambridge University Press, 2002.

Worster, Donald. "History as Natural History: An Essay on Theory and Method," *Pacific Historical Review*, 53.1 (Feb. 1984): 1–19.
"Appendix: Doing Environmental History." In Donald Worster, ed. *The Ends of the Earth: Perspectives on Modern Environmental History*. Cambridge: Cambridge University Press, 1989.

Works Cited

"Nature and the Disorder of History." In Michael E. Soulé and Gary Lease, eds. *Reinventing Nature? Responses to Postmodern Deconstruction*. Washington, DC: Island Press, 1995.

Wu Luzhen. *Dong si Menggu shiji* (Facts on the four eastern Mongolian leagues). In Neimenggu tushuguan, ed. *Neimenggu lishi wenxian congshu* (Collectanea of Inner Mongolian historical records). Volume 4. 1912–13. Reprint, Yuanfang chubanshe, 2007.

Wu Zhenchen. *Ningguta jilüe* (Notes on Ningguta). In *Xuxiu Siku quanshu* (Sequel to the complete collection of the four treasuries). Volume 731. Shanghai: Shanghai guji chubanshe, 1995–99.

Wu Zhongyao. "Tengyue ting guan ai lun" (On the passes and pales of Tengyue subprefecture). In *Yongchang fuzhi* (Gazetteer of Yongchang prefecture). Liu Yuke et al., comps. Taibei: Chengwen chubanshe, 1967.

Wucheng xianzhi (Gazetteer of Wucheng district). Zhou Xuejun et al., comps. 1881.

Wu-re-tao-ke-tao. *Mengguzu youmu jingji ji qi bianqian* (The Mongolian pastoral economy and its transformations). Beijing: Zhongyang minzu daxue chubanshe, 2006.

Wu-yun-ger-ri-le. *Shiba zhi ershi shiji chu Neimenggu chengzhen yanjiu* (Inner Mongolian urban studies from the eighteenth to the early twentieth centuries). Hohhot: Neimenggu renmin chubanshe, 2005.

Xi-yong-jiao. "'Qin fanzhong jian kan tongli, waiyu jimi qi jinqing:' Qianlong xunyou Neimenggu ji qi shige chuangzuo" ('Close relations with the vassal masses constructs a suitable similitude: How can intimacy come from loose reigns on the borderlands?': Qianlong's peregrinations to Inner Mongolia and his poetic creations). *Minzu wenxue yanjiu*, 3 (1997): 76–78.

Xi'an xianzhi (Gazetteer of Xi'an district). Fan Chongkai et al., comps. 4 volumes. 1811. Reprint, Taibei: Chengwen chubanshe, 1970.

Xiao Ruiling, Cao Yongnian, Zhao Zhiheng, and Yu Yong. *Ming-Qing Neimenggu xibu diqu kaifa yu tudi shahua* (The development and desertification of western Inner Mongolia in the Ming-Qing period). Beijing: Zhonghua shuju, 2006.

Xiao, X., D. S. Ojima, W. J. Parton, Z. Chen, and D. Chen. "Sensitivity of Inner Mongolia Grasslands to Climate Change." *Journal of Biogeography* (July–Sept. 1995): 643–48.

Xi-bozu dang'an shiliao (Archival historical materials on the Sibe ethnicity). Zhongguo diyi lishi dang'anguan, ed. 2 volumes. Shenyang: Liaoning minzu chubanshe, 1989.

Xie Huijun. "Qingdai Shengjing cheng liubu jianzhi ji zuoluo weizhi" (The establishment of the six boards in the city of Shengjing and their location). *Manzu yanjiu*, 4 (2005): 54–58.

Xin Tangshu (New history of the Tang dynasty). 20 volumes. Beijing: Zhonghua shuju chubanshe, 1975.

Xu Guangqi. *Nongzheng quanshu* (Complete treatise on agricultural administration). Chen Huanliang and Luo Wenhua, eds. 2 volumes. Changsha: Yuelu shushe, 2002.

Xu Jiagan. *Miaojiang wenjian lu* (Record of things seen and heard on the Miao frontier). Guiyang: Guizhou renmin chubanshe, 1997.

Xu Junfeng. "Qingdai Yunnan liangshi zuowu de diyu fenbu" (Regional distribution of food crops in Qing Yunnan), *Zhongguo lishi dili luncong*, 3 (1995): 85–96.

Xu, Jianchu and Andreas Wilke, "State Simplifications of Land-Use and Biodiversity in the Uplands of Yunnan, Eastern Himalayan Region." In Uli M. Huber, Harald K. M. Bugmann, and Mel A. Reasoner, eds. *Global Change and Mountain Regions: An Overview of Current Knowledge*. New York: Springer, 2005.

Xu, Jianhui and Hui Liu. "The Challenges of Malaria Elimination in Yunnan Province, People's Republic of China." *Asian Pacific Journal of Tropical Biomedicine* (2011): 1–4.

Xu Jianwei and Liu Hui. "Border Malaria in Yunnan, China." *Southeast Asian Journal of Tropical Medicine and Public Health*, 28.3 (Sept. 1997): 456–59.

Xu Shanji and Xu Jishu. *Chongkan renzi xuzhi zixiao dili xinxue tongzong* (Reprint of the compilation of what people of terrestrial principle need to know for mental cultivation that endows filial piety). China: Da wen tang, late Qing.

   Dili renzi xu zhi (What people of terrestrial principle need to know). 3rd ed. Taibei: Wuling chubanshe, 1991.

Xu Ke. *Qingbai leichao* (Notes on the Qing compiled by category). 13 volumes. 1917. Reprint, Beijing: Zhonghua shuju, 1996.

Xu Yunnan tongzhi gao (Draft of the comprehensive gazetteer of Yunnan). Wang Wenshao, comp. 14 volumes. 1900. Reprint, Taibei: Wenhai chubanshe, 1966.

Yan Chongnian. *20 shiji Manxue zhuzuo tiyao* (Abstracts of twentieth-century works of Manchu studies). Beijing: Minzu chubanshe, 2003.

Yan Deyi. "Pu Si yanbian – Yunnan xin ding ken." (The [*sic*] Southernmost Yunnan). *Dili xuebao* 6 (1939): 27–40.

Yan Gao. "The Retreat of the Horses: The Manchus, Land Reclamations and Local Ecology in the Jiangnan Plain (ca. 1700s–1850s)." In Ts'ui-jung Liu, ed. *Environmental History in East Asia*. New York: Routledge, 2014.

Ya-er-tu. "Kan bao kai ken xu shi shu" (Survey report on fake and real land clearance). In He Changling, ed. *Qing jingshi wenbian* (Collected writings on statecraft from the Qing dynasty). 3 volumes. 1826. Reprint, Beijing: Zhonghua Shuju, 1992.

Yan Li. "Fajia sixiang zai Zhongguo zhengzhi wenhua chuantong zhong de diwei" (On position of Fajia's thought in Chinese political and cultural tradition [*sic*]). *Hefei gongye daxue xuebao (shehui kexue ban)*, 20.6 (Dec. 2006): 112–13.

Yan Shaomei and Zhang Xinchang. "Qingdai Yunnan Yizu diqu senlin shengtai baohu beike dang'an yanjiu" (A study of stele carving records of forest environmental protection in Yi areas of Qing Yunnan). *Dang'anxue yanjiu*, 3 (2004): 37–40.

Yan tie lun (Discourses on salt and iron). In *Wenyuan ge Siku quanshu* (Wenyuan ge edition of the complete collection of the four treasuries). Volume 695. Shanghai: Shanghai guji chubanshe, 2003.

Works Cited

Yang Bin. *Liubian jilüe* (Notes on the Willow Palisade). In Jin Yufu, comp. *Liao Hai cong shu* (Liaohai Collectanea). Taibei: Yiwen yinshuguan, c. 1970.

Yang Hu. *Mingdai Liaodong dusi* (The Ming regional military commission in Liaodong). Zhengzhou: Zhongzhou guji chubanshe, 1988.

Yang, Lien-sheng. *Studies in Chinese Institutional History*. Cambridge MA: Harvard University Press, 1961.

Yang Nianqun. *Hechu shi 'Jiangnan'?* (Where is Jiangnan?). Beijing: Renmin Daxue chubanshe, 2010.

Yang Qiang. *Qingdai Mengguzu mengqi zhidu* (The Mongol league-banner system of the Qing dynasty). Beijing: Minzu chubanshe, 2004.

Yang, Xiu and Ming Xu. "Biodiversity Conservation in Changbai Mountain Biosphere Reserve, Northeastern China: Status, Problem and Strategy." *Biodiversity and Conservation* 12.5 (May 2003): 883–903.

Yang Xulian. "Jianlun Qingdai Kangxi shiqi de xin Manzhou yu Bu-te-ha Baqi" (A brief discussion of New Manchus and the Hunting Eight Banners in the Qing Kangxi period). *Shehui kexue zhanxian*, 4 (1980): 192–96.

et al. *Qingdai dongbei shi* (A History of the Qing northeast). Shenyang: Liaoning jiaoyu chubanshe, 1991.

Yao, C. T., C. C. Wu, and Y. S. Pei. "Some Epidemiological Factors of Malaria in Mangshih, Yunnan, with Remarks on the Occurence of Blackwater Fever." *Chinese Medical Journal*, 61.3(1943): 197–211.

Yao, Y. T., L. C. Ling, and K. B. Liu. "Studies on the So-Called *Changch'i*: Part I. *Changch'i* in Kweichow and the Kwangsi Border." *Chinese Medical Journal* 50 (1936): 726–38.

"Studies on the So-Called *Changch'i*: Part II. *Changch'i* in Yunnan." *Chinese Medical Journal* ,50 (1936): 1815–28.

Yee, Cordell D. K. "Chinese Maps in Political Culture." In J. B. Harley and David Woodward, eds. *The History of Cartography, Volume 2, Book 2: Cartography in the Traditional East and Southeast Asian Societies*. Chicago: University of Chicago Press, 1994.

"Reinterpreting Traditional Chinese Geographic Maps." In J. B. Harley and David Woodward, eds. *The History of Cartography, Volume 2, Book 2, Cartography in the Traditional East and Southeast Asian Societies*. Chicago: University of Chicago Press, 1994.

Yi-du-he-xi-ge et al. *Menggu minzu tongshi, disi juan* (A complete history of Mongolia, volume 4). Hohot: Neimenggu daxue chubanshe, 1993.

Yin Shaoting. *People and Forests: Yunnan Swidden Agriculture in Human-Ecological Perspective* Magnus Fiskesjo, trans. Kunming: Yunnan Education Publishing House, 2001.

Yin-ji-shan. "Chouzhuo Pu-Si-Yuan-Xin shanhou shiyi shu" (Deliberation on the proper arrangements for the reconstruction of the Pu-Si-Yuan-Xin region). In Fang Guoyu, ed. *Yunnan shiliao congkan* (Collectanea of Yunnan historical materials). Volume 8. Kunming: Yunnan daxue chubanshe, 1998.

Yongchang fuzhi (Gazetteer of Yongchang prefecture). Liu Yuke et al., comps. 1885. Reprint, Taibei: Chengwen chubanshe, 1967.

Works Cited

Yongzhengchao Hanwen zhupi zouzhe huibian (The collected Chinese-language palace memorials of the Yongzheng reign). Zhongguo diyi lishi dang'anguan, ed. 40 volumes. Nanjing: Nanjing Guji Shudian, 1989–91.

Yongzhengchao Manwen zhupi zouzhe quan yi (Complete translation of the Yongzheng court's Manchu palace memorials). Guan Xiaolian and Qu Liusheng, eds. 2 volumes. Hefei: Huangshan shushe, 1998.

You Zhong. *Zhongguo xinan gudai minzu* (China's southwestern ethnic minorities in antiquity). Kunming: Yunnan renmin chubanshe, 1979.

Yunnan minzu shi (An ethnic history of Yunnan). Kunming: Yunnan daxue chubanshe, 1994.

Young, Robert J. C. *Postcolonialism: An Historical Introduction*. Oxford: Blackwell, 2001.

Yu Fengchun. "Hua-yi yanbian yu da yitong sixiang kuangjia de gouzhu – yi *Shiji* youguan jishu wei zhongxin" (The structure of Han-Barbarian conceptual changes and the conceptual framework of the great unity – with a focus on related narratives in the *Shiji*). *Zhongguo bianjian shidi yanjiu*, 17.2 (2007): 21–34.

Yu Tongyuan and Wang Laigang. "Qingdai zhongyuan renkou bei yi yu nongmu jingji eryuan yitihua fazhan" (The Qing northern migration of the central plains population and the development the integration of the agro-pastoral dual economy). *Ming Qing luncong*, 6 (2005): 327–40.

Yu Xijian and Yu Tong. *Zhongguo gudai fengshui de lilun yu shijian* (Chinese fengshui in theory and practice). 2 volumes. Beijing: Guangming ribao chubanshe, 2005.

Yu Zhiyong. "Qingdai Neimenggu xibu diqu de huangzheng chutan" (Preliminary investigation of famine administration in western Inner Mongolia in the Qing dynasty). *Neimenggu shifan daxue xuebao* (zhexue, shehui kexue ban), 33.1 (Feb. 2004): 32–36.

"Qingdai Neimenggu diqu de ziran zaihai qianxi" (Preliminary analysis of natural disasters in western Inner Mongolia in the Qing dynasty). *Neimenggu shifan daxue xuebao* (zhexue, shehui kexue ban), 33.4 (July 2004): 35–40.

Yuan Lükun. *Qingdai qian shi* (A history of Pre-Qing dynasty [*sic*]). 2 volumes. Shenyang: Shenyang chubanshe, 2004.

Yuan Shouding. *Dili dan zhe lu* (Getting to the essence of terrestrial principles). Taibei: Wu ling chuban gongsi, 1996.

Yule, Henry and A. C. Burnell. *Hobson-Jobson*. 1886. Reprint, Calcutta: Rupa and Co., 1985.

Yun Heyi. "Qingdai yilai Neimenggu daliang kaiken tudi de zhuyao yuanyin" (Primary causes for large-scale land clearance for agriculture in Inner Mongolia since the Qing). *Neimenggu nongye keji*, 6 (Dec. 1999): 8–11.

Zelin, Madeleine. "The Yung-Cheng Reign." In Willard J. Peterson, ed. *The Cambridge History of China, Volume 9, Part 1: The Ch'ing Dynasty to 1800*. Cambridge: Cambridge University Press, 2002.

Zeng, Y. T. and S. Z. Huang. "Disorders of Haemoglobin in China." *Journal of Medical Genetics*, 24 (1987): 578–83.

Zhang, David D., Jane Zhang, Harry F. Lee, and Yuan-qing He. "Climate Change and War Frequency in Eastern China over the Last Millennium." *Human Ecology*, 35.4 (Aug. 2007): 403–14.

Works Cited

315

Zhang Hong. *Diannan xin yu* (New topics about Yunnan). In Fang Guoyu, ed. *Yunnan shiliao congkan* (Collectanea of Yunnan historical materials). Volume 8. Kunming: Yunnan Daxue chubanshe, 1998.

Zhang Jiana, Wei Jie, and Chen Quangong. "Mapping the Farming-pastoral Ecotones in China." *Journal of Mountain Science*, 6.1 (Mar. 2009): 78–87.

Zhang Jie. "Qing chu zhaofu Xin Manzhou shulue" (A brief overview of new Manchu recruitment in the Early Qing). *Qingshi yanjiu*, 1 (1994): 23–30.

Zhang Jie and Zhang Danhui. *Qingdai dongbei bianjiang de Manzu* (The Manchus of the Qing northeastern frontier). Shenyang: Liaoning minzu chubanshe, 2005.

Zhang Jingshu. "*Shangjunshu* nongye jiaoyu ixiang tanxi" (Analysis of agricultural education thought in the *Book of Lord Shang*). *Zhongguo nongshi* 22.1 (2003): 124–27.

Zhang Linxiang. "20 shiji *Shangjunshu* yanjiu shuping" (Critical comment on studies of *Shangjunshu* in the 20th century). *Gansu guangbo dianshi daxue xuebao*, 16.3 (Sept. 2006):10–14.

Zhang Mu. *Menggu youmu ji* (Record of the Mongol herders). Taiyuan: Shanxi renmin chubanshe, 1991.

Zhang Pufan and Guo Chengkang. *Qing ruguan qian guojia falü zhidu shi* (A history of the Qing state legal system prior to the conquest). Shenyang: Liaoning renmin chubanshe, 1988.

Zhang Ruizhi and Xu Lizhi, eds. *Shengjing Manwen dang'an zhong de lüling ji shaoshu minzu falü* (Decrees and laws for ethnic minorities in the Shengjing Manchu archives). In Liu Hainian and Yang Yifan, eds. *Zhongguo zhen xi fa lü dian ji ji cheng, bing bian* (Collection of rare Chinese legal compendiums, third series). Volume 2. Beijing: Kexue chubanshe, 1994.

Zhang Shizun. "Kangxi shiyi nian 'Dongbei hu' zai dongbei nanbu diqu de fenbu" (The distribution of 'northeastern tigers' in the southern Manchurian region in the eleventh year of the reign of the Kangxi emperor). *Manzu yanjiu*, 2 (2005): 99–100, 121.

Zhang Shuangzhi. "Qingchao huangdi de Hua-yi guan" (The Han-barbarian concept of the Qing emperors). *Lishi dang'an* 3 (2008): 32–42.

Zhang Wen. "Diyu pianjian yu zuqun zhishi: Zhongguo gudai zhangqi yu zhangbing wenhua xue jiedu" (Regional preconceptions and ethnic group discrimination: An interpretive reading of cultural studies of *zhangqi* and *zhangbing* in ancient China). *Minzu yanjiu*, 3 (2005): 68–77.

Zhang Yan. *Qingdai jingji jianshi* (A short economic history of the Qing dynasty). Zhengzhou: Zhongzhou guji chubanshe, 1998.

Zhang Yanli. *Jia Dao shiqi de zaihuang yu shehui* (Disaster and society in the Jiaqing and Daoguang periods). Beijing: Renmin chubanshe, 2008.

Zhang Yihe. *Zhongguo huangzai shi* (A history of locust plagues in China). Hefei: Anhui renmin chubanshe, 2008.

Zhang Yingtai. "Tengyue Nandian ying xiujian chengdan bei ji" (Stele record of the repair of the town walls for Tengyue's Nandian garrison). In Li Genyuan, comp. *Yongchang fu wenzheng* (Anthology of writings on Yongchang prefecture). Kunming: Teng chong Li shi, 1941.

316 *Works Cited*

Zhang Yongjiang. "Lun Qingdai monan Menggu diqu de eryuan guanli tizhi" (Discussing the dual administrative system of the Qing dynasty in the Mongol territory south of the Gobi). *Qingshi yanjiu*, 2 (1998): 29–40.

Qindai fanbu yanjiu: yi zhengzhi bianqian wei zhong xin (A study of Qing dependencies from the perspective of political transformation). Harbin, Heilongjiang jiao yu chubanshe, 2001.

"Liangshi xuqiu yu Qingchu Neimenggu nongye de xingqi" (The demand for grain and the rise of agriculture in Inner Mongolia in the early Qing dynasty). 3 (Aug. 2003): 30–42.

"Neidihua yu yitihua: lüelun Qingdai fanbu diqu zhengzhi fazhan de yiban qushi" (Interiorization and homogenization: On the general trends in the regional political development of vassal tribes during the Qing dynasty). *Ming-Qing luncong*, 6, (2005): 298–326.

Zhang Yuan. "Qian lun zhangli dui Qianlong sanci zheng Mian zhanyi de yingxiang" (Overview of the influence of malaria on the Qianlong reign's three attacks on Myanmar). *Zhongguo bianjiang minzu yanjiu*, 1 (2008): 62–70.

Zhang Yunsui. "Zhang Yunsui zougao" (Draft memorials of Zhang Yunsui). In Fang Guoyu, ed. *Yunnan shiliao congkan* (Collectanea of Yunnan historical materials). Volume 8. Kunming: Yunnan Daxue chubanshe, 1998.

Zhang Zhidong. *Zhang Zhidong quanshu* (Complete works of Zhang Zhidong). Zhao Dexin, ed. 12 volumes. Wuhan: Wuhan chubanshe, 2008.

Zhao Jinsheng. "Longling jiangyu xu" (The boundaries of Longling, preface). In Li Genyuan, comp. *Yongchang fu wenzheng* (Anthology of writings on Yongchang prefecture). Kunming: Teng chong li shi, 1941.

Zhao-lian. "Mu-lan xingwei zhidu" (The Mu-lan battue hunting system). *Xiaoting zalu* (Random notes from the whistling pavilion). Beijing: Zhonghua shuju, 1997.

Zhaoqing Han. "Maize Cultivation and its Effect on Rocky Desertification." In Ts'ui-jung Liu, ed. Environmental History in East Asia. New York: Routledge, 2014.

Zhao Shenzhen. *Yuechao zazhi* (A miscellany from the elm nest). Beijing: Zhonghua shuju, 2001.

Zhao Tingdong. *Dili wujue* (The five arcana of terrestrial principles). Taibei: Woolin Publishing Co., 1989.

Zhao Yi. "Chang'an diqi" (The terrestrial qi of Chang'an). In He Changling, ed. *Qing jingshi wenbian* (Collected writings on statecraft from the Qing dynasty). Volume 3. 1826. Reprint, Beijing: Zhonghua shuju, 1992.

"Menggu shi lao" (Mongolian consumption of dairy products). *Yanpu zaji* (A miscellany from sunning under the eaves). Beijing: Zhonghua shuju, 1997.

"Menggu zha ma xi" (The Mongols' cunning horse tricks). *Yanpu zaji* (A miscellany from sunning under the eaves). Beijing: Zhonghua shuju, 1997.

Nianer shi zhaji (Noteworthy notes on the twenty-two histories). Beijing: Zhonghua shuju, 2008.

Zhao Yuntian. *Qingdai zhili bianchui de shuniu: Lifanyuan* (Axis of Qing frontier rule: The Lifan Yuan). Urumqi: Xinjiang renmin chubanshe, 1995.

Works Cited

"Qing zhi Mingguo guanli Menggu shiwu jigou de yanbian" (Evolution of the structure for the management of Mongol affairs, Qing to Republican periods). *Menggu shi yanjiu*, 6 (2000): 208–17.

Zhao Zhen. "Qingdai Shaan Gan diqu de senlin shengtai baohu yishi he cuoshi" (Concepts and measures for environmental protection of forests in the Shaan-Gan region during the Qing). *Ming-Qing luncong*, 4 (2004): 262–72.

Qingdai xibei shengtai bianqian yanjiu (Studies in ecological change in the Qing dynasty's northwest). Beijing: Renmin Daxue chubanshe, 2005.

"Zhongguo huanjing shi yanjiu de xin liang dian" (New highlights in research on Chinese environmental history). *Qingshi yanjiu*, 2.1 (2007): 122–24.

"Qingdai saiwai weichang de ziyuan guanli" (The resource management of the paddock in north great wall in Qing dynasty [sic]). *Zhongguo renmin daxue xuebao*, 5 (2008): 149–54.

Ziyuan, huanjing yu guojia quanli: Qingdai weichang yanjiu (Resources, environment and state power: A study of the Qing hunting preserves). Beijing: Zhonghua shuju, 2012.

Zhao Zhiheng, ed. *Neimenggu tongshi* (A complete history of Inner Mongolia). Volumes 3 and 4. Hohhot: Neimenggu daxue chubanshe, 2007.

Zheng Jiaju, Gong Zhengliang, Xue Liansheng, and Zhi Xiashuang. "Lactose Malabsorption and Its Ethnic Differences in Hans and Uygurs [sic]." *Chinese Medical Journal*, 101.4 (1988): 284–86.

Zheng, Jiaju and Irwin H. Rosenberg. "Lactose Malabsorption in Healthy Chinese Adults." *Ecology of Food and Nutrition*, 15 (1984): 1–6.

Zheng Zuyou, Zhang Zaixing, and Yang Henglin. *Yunnan Nüeji: tezheng yu fangzhi*, (Malaria characteristics and control in Yunnan). Kunming: Yunnan kexue jishu chubanshe, 2003.

Zhong Han. "Beimei 'Xin Qingshi' yanjiu de jishi hezai?" (Where does the cornerstone of the new Qing history lie?) *Zhongguo bianjiang minzu yanjiu*, 7 (2014): 156–213.

Zhou Ailian. *Xizang jiyou* (Travel notes from Tibet). Beijing: Zhongguo Zangxue chubanshe, 2006.

Zhou Huafeng. "Shang zongdu Yongchang shiyi tiaoyi" (Proposal to the governor-general for arrangements in Yongchang). In Li Genyuan, comp. *Yongchang fu wenzheng* (Anthology of writings on Yongchang prefecture). Kunming: Teng chong li shi, 1941.

Zhou Qiong. *Qingdai Yunnan zhangqi yu shengtai bianqian yanjiu* (A study of zhangqi and environmental change in Qing Yunnan). Beijing: Zhongguo shehui kexue chubanshe, 2007.

Zhou Qiong and Li Mei. "Qingdai zhong hou qi Yunnan shanqu nongye shengtai tanxi" (Analysis of the ecology of mountain agriculture in Yunnan during the mid- and late Qing). *Xueshu yanjiu*, 10 (2009): 123–30.

"Qingdai Yunnan neidihua shengtai bianqian houguo chutan." In Yang Weibing, ed. *Ming Qing yilai Yun Gui gaoyuan de huanjing yu shehui* (Environment and society on the Yun-Gui plateau from the Ming-Qing period). Shanghai: Dongfang chuban zhongxin, 2010).

Zhou Rong. "Kang, Qian shengshi de renkou pengzhang yu shengtai huangjing wenti" (Enivironmental problems and the population expansion in the

Works Cited

Kangxi and Qianlong periods of the high Qing). *Shixue yuekan*, 4 (1990): 110–15.

Zhou Shu. "Tengyue bianfang ji" (Notes on border defense in Tengyue). In Li Genyuan, comp. *Yongchang fu wenzheng* (Anthology of writings on Yong-chang prefecture). Kunming: Teng chong li shi, 1941.

Zhou Shunwu. *China Provincial Geography*. Beijing: Foreign Languages Press, 1992.

Zhou Xifeng. *Qingchao qianqi Heilongjiang minzu yanjiu* (A study of ethnic groups in Heilongjiang in the early Qing). Beijing: Zhongguo shehui kexue chubanshe, 2007.

Zhou Yu. "Cong zheng Miandian riji" (Diary of a member of the expedition to Myanmar). In Fang Guoyu, ed. *Yunnan shiliao congkan* (Collection of Yunnan historical materials). Volume 8. Kunming: Yunnan daxue chu-banshe, 2001.

Zhou Yuli. "Tiao chen zheng Mian shi yi shu" (Detailed memorial of the Myan-mar campaigns). In He Changling, ed. *Qing jingshi wenbian* (Collected writings on statecraft from the Qing dynasty). Volume 3. 1826. Reprint, Beijing: Zhonghua shuju, 1992.

Zhou, Zu-jie. "The Malaria Situation in the People's Republic of China." *Bulletin of the World Health Organization*, 59.6 (1981): 931–36.

Zhu Shiguang. "Qingdai shengtai huanjing yanjiu chulun" (Preliminary discus-sion of Qing ecological and environmental studies). *Shaanxi shifan daxue xuebao*, 36.1 (Jan. 2007): 51–54.

Zhuang Jifa. *Qing Gaozong shi quan wu gong yanjiu* (Research on the Qing emperor Qianlong's ten complete military victories). Taipei: National Palace Museum. 1982.

"Qing Gaozong shidai de Zhong Mian guanxi" (Sino-Myanmar relations during the Qing dynasty Qianlong period). *Dalu zazhi* 45.2 (1972): 11–37.

Zhu Hu. "Ershi shiji Qingdai zaihuang shi yanjiu shuping" (Review of twentieth-century research on the history of Qing natural disasters). *Qingshi yanjiu*, 2 (May 2003): 104–19.

Zhu Qiqian. *Dong San Sheng Meng wu gong du huibian* (Compilation of official documents on Mongol affairs in the three Eastern Provinces). In Xu Lihua, ed. *Zhongguo shaoshu minzu guji jicheng*. Chengdu: Sichuan minzu chu-banshe, 2002.

Zhu Yue Baqi zhi (Gazetteer for the eight-banner garrisons in Guangzhou). Chang Shan et al. comps. 1875. Reprint, Shenyang: Liaoning Daxue chubanshe, 1992.

Zhu-sa. 18–20 shiji chu dongbu Neimenggu nonggeng cunluohua yanjiu (A study of the transformation of eastern Inner Mongolia into farming villages 18th to early 20th centuries). Hohhot: Neimenggu renmin chubanshe, 2009.

Zimmerer, Karl S. "The Reworking of Conservation Geographies: Nonequili-brium Landscapes and Nature-Society Hybrids." *Annals of the Association of American Geographers*, 90.2 (June 2000): 356–69.

Žižek, Slavoj. *The Sublime Object of Ideology*. London: Verso Press, 1989.

ed. *Mapping Ideology*. London: Verso Press, 1994.

Works Cited

Znamenski, Andrei. "The Ethic of Empire on the Siberian Borderland." In Nicholas B. Breyfogle, Abby Schrader, and William Sunderland, eds. *Peopling the Russian Periphery: Borderland Colonization in Eurasian History.* New York: Routledge, 2007.

Zou Yilin. "Lun Qing yidai dui jiangtu bantu guannian de shanbian" (On the evolution of the Qing dynasty's concept of territorial incorporation). *Higashi Ajia bunka kōshō kenkyū*, supplementary issue 4, 2009: 183–96.

Index

Actor-Network Theory (ANT, Latour), 5
adame jergilefi, 22
agarts, 164
agriculture/cultivation, 10, 12, 21, 42, 67–68,
    131, 176, 179, 203, 207, 226, 251,
    253, 254, 267
  administration of, 78, 149, 151, 153,
    232, 235
  barley, 44, 181
  beans, 181
  borderland expansion of, 45, 55, 144,
    170, 189, 222, 253–54, 272
  buckwheat, 149, 180, 181, 238
  cotton, 77, 79, 243
  corn, 243
  as environmental relation, 2, 13, 22, 23,
    39–44 passim, 48, 137, 158, 164,
    170, 221, 224, 227, 235–38, 257, 273
  foraging and, 22, 48, 60, 69–70, 73,
    76–77, 80, 89–95 passim, 101,
    213, 230–31
  as habitat, 35, 196
  maize, 9, 44, 242, 244–45
  Manchurian ecology for, 77, 79, 260
  millet, 22, 44, 47, 146, 149, 182, 238, 243
  Mongol versus Han, 45–48, 147, 150
  mushrooms, 185, 272
  New World crops, 8, 59, 227, 242, 262
  oats, 181
  opium poppy, 246
  pastoralism and, 116, 125, 133, 139, 147,
    150–52, 154–55, 238–41 passim
  peanuts, 44, 182

  potatoes, 44, 182 (sweet), 183, 184, 242,
    245
  rollback of, 253, 273
  rotation, 182, 243
  sedentary, 47, 151, 176, 182
  shifting/swidden, 8, 14, 15, 170, 180–86
    passim, 188, 190, 207, 242–46,
    249, 257 passim, 272–73
  statistics, 105, 149, 153, 158, 159, 221,
    238, 255, 257
  taro, 184
  tubers, 183, 245
  wheat, 22, 42, 44, 47, 181
aimag (aimaγ), xv, 118, 122, 164
aiman, xv, 69, 75, 76, 78, 81, 85–87 passim,
    90, 93, 95, 97, 113
Ainu, 106, 137, 176
alban, 78, 81, 98
Altan Khan (r. 1521–82), 145
amanat, 85, 111
angga sulfame banjire Monggoso, 136
Anhui, 42, 48, 244
anthropocentricity, 2–7 passim, 28, 55, 103,
    135, 156, 170, 176, 209, 222
  Qing expressions of, 2, 4, 5, 103, 135,
    156, 170, 209
anthrozoology (defined), 16
Arablism, 14, 15, 23, 49, 224, 252, 268
  in China proper, 22, 39–42, 44, 227, 234,
    243
    defined 13, 226–27
    identity formation and, 23, 43, 47, 48,
     54, 101, 185–90, passim, 245

322 *Index*

Arablism (cont.)
    in Manchuria, 49, 77, 81, 89–92,
      passim, 230, 231, 233, 253, 264, 271
    in Mongolia, 45–47, passim, 117, 137,
      234–41 passim, 272
    radiation of, 55, 145, 150, 220–21,
      225–26, 231, 234, 239, 240, 257, 268
    in Yunnan, 170, 178, 180–84, 192–94
      passim, 206, 208, 246, 249–50, 272
aragoul, 164
Aru Khorchin, 120
Atwood, Christopher P., *xv*
Awei 阿魏 (*Ferula assa foetida L.*), 216

ba guan 八關, 201
ba na i muke boihon ehe, 204
Bagou 八溝, 146, 158, 168
Bahai 巴海 (d. 1696), 82, 87
banners (qi, 旗)
    Alashan Ööled, 121
    Baarin, 153
    bondservant, 71, 112
    Bordered
      Yellow, 71
    Dörbed, 131–33 passim
    Ejene Gool Torghut, 121
    five inferior, 71, 73
    Forty-nine, 50, 117, 120
    Gorlos, 238
    gūsa, 50, 64, 65, 78, 97, 118, 120, 121,
      123, 143
    hoshuu (*qošiyu*), 50, 52, 118, 121, 123,
      132, 137, 143
    Hunting Eight (*bu-te-ha baqi* 布特哈八
      旗), 64, 88
    Khalkha, 117, 118, 121, 136–39 passim
    Kheshigten, 152–56 passim
    Khorchin, 118, 131, 239
    Ongni'ud, 153
    Pastoral Chakhar, 21, 50–52, 117,
      122, 135–36, 149–50, 151, 153,
      238
    (*Neiwufu*) Plain
      White, 71, 104
      Yellow, 71, 135
    Right Ujumchin, 266
    Taipusi, 116, 270
    three superior (Plain Yellow, Bordered
      Yellow, Plain White), 71, 73
    Tümed, 59, 101, 117, 118, 147, 151, 158,
      212, 224
    Urad, 121, 133, 139, 152

Bao Shichen 包世臣 (1775–1855), 243–44,
    245, 272
baogu zhi lei 包穀之類, 245
baojia 保甲, 158, 188, 245, 249
Bargut (巴爾虎; Ma: Barhū:), 60, 64, 96,
    113, 142, 232, 233, 272
Bayaguut, 266
beans, 181
bears Manchurian, brown (*Ursus arctos
    manchuricus; xiong* 熊), 70
Bedune, 230–31
beijie 北戒, 28
Beijing, 21, 35, 54, 70–71 passim, 83, 88,
    97, 105, 112, 124, 141, 151, 153,
    156, 202, 222, 230, 269
Belin (1747–1824), 173, 213, 223, 247
*Beyond the Passes Outposts of Civilization
    Steadily Become Settlements*
    (*Kouwai she tun gengzhi juluo jian
    cheng, Kangxi emperor*), 47
bianmin 邊民 (defined), 106
bianwai 邊外, 202, 216, 247
bianzhong 遍種, 188
Bičan River (Bizhan he 毕瞻河), 88, 90
Binlang River 檳榔江, 201, 207, 251
biopower/biosociality, 174
biota, portmanteau, 6, 17
Birar, 229
Board of Rites, 71
borderlands, 4, 12, 19, 53, 55, 153, 170,
    171, 227, 237–38, 241, 262, 265,
    268, 270, 273, 274
    animal-human interdependencies in, 2–3, 54
    and agriculture, 39, 45, 47, 55, 178–90,
      210, 220, 221, 227, 253, 254, 257
    defined, 12
    disease and, 176, 178, 190–206,
      208–09, 250
    environmental relations, 10–16, 157,
      266, 267, 271
    identity and, 5, 7, 13–15, 48, 49, 170,
      233, 249, 270
    Inner Asian consolidation of, 50
    Manchurian consolidation of, 64–65, 69,
      74, 78, 79, 82, 93, 96–100, 105,
      106, 229, 231, 233
    Mongolian consolidation of, 116, 118,
      121, 125, 135–39, 143, 146, 234,
      237, 238, 240
    southwestern consolidation of, 5, 159,
      169, 170, 172, 174, 180, 187, 190,
      225, 247, 249, 250

Index

Buddhism, 51
Buhi (fl. 1749), 52, 269
buluo 部落, xv
Burni, 118
Butha Ula (Da-sheng wu-la 打生烏拉), 46, 64, 67, 71, 73, 97, passim, 229–31, 271
butter, 165

Cai Yurong 蔡毓榮 (1633–1699), 178–81, 208, 250, 272
caibu shan 採捕山, 72
Campbell, Cameron, 220
Cangde (fl. 1727), 274
Cao Yishi 曹一士 (1678–1736), 256
cereal
   cultivation, 47, 77, 227
   Japanese cultivated, 137
   plants, 2, 22, 35
Chang Deshou 常德壽 (fl. 1725), 188, 268
Chang, Chia-feng, 177
Chang'an, 29, 32
Changbai(shan) 長白山 (Ma: Golmin Šanggiyan Alin), 37–38, 63, 80, 101, 115
Changchun, 239
chaogong 朝貢, 57
Chen Hongmou 陈宏谋 (1696–1771), 208
Chen Jian, 41
Chen Shen 陳詵 (1644–1722), 4
Chengde 承德, 50, 61, 146, 153
Chengde-Muran (Mountain Retreat, Shanzhuang), 50, 146
chifa yeren 赤髮野人, 213
China proper, 1, 14, 21, 39, 45, 59, 66, 69, 75, 87, 106, 129, 162, 167, 176, 177, 216, 254, 256, 274
   and Imperial Arablism, 13, 22, 40–44, passim, 54–55, 221, 227, 233, 237, 239, 257, 264
   and Imperial Foraging, 70, 78, 81–82, 95, 101, 271
   In Hanspace thought, 23–36, passim, 39
   and Imperial Indiginism, 184, 197
   and Imperial Pastoralism, 129, 131, 132, 145–53, passim
   inter-regional comparisons, 2–13, passim, 22, 48, 63, 78, 95, 131, 132, 146, 159, 186, 226–27, 239, 254, 261, 266, 273
   swidden agriculture in, 182, 184, 186
   and venery, 48, 51, 55, 176
   As Zhongxia (中夏), 38
Chu, 39

chun 純, 35
climate, 3, 10, 22, 42, 222
   change, 43, 130, 161, 220, 254
   effects on horses, 148
   Manchurian, 60, 77, 79, 105, 108
   microclimates, 50, 72, 147, 233
   Inner Mongolian, 14, 48, 128–31, passim, 147, 162, 241
   Yunnan, 189–93, passim, 198, 203
colonialism and imperialism, 7, 147, 176, 229, 248
   ecological (Crosby), 6
Confucianism, 38
copper, 42, 179–80, 216
Cossacks, 73–74, 79, 83, 85–88, 90
cotton, 243
Country Inns (Ye Dian 野店, Qianlong emperor), 146
Cronon, William, 6
Crosby, Alfred W., 6
Crumley, Carol L., 13
culture-nature, 4, 169
cultured nature, 14, 65, 100, 105
cun 寸, 162

da yitong 大一統, 30
Dagur (達幹爾; Ma: Dagūr), 47, 53, 54, 60, 110, 272, 273
   as Cossack captives and servitors, 78, 85–86, 111
   as Qing subjects, 64, 79, 81, 95, 96, 101, 112, 142, 232
   as Qing deserters and poachers, 92, 268

Dai (Tai) 傣, 207
Daniels, Christian, 186
Daoguang period (1821–50), 200, 220, 260, 264
   depression (*Daoguang xiaotiao* 道光蕭條), 220
Daoyi tun 道 屯, 220
Daqing(shan) 大青山, 153, 260, 273
Daši (fl. 1749), 142
Dasungga (fl. 1748), 130, 131
Datong 大同, 123, 146
Dayao 大姚, 185, 272
Dayi juemi lu (*Record of the great counsel to enlighten the deluded*, Yongzheng emperor), 36, 37, 219, 228
deforestation 8, 9, 252, 257, 263, 268–69, 271

Index

deforestation (cont.)
  in Manchuria 92, 93, 102–05 passim, 230–32, 260
  in Inner Mongolia, 153, 156, 157, 222–23, 230
  in Yunnan 183–85 passim, 193, 196, 242, 272
Denggeng 登埂, 198
desertification, 10, 144, 147, 240, 262
destruction, creative, 8
Di 狄, 28, 30, 34, 38, 39
diaobao 碉堡, 251
diji 地紀, 33
dili 地理, 25
diluo 地絡, 28
dingjie 定界, 247
diqi 地氣, 31
disasters, 36, 145, 162, 163, 165, 178, 179, 220, 234, 254–55
  drought, 5, 8, 44, 124, 128–32, 145, 152, 158, 220, 229, 230, 234
  dust storms, 264
  dzud and snowstorms, 5, 128–35 passim, 138, 142, 152, 269–70
  flood, 8, 26, 128, 145, 182, 220, 225, 244
  plague, 176, 193, 214, 271
  (non-pastoral) relief of, 9, 44, 234, 254–55, 262, 264
  sandstorms, 131, 142
disease
  blackwater fever, 190
  chill and fever (Ma: *shahūrun halhūn*), 192
  dysentery (Ma: *hefeliyenere*), 192
  marmots (*Marmota sibirica*) as vector for, 271
  plague, 176, 193, 271
  smallpox, 17, 172, 176–78 (*variola major*), 273
  transhumance and, 176
  yellow fever, 175–76
Dolon Nuur, 118, 146, 153
Domain of
  Pacification (*Suifu* 綏服), 26, 27, 30
  Restraint (*Yao fu* 要服), 26, 30
  the Nobles (*Hou fu* 候服), 26, 30
  the Sovereign (*Dian Fu* 甸服), 26
  the Wild (*Huang fu* 荒服), 26, 30
Dongbei sanbao 東北三寶, 67
Dongchuan 東川, 179
Dongting Lake 洞庭湖, 226
dorgi ba, 21

Draft History of the Qing (*Qingshigao*), 1
dragon's true lair (*long zhen xue*, 龍真穴), 15, 24, 257, 270
du 度, 128
Du tongjian lun (Wang Fuzhi), 33
Dushikou 獨石口, 146, 156
Duyusi 都虞司 (Office of the Imperial Hunt (Caibuyamen 採捕衙門, Ma, Buthai Jurgan), 71, 102

e-bo 鄂博 (Mo: *obō*), 120
Ecological Imperialism. The Biological Expansion of Europe, 900–1900 (Crosby), 6
ecology/ecological concepts, 258
  dichotomies with culture, 2, 3, 12, 13, 15, 35, 40, 55, 100, 104–05, 169, 228, 270
  disease and, 170, 174–75
  disharmony dynamics, 9, 14, 225, 226, 240
  diversity, 5, 6, 73, 128, 147, 149, 163, 181, 193, 252
  ecotone, 10–12, 18, 144, 147, 157, 159, 231, 234, 236, 270, 272
  environmental determinism, 4, 17, 24
  environmental determinism subheadings:
    Hanspace and, 24
    versus cultural, 4
  Malthusian perspectives and, 220, 226, 257
  new, 9
  nonequilibrium, 9, 129, 226, 244
  patchiness, 7, 8, 12, 19, 147, 191, 202–204, 229, 231, 245, 260, 267
  qi and, 35
  recursive, 12, 14, 19, 269
  SAH biodiversity, 63, 79–80, 84, 93, 96
  steady state, 9, 12, 18, 19, 31, 130, 137, 161, 219, 228, 269
  steppe, 124
ehe sukdun, 192, 202, 270
Elvin, Mark, *xiii*, 8, 224, 227
environmental history, 3–7, 220, 222
  China proper of, 9–10, 40
  Malthusian perspectives and, 220
  Qing empire and, 7–10, 15, 23
environmental relations, 2, 3, 9, 22, 176, 235, 249, 266, 271, 273
  empire and, 4–7, 41, 54–55, 154, 227, 239, 268, 269
  Han, 8, 10, 22, 33, 34, 36, 44, 239
  Inner Asian, 51, 142, 229
  Manchu, 65, 78–81, 228, 232

Index

Mongol, 46–47, 121, 123, 135, 139, 140, 146, 151, 153, 157, 158, 164, 235, 236
Qing borderlands and, 10–16, 267, 273
southwestern indigenous, 159, 175, 178, 185, 189, 207, 225
environmentality, Qing, 15, 266–74 passim
Erdene Juu, 137
ethnic diversity, 10, 22–23, 27, 30, 35, 39, 205, 257
erosion, 8, 128, 147, 182–85 passim, 206, 242, 243, 252, 253, 262

falconry, 53, 97
fanbu 藩部, 146
fen 分, 124
fengjian 封建, 187
fengjin zhengce 封禁政策, 68
fengshui 風水, 24–25, 58, 101
Fengtian (Liaoning) 奉天, 66, 70, 72, 97, 98, 102, 105, 122, 134, 221, 228, 239
field allocation system (*fenye* 分野), 27, 28, 57
fire, 9, 149, 231–32, 245
fish and fishing, 7–8, 68–74 passim, 81, 90, 94–104 passim, 152, 155, 229–30, 236, 256
carp, 152
catfish, 152
perch, sea, 71
salmon, 98
chum (*Oncorhynchus keta*; Ma: *dafaha*), 108
Siberian (*Brachymystax lenok*; Ma: *niomošon*), 97, 108
Five Domains (Wufu 五服), 31
Five Sacred Peaks (Marchmounts, *Wuyue* 五岳), 28, 37–38
Fiyaka (Ma, *Fiyaka*) 費雅喀, xv, 72, 81–83, 86, 93, 106, 268
forage and foraging, 12, 47, 48, 64, 79, 80, 84, 176, 185–86, 196, 209, 227, 229, 256–57
Ainu, 137
bears, 52, 70 (Manchurian brown; *Ursus arctos manchuricus; xiong* 熊)
bureaucratized/quotas and equivalents, 96–106
deer antlers, 223
of human resources, 75–78, 95
imperial, 3, 13, 14, 65, 69–74, 79, 96, 101, 103, 104, 106, 114, 135, 170, 209,

221, 229, 233, 234, 241, 252, 268, 271, 272
leopards, Amur (*Panthera pardus orientalis*), 70
Manchu identity and, 15, 48, 60, 66–74, 80, 89, 95, 100, 229, 230
Manchurian moose, 70–71
sustainability, 101–06, 223, 268, 271–72
red pine and, 231
sedentary conditions and, 95, 96
spatial and administrative issues, 69–74, 228–34, 235, 269, 270
tigers, 70
forest, 3, 34, 39, 79, 90, 94, 95, 143, 170, 206, 209, 266–74, passim
conservation policies, 9, 234
disease and, 194
as habitat, 47–55, passim, 74, 80, 264
(indigenous) swidden agriculture and, 182–84, 224, 242, 249
resources, 67, 93, 115
four seas, 30
frontier(s), 1, 15, 97, 120, 154, 171–72, 188, 191, 202–206 passim, 219, 220, 230, 236, 247, 250, 270
defined, 12, 58
ecological, 8, 172, 190, 206
ethnic, 39
inner and outer, 27, 173, 186, 198, 201, 204–10 passim, 211, 215, passim, 248–51 passim
Miao, 188
Sino-Russian, 229, 236
transfrontier conditions, 155, 201, 207
Fujian, 29, 77, 195
furdan i dolo, 215
furdan i tule, 215
Fusengga (d. 1775), 53
Fushun 撫順, 70
Fuzhou 福州 148

Galdan (r. 1671–1697), 87, 118, 121
Galdan Tseren (r. 1727–1745), 121
gan 幹, 29
Gansu, 10, 29, 43, 164, 179
Ganya 干崖, 248
Gao Qizhuo 高其倬 (1676–1738), 188, 189, 204, 225, 250, 268, 272
Gao Shiqi 高士奇 (1645–1704), 46, 52, 77
gen 艮, 29
Gengma 耿馬, 172, 198, 201, 246–47 passim
Ghilyak, xv

326 *Index*

Giddens, Anthony, 19
Gimi peoples (Papua New Guinea), 3
ginseng, Korean (Panax ginseng C.A.
    Meyer; *renshen* 參; Ma: *orhoda*), xvi,
    67–68, 74, 76, 80, 97–105, passim,
    112, 114, 233, 260
  as currency, 223
  exhaustion/depletion of, 99, 101–02, 105,
    112, 260
  mountains (*renshenshan shenshan*), 63,
    68, 72, 102
  poaching of, 67, 101–02, 104, 107, 260
  Siberian (*Eleutherococcus senticosus*), 114
Giohoto (d. 1752), 155, 236, 268
gong 公 (duke), 78, 81
Gongbu (工部 Board of Works), 71
grain, 10, 21, 43, 55, 71, 101, 113, 121,
    185, 189, 207, 222, 235, 236, 244,
    245, 253, 256
  defined, 44
  as disaster relief, 14, 129–39 passim, 162,
    163, 165, 237–45 passim, 253, 260,
    269, 272
  as Hanspace crop (five grains), 23, 40, 42,
    221, 273
  identity and, 40, 45–49 passim, 64, 95,
    142, 148, 158
  as revenue, 40, 78, 151, 255
  as tribute, 101
grasshoppers (*Chorthippus*), 6
grassland, 44, 52, 131, 134, 138, 144,
    146–47, 149, 151, 166, 238, 273
  ecology, 77, 124, 128–30, 147, 241, 261
  identity and, 116, 123, 239, 267
Great Wall, 1, 22, 28, 31, 45, 48, 50, 52, 54,
    63, 66, 70, 116–17, 138, 143–57
    passim, 157, 177, 209, 238
Greater Hinggan Mountains, 2
Guangdong, 29, 77, 191, 216, 249
Guangnan 廣南, 245
Guangren 廣人, 249
Guangxi, 29, 191, 249
Guangzhou, 148
Gui(hua)-Sui(yuan) Liu Ting 歸綏六廳, 146
Guihua 歸化 (Hohhot), 118, 121, 146, 152,
    157–59, 166, 224, 239
Guizhou, 4, 29, 35, 182, 187, 188, 191,
    195, 205, 244, 245, 250, 257–58
Gulf of Bohai, 37
gumlao, 186, 207, 211, 248, 250, 271
Gungsangnorbu (1871–1930), 240, 268

Hainan Island, 2, 215
Hakka, 182
Hale, Henry E., 16, 55, 174
Han dynasty (206 BCE-220 CE), 38–39
Han-barbarian discourse (*Xia-yi lun*夏夷
    論), 25–26, 30, 31, 38, 39, 57
Han migration, 10, 34, 43–45 passim, 131,
    159, 246, 249, 272
  borderland, 220, 227, 238
  Inner Mongolia, 14, 117, 144–47 passim,
    151, 156, 158, 166, 224, 236
  Manchuria, 39, 65–66, 74, 102, 105, 106,
    228, 230
  Yunnan, 170, 180, 182–84 passim, 196,
    242, 245, 249
Hangzhou 杭州, 148–149
Hangzhou Bay, 226
hanhai 瀚海, 258
hanhua 漢化, 191
Hanjun 漢軍, 113, 117, 149
Hanspace, 54, 55, 81, 219, 225, 258, 265,
    273
  accommodationist, 26–31, 219
  arablism and, 40, 225, 231, 239, 257, 268
  borderlands and, 50, 150, 157–59, 179,
    189, 204, 231, 232, 239, 267
  defined, 23–26, 40, 55
  dissident, 31–36, 219, 252
  Qing state revisions of, 36–40
hawking and hawks, 70, 73
He Zikai 何自岂 (fl. 1817), 251
Heihe 黑河, 10
Heilongjiang, 10, 47–48, 53–61 passim, 69,
    73, 77–88 passim, 95–05 passim,
    132, 229–30, 233, 234, 268–69
Hejen (赫哲 Ma: Heje), xv, 72, 81–86
    passim, 90–93, 106, 268
Henan, 29, 33, 37, 41, 259, 263
Hexi Corridor, 253
Hong Taiji, 60, 67, 70, 75, 81, 177, 233
hongshan 紅山, 185
horses, 22, 49, 53, 70, 73, 83, 120, 205,
    206, 228
  disaster relief and, 131, 135–36, 142
  erma 兒馬(Ma: *ajirgan*), 123
  herds and pastures, 123–24, 131, 136, 150
  habitat limitations of, 148–49
  kema 騍馬(Ma: *geo*), 123
  milk and, 140–44
  qun 群(Ma: *adun*), 123
  shanma 騸馬(Ma: *akta*), 123

Index

sun sara geo, 141
tribute relations and, 83, 117
Hoton Nuur, 138
Hu Han 胡翰 (1307–81), 33
Hu Huanyong, 10
Hu Line (Hu *Huanyong xian* 胡煥庸線), 10–12, 147
Hu Qirong 胡啟榮 (fl.1820), 250–51
Hu Wei 胡渭 (1633–1714), 25, 29–34 passim, 258
Hua y 華夷, 37
Huangchao jinshi wenbian, 25
Huangshu (Wang Fuzhi), 23, 33
Huaxia 華夏, 24
Hubei, 7, 39, 245, 258
Hubu (戶部 Board of Review), 79, 231
Huguang, 29, 188
Huise (fl. 1749), 188
hule (*shi* 石), 131, 133
hūlhame sun be jetere, 140
Hulun Buir, 47, 64, 96, 142, 230, 112, 271
Hunan, 36, 39, 182, 226, 244, 251, 258
hunting (Ma: *buthai*), 46, 48, 95
battue, 51, 61, 72
Huolun River 霍伦河, 231
Hūrha (Hu-er-ha 呼爾哈), 75–76, 82, 83, 108
Huzhou 湖州, 182
identity
animal, 53
borderland, 2, 63–65, 237
contradictions, 23, 36, 151, 159, 170, 188, 190, 229, 249, 257, 267
Cossack and variants, 86–87
cultural and ecological, 3
disease and, 172–76, 178, 206–09 passim
formation of, 2–3, 7–8, 13, 55
Han 漢, 8, 10, 22–26 passim, 31–40 passim, 44, 170, 176
(Han) contamination (Ma: *icembi*) and, 106, 158, 159, 177–78, 228, 232
hybridization, 66
Inner Asian, 13, 22, 50–54, 228–29, 268–69
liangmin 良民, 22, 40, 42
Manchu (Ma: *Manju*), 3, 15, 49, 62, 63–78 passim, 83, 95, 159, 228
Manchu, borderland, 3, 5, 7, 13–14, 48, 54, 63–66 passim, 57, 100, 105, 110, 178, 232, 233, 260, 270, 274

Manchu, New (Xin Manzhou 新滿洲; Ma: *Ice Manju*), 53, 64, 65, 75, 82, 87–95, 106, 109 passim, 215, 232, 233
Manchu, Old, (Jiu Manzhou 舊滿洲; Ma: Fe Manju), 109
Mongol, 46, 116, 123, 134, 135, 144, 150–51, 236
Mongol, banner, 3, 5, 14, 48, 113, 123, 136–39 passim, 159, 237, 270, 274
Pan-Qing, 22–23, 51
Qing environmentality, 270
Shack people (*pengmin* 棚氏), 10–11, 181–86 passim, 237, 242–49 passim, 257, 262
southwestern indigenous, 170, 174, 178, 183, 187, 206–208, 247–48
civilized tribal, 3, 5, 14, 171, 207
space and, 33–35, 208, 252–53

Ilan Hala (San-xing 三姓), 64, 81, 88, 177
Ilibu (1775–1843), 244, 246, 249
indigenism, imperial, 3, 14, 170–172, 175, 178, 179, 183, 187, 190, 191, 204, 206–08, 251, 252
Inner Asia 1, 2, 21–24 passim, 38, 54, 261, 274
conquest dynasties, 23, 25, 27, 31–32, 36
and disease, 58, 177–79, 197
environmental relations issues, 16, 17, 18–19, 40, 45, 51–55 passim, 77, 120, 222–24, 233, 239
interiorization (neidihua 內地化), 146, 225, 239
irgen, 114

Janhunen, Juha, xv
Januka (fl. 1676), 88
Jaocang (fl.1755), 157
jasag (jasay) 扎薩克, 3, 39, 50, 118, 120–21, 131, 139
leagues (meng 盟), 116–118, 120–21 passim, 125, 132, 157, 253
nei zha-sa-ke 內扎薩克 (inner), 117, 134, 136–37 passim, 155
wai zha-sa-ke 外扎薩克 (outer), 136, 137, 159
ji 紀, 28–29
jian kan tongli 建堪同例, 53
jiangli 疆理, 30
Jiangnan 江南, 38, 220, 239, 253, 254, 256
Jiangsu, 255

328 Index

Jiangxi, 29, 56, 182
jiao 傲, 247
Jiaodong 角董, 216
jiaohua 教化, 208
Jiaqing emperor, 103–04, 223, 271, 272
   regnal events of, 186–87, 200, 207, 244,
      257, 260, 264
jibca, 79
Jilin, 46, 63–69 passim, 72, 73, 81, 82, 86,
      94–105 passim, 122, 177, 228–31
      passim, 268
jin 斤, 99
Jin dynasty (1115–1234), 32, 35, 38
jing 境, 247
Jingdong, 272
Jingqili River 精奇哩江 (Ru: Zeia River), 85
jingshen zhongnongzhuyi 精神重農主義, 41
Jingzhou, 148
jinqing 近情, 53
Jinsha River, 179
juhiyan (*zhu-xuan* 珠軒), 71, 73, 97
jun 郡, 146
Jungfoboo (fl. 1750), 158–59, 224, 268
junqi 均齊, 123
junxian 郡縣 system, 3, 35, 39, 249
   in Manchuria, 231
   in Inner Mongolia, 144, 147, 238
   in Yunnan, 174, 178, 186, 188, 191,
      196–205 passim, 208, 247, 249, 270
Jurchen 女真, 32, 35, 37, 49, 63, 66–69, 76,
      88, 120
   Donghai Jurchen 東海女真, 75, 76
Juu Uda, 152, 155, 224
juwen, 135

Kachin (Ch, Jingpo 景頗族), 173, 186, 187,
      270
Ka-er-ji-shan (d.1757), 166
Kaifeng, 29
Kaihua 開化, 183, 201, 245
Kaiping 開平, 154, 156
Kaiyuan 開元, 67
Kangxi emperor (r. 1662–1722), 4–5, 82, 233
   on agricultural issues, 42–47
   on disaster relief, 132
   on foraging issues, 73, 95, 100–01, 103
   on Hanspace issues, 37, 56
   on malaria, 204
   reign events of, 71, 76, 81, 99, 105, 108,
      144, 145, 154, 156, 166
   on venery issues, 50–53 passim, 61

kanyu 堪輿, 25
kao tian tian 靠天田, 45, 243
Kawa (Wa 佤族), 173, 187, 250
Khabarov, Erofei (ca. 1610–67), 84–86
Khalkha otog, 49, 118
Khordarkovsky, Michael, 111
Kiler-Ewenki, xv, 81, 93–94
   women and children, 95
King Injo (Renzu 仁祖, r. 1623–49), 68
King Wen, 33
Kododo, 154–55, 266
Konbaung Dynasty (1752–1885), 19, 169,
      207, 246–47
Korea, 28, 66–9, 100, 111
   Chosŏn dynasty, 68
   flora, 72, 80
   as source of human resources, 76, 77
Koubei San Ting 口北三廳, 122, 146, 154
koumiss, 165
Kunming Massacre, 242
kūru (*rubing* 乳餅), 140, 143, 165

lactose intolerance (Han), 44
Lahu, 186
Lanna (Chiangmai), 247
laobaixing 老百姓, 44
Latour, Bruno, 5
Lattimore, Owen, 18
Leach, E. R., 173
lead, 179–80
Lee, James Z., 220
lei 類, 34
Letting Deer Go (Qianlong emperor), 53
letu 樂土, 155, 189, 267
li 里, 26, 52, 224, 230
Li Bozhong, 220, 254, 258
Li Chunfeng 李淳風 (602–670), 27
Li Guangdi 李光地 (1642–1718), 37
lianbing 練兵, 236
liang 糧, 165
Liangguang, 182, 245, 246
Liangjiang, 245–46
Lifanyuan (Court of Territorial Affairs),
      118–23, 132, 136, 156, 258
Lin Zexu 林則徐 (1785–1850), 251
Lingdan Khan (1604–34), 118
Lingnan, 28, 178, 253, 254
Little Ice Age, 130, 254
Liu Bin 劉彬 (fl. 1692), 172, 208
Liu Kun 劉崑 (fl. 1680), 181, 197
Liu Min, 185

Index

Liu Shiyong, 10
Liu Xiaomeng, 67
Liu Zao 劉藻 (1701–1766), 179
liubi 流弊, 237
liumin 流民, 245
liuyu 流寓, 196
livestock, 2, 12, 14, 70, 76, 79, 108, 117,
    121, 130, 151, 152, 170, 209, 239,
    240, 256, 266, 272
  camels, 123, 124, 156
  cattle, 89, 122, 123, 132–35 passim, 137,
    138, 142, 153, 155
  chickens, 243
  cows (Ma: *uniyen*), 123, 142
  as disaster relief, 5, 129–39 passim
  herds, 5, 14, 120–27, 131, 134, 138, 163
  management, 121–27, 222, 236
  milk and, 140–44
  mortality, 123–27 passim, 134, 136,
    148–49, 163, 269
  personal property (Ma: *hethe ulha*), 135,
    156
  pigs, 243
  in poetry, 46, 47
  penalty, 120, 131, 132
  salt and, 154–57
  sheep, 10, 122–26, 131–38 passim, 142,
    153, 155
  six domesticates, the (*liu chu* 六畜), 273
Livingstone, Frank B., 196–97
locusts, 21–22, 42
  control by ducks, chickens, frog or
    swallows, 42, 54
  cult, 42
Longchuan 龍川, 198, 248
Longling 龍陵, 203–05, 225
Lubsang Darja (fl. 1732), 139, 238
Lü Liuliang 呂留良 (1629–83), 25, 32, 36
Lujiang 潞江, 198, 263
Lujiang River 潞江, 205
Lukuishan 魯魁山, 204
Luo Kanglong, 10
Luohei 倮黑 (Wa 佤族), 173, 187, 250
Luoyang, 29

macroregions, 19, 220, 244–246, 254
Malaria (*zhangqi* 瘴氣; Ma: *indehen*), 2, 171,
    175–76, 189, 201, 205, 249, 273
  differential resistance to, 14, 170–78
    passim, 183, 195, 197, 208, 215,
    272–73

  as *ehe sukdun*, 192, 194, 202, 270
  falciparum, 190, 192, 194
  imperial indigenism and, 169–71, 178–81
    passim, 186, 190, 200–1, 206, 209,
    251
  mortality rates, 197
  opium smoking and, 195
  spatial distribution of, 183, 196,
    198–204, 245
  vectors (mosquitos, *plasmodium* blood
    parasites), 2, 5, 14, 16, 17, 169–76
    passim, 190–96 passim, 201, 204,
    205, 210, 214, 216, 221, 248, 272
  yanzhang 煙瘴and, 189, 191, 192, 198
  zhangqi and, 169, 190–4, 210
Man 蠻, 28, 30, 38, 195
Manchu
  agriculture, 46–9 passim, 229–31
  cavalry, 148, 206
  cultural significance, 7
  cultured nature, 100–6
  diaspora, 7, 66, 74, 159, 177–78
  sources, 15, 159, 163, 167, 192
Manchuria, 13, 68, 70, 74, 75, 77, 78, 83,
    96, 105, 113, 128, 197, 209, 253,
    271–273
  ecology of, 72, 77, 84, 114, 229–30
  demographic issues, 12, 39, 105
  Hanspace and, 37–8
  identity formation in, 63–4, 66, 68,
    88–89, 105–106, 135, 228–9, 233
  inter-regional comparisons, 2, 12, 45,
    142, 159, 170, 197–98, 208, 232,
    269
Mang 莽, 213
Mangshi 芒市, 196, 198, 203, 224
manyan 蠻煙, 195
Marks, Robert B., 9, 43, 254, 258
marmots (Marmota sibirica), 271
marten (*mishu* 蜜鼠; Ma: *harsa*), 67, 105,
    106, 112
McNeill, John Robert, 175–76
Mekong River (Lancang 瀾滄河, Jiulong 九
    龍河), 172, 187–189, 200–202, 207,
    251
Mengding 孟定, 198, 248
Menggu yishi 蒙古醫士, 123
Menglian (Muong Laem) 孟連, 204, 216,
    247, 250
Mengmao (Muong Mao) 孟卯, 198, 248
Mengmeng 孟孟, 198, 201, 250

Index

Mengmian 孟緬, 248
mentuhun urse, 83
Mergen, 230, 266
Mianning 緬寧, 201, 202, 205, 263
Miao 苗, 39, 182–3, 188, 205, 210, 225, 251
  defined, 17
middle ground, 12, 171, 173
Migration, 194, 226
  Manchu, 159
  wild tribal, 206–7
Min (Zhejiang), 31
Ming Chenghua emperor (1464–87), 76
Ming dynasty (1368–1644), 1, 13, 52, 129, 185
  arablist concepts, 41
  borderland relations, 23, 46, 48–9, 120, 145, 146, 184–5, 201
  disease and, 177–8 passim, 195
  Hanspace concepts and, 27–39 passim, 219
  Jurchen relations, 67–8, 69, 76, 82, 109
Ming Jiajing reign (1522–1566), 219
Ming Taizu, 32–33, 219
Ming Wanli period (1573–1620), 186
Ming-de (d. 1788), 216
Min-Zhe, 58
Mitchell, Timothy, 6
Mo-luo-hong (fl. 1669), 87
monan 漠南, 117
Mongolia, 133, 135, 136, 142, 158, 160, 162, 170, 209, 239–41
Mongolian Fields (Menggu tian, Qianlong emperor), 45
mu 畝, 148, 149, 238, 256, 264
Mukden, 100
muke boihon de acharakū, 197
Muna 木納, 152–3, 273
muong (*meng* 孟), 173, 198
Muran (Mu-lan 木蘭), xv, 45, 50–51, 52, 53, 142, 176, 222–3, 224
Muran i ejebun (Record of Muran, Mu-lan ji, Jiaqing emperor), 223
mussels (*Unio or Margaritifera dahuricus*), 113
mutton, 142
Myanmar (Miandian 緬甸), 14, 171, 186, 194, 207, 230, 247–8
  campaigns, 169, 198, 202–5 passim
  defined, 19
  disease environment, 192, 195, 197, 198, 202–4 passim

indigenous peoples and, 173, 174, 200, 206–09 passim

Nanai, xv
nanjie 南戒, 28
Nanyuan 南苑, 70
native chieftainships (tusi 土司), 4, 39, 170–5 passim, 178, 186, 198–3 passim, 206–10, 246–51 passim, 251, 274
  administrative concepts of, (*tusi zhidu* 土司制度, tusi dai土司帶), 248
  centralized (*gumsa* and Shan), 173, 187, 246, 248, 250
  conversion of, (*gaitu guiliu* 改土歸流), 187–9, 191, 198, 199, 205, 207
  and *gumlau* organizations, 173, 186–87, 248, 250
Nayanceng 那彥成 (1764–1833), 228, 232–234, 268
neidi 內地 (Yunnan proper, or Hanspace), 164, 189, 198, 246
Neiwufu (內務府 Imperial Household Department), 71–72, 100, 109, 117, 121, 123, 135, 154
nengyuan jidi 能源基地, 267
Nerchinsk, 94
  Treaty of, 73, 94
New Qing History, 7
Ni Tui 倪蛻 (b. 1668), 200
nimeku aku oho, 197
Nine Provinces (Jiuzhou 九州), 26–31 passim, 35
Ningguta, 76, 81, 82, 86–95 passim, 99
Niuzhuang 牛莊, 97
niyahašara urse, 113
niyalma, 113
niyalma i hūsun eterakū, 22
Non River (Nenjiang 嫩江), 83, 88
Norman, Jerry, xv
nüe 瘧, 191
Nurhaci (r. 1616–26), 49, 66, 120

Oirad (Ma: Ūlet), 118, 197, 215
Oning (d. 1770), 205, 206
Ordos, 5, 46, 132–33, 138, 152, 212, 253
Orochen (鄂倫春; Ma: Orončo), 64, 81, 94, 103, 229, 273
Ortai 鄂爾泰 (1680–1745), 187–88, 191, 196, 200, 208, 268
Osborne, Anne, 8, 182, 184
otog (*otoγ*), xvi, 118, 268

Index

331

outposts (Ma: *karun*), 95, 121, 231, 260
Oyonggo 鄂容安 (1714–55), 42

Pamirs, 2
Pan River 盤江, 205
Panthay Rebellion (1856–73), 242, 246, 250
Passing through the Mongol Tribes (*Guo Menggu zhubu* 過蒙古諸部, Qianlong emperor), 143
pastoralism, 14, 39, 77, 257, 269
 consolidating banners and herds, 118–27
 cultivation and, 44–48 passim, 90, 144–51 passim, 155, 237, 239, 260
 disease and, 176
 disaster relief for, 5, 14, 117, 120, 129–39, 238–41, 260, 269, 272
 ecotone, 10–12, 147, 157
 forage and, 128, 130, 141, 154, 169
 imperial, 3, 14, 116, 121, 124, 137, 144, 159, 170, 209, 221, 235–36, 237–39, 241, 252
 sedentarization of, 240
 steppe conditions for, 12, 116, 124, 128–31, 154–57 passim
 sustainability, 239–40, 241, 268
pearls (*dongzhu* 東珠), xiii, 66–68 passim, 74, 96–98 passim, 100
 exhaustion/depletion of, 102, 260
 pearl rivers, 63, 68
perch, sea, 71
Perdue, Peter C., 17, 84
pheasants, 271
physiocracy, spiritual, 41
pian'an 偏安, 38
Pingnan, 242
Pomeranz, Kenneth, 220
Potala temple (*Putuozongcheng miao* 普陀宗乘庙), 153
Poiarkov, Vasilii, (d. 1668), 74, 84–85
pu 樸, 41
Pu('er)-Si(mao)-Yuan(jiang)-Xin(ping) uprising, 198
Pu'er 普洱, 173, 186–87, 189, 191, 198 passim, 207, 245, 249 passim, 272
qi 氣
 defined, 24
 historical mechanics of, 31–36, 39, 57, 219, 252
 royal, 36

terrestrial, 31, 257
 three dragon trunks of terrestrial, 29–30

Qi Xizao 祁藻 (1793–1866), 253
Qianlong emperor, 1, 4, 61, 153, 176
 on agricultural issues, 41–42, 45–48 passim, 77, 146, 222
 on disaster relief, 136, 138, 238, 239
 on ethnic identity, 62, 136, 155, 239, 260
 on Hanspace issues, 38
 poetry, 1, 45, 47, 60, 68, 143, 146, 222, 223
 reign events of, 36, 64, 112, 144, 145, 153, 167, 186, 230, 253, 255–56, 268
 on tributary issues, 143
 on venery issues, 45–48 passim, 50–54 passim, 61, 77, 103, 142, 165, 211, 222, 223
 on southwestern disease environment, 169, 197, 198, 204, 216
Qiantang River 錢塘江, 226
qimin 齊民, 146
qin 親 (close relations), 53
qin 勤 (diligence), 41
Qin Heping, 9
Qing Empire (dynasty, 1644–1912), 1, 23, 54, 80, 118, 143, 187, 252, 255
 borderland environmental relations, 10–16, 19, 21–22, 50, 51, 80, 140, 141, 145, 157, 163, 166, 172–81 passim, 186, 189, 205–06, 209, 238–44 passim, 250, 252, 268, 269, 273
 Chosŏn Korea, relations with, 67–68
 diversity and, 2, 6, 16, 23, 39, 40, 78, 86, 149, 158, 169, 172, 181, 190, 219–20, 227–28, 235, 270
 environmental perspectives and perceptions, 6, 10, 22, 23, 43, 106, 129, 167, 222, 226, 232, 243, 249, 254, 257, 258, 268
 Hanspace and, 25, 32–33, 36–40, 258
 identity formation within, 3, 5, 24, 33, 44, 48, 51, 53, 66, 83, 87–92 passim, 116–17, 123, 135, 138, 170–74 passim, 206, 208, 209, 233, 239
 Konbaung Myanmar, relations with, 169, 202, 247
 as Later Jin (Hou Jin, 1616–1635), 67–69, 75, 77

Qing Empire (dynasty, 1644–1912) (cont.)
   Romanov Russia, relations with, 64,
      74–78, 83–96 passim, 229
   spatial issues, 2–4, 43, 46, 49, 55, 69, 71,
      96, 164, 173–74, 207, 248
   Zunghar Mongols, relations with, 121,
      137, 138
qing ye 清野, 229
Qinghai, 129, 160, 212
qiongyi 窮夷, 142
Qiqihar (Ma: Cicigar), 81, 101, 268
qishu 氣數, 258

resources, 86, 92, 95, 131, 133, 139, 175,
    223, 237, 241, 268
   administration, 4, 80, 96, 144–57 passim,
    188
   competition for, 66–68, 72, 74, 77, 78,
    88, 117, 121, 140–57 passim, 200,
    222, 226, 228, 229, 246, 254,
    266–67
   concentration of, 8–9, 40, 131, 224–26
    passim, 235, 240, 257, 268, 271
   exhaustion/depletion of, 102–06, 235,
    236, 252, 268–69
   human, 3, 14, 64, 65, 75–77, 80, 93, 95,
    105, 136, 138, 223, 227–28
   natural, 3, 75–76, 79, 186, 188, 267
rice, 10, 22, 42, 182, 220–21
   Champa, 44
   disaster relief for, 238
   double-cropping paddy, 43
   glutinous and nonglutinous, 184, 209,
    245, 249
   paddy (wet), 7, 43, 44, 181, 189, 234,
    253, 254
   rice porridge/gruel, 142, 185
   in Yunnan, 179–81, 184, 189, 204–09
    passim
Rong 戎, 28, 30, 34–39
Rowe, William T., 7
rubing 乳餅, 165
Russia (Romanov Dynasty (1613–1917)),
    99, 103, 228, 236
   economic role of pelts in, 83–85
   imperial space of, 74, 83–88 passim, 94,
    236
   Qing China and, 13, 15, 64, 73–78,
    82–96 passim, 147, 228–29, 233, 247
   SAH basin expeditions of, 74, 83–87
    passim

   SAH indigenous peoples and, 75, 78,
    82–86, 88, 92–94, 113
   as Tsardom of Muscovy, 108

sable (*Martes zibellina*; *diao* 貂; Ma: *seke*),
    xvi, 66–67, 78, 107–80, 85, 100,
    230, 233
   as currency, 93
   pelt tribute (Ma: *seke alban*), 13–14, 64,
    78, 81–8, 93–5, 177, 229, 268
Sabsu (d. ca. 1700), 99
SAH (Sahaliyan (Ma)-Amur (Ru)-Heilong)
   river basin (north-central
   Manchuria), 13, 64, 65, 83, 233
   Cossack incursion and settlement into,
    73, 74, 84, 87, 94–95
   and disease, 177
   ecological conditions in, 72, 80, 95, 112,
    114, 229–30
   indigenous settlements in, 64, 74, 78, 82,
    86
   manpower raids into, 75–77
   pacification, mobilization and resettlement
    policies in, 84, 87–96, 229
   resource exploitation of, 96-100, 229-33
   and tribute, 78, 79, 80–83
Sakhalin Island, 2, 106, 82
salt, 58, 71, 151, 154–57 (lakes), 189, 199,
    236
Salween River, 201, 203, 247
saohpa (Burmese *sawbwa*), 173
Šarhūda 沙爾虎達 (1599–1659), 86, 233
Satsuma, 262
Scott, James C., 92, 183, 211, 248
Shaan(xi)-Gan(su) region, 9
Shaanxi, 29, 37, 52, 59, 152, 154, 244, 253,
    255, 273
Shahukou 殺虎口, 152
Shan, 184, 186, 187, 211, 247
shanchuan zhi xiang 山川之像, 28
Shandong, 29, 42–44 passim, 145, 158,
    238, 259
Shang dynasty (1556–1046 BCE), 26
Shangsiyuan (上駟院; Palace Stud), 141
Shangxia Meng 上下孟, 216
Shangjunshu (Book of Lord Shang), 40
Shanxi, 21, 29, 39, 137, 145, 152–154, 166,
    235, 239, 253, 258, 273
shaohuang 燒荒, 120
shen 神, 24
Shen Hao 沈鎬 (1648?-1725?), 25

Index

333

sheng 升, 42
sheng, 172, 211
sheng shen 生身, 177
shengjiao 聲教, 30–31, 34, 81, 258
Shengjing 盛京, 66, 71, 77, 97–103 passim,
112, 140, 260
shi 石, 149, 205, 239
shibian 實邊, 241
Shili-yin Gool League, 116, 270
Shiquan 使犬, 81
shu 熟, 172, 189, 211
shu shen 熟身, 177
Shun, 33, 36
Shunning 順寧, 172, 173, 186, 187, 216,
201, 202, 207, 250
Shunzhi emperor, 70
reign events of, 36, 161
Shuoping 朔平, 146
Shurungga (fl. 1742), 232, 268
Shuwangju (fl. 1748), 156
shuyi 熟夷, 208
Sibe 錫伯, 92, 215
Sichuan, 10, 29, 37, 166, 179, 182, 187,
221, 239, 244, 245, 249, 251, 254
Sihe River 四合川, 231
siken 私墾, 237
Siku quanshu, 25
silver, 14, 40, 54, 67, 78, 97, 129–34
passim, 137–39 passim, 180, 238,
239, 269
Simao 思茅, 200, 202, 251
Sinification, 7, 31, 56, 257, 273
Sipsongpanna, 202, 251
Six Dynasties, 38
Skinner, G. William, 254
soil, 22, 200, 255
black (phaeozem), 253
conservation, 182, 183, 236, 243
deficiencies/degradation, 147, 148, 182,
185–86, 200, 224, 234, 244, 252,
256, 264
identity formation and, 42, 46–47,
189–90, 222
as alkali resource, 155, 156
Solon 索倫, 88, 95, 197, 232
Solon-Ewenki, xv, 47, 53, 54, 64, 75, 79,
81, 87, 95, 101, 142, 197, 215, 230,
233, 268, 272
Song dynasty (960-1279), 1, 13, 27, 28, 32,
38–39, 56
Song lun (Wang Fuzhi), 33

Song Yihan 宋一韓 (fl. 1592), 49
Songnen 松嫩, 77
Šongqor, 120–21
Šose (d. 1759), 42
Stepanov, Onufrii (fl. 1653), 87
Steward, Julian, 5
structuration theory (Giddens), 19
Šuhede (1710–1777), 205, 206
Suiyuan 綏遠, 145, 146, 153, 236
sun 巽, 29
Sun Jiagan 孫嘉淦 (1683-1753), 152–55,
159, 268, 273
Sungari River, 74, 86
Sungari-Hūrha confluence, 75, 112
sustainability, 153, 221, 226, 252, 258,
267, 268
of cultured nature, 100–06
problems, 15, 59, 70, 79, 86, 101, 104,
105, 130, 223–27 passim, 239, 240,
246, 252–53, 256–57
strategies for, 40, 53, 63, 85, 139, 141,
143–44, 157, 169, 271
of swiddening, 8, 181–85 passim,
242–44, 272

Tai (Dai 傣族), 173, 207, 213
Taipusi 太僕寺 (Court of the Imperial Stud),
122, 141, 163
Tang dynasty (618–907), 1, 2, 13, 25,
27–28, 31–32, 36, 38–39, 50, 57
Tao Zhu 陶澍 (1778–1839), 244
Tarai, 178
techno-politics (Mitchell), 6
"Ten Measures for Providing for Yunnan"
(Cai Yurong), 178
Tengchong 騰沖, 10
Tengyue 騰越, 173, 186, 187, 198, 201,
203, 250
Tharu, 178
Thongchai Winichakul, 173
Three Feudatories Rebellion, 77, 178, 203,
218
tiangu 天固, 34
tianji 天紀, 34
tianwen 天文, 25
Tibet, 230
tidu 提督, 188
Tigershoot River (*Shehu chuan* 射虎川,
Qianlong emperor), 46
tin, 180
tokso, 77

334   *Index*

Tokugawa, 176, 262
Tolga, 85
Ton River (*Tun he* 屯河), 88
tonglei 同類, 35
trees, 147, 229
   felling, 104, 110, 155–56, 167, 185, 231, 245
   as habitat, 80, 89
   identity and, 103–05, 113, 153, 183, 186
   Korean pine (*Pinus koraiensis*), 80
   larch, 80
   Chinese red pine (*Pinus tabulaeformis*), 147, 231, 232
   siviculture, 42
   as timber, 152–53, 167, 188, 223, 245, 272
tribute (*gong* 貢, Ma: *alban*), 30–31, 49, 105, 117, 119–120, 258
   beaver pelts, 84, 85
   dairy, 143
   defined, 30, 78–79
   eagles, 73, 100 (sea), 114 (sea)
   ermine pelts, 85
   fox pelts, 81, 83, 85, 100, 101, 112
   general pelt, 66, 72, 83–86
   honey (Chinese/ Ma: *nikan* and wild), 97–99, 102, 104, 105, 229–30, 271
   hua fish 魚匕, 230
   lynx pelts, 66
   Nine Whites (*jiubai* 九白), 117
   otter pelts, 66, 72, 85, 97, 99
   pheasant, 103, 104, 112, 233, 271
   pine nut, 67, 102, 105, 229
   poaching, 67–68, 102–03, 232, 260, 268
   squirrel pelts, 66
   storks (*Ciconia boyciana*; *guan* 鸛), 97–100 passim, 103, 104, 106, 233, 271
   sturgeon (*Huso dauricus*, Ma: *kirfu*), 71–73, 97, 108
   tiger pelts, 66
   wolf pelts, 66
   yasak (*iasak*), 84–85, 87, 88
Tsardom of Muscovy, 108
Tsewang Rabdan (r. 1697–1727), 121
tubers, 245
Tuhuru River 圖呼勒河, 94
tumu 土目, 200
tunmu 屯牧, 236
military agricultural colonies (tuntian 屯田), 60, 236, 237, 251
Two Verses on Antiquity (*Yonggu er shou* 永古二首, Qianlong emperor), 1

Ulaanchab League, 133, 152
Uliastai, *xvi*, 122, 138, 258, 268
Unified Mongol Tribes of the Marches (*waifan Menggu tongbu* 外藩蒙古統部), 159
urgun (or *urhun*), 162
Urianghai *otog*, 268
Ušiba (fl. 1747), 140, 150, 151, 238
Usihun River 武斯渾河, 112
Ušish (fl. 1736), 140–41

venery and hunting (Ma: *butha*), 48–54 passim, 142
   agriculture and, 49, 54–55, 70, 88–89, 213, 231, 272
   battue, 22, 50–52 passim, 53, 54, 72, 101, 222, 223, 269
   definitions, 13, 49
   deer hunting, 113
   hunting dogs, 52, 79, 100
   hunters as soldiers, 49, 51, 54–55 passim, 60, 64, 88, 95, 96, 106, 197, 228, 230
   pacification through, 51, 52, 62, 223
   poaching, 68, 104, 222, 223, 268, 274
   poetic references, 45–46, 146
   predator-prey networks, 53
   regulations, 54, 67, 73, 177, 223, 268
   tiger hunting, 60, 52, 113
   wild boar hunting, 113

waidi 外地, 164
Wandian 灣甸, 198
wang (prince) 王, 67
Wang Fuzhi 王夫之 (1619–92), 23, 25, 31, 33–36, 38, 54, 56, 257, 273
Wang Lüjie 王履階, 188
Wang, Yen-chien, 253
wang qi 王氣, 36
wang tian shou 望天收, 48
Warka 瓦爾喀, 74–76, 82, 88–93, 224, 233, 268, 270
water, 7, 8, 30, 147, 164, 179, 182, 190, 239, 265
   as agricultural resource, 42, 132, 182, 189, 225–27, 234, 235, 243, 253–54, 256, 262, 264, 267
   as disease environment, 198
   as mosquito habitat, 193, 194
   as pastoral resource, 45, 124, 129–31 passim, 140, 148, 151

Index

335

in poetry, 45
salt and, 155
as steppe limiting factor, 130
as venery resource, 52
wei chudou 未出痘, 177
weilie shan 圍獵山, 72
Weiyuan 威遠, 189, 204
Weji 窩集, 75
Wenzhou 溫州, 182
Western Regions (*Xiyu* 西域), 31
What I Saw (*Liutiaobian* 柳條邊, Qianlong
    emperor), 46
What I Saw (*Suo jian* 所見, Qianlong
    emperor), 46, 222
White Lotus, 251
Wild Fields (*Huang tian*, Qianlong
    emperor), 45, 46
Wildlife
    deer, 60, 53
    enclave management of, 63
    foxes, 53
    gazelles, 53
    as game bagged, 52
    leopards, Amur (*Panthera pardus
        orientalis*), 80
    rabbits, 52–53, 132–33
    tigers (*hu* 虎), 52, 60, 80, 151, 264,
        273
    wolves, 135, 150, 272
Will, Pierre-Etienne, 254
Wills, John E., Jr., 79
Wuchang 武昌, 7
Wutaishan, 46
wuyong shengwu 無用牲物, 97

Xia, 15, 35
Xia dynasty (ca. 2070–ca. 1600 BCE), 26,
    31
xian 縣, 146
Xianfeng reign, 231, 264
xiao min 小民, 43
Xiao Ruiling, 10
xidi 隙地, 59
xiguan 習慣, 196
Xingyi 興義, 205
Xinjiang, 121, 195, 230
Xinping 新平, 137
xiuyang shengxi 休養生息, 146
xiyou 嬉遊, 48
Xu Bingyi 徐秉義 (1633–1711), 31
Xuanhua 宣化, 123
xunshou 巡守, 51

Yaksa 雅克薩 (Ru: Albazin), 74, 79, 88, 94
Yalu River, 265
yan 煙, 195
Yan Gao, 148
Yan Wenlong, 266
yang 陽, 24, 28, 34, 38
Yang Mingshi 楊名時 (1661–1737), 189
Yangzi River, 7, 28, 29, 33, 34, 44, 148,
    195, 226, 235, 254
    basin, 9
    delta, 7, 8, 43, 57, 132, 182, 185
    highlands, 182, 244–45, 253
    macroregion, 244
yanzhang 煙瘴, 189, 191, 198
Yellow River, 28, 29, 147, 225, 226, 259
Yerenshan 野人山, (Wild People
    Mountains), 186, 251
yeyi 野夷, 172, 213
yi 夷 (tribal, barbarian), *xvi*, 28 & 30 & 38
    as Eastern Barbarian (*Yi*), 38, 170
yi 疫 (plague), 193
Yi彝 (the Yi or Lolo ethnicity), 181, 188,
    189, 191, 242, 249, 268, 272
Yidi 夷狄, 24
yilei 異類, 35
yin 陰, 24, 28, 34, 38
Yin Shaoting, 181
Yin-ji-shan 尹繼善 (1694–1770), 198
yiren 夷人, 155
Yixing 一行 (673–727), 27–28, 31, 33, 55
Yizhou 沂州, 264
Yongbei 永北, 185, 272
Yongchang 永昌, 172, 173, 186, 187, 198,
    201, 203, 205, 248, 250
Yongyou temple 永佑, 50, 51
Yongzheng emperor, 36–38, 43, 54, 61, 66,
    138, 148, 149, 219, 228, 258
Youle 攸樂, 200
youmin 莠民 (bad people, weed people,
    green bristle grass people), 237
Young Mongols and Vigilantes (Atwood), *xv*
Yu the Great, 258
Yuan dynasty (1271–1368), 32, 33, 35, 38,
    58, 156, 185, 234
Yuanjiang 元江, 189, 196, 198, 204
Yuanming Yuan, 153
Yue Chaolong 岳超龍 (d. 1732), 188
Yue Fei 岳飛 (1103–42), 37
Yue Zhongqi 岳鐘琪 (1686–1784), 37
Yugong 禹貢, 26
Yugong chuizhi (*A Peep-hole View of the
    Tribute of Yu*, Hu Wei), 26, 31

Yumachang (御馬廠; Imperial Horse Pastures), 123
Yun(nan)-Gui(zhou), 178, 188, 244–45
Yunmeng 允孟, 216
Yunnan, 10, 29, 169, 180–81, 200, 201, 207
  agriculture, 9–10, 178–90, 196, 210, 241–46, 253, 272
  as a disease environment, 12, 14, 169–78 passim, 181, 183, 184, 187–205 passim, 206, 208–09, 224–25, 241, 248–52, 272, 275
  inter-regional comparisons, 2–3, 12, 159, 170, 175, 178, 180, 182–83, 187, 192, 194–196, 209, 225, 241, 243, 244, 246, 253, 272, 273
  migration, 170, 180, 182–85 passim, 206–07, 242, 244, 245–46, 249
  mining, 179–81, 242
  nature and culture compromise in, 210
  opium in, 246
  pastures, 148–49
Yuchashanfang 御茶膳房 (Palace Larder), 71

za 雜, 35
zaliang 雜糧, 245
Zeng Jing 曾靜 (1679–1735), 32, 36
Zengfu (fl. 1745), 156
Zhanda 盞達, 198
zhang 瘴, 191
Zhang Fuguo 張輔国 (1768–1812), 201
Zhang Yongjiang, 146
Zhang Yunsui 張允隨 (1693–1751), 179, 212, 213, 263
Zhang Zhidong 張之洞 (1837–1909), 234–39, 244, 257, 268, 270

Zhang, David D., 220
Zhangjiakou 張家口, 121, 137, 146, 148
zhanzhou 饘粥, 142
Zhao Shenzhen 趙慎畛(1761–1825), 58
Zhao Yi 趙翼 (1727–1814), 25, 31–33, 36, 51, 142
Zhao Zhen, 9–10
Zhao-lian 昭槤 (1780–1833), 51
Zhaotong 昭通, 179, 188, 225
Zhefang 遮放, 198, 248
Zhejiang, 31, 182, 244, 258
zhen 震, 29
Zhenfeng 貞豐, 205
zhengjiao 政教, 27, 271
Zhili, 29, 42, 43, 122, 137, 145–46, 152–55 passim, 230, 234, 259
zhongbang 中邦, 27, 271
Zhonghua 中華, 32
zhongqu 中區, 23
zhongren 種人, 186
zhongwai 中外, 37
zhongwai yi jia 中外一家, 51
Zhou dynasty (1046–256 BCE), 26–27
Zhou Huafeng 周化鳳 (fl.1694), 174, 248
Zhou Yu 周裕 (fl. 1766), 169
zinc, 180
Zomia, 3, 183, 184, 209, 212–13, 235, 248, 262, 269, 270
  Zomi-culture, 209–10, 257, 268, 272
Zunghar 準噶爾, 38, 61, 84, 87, 118, 121, 163, 137–139, 145, 155, 158, 176, 215, 270
zushan 祖山, 58

Printed in the United States
By Bookmasters